2012

by
Jack Gillis

with
Amy Curran,
Julia Redmon
and
Eric Glenn

Foreword by
Clarence Ditlow
Center for Auto Safety

A Center for Auto Safety Publication

ACKNOWLEDGMENTS

In the 32 years we've been publishing *The Car Book* not only have cars become much more sophisticated, but so has the task of collecting and organizing the massive amount of data necessary to bring you straightforward car buying information. For four years, Julia Redmon has been managing and organizing this extraordinary effort. Her competent command of thousands of data points will enable car buyers to make some excellent choices. For 21 years, Amy Curran has been expertly preparing all the graphics necessary to clearly present the data, managing the logistics necessary to get a printed book in the hands of the public, and keeping the project on track. This year we were thrilled to add Eric Glenn to the team. He effectively compiled and analyzed an amazing amount of vehicle data and no doubt pushed Microsoft Excel to its limits! Thanks to Amy, Julia, and Eric, consumers have the information they need to make a smart, sensible new car choice.

As has been the case for 31 years, this year's edition would not have been possible without the essential contributions from Clarence Ditlow and the staff of the Center for Auto Safety, including Michael Brooks and John Robinson.

As always, the most important factor in being able to bring this information to the American car buyer for 32 years is the encouragement, support, and love from my brilliant and beautiful wife, Marilyn Mohrman-Gillis. For her and four terrific children–Katie, John, Brian and Brennan–I am eternally grateful.

—*J.G.*

As Always,

for Marilyn &
Katie, John, Brian, and Brennan

CONTENTS

4 FOREWORD
BY CLARENCE DITLOW, CENTER FOR AUTO SAFETY

5 INTRODUCTION

6 BUYING GUIDE
USING THE BUYING GUIDE/6   2012 BUYING GUIDE/6

13 BEST BETS

18 SAFETY
CRASH TESTS: HOW THE CARS ARE RATED/18   CRASH TEST RESULTS/19   AUTOMATIC CRASH PROTECTION/28   CHILD SAFETY/29   ROLLOVER/30   ROOF CRUSH/31
STATIC STABILITY FACTOR/32

33 FUEL ECONOMY
TWELVE WAYS TO SAVE MONEY AT THE PUMP/34
FUEL ECONOMY MISERS AND GUZZLERS/35

36 WARRANTIES
COMPARING WARRANTIES/37   SECRET WARRANTIES/38

39 MAINTENANCE
KEEPING IT GOING/39   MAINTENANCE COSTS/40   SERVICE CONTRACTS/44   TIPS FOR DEALING WITH A MECHANIC/45

46 TIRES
TIRE RATINGS/46   HOW TO READ A TIRE/47   TIRE TABLE/48

49 INSURANCE
REDUCING INSURANCE COSTS/50   BUMPERS/52

53 COMPLAINTS
COMPLAINT INDEX/55   CENTER FOR AUTO SAFETY/56   CONSUMER GROUPS AND GOVERNMENT/57   AUTOMOBILE MANUFACTURERS/58   LEMON LAWS/59

64 SHOWROOM STRATEGIES
5 BASIC STEPS/64   IN THE SHOWROOM/65   GETTING THE BEST PRICE/66   CARBARGAINS' BEST PRICE SERVICE/68   FINANCING/69   LEASING VS. BUYING/71
USING THE INTERNET/73   DEPRECIATION/74   CORPORATE TWINS/75

76 RATINGS
HOW TO USE THE RATINGS/76   THE CAR PAGES/81   YOUR NOTES/271

272 INDEX

BY CLARENCE DITLOW

The Great Recession or Auto Safety Improvements - which is the life saver? In 2010, traffic deaths declined to 32,885, the lowest since 1949. The United States had large traffic death declines during economic downturns in 1981-83 and 1991-93 only to see traffic deaths rebound when the economy improved. But each time after the recession, deaths did not climb up to levels before the recession. Why? Because the long term trend is downward thanks to safety improvements in vehicles, roads and safety laws which save over 20,000 lives each year and climbing as advanced safety features are built into cars.

Deaths go down in recessions because people cut back on discretionary driving like going out in the evening when death rates are the highest. Crashes involving teenage drivers saw the biggest drop in deaths during the Great Recession, 39% compared to 23% overall. All the more remarkable because in 2006, teenagers weren't texting behind the wheel. Going to work is not discretionary so safer work commutes cannot be cut back nearly as much.

During the Great Recession, new vehicles got major safety improvements - electronic stability control, side curtain airbags and even advanced braking systems that slow a car down more than the driver would or could when a crash is about to occur. And more improvements are coming like stronger roofs, backup cameras and dynamic tuning of a vehicle for optimum occupant protection in the split seconds before a crash. Further down the roads, cars will "talk" to each other much like airplanes warn about a collision course. Even if a distracted driver is about to run a red light, his or her car will send an electronic signal to cars with the green light that it is about to run the red light.

Safety technology and laws combined with the Great Recession to push traffic deaths down in 2010 but no one believes recessions are the answer to auto safety. And 32,885 traffic deaths are 32,885 too many. In the latest available year for world figures 2008, US traffic deaths per 100,000 population were 12.3 Other developed countries had death rates less than half that with Sweden at 4.8, the Netherlands at 3.9, Germany at 5.2, Japan at 5.4, Great Britain at 5.1 and Norway at 4.9. If the US had a 5.0 death rate, we would have saved 16,000 more lives in 2010.

The Center has a Vision of Zero Traffic Deaths - we want to eliminate traffic deaths. Sweden adopted a Zero Traffic Deaths Vision in 1997. Volvo has adopted Vision Zero as has New York City's Transportation Alternatives. Traffic deaths should be treated like a terrible disease to be wiped from the face of the earth. Every consumer should have the right to buy a vehicle whose occupants survive 50-mph front, rear and side impact crashes – goals which were set by NHTSA in 1970 but which were derailed by industry lobbyists and bureaucratic inertia. No one should be killed in a rollover and pedestrians should have the rights to safe streets. Our mission is to dream the impossible and achieve it.

How does the US get to Zero Traffic Deaths. Doing as well as slow driving Great Britain or Zoom, Zoom Germany would get us half way there. The single biggest step would be to transform the National Highway Traffic Safety Administration into an adequately funded and staffed regulatory agency instead of one with about a nickel per vehicle on the road for enforcement and rulemaking and rents testing and research facilities from Honda. One of the biggest battles will be over distracted driving where more drivers have their eyes and minds off the road as auto companies introduce more electronic devices that overwhelm the driver with too many inputs.

Consumers need to do more to drive safely in the new car since advanced safety features like lane departure, radar braking and adaptive cruise control, active pre-crash safety and automatic crash notification will be options only on some models. Use *The Car Book* and its new comprehensive crash safety rating to buy the safest car in a crash. Use the Safety Chapter to find all the optional safety features and which models have them when you buy a new vehicle. Your buying decision not only may save your life but also sends a message to automakers not to withhold vital safety features.

By using *The Car Book* to buy a safer car, you have taken an important first step toward your personal vehicle safety and helping CAS reach our Vision. The next step is to support the Center for Auto Safety which works every day on your behalf to ensure that all Americans ride in safe and reliable vehicles. Go to our Website www.autosafety.org and find out how you can support the Center and have CAS be your safety and lemon insurance.

BY JACK GILLIS

As consumers start going back into the showrooms and the car industry gets back on its feet, the 32nd edition of *The Car Book* will guide you to some of the best cars ever made!

Not only will our "*Car Book* Best Bets" lead you to some excellent vehicles, but there are numerous other choices that, while not making our top lists, will do well in meeting your demands for efficient, safe and intelligently designed vehicles. You can confidently let *The Car Book* be your guide to the best for 2012.

As it has been for 32 years, my goal is to sift through the myriad of government and industry data on cars and present it so consumers can actually use it. 32 years ago, *The Car Book* was the first publication to give consumers the ability to make an informed choice on one of the most important and complex items that they will ever purchase. Today, thanks in large part to the efforts of the Center for Auto Safety in Washington, DC, our mission has never wavered.

Working closely with the Center's Clarence Ditlow and his staff, the information in *The Car Book* has significantly changed the way carmakers build their vehicles. This is because we have always believed that if *you* knew that one car was safer than another you'd buy the safer car. We believed that your action would put enormous pressure on the auto makers to improve safety. It worked and cars today are safer than ever before!

In setting out to change the way people buy their cars, *The Car Book* was able to change the way car companies made them.

This year the government has improved the crash test program on which we base our all-important and unique safety ratings. In keeping with *The Car Book*'s philosophy of making it as easy as possible to identify the truly good performers in the government crash tests, we provide a unique *Car Book* Combined Crash Test Rating which combines all of the complex government testing into a simple, straightforward number. In addition, we take the step of comparing the vehicles on a relative basis to each other so you can easily tell the best performers from the worst.

While making improvements to the crash test program (see page 18) is a good thing, not all of the 2012 vehicles have been tested. While we (and you!) look forward to the day when all of your choices have been tested, our safety ratings will provide a good indication of which cars can be expected to protect you.

Before *The Car Book*, consumers had no idea which warranties were better, what you could expect to pay for typical repairs, which cars cost the most and least to insure, and how they stacked up in government complaints. Now you have this information all in one place.

Our exclusive car-by-car ratings at the end of the book provide an overview of all the criteria you need to make a good choice. Here, you'll be able to quickly assess key features and see how the car you're interested in stacks up against its competition so you can make sure your selection is the best car for you.

Even though the choices get better each year and safety is improved, it's still a challenge to separate the lemons from the peaches. There are notable differences in how cars protect you in a crash, how much they cost to maintain, the benefits of their warranties, and how far they'll go on a gallon of expensive gasoline. Nevertheless, if you use the information in *The Car Book*, there is no reason why your next car should not last at least 150,000 miles.

Buying a car means staying on your toes and not being "schnookered" in the showroom. *The Car Book* will help you do just that. It's not easy matching wits with a seasoned salesperson, but our "Showroom Strategies" section will give you the keys to getting the best deal. In spite of all the new car technology and the Internet, the fundamentals of buying a good, safe, reliable car remain the same: do your homework; shop around; and remember that car dealers need you more than you need them!

The information in *The Car Book* is based on data collected and developed by our staff, the U.S. Department of Transportation, and the Center for Auto Safety. With all of this information in hand, you'll find some great choices for 2012.

—*Jack*

USING THE BUYING GUIDE

T he "Buying Guide" provides a quick comparison of the 2012 cars in terms of their safety, warranty, fuel economy, complaint rating, and price range—arranged by size class. To fully understand the information in the charts, it is important to read the related section in the book.

Overall Rating: This shows how well this car stacks up on a scale of 1 to 10 when compared to all others on the market. Because safety is the most important component of our ratings, cars with no crash test results at printing are not given an overall rating.

Combined Crash Test Rating: This indicates how well the car performed in the government's frontal and side crash test programs compared to this year's vehicles tested to date. See page 18 for details.

Warranty Rating: This is an overall comparative assessment of the car's warranty.

Fuel Economy: This is the EPA city/highway mpg for, what is expected to be, the most popular model.

Complaint Rating: This is based on complaints received by the U.S. Department of Transportation. If not rated, the vehicle is too new to have a complaint rating.

Price Range: This will give you a general idea of the "sticker," or suggested retail price.

Indicates a *Car Book* Best Bet. See page 13.

Vehicle	Page #	Overall Rating	Combined Crash Test Rating	Warranty Rating	Fuel Economy	Complaint Rating	Price Range
Subcompact							
BMW Z4	100			Very Good	17/24	Very Poor	$48-$64,000
Chevrolet Sonic	**116**	**9**	**Very Good**	**Average**	**25/35**		**$13-$18,000**
Fiat 500	131	2	Very Poor	Very Poor	27/34		$15-$19,000
Ford Fiesta	137	5	Very Good	Poor	29/39	Very Poor	$13-$17,000
Honda CR-Z	149	1	Very Poor	Very Poor	35/39	Very Poor	$19-$23,000
Honda Fit	150			Very Poor	28/35	Good	$15-$19,000
Honda Insight	151			Very Poor	40/43	Poor	$18-$23,000
Hyundai Accent	**155**	**8**	**Average**	**Very Good**	**30/40**		**$12-$16,000**
Hyundai Veloster	163			Very Good	29/38		$17-$18,000
Kia Rio	179			Good	30/40		$13-$17,000
Kia Soul	182	7	Poor	Good	27/35	Average	$13-$19,000
Mazda 2	196			Very Poor	28/34	Very Good	$14-$16,000
Mazda MX-5 Miata	202			Very Poor	21/28	Very Good	$24-$29,000
Mini Cooper	209			Very Good	28/36	Very Poor	$24-$35,000

Vehicle	Page #	Overall Rating	Combined Crash Test Rating	Warranty Rating	Fuel Economy	Complaint Rating	Price Range
Subcompact (cont.)							
Mini Countryman	210			Very Good	25/30		
Nissan 370Z	214			Very Poor	19/26		$31-$40,000
Nissan Versa	228	1	Very Poor	Very Poor	28/34	Good	$10-$15,000
Scion iQ	232			Very Poor	36/37		$15-$15,000
Scion xB	234			Very Poor	22/28	Poor	$16-$17,000
Scion xD	235			Very Poor	27/33	Very Good	$15-$16,000
Smart ForTwo	236			Very Poor	33/41	Average	$12-$17,000
Suzuki SX4	243			Poor	23/30	Poor	
Toyota Yaris	258			Very Poor	30/35		$14-$17,000
Volkswagen Beetle	259			Good	22/29		$18-$29,000
Compact							
Audi A3	86			Good	21/30	Very Poor	$27-$32,000
Audi A4	87	6	Average	Good	22/30	Good	$32-$47,000
BMW 1 Series	94			Very Good	18/28	Very Poor	$30-$43,000
BMW 3 Series	95			Very Good	18/28	Average	$38-$51,000
Buick Verano	104			Good	22/31		$22-$25,000
Chevrolet Cruze	**111**	**9**	**Very Good**	**Average**	**26/38**	**Average**	**$16-$23,000**
Chevrolet Volt*	**120**	**8**	**Good**	**Average**	**35/40**	**Very Poor**	**$39-$39,000**
Dodge Caliber	125	3	Poor	Poor	23/27	Poor	$17-$18,000
Ford Focus	139	6	Average	Poor	28/38		$16-$22,000
Ford Mustang	141	3	Average	Poor	19/31	Very Poor	$22-$48,000
Honda Civic	146			Very Poor	28/39		$15-$26,000
Honda Civic Coupe	147			Very Poor	28/39		$15-$23,000
Hyundai Elantra	157	7	Poor	Very Good	29/40	Good	$15-$20,000
Kia Forte	177	8	Poor	Good	26/36	Good	$15-$19,000
Lexus CT	186			Average	43/40		$29-$31,000
Mazda 3	197	6	Good	Very Poor	24/33	Good	$15-$23,000
Mercedes-Benz C-Class	203	3	Poor	Poor	18/25	Very Good	$34-$42,000
Mitsubishi Lancer	212			Very Good	25/33	Average	$15-$27,000
Nissan Altima Coupe	216			Very Poor	23/32	Very Good	$23-$30,000
Nissan Leaf	221	6	Good	Very Poor	106/92	Very Poor	$35-$37,000
Nissan Sentra	226	4	Very Poor	Very Poor	27/34	Very Good	$16-$20,000

*Best Bet designation is for Volts produced after January 2012. Chevrolet upgraded the steel structure surrounding the battery to prevent the post crash electrical fire hazard reported by NHTSA.

Vehicle	Page #	Overall Rating	Combined Crash Test Rating	Warranty Rating	Fuel Economy	Complaint Rating	Price Range
Compact (cont.)							
Scion tC	233	7	Very Good	Very Poor	23/31	Average	$18-$19,000
Subaru Impreza	238			Poor	27/36		$17-$22,000
Suzuki Kizashi	242			Poor	23/30		
Toyota Corolla	247	5	Average	Very Poor	26/34	Poor	$16-$18,000
Toyota Matrix	250			Very Poor	25/32	Average	$18-$21,000
Toyota Prius	251	7	Very Good	Very Poor	51/48	Very Poor	
Volkswagen Golf	261			Good	24/31	Very Poor	$17-$29,000
Volkswagen Jetta	262	6	Good	Good	24/32	Very Poor	$16-$26,000
Volvo C70	266			Very Good	18/28	Very Good	$39-$43,000
Intermediate							
Acura TL	83			Average	20/29	Very Good	$35-$45,000
Acura TSX	84			Average	22/31	Poor	$29-$38,000
Audi A5	88			Good	22/30	Good	$37-$55,000
BMW 5 Series	96	9	Good	Very Good	20/30	Very Poor	$46-$64,000
Buick LaCrosse	102	9	Very Good	Good	25/36	Poor	$29-$38,000
Buick Regal	103			Good	19/31	Poor	$26-$34,000
Cadillac CTS	105	7	Very Good	Good	18/27	Average	$38-$63,000
Chevrolet Camaro	108	6	Very Good	Average	18/29	Poor	$23-$31,000
Chevrolet Corvette	110			Average	15/25	Poor	$49-$111,000
Chevrolet Impala	113	4	Good	Average	19/29	Average	$25-$30,000
Chevrolet Malibu	114	5	Average	Average	22/33	Good	$21-$30,000
Chrysler 200	121	3	Poor	Poor	20/31	Good	$18-$26,000
Dodge Avenger	124	3	Poor	Poor	21/30	Poor	$18-$25,000
Ford Fusion	140	5	Poor	Poor	23/33	Good	$19-$28,000
Honda Accord	144	8	Good	Very Poor	23/34	Poor	$21-$31,000
Honda Accord Coupe	145			Very Poor	22/33		$22-$31,000
Hyundai Azera	156			Very Good	20/29		
Hyundai Genesis	159			Very Good	19/29	Very Poor	$34-$46,000
Hyundai Sonata	161	9	Very Good	Very Good	24/35	Very Poor	$19-$26,000
Infiniti EX	165			Good	17/24	Poor	$35-$39,000
Infiniti G	167			Good	20/29	Good	$32-$45,000
Kia Optima	178	8	Very Good	Good	24/34	Very Poor	$19-$26,000
Lexus ES	187			Average	19/27	Average	$36-$36,000
Lexus GS 2013	188			Average	19/28		
Lexus HS	190			Average	35/34	Very Poor	$36-$39,000
Lexus IS	191			Average	21/30	Good	$33-$46,000
Lincoln MKZ	140	3	Poor	Average	18/27	Very Good	$34-$36,000
Mazda 6	199	7	Average	Very Poor	22/31	Very Good	$20-$29,000

Vehicle	Page #	Overall Rating	Combined Crash Test Rating	Warranty Rating	Fuel Economy	Complaint Rating	Price Range
Intermediate (cont.)							
Mercedes-Benz E-Class	204			Poor	19/28	Very Good	$50-$92,000
Mitsubishi Galant	211			Very Good	21/30	Very Good	$21-$24,000
Nissan Altima	215	6	Average	Very Good	23/32	Very Good	$20-$25,000
Nissan Maxima	222	4	Poor	Very Poor	19/26	Good	$31-$34,000
Subaru Legacy	239	2	Average	Poor	23/31	Very Poor	$19-$31,000
Subaru Outback	240			Poor	22/29	Very Poor	$23-$31,000
Toyota Avalon	245			Very Poor	20/29	Very Poor	$33-$36,000
Toyota Camry	**246**	**10**	**Good**	**Very Poor**	**25/35**		**$21-$27,000**
Volkswagen CC	260			Good	22/31	Good	$28-$40,000
Volkswagen Passat	**263**	**9**	**Very Good**	**Good**	**22/31**		**$19-$32,000**
Volvo S60	267			Very Good	18/26	Very Good	$30-$42,000
Large							
Audi A6	89			Good	25/33		$41-$49,000
Audi A7	90			Good	18/28		$59-$65,000
Audi A8	91			Good	18/28		$78-$84,000
BMW 7 Series	97			Very Good	15/22	Average	$71-$91,000
Chrysler 300	122			Poor	18/27	Average	$27-$47,000
Dodge Challenger	126			Poor	18/27	Very Poor	$24-$43,000
Dodge Charger	127			Poor	18/27	Average	$25-$45,000
Ford Taurus	142	4	Good	Poor	18/28	Poor	$25-$38,000
Hyundai Equus	158			Very Good	15/23		$58-$65,000
Infiniti M	**168**	**6**	**Average**	**Good**	**18/26**	**Poor**	**$47-$61,000**
Jaguar XF	170			Average	16/24	Very Poor	$53-$82,000
Jaguar XJ	171			Average	16/23		$73-$117,000
Lexus LS	192			Average	16/24	Very Good	$67-$112,000
Lincoln MKS	194			Average	17/25	Poor	$41-$48,000
Mercedes-Benz S-Class	208			Poor	15/25	Very Good	$92-$211,000
Volvo S80	268			Very Good	20/29	Average	$37-$45,000
Minivan							
Chrysler Town and Country	123	5	Average	Poor	17/25	Very Poor	$30-$39,000
Dodge Grand Caravan	129	5	Average	Poor	17/25	Poor	$22-$29,000
Honda Odyssey	**152**	**7**	**Good**	**Very Poor**	**18/28**	**Poor**	**$28-$43,000**
Kia Sedona	180			Good	18/25	Poor	$24-$29,000
Mazda 5	198			Very Poor	21/28	Very Poor	$19-$24,000
Toyota Sienna	254	1	Very Poor	Very Poor	19/24	Very Poor	$25-$40,000
Volkswagen Routan	264			Good	17/25	Very Poor	$27-$44,000
Small SUV							
Acura RDX	82			Average	19/24	Very Good	$32-$37,000

Vehicle	Page #	Overall Rating	Combined Crash Test Rating	Warranty Rating	Fuel Economy	Complaint Rating	Price Range
Small SUV (cont.)							
Ford Escape	133	2	Very Poor	Poor	21/28	Average	$21-$34,000
Honda CR-V	148	4	Very Poor	Very Poor	23/31		$21-$30,000
Hyundai Tucson	**162**	**8**	**Average**	**Very Good**	**23/31**	**Average**	**$19-$26,000**
Jeep Compass	172			Poor	21/26	Poor	$19-$26,000
Jeep Liberty	174			Poor	15/21	Average	$23-$28,000
Jeep Patriot	175			Poor	21/27	Poor	$15-$25,000
Jeep Wrangler	176			Poor	17/21	Very Poor	$22-$33,000
Kia Sportage	183			Good	22/32	Average	$18-$26,000
Mitsubishi Outlander	213			Very Good	23/28	Good	$22-$27,000
Nissan Cube	218			Very Poor	27/31	Very Good	
Nissan Juke	220			Very Poor	27/32	Very Good	$19-$25,000
Subaru Forester	237	5	Average	Poor	21/27	Good	$20-$29,000
Suzuki Grand Vitara	241			Poor	19/25	Poor	
Toyota RAV4	252	1	Very Poor	Very Poor	21/27	Average	
Volkswagen Tiguan	265			Good	22/27	Average	$22-$37,000
Mid-Size SUV							
Acura MDX	**81**	**8**	**Average**	**Average**	**16/21**	**Very Good**	**$42-$56,000**
Acura ZDX	**85**	**8**	**Good**	**Average**	**16/23**		**$46-$56,000**
Audi Q5	92			Good	18/23	Very Good	$35-$39,000
BMW X3	98			Very Good	19/26	Very Poor	$36-$42,000
BMW X5	99			Very Good	16/23	Good	$47-$84,000
Buick Enclave	**101**	**7**	**Very Good**	**Good**	**17/24**	**Average**	**$36-$43,000**
Cadillac SRX	**106**	**7**	**Very Good**	**Good**	**17/24**	**Poor**	**$35-$45,000**
Chevrolet Equinox	112	3	Average	Average	17/24	Poor	$23-$30,000
Dodge Journey	130	5	Average	Poor	19/26	Very Poor	$20-$29,000
Ford Edge	132	5	Poor	Poor	21/30	Good	$27-$36,000
Ford Explorer	135	6	Average	Poor	17/23	Good	$28-$37,000
GMC Terrain	112	4	Average	Average	22/32	Poor	$25-$32,000
Honda Pilot	153	4	Poor	Very Poor	17/24	Very Good	$28-$40,000
Hyundai Santa Fe	160			Very Good	20/28	Poor	$23-$30,000
Hyundai Veracruz	164			Very Good	17/22	Average	$28-$34,000
Infiniti FX	166			Good	16/21	Good	$43-$59,000
Kia Sorento	181	5	Average	Good	20/26	Very Poor	$21-$34,000
Lexus GX	189			Average	15/20	Good	$53-$58,000
Lexus RX	193	5	Average	Average	18/24	Average	$39-$46,000
Lincoln MKX	132	3	Very Poor	Average	17/23	Good	$39-$41,000
Mazda CX-7	200			Very Poor	20/28	Poor	

Vehicle	Page #	Overall Rating	Combined Crash Test Rating	Warranty Rating	Fuel Economy	Complaint Rating	Price Range
Mid-Size SUV (cont.)							
Mazda CX-9	201			Very Poor	17/24	Very Good	$29-$34,000
Mercedes-Benz GLK-Class	206			Poor	16/21	Very Poor	$35-$37,000
Mercedes-Benz M-Class	207			Poor	17/22	Average	$49-$57,000
Nissan Murano	223	3	Very Poor	Very Poor	18/23	Good	$29-$39,000
Nissan Pathfinder	224			Very Poor	14/20	Poor	$28-$43,000
Nissan Rogue	225	5	Average	Very Poor	22/26	Very Good	$21-$29,000
Nissan Xterra	229			Very Poor	15/20	Poor	$24-$31,000
Porsche Cayenne	230			Good	16/23	Very Poor	$48-$107,000
Toyota 4Runner	244			Very Poor	17/23	Good	$31-$40,000
Toyota Highlander	249	4	Average	Very Poor	17/22	Average	$28-$35,000
Toyota Venza	257	1	Poor	Very Poor	18/25	Average	$27-$37,000
Volvo XC60	**269**	**10**	**Very Good**	**Very Good**	**17/23**	**Poor**	**$32-$47,000**
Volvo XC90	270			Very Good	16/22	Poor	$38-$44,000
Large SUV							
Audi Q7	93			Good	16/22	Good	$46-$59,000
Cadillac Escalade	**118**	**7**	**Very Good**	**Good**	**13/18**	**Good**	**$63-$85,000**
Cadillac Escalade ESV	117	6	Very Good	Good	13/18	Good	$66-$85,000
Chevrolet Suburban	117	6	Very Good	Average	15/21	Good	$41-$57,000
Chevrolet Tahoe	**118**	**7**	**Very Good**	**Average**	**15/21**	**Good**	**$38-$54,000**
Chevrolet Traverse	**119**	**8**	**Very Good**	**Average**	**17/24**	**Very Good**	**$29-$38,000**
Dodge Durango	128	2	Very Poor	Poor	16/23	Very Good	$28-$40,000
Ford Expedition	134			Poor	13/18	Average	$36-$52,000
Ford Flex	138			Poor	17/24	Poor	$29-$42,000
GMC Acadia	143	6	Very Good	Average	17/24	Average	$32-$45,000
GMC Yukon	118	6	Very Good	Average	15/21	Good	$39-$61,000
GMC Yukon XL	**117**	**7**		**Average**	**15/21**	**Good**	**$43-$61,000**
Infiniti QX56	169			Good	14/20	Average	$58-$61,000
Jeep Grand Cherokee	173	6	Good	Poor	16/23	Average	$26-$54,000
Land Rover LR4	184			Poor	12/17	Very Good	$49-$58,000
Land Rover Range Rover	185			Poor	12/18	Very Good	$79-$94,000
Lincoln MKT	195			Average	17/24	Very Poor	$44-$46,000
Mercedes-Benz GL-Class	205			Poor	13/18	Good	$61-$85,000
Nissan Armada	217			Very Poor	13/19	Poor	$38-$54,000
Toyota FJ Cruiser	248			Very Poor	17/20	Very Poor	$25-$27,000
Toyota Sequoia	253			Very Poor	13/17	Average	$40-$61,000
Compact Pickup							
Chevrolet Colorado	109			Average	18/25	Very Good	$17-$30,000

Vehicle	Page #	Overall Rating	Combined Crash Test Rating	Warranty Rating	Fuel Economy	Complaint Rating	Price Range
Compact Pickup (cont.)							
GMC Canyon	109			Average	17/23	Good	$17-$32,000
Nissan Frontier	219			Very Poor	14/19	Average	$22-$32,000
Toyota Tacoma	255	1	Poor	Very Poor	16/21	Average	$16-$27,000
Standard Pickup							
Cadillac Escalade EXT	107			Good	13/18	Very Good	$63-$70,000
Chevrolet Avalanche	107			Average	15/21	Average	$36-$50,000
Chevrolet Silverado Ext.	**115**	**6**	**Good**	**Average**	**15/21**	**Very Good**	**$21-$42,000**
Ford F-150 Crew Cab	136	5	Average	Poor	14/19	Very Good	$22-$51,000
GMC Sierra Ext. Cab	**115**	**6**	**Good**	**Average**	**12/18**	**Very Good**	**$21-$42,000**
Honda Ridgeline	154			Very Poor	15/20	Good	$29-$37,000
Nissan Titan	227			Very Poor	13/18	Very Poor	$27-$40,000
Ram 1500 Crew Cab	231	1	Very Poor	Poor	14/19	Very Good	$21-$46,000
Toyota Tundra	256	3	Average	Very Poor	15/20	Good	$25-$43,000

ABOUT THE CAR BOOK BEST BETS

TIP

It is important to consult the specific chapters to learn more about how *The Car Book* ratings are developed and to look on the car pages, beginning on page 81, for more details on these vehicles. In order to be considered as a "Best Bet" the vehicle must have a crash test rating as safety is a critical factor in gaining that recognition. Vehicles with "Poor" (3 or 4) or "Very Poor" (1 or 2) in Combined Crash Tests, "Very Poor" in Front or Side Crash Test Ratings, or an additional injury warning were not concidered for as a "Best Bet." Because most people are considering vehicles in the same size category, the "Best Bets" are by size—indicating how these vehicles compared against others in the same size class.

BEST BETS

The following is our list of the highest rated vehicles in each size category. The ratings are based on expected performance in nine important categories–Combined Crash Rating, Safety Features, Rollover, Preventive Maintenance, Repair Costs, Warranty, Fuel Economy, Complaints, and Insurance Costs–with the heaviest emphasis placed on safety. (See box on previous page.)

CHEVROLET SONIC — SUBCOMPACT

Combo Crash Tests.... 10	Warranty 5
Safety Features 9	Fuel Economy 8
Rollover 6	Complaints .... –
PM .... –	Insurance 5
Repair Costs.......... –	**OVERALL RATING ...9**

Page 116

HYUNDAI ACCENT — SUBCOMPACT

Combo Crash Tests..... 6	Warranty 10
Safety Features 4	Fuel Economy 10
Rollover 7	Complaints .... –
PM 6	Insurance 1
Repair Costs......... 10	**OVERALL RATING ...8**

Page 155

CHEVROLET CRUZE — COMPACT

Combo Crash Tests.... 10	Warranty 5
Safety Features 10	Fuel Economy 9
Rollover 7	Complaints 5
PM .... –	Insurance 1
Repair Costs.......... –	**OVERALL RATING ...9**

Page 111

CHEVROLET VOLT* — COMPACT

Combo Crash Tests..... 8	Warranty 5
Safety Features 8	Fuel Economy 10
Rollover 9	Complaints 2
PM .... –	Insurance 5
Repair Costs.......... –	**OVERALL RATING ...8**

Page 120

SCION TC — COMPACT

Combo Crash Tests..... 9	Warranty 2
Safety Features 5	Fuel Economy 6
Rollover 7	Complaints 6
PM 9	Insurance 1
Repair Costs.......... –	**OVERALL RATING ...7**

Page 233

*See page 7 for details.

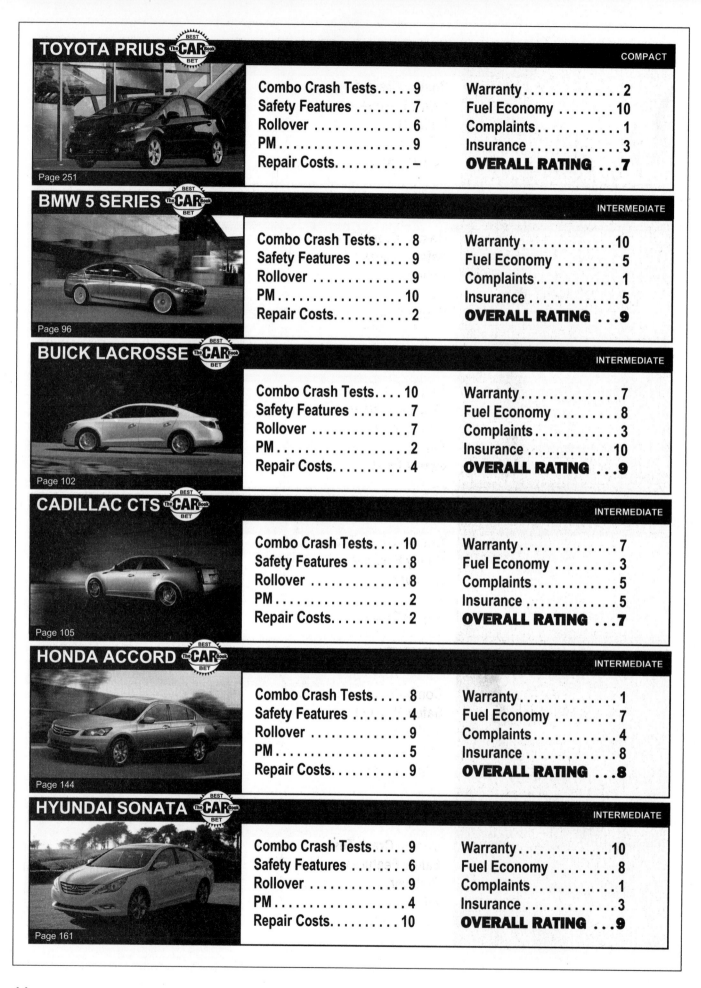

TOYOTA PRIUS

COMPACT

Combo Crash Tests	9	Warranty	2
Safety Features	7	Fuel Economy	10
Rollover	6	Complaints	1
PM	9	Insurance	3
Repair Costs	–	**OVERALL RATING**	**7**

Page 251

BMW 5 SERIES

INTERMEDIATE

Combo Crash Tests	8	Warranty	10
Safety Features	9	Fuel Economy	5
Rollover	9	Complaints	1
PM	10	Insurance	5
Repair Costs	2	**OVERALL RATING**	**9**

Page 96

BUICK LACROSSE

INTERMEDIATE

Combo Crash Tests	10	Warranty	7
Safety Features	7	Fuel Economy	8
Rollover	7	Complaints	3
PM	2	Insurance	10
Repair Costs	4	**OVERALL RATING**	**9**

Page 102

CADILLAC CTS

INTERMEDIATE

Combo Crash Tests	10	Warranty	7
Safety Features	8	Fuel Economy	3
Rollover	8	Complaints	5
PM	2	Insurance	5
Repair Costs	2	**OVERALL RATING**	**7**

Page 105

HONDA ACCORD

INTERMEDIATE

Combo Crash Tests	8	Warranty	1
Safety Features	4	Fuel Economy	7
Rollover	9	Complaints	4
PM	5	Insurance	8
Repair Costs	9	**OVERALL RATING**	**8**

Page 144

HYUNDAI SONATA

INTERMEDIATE

Combo Crash Tests	9	Warranty	10
Safety Features	6	Fuel Economy	8
Rollover	9	Complaints	1
PM	4	Insurance	3
Repair Costs	10	**OVERALL RATING**	**9**

Page 161

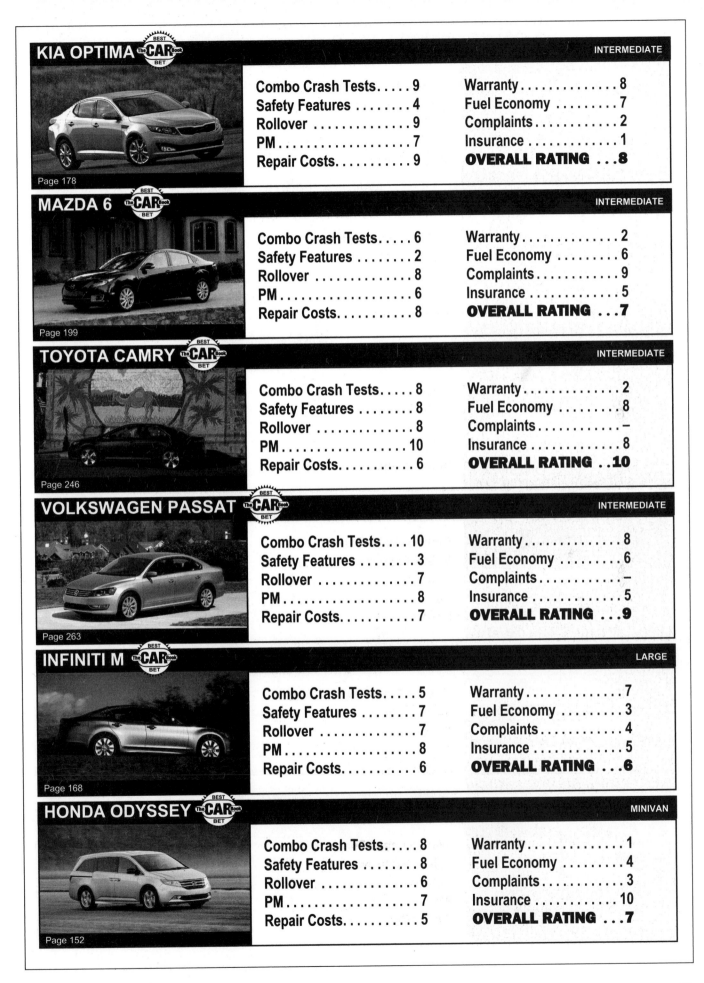

KIA OPTIMA

INTERMEDIATE

Page 178

Combo Crash Tests	9	Warranty	8
Safety Features	4	Fuel Economy	7
Rollover	9	Complaints	2
PM	7	Insurance	1
Repair Costs	9	**OVERALL RATING**	**8**

MAZDA 6

INTERMEDIATE

Page 199

Combo Crash Tests	6	Warranty	2
Safety Features	2	Fuel Economy	6
Rollover	8	Complaints	9
PM	6	Insurance	5
Repair Costs	8	**OVERALL RATING**	**7**

TOYOTA CAMRY

INTERMEDIATE

Page 246

Combo Crash Tests	8	Warranty	2
Safety Features	8	Fuel Economy	8
Rollover	8	Complaints	–
PM	10	Insurance	8
Repair Costs	6	**OVERALL RATING**	**10**

VOLKSWAGEN PASSAT

INTERMEDIATE

Page 263

Combo Crash Tests	10	Warranty	8
Safety Features	3	Fuel Economy	6
Rollover	7	Complaints	–
PM	8	Insurance	5
Repair Costs	7	**OVERALL RATING**	**9**

INFINITI M

LARGE

Page 168

Combo Crash Tests	5	Warranty	7
Safety Features	7	Fuel Economy	3
Rollover	7	Complaints	4
PM	8	Insurance	5
Repair Costs	6	**OVERALL RATING**	**6**

HONDA ODYSSEY

MINIVAN

Page 152

Combo Crash Tests	8	Warranty	1
Safety Features	8	Fuel Economy	4
Rollover	6	Complaints	3
PM	7	Insurance	10
Repair Costs	5	**OVERALL RATING**	**7**

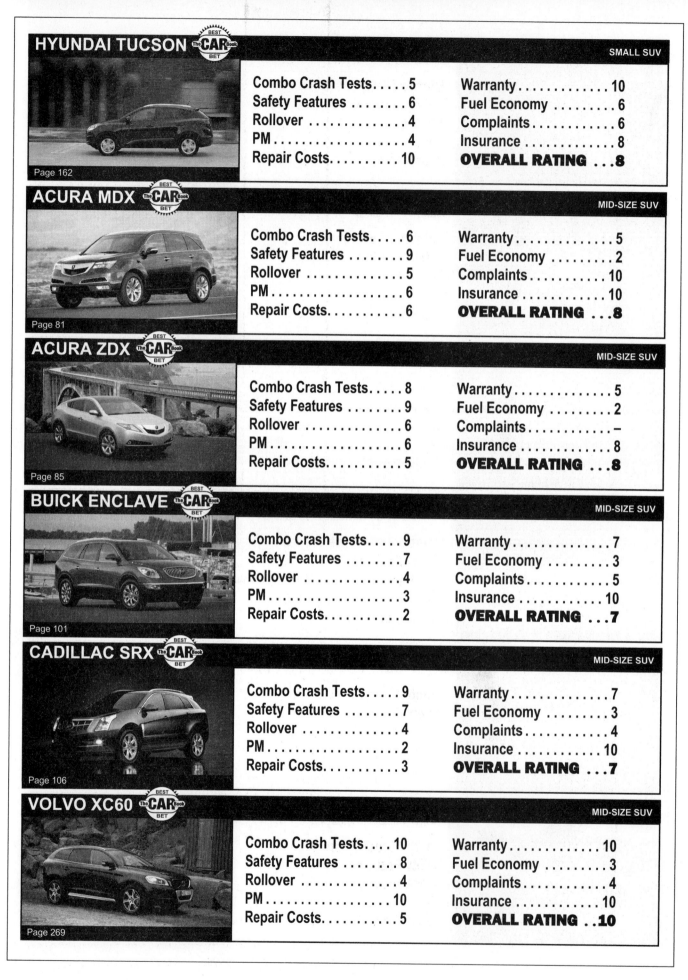

HYUNDAI TUCSON

SMALL SUV

Combo Crash Tests.....5
Safety Features 6
Rollover 4
PM.............4
Repair Costs.........10

Warranty...........10
Fuel Economy 6
Complaints..........6
Insurance 8
OVERALL RATING ...8

Page 162

ACURA MDX

MID-SIZE SUV

Combo Crash Tests.....6
Safety Features 9
Rollover 5
PM.............6
Repair Costs.........6

Warranty...........5
Fuel Economy 2
Complaints..........10
Insurance 10
OVERALL RATING ...8

Page 81

ACURA ZDX

MID-SIZE SUV

Combo Crash Tests.....8
Safety Features 9
Rollover 6
PM.............6
Repair Costs.........5

Warranty...........5
Fuel Economy 2
Complaints...........–
Insurance 8
OVERALL RATING ...8

Page 85

BUICK ENCLAVE

MID-SIZE SUV

Combo Crash Tests.....9
Safety Features 7
Rollover 4
PM.............3
Repair Costs.........2

Warranty...........7
Fuel Economy 3
Complaints..........5
Insurance 10
OVERALL RATING ...7

Page 101

CADILLAC SRX

MID-SIZE SUV

Combo Crash Tests.....9
Safety Features 7
Rollover 4
PM.............2
Repair Costs.........3

Warranty...........7
Fuel Economy 3
Complaints..........4
Insurance 10
OVERALL RATING ...7

Page 106

VOLVO XC60

MID-SIZE SUV

Combo Crash Tests....10
Safety Features 8
Rollover 4
PM.............10
Repair Costs.........5

Warranty...........10
Fuel Economy 3
Complaints..........4
Insurance 10
OVERALL RATING ..10

Page 269

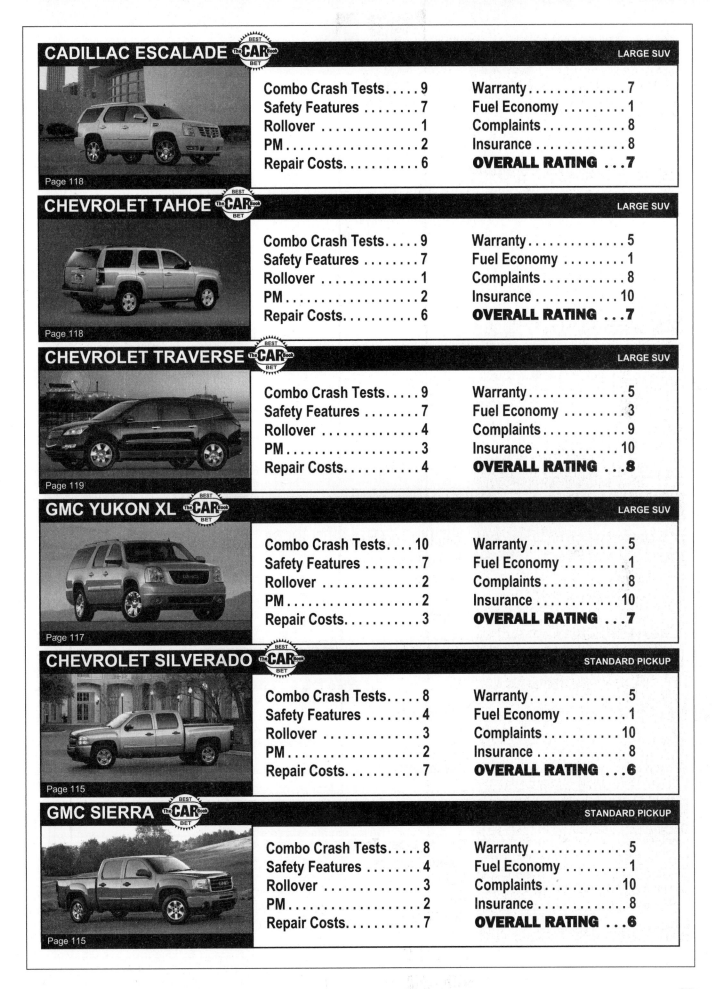

CADILLAC ESCALADE

LARGE SUV

Combo Crash Tests	9	Warranty	7
Safety Features	7	Fuel Economy	1
Rollover	1	Complaints	8
PM	2	Insurance	8
Repair Costs	6	**OVERALL RATING**	7

Page 118

CHEVROLET TAHOE

LARGE SUV

Combo Crash Tests	9	Warranty	5
Safety Features	7	Fuel Economy	1
Rollover	1	Complaints	8
PM	2	Insurance	10
Repair Costs	6	**OVERALL RATING**	7

Page 118

CHEVROLET TRAVERSE

LARGE SUV

Combo Crash Tests	9	Warranty	5
Safety Features	7	Fuel Economy	3
Rollover	4	Complaints	9
PM	3	Insurance	10
Repair Costs	4	**OVERALL RATING**	8

Page 119

GMC YUKON XL

LARGE SUV

Combo Crash Tests	10	Warranty	5
Safety Features	7	Fuel Economy	1
Rollover	2	Complaints	8
PM	2	Insurance	10
Repair Costs	3	**OVERALL RATING**	7

Page 117

CHEVROLET SILVERADO

STANDARD PICKUP

Combo Crash Tests	8	Warranty	5
Safety Features	4	Fuel Economy	1
Rollover	3	Complaints	10
PM	2	Insurance	8
Repair Costs	7	**OVERALL RATING**	6

Page 115

GMC SIERRA

STANDARD PICKUP

Combo Crash Tests	8	Warranty	5
Safety Features	4	Fuel Economy	1
Rollover	3	Complaints	10
PM	2	Insurance	8
Repair Costs	7	**OVERALL RATING**	6

Page 115

CRASH TESTS

S afety is likely the most important factor that most of us consider when choosing a new car. In the past, evaluating safety was difficult. Now, thanks to the information in The Car Book, it's much easier to pick a safe vehicle. The bottom line: For the greatest protection, you'll want the maximum number of safety features (pages 78-79) and good crash test results (the following tables).

A key factor in occupant protection is how well the car protects you in a crash. This depends on its ability to absorb the force of the impact rather than transfer it to the occupant. In 2011, the government began a new crash test program with more sophisticated dummies, additional test measurements, and a small female dummy.

In the frontal test, the vehicle impacts a solid barrier at 35 mph. In the side test, a moving barrier is crashed into the side of the vehicle at 38.5 mph. A second side test, new in 2011, simulates hitting a tree or roadside pole by smashing a vertical pole into the driver side door at 20 mph. The only occupant in this side pole test is a small female dummy in the driver seat.

In all crash tests the dummies are securely belted. Therefore, these test results do not apply to unbelted occupants. The new dummies measure impact on a different scale from previous tests, and the new test measures neck injuries and chest deflexion which were not included in the previous tests. In addition, these new test results cannot be compared with older results.

Because of the new test procedures not all 2012 vehicles have undergone the new tests. The good news is that by carrying forward new 2011 tests from cars that haven't changed, we can predict results for ninety 2012 models. The bad news is that there are 100 models for which we don't have crash test results.

How the Cars are Rated: The combined crash test ratings are based on the relative performance of the vehicles tested to date using the new test. It is best to compare the results within the size class.

The first column provides The Car Book's Combined Crash Test Rating. The cars are rated from 10 Best to 1 Worst. The front is weighted 60%, the side 36%, and the pole test 4% with results compared among all new 2012 crash tests to date.

Next are the individual front and side tests. Again, relative to all other 2012 vehicles tested, we indicate if the vehicle was Very Good, Good, Average, Poor or Very Poor. For side tests, the cars are rated separately from the trucks. Because of their construction the dynamics of a side test are different in cars and trucks.

The next five columns indicate the likelihood of the occupant sustaining a life-threatening injury. The percent likelihood is listed for the driver and front passenger in the front test, the driver and rear passenger in the side test, and the driver in the side pole test. Lower percentages mean a lower likelihood of being seriously injured. This information is taken directly from the government's analysis of the crash test results.

WHAT'S DIFFERENT IN THE 2012 GOVERNMENT CRASH TEST PROGRAM?

The 2012 crash test program contains some important improvements over the 1990-2010 program.

New Dummies: Three new dummy types are used which contain more sophisticated measuring devices.

Female Dummies: Previously, only male sized dummies were used. These new dummies better measure the impact on a smaller female body.

New Test Measurements: The new dummies measure neck injuries, chest deflection and impact on the abdomen.

While the new test procedures provide a better indication of crash protection, relatively few 2012 vehicles have been tested. As such, we've included the previous test results for untested vehicles which haven't changed in 2012. Because of test differences, you can't compare new results with previous results.

CRASH TESTS

Crash Test Performance (10=Best, 1=Worst)	Combined Car Book Crash Test Rating	Test Type	Car Book Crash Test Rating - Index (Lower numbers are better)	Likelihood of Life Threatening Injury				
				Front Fixed Barrier		Side Moving Barrier		Side Pole
				Front Driver	Front Pass.	Side Driver	Side Pass.	Pole Driver
Subcompact								
Chevrolet Sonic	10	Front	Very Good - 165	8.5%	8.8%			
		Side	Very Good - 113		7.0%	4.5%	7.0%	
Fiat 500	2	Front	Poor - 256	11.4%	16.0%			
		Side	Very Poor - 372			5.8%	31.9%	15.8%
Ford Fiesta*	9	Front	Good - 199	8.2%	12.8%			
		Side	Good - 121			10.1%	1.8%	11.8%
Honda CR-Z	2	Front	Very Poor - 336	15.5%	21.4%			
		Side^	Average - 166			19.1%		6.5%
Hyundai Accent	6	Front	Good - 209	9.2%	12.9%			
		Side	Poor - 234			8.5%	17.0%	4.3%
Kia Soul	4	Front	Poor - 267	14.2%	14.4%			
		Side	Average - 171			12.1%	6.6%	7.9%
Nissan Versa	1	Front	Very Poor - 330	15.2%	21.0%			
		Side	Very Poor - 581			37.1%	36.8%	20.1%
Compact								
Audi A4/S4	5	Front	Poor - 268	16.5%	12.3%			
		Side	Good - 152			12.8%	4.8%	3.8%
Chevrolet Cruze	10	Front	Very Good - 161	8.0%	8.8%			
		Side	Very Good - 114		7.1%	4.8%	6.6%	

^Vehicle has no back seat, side rating based on injury results for the driver in the side impact barrier test and side impact pole test.

*Additional Injury Potential: Due to the intrusion of the left rear door during the side impact test, the interior door panel struck the torso of the rear passenger dummy, causing impact on lower spine acceleration to exceed government limit resulting in higher likelihood of thoracic injury.

CRASH TESTS

Crash Test Performance (10=Best, 1=Worst)	Combined Car Book Crash Test Rating	Test Type	Car Book Crash Test Rating - Index (Lower numbers are better)	Likelihood of Life Threatening Injury				
				Front Fixed Barrier		Side Moving Barrier		Side Pole
				Front Driver	Front Pass.	Side Driver	Side Pass.	Pole Driver
Compact (cont.)								
Chevrolet Volt^^	8	Front	Good - 205	8.8%	12.9%			
		Side	Good - 141			7.9%	7.9%	2.0%
Dodge Caliber	3	Front	Poor - 245	12.2%	14.0%			
		Side	Very Poor - 319			19.6%	8.1%	51.1%
Ford Focus	6	Front	Average - 219	9.2%	14.0%			
		Side	Average - 182			14.1%	7.5%	1.8%
Ford Mustang	6	Front	Good - 211	12.4%	9.8%			
		Side	Poor - 260			7.7%	18.6%	14.7%
Hyundai Elantra	3	Front	Very Poor - 324	9.2%	25.6%			
		Side	Good - 146			12.0%	3.9%	7.8%
Kia Forte**	4	Front	Poor - 246	9.0%	17.2%			
		Side	Poor - 235			17.1%	6.2%	23.7%
Nissan Leaf	8	Front	Good - 202	10.4%	10.9%			
		Side	Very Good - 109		6.7%	3.8%	10.2%	
Mazda 3	7	Front	Very Good - 186	7.2%	12.3%			
		Side	Very Poor - 311			13.2%	19.9%	16.7%
Mercedes-Benz C-Class	3	Front	Very Poor - 302	12.7%	20.1%			
		Side	Average - 162			3.1%	12.2%	10.3%
Nissan Sentra	2	Front	Poor - 287	12.3%	18.7%			
		Side	Very Poor - 291			7.5%	23.3%	8.0%

^^NHTSA reported that the May 2011 Volt crash test damaged the battery which led to a fire three weeks after the test was completed. Additional testing of the battery packs resulted in a subsequent fire and the agency has launched a safety defect investigation. For Volts produced after January 2012, Chevrolet upgraded the steel surrounding the battery to prevent the post crash electrical fire hazard reported by NHTSA.

** Additional Injury Potential: Due to the intrusion of the rear door during the side impact barrier test, the interior door panel struck the torso of the rear passenger dummy, causing impact on lower spine acceleration to exceed government limit resulting in higher likelihood of thoracic injury. Although not included in the rating, the rear passenger dummy's thoracic rib deflection reading was elevated

CRASH TESTS

Crash Test Performance (10=Best, 1=Worst)	Combined Car Book Crash Test Rating	Test Type	Car Book Crash Test Rating - Index (Lower numbers are better)	Likelihood of Life Threatening Injury				
				Front Fixed Barrier		Side Moving Barrier		Side Pole
				Front Driver	Front Pass.	Side Driver	Side Pass.	Pole Driver
Compact (cont.)								
Scion tC	9	Front	Good - 201	9.1%	12.1%			
		Side	Very Good - 89			2.7%	6.1%	4.0%
Toyota Corolla	5	Front	Good - 210	8.8%	13.4%			
		Side	Very Poor - 407			4.7%	31.8%	46.8%
Toyota Prius	9	Front	Very Good - 191	9.1%	11.0%			
		Side	Good - 137			5.6%	8.2%	7.2%
Volkswagen Jetta	7	Front	Good - 201	10.1%	11.1%			
		Side	Average - 181			10.6%	9.6%	4.7%
Intermediate								
BMW 5 Series	8	Front	Average - 233	13.1%	11.7%			
		Side	Very Good - 85			8.4%	0.8%	5.5%
Buick LaCrosse	10	Front	Very Good - 169	8.0%	9.7%			
		Side	Good - 158			5.0%	10.4%	10.3%
Cadillac CTS	10	Front	Very Good - 170	8.9%	8.8%			
		Side	Good - 130			5.4%	7.6%	7.6%
Chevrolet Camaro	10	Front	Very Good - 171	9.7%	8.2%			
		Side	Very Good - 67			5.7%	1.5%	3.2%
Chevrolet Impala	7	Front	Good - 194	8.4%	12.0%			
		Side	Poor - 230			22.8%	4.7%	5.0%
Chevrolet Malibu	5	Front	Average - 235	8.7%	16.2%			
		Side	Average - 170			14.9%	5.3%	2.7%
Chrysler 200	3	Front	Poor - 245	10.5%	15.6%			
		Side	Very Poor - 281			8.9%	10.3%	63.7%

CRASH TESTS

Crash Test Performance (10=Best, 1=Worst)	Combined Car Book Crash Test Rating	Test Type	Car Book Crash Test Rating - Index (Lower numbers are better)	Likelihood of Life Threatening Injury				
				Front Fixed Barrier		Side Moving Barrier		Side Pole
				Front Driver	Front Pass.	Side Driver	Side Pass.	Pole Driver
Intermediate (cont.)								
Dodge Avenger	3	Front	Poor - 239	9.9%	15.5%			
		Side	Poor - 245			16.6%	8.8%	20.1%
Ford Fusion & Hybrid	3	Front	Poor - 283	13.9%	16.8%			
		Side	Poor - 222			7.9%	15.1%	10.2%
Honda Accord	8	Front	Very Good - 187	9.8%	9.8%			
		Side	Average - 172			13.0%	5.6%	9.6%
Hyundai Sonata	9	Front	Good - 197	8.9%	11.9%			
		Side	Very Good - 103		7.6%	2.6%	9.2%	
Kia Optima & Hybrid	9	Front	Very Good - 174	8.6%	9.6%			
		Side	Average - 167			16.8%	2.0%	7.9%
Lincoln MKZ & Hybrid	3	Front	Poor - 283	13.9%	16.8%			
		Side	Poor - 222			7.9%	15.1%	10.2%
Mazda 6	6	Front	Poor - 286	12.0%	18.9%			
		Side	Very Good - 92			6.4%	0.5%	17.6%
Nissan Altima	5	Front	Average - 234	10.6%	14.3%			
		Side	Average - 181			12.7%	8.0%	3.8%
Nissan Maxima	3	Front	Very Poor - 299	11.2%	21.0%			
		Side	Average - 168			15.6%	4.0%	4.3%
Subaru Outback/Legacy	5	Front	Average - 227	12.2%	12.0%			
		Side	Poor - 222			8.3%	13.7%	15.8%
Toyota Camry & Hybrid	8	Front	Good - 201	9.0%	12.2%			
		Side	Good - 122			7.4%	5.3%	6.9%

CRASH TESTS

Crash Test Performance (10=Best, 1=Worst)	Combined Car Book Crash Test Rating	Test Type	Car Book Crash Test Rating - Index (Lower numbers are better)	Likelihood of Life Threatening Injury				
				Front Fixed Barrier		Side Moving Barrier		Side Pole
				Front Driver	Front Pass.	Side Driver	Side Pass.	Pole Driver
Intermediate (cont.)								
Volkswagen Passat	10	Front	Very Good - 154	7.7%	8.4%			
		Side	Good - 137			13.0%	2.7%	3.9%
Large								
Ford Taurus	7	Front	Average - 217	9.6%	13.3%			
		Side	Good - 154			8.3%	8.3%	5.8%
Infiniti M37 & M56	5	Front	Poor - 241	9.1%	16.5%			
		Side	Good - 152			13.9%	4.2%	1.6%
Minivan								
Chrysler Town & Country	6	Front	Good - 207	11.2%	10.7%			
		Side	Poor - 152			7.4%	8.8%	5.5%
Dodge Grand Caravan	6	Front	Good - 207	11.2%	10.7%			
		Side	Poor - 152			7.4%	8.8%	5.5%
Honda Odyssey	8	Front	Very Good - 176	8.6%	9.9%			
		Side	Average - 96			6.0%	3.5%	7.6%
Toyota Sienna	2	Front	Very Poor - 349	9.0%	28.4%			
		Side	Average - 80			4.5%	2.2%	11.5%
Small SUV								
Ford Escape & Hybrid	1	Front	Very Poor - 293	20.4%	11.2%			
		Side	Very Poor - 308			18.6%	15.7%	14.8%
Honda CR-V	2	Front	Poor - 265	10.2%	18.1%			
		Side	Very Poor - 232			15.0%	8.2%	21.5%
Hyundai Tucson	5	Front	Average - 231	11.5%	13.2%			
		Side	Average - 104			8.5%	2.3%	7.5%

CRASH TESTS

Crash Test Performance (10=Best, 1=Worst)	Combined Car Book Crash Test Rating	Test Type	Car Book Crash Test Rating - Index (Lower numbers are better)	Likelihood of Life Threatening Injury				
				Front Fixed Barrier		Side Moving Barrier		Side Pole
				Front Driver	Front Pass.	Side Driver	Side Pass.	Pole Driver
Small SUV (cont.)								
Subaru Forester	5	Front	Good - 200	11.6%	9.5%			
		Side	Very Poor - 321			5.5%	23.2%	36.2%
Toyota RAV4	1	Front	Very Poor - 303	12.8%	20.1%			
		Side	Very Poor - 263			5.5%	19.0%	22.5%
Mid-Size SUV								
Acura MDX	6	Front	Average - 227	9.3%	14.8%			
		Side	Average - 84			4.4%	3.4%	7.9%
Acura ZDX	8	Front	Good - 198	9.4%	11.5%			
		Side	Average - 90			6.7%	2.8%	5.2%
Buick Enclave	9	Front	Good - 193	9.3%	11.0%			
		Side	Very Good - 49			2.1%	2.2%	5.2%
Cadillac SRX	9	Front	Very Good - 184	8.2%	11.1%			
		Side	Good - 67			2.6%	1.7%	14.9%
Chevrolet Equinox	6	Front	Average - 216	9.5%	13.4%			
		Side	Average - 120			11.7%	2.0%	4.5%
Dodge Journey	5	Front	Average - 222	9.6%	14.0%			
		Side	Poor - 168			3.7%	11.9%	13.5%
Ford Edge	3	Front	Very Poor - 313	16.1%	18.1%			
		Side	Average - 81			5.3%	2.3%	8.3%
Ford Explorer	6	Front	Average - 237	11.0%	14.2%			
		Side	Good - 63			4.2%	1.6%	7.1%

CRASH TESTS

Crash Test Performance (10=Best, 1=Worst)	Combined Car Book Crash Test Rating	Test Type	Car Book Crash Test Rating - Index (Lower numbers are better)	Likelihood of Life Threatening Injury				
				Front Fixed Barrier		Side Moving Barrier		Side Pole
				Front Driver	Front Pass.	Side Driver	Side Pass.	Pole Driver
Mid-Size SUV (cont.)								
GMC Terrain	6	Front	Average - 216	9.5%	13.4%			
		Side	Average - 120			11.7%	2.0%	4.5%
Honda Pilot	4	Front	Average - 222	9.4%	14.1%			
		Side	Very Poor - 185			6.4%	12.3%	9.9%
Kia Sorento	5	Front	Average - 221	9.4%	14.0%			
		Side	Poor - 136			5.0%	8.8%	6.6%
Lexus RX350 & RX450h	5	Front	Average - 234	11.5%	13.4%			
		Side	Poor - 148			3.2%	10.8%	9.9%
Lincoln MKX	-	Front	Very Poor - 313	16.1%	18.1%			
		Side	N/A					
Nissan Murano	2	Front	Poor - 270	13.3%	15.8%			
		Side	Poor - 165			4.4%	11.5%	10.7%
Nissan Rogue	5	Front	Poor - 238	10.3%	15.1%			
		Side	Good - 65			3.8%	3.0%	2.9%
Toyota Highlander & Hybrid	5	Front	Poor - 260	14.9%	13.1%			
		Side	Good - 77			3.0%	4.0%	7.2%
Toyota Venza	3	Front	Very Poor - 316	14.1%	20.4%			
		Side	Average - 94			4.9%	3.9%	9.0%
Volvo XC60	10	Front	Very Good - 165	8.2%	9.0%			
		Side	Good - 60			4.0%	2.1%	4.0%

CRASH TESTS

Crash Test Performance (10=Best, 1=Worst)	Combined Car Book Crash Test Rating	Test Type	Car Book Crash Test Rating - Index (Lower numbers are better)	Likelihood of Life Threatening Injury				
				Front Fixed Barrier		Side Moving Barrier		Side Pole
				Front Driver	Front Pass.	Side Driver	Side Pass.	Pole Driver
Large SUV								
Cadillac Escalade & Hybrid	9	Front	Very Good - 185	9.3%	10.1%			
		Side	Good - 53			4.7%	0.3%	6.5%
Cadillac Escalade ESV	10	Front	Very Good - 181	9.0%	9.9%			
		Side	Very Good - 33			2.2%	0.3%	6.3%
Chevrolet Suburban/Yukon XL	10	Front	Very Good - 181	9.0%	9.9%			
		Side	Very Good - 33			2.2%	0.3%	6.3%
Chevrolet Tahoe	9	Front	Very Good - 185	9.3%	10.1%			
		Side	Good - 53			4.7%	0.3%	6.5%
Chevrolet Traverse	9	Front	Good - 193	9.3%	11.0%			
		Side	Very Good - 49			2.1%	2.2%	5.2%
Dodge Durango	2	Front	Poor - 275	11.7%	17.9%			
		Side	Very Poor - 193			9.7%	11.9%	2.9%
GMC Acadia	9	Front	Good - 193	9.3%	11.0%			
		Side	Very Good - 49			2.1%	2.2%	5.2%
GMC Yukon	9	Front	Very Good - 185	9.3%	10.1%			
		Side	Good - 53			4.7%	0.3%	6.5%
Jeep Grand Cherokee	7	Front	Good - 196	9.9%	10.8%			
		Side	Average - 94			8.4%	2.3%	2.4%
Compact Pickup								
Toyota Tacoma	3	Front	Poor - 283	14.9%	15.8%			
		Side	Poor - 134			11.5%	1.9%	12.9%
Standard Pickup								
Chevrolet Silverado Reg. Cab	8	Front	Average - 228	9.9%	14.3%			
		Side^	Very Good - 39			2.8%		8.6%

^Vehicle has no back seat, side rating based on injury results for the driver in the side impact barrier test and side impact pole test.

CRASH TESTS

Crash Test Performance (10=Best, 1=Worst)	Combined Car Book Crash Test Rating	Test Type	Car Book Crash Test Rating - Index (Lower numbers are better)	Likelihood of Life Threatening Injury				
				Front Fixed Barrier		Side Moving Barrier		Side Pole
				Front Driver	Front Pass.	Side Driver	Side Pass.	Pole Driver
Standard Pickup (cont.)								
Chevrolet Silverado (cont.)								
Extended Cab	7	Front	Average - 228	9.9%	14.3%			
		Side	Very Good - 46			2.8%	0.7%	8.6%
Crew Cab & Hybrid Crew	7	Front	Average - 213	10.7%	11.9%			
		Side	Good - 52			4.5%	0.4%	6.3%
Ford F-150 Regular Cab	4	Front	Very Poor - 319	14.1%	20.8%			
		Side^	Very Good - 45			2.2%		13.9%
Crew Cab	5	Front	Very Poor - 309	14.3%	19.3%			
		Side	Very Good - 37			1.4%	0.7%	9.7%
Super Cab	4	Front	Very Poor - 319	14.1%	20.8%			
		Side	Good - 58			2.2%	1.4%	13.9%
GMC Sierra Regular Cab	8	Front	Average - 228	9.9%	14.3%			
		Side^	Very Good - 39			2.8%		8.6%
Extended Cab	7	Front	Average - 228	9.9%	14.3%			
		Side	Very Good - 46			2.8%	0.7%	8.6%
Crew Cab	7	Front	Average - 213	10.7%	11.9%			
		Side	Good - 52			4.5%	0.4%	6.3%
Ram 1500 Reg. Cab	5	Front	Average - 213	10.8%	11.9%			
		Side^	Poor - 170			7.6%		54.5%
Crew Cab***	1	Front	Very Poor - 389	16.0%	27.3%			
		Side	Very Poor - 183			6.2%	0.4%	65.1%
Quad Cab	4	Front	Average - 213	10.8%	11.9%			
		Side	Very Poor - 173			7.6%	0.3%	54.5%
Toyota Tundra Regular Cab	6	Front	Poor - 270	10.6%	18.3%			
		Side^	Very Good - 32			1.6%		9.5%
Extended Cab	6	Front	Poor - 270	10.6%	18.3%			
		Side	Very Good - 40			1.6%	0.9%	9.5%

^Vehicle has no back seat, side rating based on injury results for the driver in the side impact barrier test and side impact pole test.
***Additional Injury Potential: Due to the intrusion of the driver door during the side impact pole test, the interior door panel struck the torso of the driver dummy, causing impact on lower spine acceleration to exceed government limit resulting in higher likelihood of thoracic injury. Although not included in the rating, the driver dummy's abdomen rib deflection and thoracic rib deflection readings were elevated.

AUTOMATIC CRASH PROTECTION

The concept of automatic safety protection is not new. Automatic fire sprinklers in public buildings, oxygen masks in airplanes, purification of drinking water, and pasteurization of milk are all commonly accepted forms of automatic safety protection. Airbags provide automatic crash protection in cars.

Automatic crash protection protects people from what is called the "second collision," when the occupant collides with the interior of the vehicle. Because the "second collision" occurs within milliseconds, providing automatic rather than manual protection dramatically improves the chances of escaping injury.

Automatic crash protection comes in two basic forms, airbags and automatic control of safety features.

Since airbags were introduced over 30 years ago, they have been so successful in saving lives that car makers now include a variety of types which deploy from 4 to 8 different points.

The automatic control of safety features was first introduced with anti-lock brakes. Today, Electronic Stability Control (ESC) and other automatic functions are improving the safety of new cars.

Electronic Stability Control (ESC) takes advantage of anti-lock brake technology and helps minimize the loss of control. Each car maker will have its own name for this feature, but they all work in a similar fashion.

For ESC, anti-lock brakes work by using speed sensors on each wheel to determine if one or more of the wheels is locking up or skidding. ESC then uses these speed sensors and a unit that determines the steering angle to monitor what's happening with the vehicle. A special control device measures the steering and rotation of the tires in order to detect when a vehicle is about to go in a direction different from the one indicated by the steering wheel–or out of control! This will typically occur during a hard turn or on slippery surfaces. The control unit will sense whether the car is over-steering (turning sharper than you intended resulting in the back wheels slipping sideways) or under-steering (continuing to move forward despite your intended turn).

When either of these events occur, the control unit will automatically apply the brakes to the appropriate wheels to correct the situation and, in some cases, automatically slow down the engine.

As amazing as this device is, it will not keep the vehicle under control in severely out of control situations. Nevertheless, according to the IIHS, ESC can reduce the chance of a single vehicle crash by over 50%. Its benefit is that it will prevent more typical losses of control from escalating into a crash. It is an extremely important and recommended safety feature.

TELEMATICS

Telematic systems are subscription-based services ($200-$300 per year) that use a combination of cellular technology and global positioning systems to provide a variety of safety and convenience features. The main safety feature is automatic crash notification (ACN) which connects the vehicle's occupants to a private call center that directs emergency medical teams to the car. This system can be activated by pressing a button on the dash or rear view mirror or it is automatically activated if the airbag deploys. Once the system is activated, the call center receives the exact location of your vehicle and notifies the local emergency response team. This can potentially reduce the time it takes for an emergency team to reach your vehicle. Other safety features can include roadside assistance, remote door unlocking, stolen vehicle tracking, and driving directions.

Caution! Some manufacturers are adding cell phone capability to the ACN system which increases the risk of a crash 4-fold when talking on the ACN cell phone. This is about the same effect as drinking and driving. Don't drink and drive or telephone and drive!

CHILD SAFETY

Seat Belts for Kids: How long should children use car seats? For school-age children, a car seat is twice as effective in preventing injury as an adult lap and shoulder harness—use a booster as long as possible. Most children can start using seat belts at 4'9" and when tall enough for the shoulder belt to cross the chest, not the neck. The lap section of the belt should be snug and as low on the hips as possible. If the shoulder belt does cross the face or neck, use a booster seat.

Never:

☒ Use the same belt on two children.

☒ Move a shoulder belt behind a child's back or under an arm.

☒ Buckle in a pet or any large toys with the child.

☒ Recline a seat with a belted child.

☒ Use a twisted seat belt. The belt must be straight and flat.

☒ Use pillows or cushions to boost your child.

☒ Place a belt around you with a child in your lap. In an accident or sudden stop, your child would absorb most of the crash force.

Incorrect Installation: Surveys show up to 85 percent of parents do not install their child seats properly. Incorrect installation of a child safety seat can deny the child lifesaving protection and may even contribute to further injuring the child. Read the installation instructions carefully. If you have any questions about the correct installation in your particular car, contact the National Highway Traffic Safety Administration's website at www.nhtsa.gov. They can direct you to the nearest child seat inspection station that will check to see if you have installed your child seat correctly and instruct you on the proper way to install the seat if you have any questions. There is no charge for this service.

Following are some common mistakes parents make when installing a child safety seat.

☒ Infant is in safety seat facing forward, rather than to the rear.

☒ Child safety seat in front with an airbag.

☒ Child is not secured by safety seat harness and is sitting loose in safety seat.

☒ Booster seat used without a shield or a shoulder belt.

☒ Safety belt is fastened to or around wrong part of safety seat.

☒ Tether strap is not used, missing, or at wrong angle of attachment, when required.

☒ Use of incompatible safety belts.

☒ Safety belt is not used to secure safety seat in vehicle. The safety seat is loose on vehicle seat.

☒ Harness strap adjustment slides are not securely locked, permitting straps to release in a crash.

Warning: After an accident, rescue experts suggest that the entire seat be removed from the car, rather than unbuckling the child first.

CHILD SAFETY SEAT RECALLS

Manufacturers are required to put address cards in child seat packages. Mail the registration card as soon as you open the box! This is the only way you will receive notification of a seat recall. Keep a copy of the manufacturer's address and contact the manufacturer if you move. To find out if the seat you are using has ever been recalled go to http://www-odi.nhtsa.dot.gov/cars/problems/recalls/childseat.cfm. You can also contact the Auto Safety Hotline at 800-424-9393, (D.C. call 202-366-0123.)

ROLLOVER

The risk of rollover is a significant safety issue, especially with sport utility vehicles. Because of their relatively high center of gravity, they don't hug the road like smaller, lower automobiles and trucks. As a result, they are more likely to turn over on sharp turns or corners. Not only does a rollover increase the likelihood of injuries, but it also increases the risk of the occupant being thrown from the vehicle. In fact, the danger of rollover with sport utilities is so severe that manufacturers are now required to place a sticker where it can be seen by the driver every time the vehicle is used. Each year, approximately 10,000 people die in rollover-related accidents.

To understand the concept behind these vehicles' propensity to roll over, consider this: place a section of 2x4 lumber on its 2-inch side. It is easily tipped over by a force pushing against the side. But if you place it on its 4-inch side, the same force will cause it to slide rather than tip over. Similarly, in a moving vehicle, the forces generated by a turn can cause a narrow, tall vehicle to roll over. This is why SUVs are more susceptible to rolling over.

This year in the safety checklist we include a feature called roll-sensing side airbags. Roll-sensing side airbags are a special side airbag system which keeps the side airbags inflated longer in the event of a rollover. This feature is found in many SUVs and can reduce the likelihood of injury when a vehicle flips. See the car pages (81-270) for which 2012 models have this feature.

Congress required the U.S. Department of Transportation to develop a dynamic (moving) rating system to accompany the static (stationary) rating system. To date, this complex test has resulted in a simple "tip" or "no-tip" rating. Consumers are never told the speed of the tip and certain vehicles are not tested, just listed as "no tip."

Following are rollover ratings for many 2012 vehicles. We have been publishing these ratings for a number of years and recently, the National Highway Traffic Safety Administration adopted this rating system.

The rollover rating is based on the Static Stability Factor (SSF) and consists of a formula that uses the track width of the vehicle (tire to tire) and height to determine which vehicles are more or less likely to roll over when compared to each other. You can't use this information to exactly predict rollovers. However, all things being equal, if two vehicles are in the same situation where a rollover could occur, the one with a high SSF is less likely to roll over than one with a lower SSF. Because this formula doesn't consider such things as driver behavior and the weight of the vehicle, among other factors, some experts do not believe it tells the whole story. We agree, and urged the government to provide an even better rollover rating system.

In the meantime, knowing how the vehicles rate using the SSF can be a key consideration in your evaluation of the vehicle.

! ROOF CRUSH !

The government standard for roof crush (the ability of the roof to keep from collapsing in a rollover) is woefully inadequate. Roofs often crush in rollover accidents and seriously injure seat-belted occupants. Rollovers and roof crush break windshields and windows creating portals for occupants to be ejected from the vehicle. See next page for more details.

! GOVERNMENT WARNING !

To alert consumers to rollover, the following warning is required on certain vehicles:

This is a multipurpose passenger vehicle which will handle and maneuver differently from an ordinary passenger car, in driving conditions which may occur on streets and highways and off road. As with other vehicles of this type, if you make sharp turns or abrupt manuevers, the vehicle may roll over or may go out of control and crash. You should read driving guielines and instructions in the Owner's Manual, and wear your seat belt at all times.

ROOF CRUSH

Since 1970, the auto industry has fought efforts by the National Highway Traffic Safety Administration to issue a dynamic roof crush standard to protect occupants in rollover crashes. From 1970 to 2007, the number of deaths to occupants in rollover crashes climbed from 1,400 to over 10,000 each year while annual occupant fatalities declined from 43,200 to 28,900. NHTSA has stuck with the outdated, static roof crush standard issued in 1971 even though it was to have been phased out by 1977 for a dynamic standard. On the other hand, NHTSA has issued effective dynamic front and side crash test standards that have significantly reduced death and serious injury.

The current standard calls for roofs to withstand 1.5 times the weight of the vehicle, applied to one side of the roof, for vehicles up to 6,000 pounds. Vehicles weighing more need not meet any standard. A new standard will be phased in for 2013 to 2017 models which will double the roof strength requirement for vehicles weighing up to 6,000 pounds. Both the driver and passenger sides of the roof will have to withstand a force equal to three times the weight of the vehicle. While an improvement, the new standard falls short of requiring a dynamic crash test that better replicates what happens in real world crashes.

Today, some vehicles have strong roofs but all too many have weak roofs. In a rollover crash, the first side of a vehicle that hits the ground generally does not crush but the second, or trailing side, that hits the ground often does crush. This failure will either break the windows and allow the occupants to eject or crush the occupants that stay in the vehicle. To identify which vehicles today have strong roofs, the Center for Auto Safety (CAS) had the Center for Injury Research (CfIR) conduct dynamic rollover roof crush tests using the Jordan Rollover System (JRS).

The table below shows the results of the CAS testing. The cumulative crush is how much the roof will crush inward after two full rolls. More than 5 inches of roof crush is unacceptable because an occupant's head is likely to be hit. The Strength to Weight Ratio (SWR) is how much weight the roof on one side will support before crushing inward 5 inches when tested in a static fashion as the government does.

The dynamic rollover test shows that good roof design can result in a vehicle with a lower static SWR outperforming a vehicle with a higher static SWR in limiting roof intrusion in a rollover, demonstrating the problem with the static government test. CAS has developed a comparative rating for the roof strength that ranges from Very Good to Very Poor.

Dynamic tests, such as the JRS, show how vehicle geometry effects safety. Vehicles with the very square roofs such as the Ridgeline are more vulnerable to roof crush. A vehicle with a more rounded roof, such as the XC90, will roll more like a barrel with less force on the corners of the roof.

The design of the roof in unison with the body of the vehicle is critical to its ability to protect occupants. If any of the critical roof structural elements buckles the roof will collapse and injure belted occupants who are seated underneath.

Good design will also keep windows in place to prevent occupants from being ejected in rollovers. Only a dynamic test can demonstrate whether seat belts, pre-tensioners and side curtains function together to protect occupants from ejection and injury in rollovers.

Center for Auto Safety Roof Crush Test Results

Vehicle*	Cumulative Crush (in.)	Dynamic SWR	Static SWR	Rating
Volvo XC90 2005-09	1.8	5.2	4.6	Very Good
VW Tiguan 2009-11	2.4	4.9	4.4	Very Good
VW Jetta 2007-09	3.4	4.4	5.1	Good
Honda CR-V 2007-10	3.6	4.3	2.6	Good
Toyota Camry Hybrid 2007-10	4.3	4.2	3.9	Good
Toyota Prius 2010	3.8	4.2	4.2	Good
Toyota Camry 2007-09	4.3	4	4.3	Good
Nissan Versa 2009-10	4.4	4	3.7	Good
Subaru Forester 2003-08	4.6	3.9	4.3	Moderate
Hyundai Sonata 2006-09	4.6	3.9	3.2	Moderate
Chevrolet Mailbu 2009-10	5	3.7	4.4	Moderate
Pontiac G6 2006-09	7	2.8	2.3	Poor
Chrysler 300 2006-09	7.4	2.6	2.5	Poor
Jeep Gr. Cherokee 2007-10	9.1	1.8	2.2	Very Poor
Scion xB 2008-10	10.4	1.2	6.8	Very Poor
Chevy Tahoe 2007-09	10.9	1	2.1	Very Poor
Honda Ridgeline 2006-09	10.9	1	2.4	Very Poor

*Year tested is first model year listed with later models having similar roof strength and design.

This work was funded by the Santos Family Foundation on sixteen vehicles donated by the State Farm Insurance Company.

STATIC STABILITY FACTOR

Vehicle	SSF (High=Better)	Chance of Rollover	Vehicle	SSF (High=Better)	Chance of Rollover	Vehicle	SSF (High=Better)	Chance of Rollover
Acura MDX	1.3	Moderate	GMC Sierra 4WD	1.2	High	Merc.-Benz GL-Class	1.17*	Very High
Acura RDX	1.24*	High	GMC Sierra RWD	1.19	High	Merc.-Benz GLK-Class	1.19*	High
Acura TL	1.48*	Very Low	GMC Terrain AWD	1.22	High	Merc.-Benz M-Class	1.2*	High
Acura TSX	1.46*	Low	GMC Terrain FWD	1.19	High	Merc.-Benz S-Class	1.45*	Low
Acura ZDX	1.33	Moderate	GMC Yukon RWD	1.12	Very High	Mini Cooper	1.38*	Low
Audi A3	1.43*	Low	GMC Yukon 4WD	1.14	Very High	Mini Countryman	1.31*	Moderate
Audi A4/S4	1.46	Low	Honda Accord	1.48	Very Low	Mitsubishi Galant	1.43*	Low
Audi A5	1.54*	Very Low	Honda Accord Coupe	1.47*	Very Low	Mitsubishi Lancer	1.38*	Low
Audi A6	1.47*	Very Low	Honda Civic	1.4*	Low	Mitsubishi Outlander	1.19*	High
Audi A7	1.54*	Very Low	Honda Civic Coupe	1.44*	Low	Nissan 370Z	1.59*	Very Low
Audi A8	1.5*	Very Low	Honda CR-V	1.23*	High	Nissan Altima	1.43	Low
Audi Q5	1.27*	Moderate	Honda CR-Z	1.48	Very Low	Nissan Altima Coupe	1.46*	Low
Audi Q7	1.25*	High	Honda Fit	1.3*	Moderate	Nissan Armada	1.14*	Very High
BMW 1 Series	1.4*	Low	Honda Insight	1.38*	Low	Nissan Cube	1.19*	High
BMW 3 Series	1.44*	Low	Honda Odyssey	1.34	Moderate	Nissan Frontier	1.14*	Very High
BMW 5 Series	1.49	Very Low	Honda Pilot 4WD	1.24	High	Nissan Juke	1.29*	Moderate
BMW 7 Series	1.47*	Very Low	Honda Pilot FWD	1.22	High	Nissan Leaf	1.41	Moderate
BMW X3	1.27*	Moderate	Honda Ridgeline	1.24*	High	Nissan Maxima	1.44*	Low
BMW X5	1.2*	High	Hyundai Accent	1.35	Moderate	Nissan Murano AWD	1.2	High
BMW Z4	1.57*	Very Low	Hyundai Azera	1.46*	Low	Nissan Murano FWD	1.21	High
Buick Enclave AWD	1.26	High	Hyundai Elantra	1.41	Low	Nissan Pathfinder	1.11*	Very High
Buick Enclave FWD	1.23	High	Hyundai Equus	1.45*	Low	Nissan Rogue AWD	1.21	High
Buick LaCrosse	1.37	Low	Hyundai Genesis	1.47*	Very Low	Nissan Rogue FWD	1.18	High
Buick Regal	1.43*	Low	Hyundai Santa Fe	1.22*	High	Nissan Sentra	1.38	Low
Buick Verano	1.39*	Low	Hyundai Sonata	1.47	Very Low	Nissan Titan	1.18*	High
Cadillac CTS	1.44	Low	Hyundai Tucson FWD	1.21	High	Nissan Versa	1.3	Moderate
Cadillac Escalade AWD	1.14	Very High	Hyundai Tucson AWD	1.22	High	Nissan Xterra	1.07*	Very High
Cadillac Escalade RWD	1.12	Very High	Hyundai Veloster	1.49*	Very Low	Porsche Cayenne	1.26*	High
Cadillac SRX	1.21	High	Hyundai Veracruz	1.2*	High	Ram 1500 2WD	1.18	High
Chevrolet Avalanche	1.15*	Very High	Infiniti EX	1.36*	Moderate	Ram 1500 4WD	1.15	Very High
Chevrolet Camaro	1.53	Very Low	Infiniti FX	1.29*	Moderate	Scion iQ	1.3*	Moderate
Chevrolet Colorado	1.15*	Very High	Infiniti G	1.4*	Low	Scion tC	1.41	Low
Chevrolet Corvette	1.67*	Very Low	Infiniti M	1.39	Low	Scion xB	1.23*	High
Chevrolet Cruze	1.41	Low	Infiniti QX56	1.16*	Very High	Scion xD	1.3*	Moderate
Chevy Equinox AWD	1.22	High	Jaguar XF	1.44*	Low	Smart ForTwo	1.15*	Very High
Chevy Equinox FWD	1.19	High	Jaguar XJ	1.49*	Very Low	Subaru Forester	1.19*	High
Chevrolet Impala	1.39	Low	Jeep Compass	1.19*	High	Subaru Forester	1.21	High
Chevrolet Malibu	1.41	Low	Jeep Gr. Cherokee 2WD	1.17	Very High	Subaru Impreza	1.38*	Low
Chevy Silverado 4WD	1.2	High	Jeep Gr. Cherokee 4WD	1.23	High	Subaru Legacy	1.39*	Low
Chevy Silverado RWD	1.19	High	Jeep Liberty	1.12*	Very High	Subaru Outback	1.27*	Moderate
Chevrolet Sonic	1.34	Moderate	Jeep Patriot	1.19*	High	Suzuki Grand Vitara	1.19*	High
Chevrolet Suburban	1.14*	Very High	Jeep Wrangler	1.13*	Very High	Suzuki Kizashi	1.41*	Low
Chevrolet Tahoe AWD	1.14	Very High	Kia Forte	1.44	Low	Suzuki SX4	1.29*	Moderate
Chevrolet Tahoe RWD	1.12	Very High	Kia Optima	1.48	Very Low	Toyota 4Runner	1.17*	Very High
ChevyTraverse AWD	1.26	High	Kia Rio	1.39*	Low	Toyota Avalon	1.41*	Low
ChevyTraverse FWD	1.23	High	Kia Sedona	1.24*	High	Toyota Camry	1.42*	Low
Chevrolet Volt	1.49	Very Low	Kia Sorento AWD	1.23	High	Toyota Corolla	1.36	Moderate
Chrysler 200	1.4	Low	Kia Sorento FWD	1.21	High	Toyota FJ Cruiser	1.14*	Very High
Chrysler 300	1.45*	Low	Kia Soul	1.31*	Moderate	Toyota Highlander AWD	1.22	High
Chrysler Town & Cntry	1.24	High	Kia Sportage	1.28*	Moderate	Toyota Highlander FWD	1.18	High
Dodge Avenger	1.37	Low	Land Rover LR4	1.14*	Very High	Toyota Matrix	1.31*	Moderate
Dodge Caliber	1.26	High	Land Rover Range Rover	1.13*	Very High	Toyota Prius	1.36	Moderate
Dodge Challenger	1.47*	Very Low	Lexus CT	1.41*	Low	Toyota RAV4	1.2*	High
Dodge Charger	1.45*	Low	Lexus ES	1.46*	Low	Toyota Sequoia	1.19*	High
Dodge Durango	1.17*	Very High	Lexus GS	1.45*	Low	Toyota Sienna	1.3	Moderate
Dodge Grand Caravan	1.24	High	Lexus GX	1.09*	Very High	Toyota Tacoma 2WD	1.28	Moderate
Dodge Journey 4WD	1.21	High	Lexus HS	1.36*	Moderate	Toyota Tacoma 4WD	1.19	High
Dodge Journey FWD	1.2	High	Lexus IS	1.44*	Low	Toyota Tundra 2WD	1.17	Very High
Fiat 500	1.29	Moderate	Lexus LS	1.46*	Low	Toyota Tundra 4WD	1.18	High
Ford Edge FWD	1.25	High	Lexus RX AWD	1.24	High	Toyota Venza AWD	1.29	Moderate
Ford Edge AWD	1.3	Moderate	Lexus RX FWD	1.21	High	Toyota Venza FWD	1.26	High
Ford Escape 2WD	1.13	Very High	Lincoln MKS	1.41*	Low	Toyota Yaris	1.31*	Moderate
Ford Escape 4WD	1.17	Very High	Lincoln MKT	1.26*	High	Volkswagen Beetle	1.4*	Low
Ford Expedition	1.13*	Very High	Lincoln MKX AWD	1.3	Moderate	Volkswagen CC	1.46*	Low
Ford Explorer	1.23*	High	Lincoln MKX FWD	1.25	High	Volkswagen Golf	1.38*	Low
Ford F-150 2WD	1.18	High	Lincoln MKZ AWD	1.5	Very Low	Volkswagen Jetta	1.4	Low
Ford F-150 4WD	1.14	Very High	Lincoln MKZ FWD	1.43	Low	Volkswagen Passat	1.42	Low
Ford Fiesta	1.29	Moderate	Mazda 2	1.33*	Moderate	Volkswagen Routan	1.26*	High
Ford Flex	1.25*	High	Mazda 3	1.41	Low	Volkswagen Tiguan	1.22*	High
Ford Focus	1.38	Low	Mazda 5	1.23*	High	Volvo C70	1.48*	Very Low
Ford Fusion AWD	1.5	Very Low	Mazda 6	1.44*	Low	Volvo S60	1.42*	Low
Ford Fusion FWD	1.43	Low	Mazda CX-7	1.28*	Moderate	Volvo S80	1.41*	Low
Ford Mustang	1.53	Very Low	Mazda CX-9	1.24*	High	Volvo XC60	1.22	High
Ford Taurus	1.39	Low	Mazda MX-5 Miata	1.6*	Very Low	Volvo XC90	1.19*	High
GMC Acadia AWD	1.23	High	Merc.-Benz C-Class	1.43	Low			
GMC Acadia FWD	1.26	High	Merc.-Benz E-Class	1.46*	Low	*Calculated		

As gas prices bounce up and down, regular drivingstill takes a big bite out of our pocketbooks. The good news is that higher fuel efficiency standards are forcing car companies to provide more fuel efficient vehicles. Buying right and practicing more fuel efficient driving will make a huge difference in your vehicle's operating costs.

Using the EPA ratings is the best way to incorporate fuel efficiency in selecting a new car. By comparing these ratings, even among cars of the same size, you'll find that fuel efficiency varies greatly. One compact car might get 36 miles per gallon (mpg) while another compact gets only 22 mpg. If you drive 15,000 miles a year and you pay $3.23 per gallon for fuel, the 36 mpg car will save you $856 *a year* over the "gas guzzler."

In 2008, the EPA changed the way it estimates miles per gallon to better represent today's driving conditions. Their new method adjusts for aggressive driving (high speeds and faster acceleration), air conditioning use, and cold temperature operation.

Octane Ratings: Once you've purchased your car, you'll be faced with choosing the right gasoline. Oil companies spend millions of dollars trying to get you to buy so-called higher performance or high octane fuels. Using high octane fuel can add considerably to your gas bill, and the vast majority of vehicles do not need it. Check your owner's manual and only use what's recommended, which is usually 87. Very few vehicles require "premium" gasoline.

The octane rating of a gasoline is not a measure of power or quality. It is simply a measure of the gas' resistance to engine knock, which is the pinging sound you hear when the air and fuel mixture in your engine ignites prematurely during acceleration.

Your engine may knock when accelerating a heavily loaded car uphill or when the humidity is low. This is normal and does not call for a higher-octane gasoline.

FIVE FACTORS AFFECTING FUEL ECONOMY

1. Engine Size: The smaller the engine the better your fuel efficiency. A 10% increase in the size of your engine can increase your fuel consumption rate by 6%. Smaller engines can be cheaper to maintain as well.

2. Transmission: If used properly, manual transmissions are generally more fuel-efficient than automatics. In fact, a 5-speed manual can add up to 6.5 mpg over a 4-speed automatic transmission. Getting an automatic with an overdrive gear can improve your fuel economy by up to 9 percent.

3. Cruise Control: Using cruise control can save fuel because driving at a constant speed uses less fuel than changing speeds frequently.

4. Trim Packages and Power Options: Upgrading a car's trim level and adding options such as power steering, brakes, windows, or a sunroof can increase the weight of your car. Every 200 pounds of weight shaves off about 1 mile per gallon off your mileage. The weight of the average car in 1981 was 3,202 pounds, today it's around 4,000 pounds.

5. Hybrids: Most manufacturers offer hybrid vehicles that have both gasoline and electric engines. Hybrids can offer 30% better fuel economy and lower emissions. [Beware, until they are more readily available, you'll still have to pay considerably more to buy them.]

TWELVE WAYS TO SAVE MONEY AT THE PUMP

Here are a few simple things you can do that will save you a lot of money. Note: Savings are based on gas at $3.23.

1. Make Sure Your Tires are Inflated Properly: 27% of vehicles have tires that are under-inflated. Properly inflated tires can improve mileage by 3%, which is like getting 9 cents off a gallon of gas. Check the label on your door or glove box to find out what the pressure range should be for your tires. Don't use the "max pressure" written on your tire. Electronic gauges are fast, easy to use and accurate. Don't rely on the numbers on the air pump.

2. Check Your Air Filter: A dirty air filter by itself can rob a car by as much as 10% percent of its mileage. If an engine doesn't get enough air, it will burn too much gasoline. Replacing a dirty filter can knock 32 cents off a gallon of gas.

3. Get Your Alignment Checked: Not only does poor alignment cause your tires to wear out faster and cause poor handling, but it can cause your engine to work harder and reduce your fuel efficiency by 10%.

4. Don't Use High Octane Gasoline: Check your owner's manual. Very, very few cars actually need high-octane gas. Using 87-octane gas will save you over 10 cents per gallon over mid-grade and 20 cents over premium.

5. Get a Tune Up: A properly tuned engine is a fuel saver. Have a trusted mechanic tune your engine to exact factory specifications and you could save up to 13 cents a gallon.

6. Check Your Gas Cap: It is estimated that nearly 17 % of the cars on the road have broken or missing gasoline caps. This hurts your mileage and can harm the environment by allowing your gasoline to evaporate.

7. Don't Speed: A car moving at 55 mph gets better fuel economy than the same car at 65 mph. For every 5 mph you reduce your highway speed, you can reduce fuel consumption by 7% which is like getting 23 cents off a gallon of gas.

8. Avoid Excess Idling: An idling car gets 0 mpg. Cars with larger engines typically waste more gas at idle than cars with smaller engines.

9. Drive Smoother: The smoother your accelerations and decelerations, the better your mileage. A smooth foot can save 57 cents a gallon.

10. Combine Trips: Short trips can be expensive because they usually involve a "cold" vehicle. For the first mile or two before the engine gets warmed up, a cold vehicle only gets 30 to 40% of the mileage it gets at full efficiency.

11. Empty your Roof Rack and Trunk: 50% of engine power, traveling at highway speed, is used in overcoming aerodynamic drag or wind resistance. Any protrusion on a vehicle's roof can reduce gas mileage, typical roof racks reduce fuel economy by about 6 mpg. 100 lbs. of extra weight will reduce your mileage by .5 mpg.

12. Choose Your Gas Miser: If you own more than one vehicle, choosing to drive the one with better gas mileage will save you money. If you drive 15,000 miles per year, half in a vehicle with 20 mpg and half with a 30 mpg vehicle and switch to driving 75% of your trips in the 30 mpg vehicle, you will save $202 annually with gas at $3.23.

TIP

FUEL ECONOMY

Get up-to-date information about fuel economy at www.fueleconomy.gov, a joint website created by the U.S. Department of Energy and the EPA. There you'll find the EPA's Fuel Economy Guide, allowing you to compare fuel economy estimates for 2012 models back to 1985 models. You'll also find out about the latest technological advances pertaining to fuel efficiency. The site is extremely useful and easy to navigate. We've added fuel economy ratings and a Fuel Factor section to the At-a-glance box on our car rating pages.

FUEL ECONOMY MISERS AND GUZZLERS

Because the success of the EPA program depends on consumers' ability to compare the fuel economy ratings easily, we have included key mileage figures on our ratings pages. Listed below are the best and worst of this year's ratings according to annual fuel cost. The complete EPA fuel economy guide is available at www.fueleconomy.gov.

FUEL ECONOMY MISERS AND GUZZLERS

Vehicle	Specifications	MPG (city/hwy)	Annual Fuel Cost
THE BEST			
Electric			
Mitsubishi i-MiEV	Automatic, RWD	126/99^	$433
Nissan Leaf	Continuously Variable, FWD	106/92^	$489
Chevrolet Volt (All Electric)	Continuously Variable, FWD	95/93^	$515
Gas			
Chevrolet Volt (Overall)*	1.4L, 4 cyl., Continuously Variable, FWD	68/69	$922
Toyota Prius	1.8L, 4 cyl., Continuously Variable, FWD	51/48	$969
Honda Civic Hybrid	1.5L, 4 cyl., Continuously Variable, FWD	44/44	$1,101
Lexus CT 200h	1.8L, 4 cyl., Continuously Variable, FWD	43/40	$1,154
Toyota Prius V	1.8L, 4 cyl., Continuously Variable, FWD	44/40	$1,154
Ford Fusion Hybrid	2.5L, 4 cyl., Continuously Variable, FWD	41/36	$1,242
Lincoln MKZ Hybrid	2.5L, 4 cyl., Continuously Variable, FWD	41/36	$1,242
Scion iQ	1.3L, 4 cyl., Continuously Variable, FWD	36/37	$1,309
Chevrolet Volt (All Gas)	1.4L, 4 cyl., Continuously Variable, FWD	35/40	$1,419
Ford Fiesta	1.6L, 4 cyl., 6 sp. Automated Manual, FWD	29/39	$1,468
Ford Fiesta SFE	1.6L, 4 cyl., 6 sp. Automated Manual, FWD	29/40	$1,468
Ford Focus SFE	2L, 4 cyl., 6 sp. Automatic, FWD	28/40	$1,468
Honda Civic HF	1.8L, 4 cyl., 5 sp. Automatic, FWD	29/41	$1,468
Hyundai Accent	1.6L, 4 cyl., 6 sp. Automatic, FWD	30/40	$1,468
Kia Rio	1.6L, 4 cyl., 6 sp. Automatic, FWD	30/40	$1,468
Nissan Versa	1.6L, 4 cyl., Continuously Variable, FWD	30/38	$1,468
Toyota Yaris	1.5L, 4 cyl., 5 sp. Manual, FWD	30/38	$1,468
Chevrolet Cruze ECO	1.4L, 4 cyl., 6 sp. Manual, FWD	28/42	$1,468
Hyundai Elantra	1.8L, 4 cyl., 6 sp. Automatic, FWD	29/40	$1,468
Honda Civic	1.8L, 4 cyl., 5 sp. Automatic, FWD	28/39	$1,514
Hyundai Veloster	1.6L, 4 cyl., 6 sp. Automated Manual, FWD	29/38	$1.514
THE WORST**			
Mercedes-Benz G 550	5.5L, 8 cyl., 7 sp. Automatic, 4WD	8/15	$4,038#
Audi R8	4.2L, 8 cyl., 6 sp. Manual, AWD	8/20	$3,750#
Cadillac CTS/CTS Wagon	6.2L, 8 cyl., 6 sp. Semi-Automatic, RWD	8/18	$3,750#
BMW X5 xDriveM	4.4L, 8 cyl., 6 sp. Semi-Automatic, AWD	8/17	$3,750#
BMW X6 xDriveM	4.4L, 8 cyl., 6 sp. Semi-Automatic, AWD	8/17	$3,750#
Jeep Grand Cherokee SRT8	6.4L, 8 cyl., 5 sp. Automatic, 4WD	8/18	$3,750#
Land Rover LR4	5L, 8 cyl., 6 sp. Semi-Automatic, 4WD	8/17	$3,750#
Land Rover Range Rover	5L, 8 cyl., 6 sp. Semi-Automatic, 4WD	8/18	$3,750#
Land Rover Range Rover Sport	5L, 8 cyl., 6 sp. Semi-Automatic, 4WD	8/17	$3,750#
Mercedes-Benz GL 550 4MATIC	5.5L, 8 cyl., 7 sp. Automatic, 4WD	8/17	$3,750#
Nissan Pathfinder	5.6L, 8 cyl., 5 sp. Semi-Automatic, 4WD	8/18	$3,750#
Mercedes-Benz C 63 AMG	6.2L, 8 cyl., 7 sp. Automatic, RWD	8/19	$3,500#
Mercedes-Benz GL 450 4MATIC	4.7L, 8 cyl., 7 sp. Automatic, 4WD	8/18	$3,500#
Chevrolet Silverado C15/K15	6.2L, 8 cyl., 6 sp. Automatic	8/18	$3,461
GMC Sierra C15/K15	6.2L, 8 cyl., 6 sp. Automatic	8/18	$3,461
Nissan Titan	5.6L, 8 cyl., 5 sp. Automatic, 4WD	8/17	$3,461
Toyota Tundra	5.7L, 8 cyl., 6 sp. Semi-Automatic, PWD	8/17	$3,461
Cadillac Escalade ESV	6.2L, 8 cyl., 6 sp. Automatic, AWD	8/18	$3,461
Cadillac Escalade EXT	6.2L, 8 cyl., 6 sp. Automatic, AWD	8/18	$3,461
GMC Yukon	6.2L, 8 cyl., 6 sp. Automatic, AWD	8/18	$3,461

Note: 2012 annual fuel cost is based on driving 15,000 miles per year and a projected regular gas price of $3.23. # Premium required at $3.50; ^We've converted electricity to MPG for comparison. For electric cars 1 MPG = 33.7 kWh; *Chevrolet Volt (Overall) calculated using 45% MPG with fuel and 55% MPG with electricity; **Low volume exotic vehicles (over $120,000) and cargo vans were excluded.

COMPARING WARRANTIES

After buying your car, maintenance will be a significant portion of your operating costs. The strength of your warranty and the cost of repairs after the warranty expires will determine these costs. Comparing warranties and repair costs, before you buy, can save you thousands of dollars down the road.

Along with your new car comes a warranty which is a promise from the manufacturer that the car will perform as it should. Most of us never read the warranty until it is too late. In fact, because warranties are often difficult to read and understand, most of us don't really know what our warranty offers.

To keep your warranty in effect, you must operate and maintain your car according to the instructions in your owner's manual. It is important to keep a record of all maintenance performed on your car.

Be careful not to confuse a warranty with a service contract. A service contract must be purchased separately while a warranty is yours at no extra cost when you buy the car.

Warranties are difficult to compare because they contain fine print and confusing language. The following table will help you compare this year's new car warranties. Because the table does not contain all the details about each warranty, review the actual warranty to understand its fine points. You have the right to inspect a warranty before you buy—it's the law.

The table provides information on four critical items in a warranty:

The Basic Warranty covers most parts against manufacturer's defects. Tires, batteries, and items you add to the car are covered under separate warranties. The table describes coverage in terms of months and miles. For example, 48/50 means the warranty is good for 48 months or 50,000 miles, whichever comes first. This is the most important part of your warranty.

The Power Train Warranty usually lasts longer than the basic warranty. Because each manufacturer's definition of the power train is different, it is important to find out exactly what your warranty will cover. Power train coverage should include parts of the engine, transmission, and drive train. The warranty on some luxury cars will often cover some additional systems such as steering, suspension, and electrical systems.

The Corrosion Warranty usually applies only to actual holes due to rust. Read this section carefully because many corrosion warranties do not apply to what the manufacturer may describe as cosmetic rust or bad paint.

The Roadside Assistance column indicates whether or not the warranty includes a program for helping with problems on the road. In addition to mechanical failures, these programs cover such things as lockouts, jump starts, flat tires, running out of gas, and towing. Most are offered for the length of the basic warranty. Some have special limitations or added features, some of which we point out. Because each one is different, check yours carefully. If it is an option that you have to pay extra for, we don't list it.

The last column, the **Warranty Rating Index**, provides an overall assessment of this year's warranties. **The higher the Index number, the better the warranty.** The Index number incorporates the important features of each warranty. In developing the Index, we gave the most weight to the basic and power train components of the warranties. The corrosion warranty was weighted somewhat less, and roadside assistance received the least weight. We also considered special features such as the manufacturer offering free scheduled maintenance or if rental cars were offered when warranty repairs were being done.

The best ratings are in **BOLD**.

WARRANTY OFFERS THAT CAN SAVE YOU HUNDREDS

This year a few manufacturers are offering free maintainance and free wear and tear part replacement for the first three, four and even five years. These programs will save you hundreds of dollars in ownership costs.

WARRANTY COMPARISON

Manufacturer	Basic Warranty	Power Train Warranty	Corrosion Warranty	Roadside Assistance	Index	Warranty Rating
Acura	48/50	72/70	60/Unlimited	48/50	1295	Average
Audi	48/50	48/50	144/Unlimited	48/Unlimiti	1676	Good
BMW[6]	48/50[7]	48/50	144/Unlimited	48/Unlimited	1868	Very Good
Buick	48/50	60/100	72/100	60/100	1456	Good
Cadillac	48/50	60/100	72/100	60/100	1456	Good
Chevrolet	36/36	60/100	72/100	60/100	1352	Average
Chrysler	36/36	60/100	60/100	36/36[13]	1220	Poor
Dodge	36/36	60/100	60/100	36/36[13]	1220	Poor
Ford[14]	36/36	60/60	60/Unlimited	60/60	1158	Poor
GMC	36/36	60/100	72/100	60/100	1352	Average
Honda	36/36	60/60	60/Unlimited	Optional	978	Very Poor
Hyundai[12]	60/60	120/100	84/Unlimited	60/Unlimited	1862	Very Good
Infiniti	48/60	72/70	84/Unlimited	48/Unlimited	1518	Good
Jaguar[4]	60/50[2]	60/50	48/58	60/50	1357	Average
Jeep	36/36	60/100	60/100	36/36[13]	1220	Poor
Kia	60/60	120/100	60/100	60/60	1640	Good
Land Rover	48/50	48/50	72/Unlimited	48/50	1229	Poor
Lexus	48/50	72/70	72/Unlimited	48/Unlimited	1412	Average
Lincoln	48/50	72/70	60/Unlimited	72/70	1361	Average
Mazda	36/36	60/60	60/Unlimited	36/36	1086	Very Poor
Mercedes-Benz	48/50	48/50	48/50	Lifetime[5]	1179	Poor
MINI[9]	48/50	48/50	144/Unlimited	48/50	1697	Very Good
Mitsubishi	60/60	120/100	84/100	60/Unlimited	1756	Very Good
Nissan	36/36	60/60	60/Unlimited	36/36	1086	Very Poor
Scion	36/36[10]	60/60	60/Unlimited	24/25	1088	Very Poor
Smart	24/24	24/24	48/50	24/24	604	Very Poor
Subaru[9]	36/36	60/60	60/Unlimited	36/36	1158	Poor
Suzuki	36/36	84/100	60/Unlimited	36/36	1278	Poor
Toyota[14]	36/36[10]	60/60	60/Unlimited	24/25	1088	Very Poor
Volkswagen[11]	36/36[8]	60/60	144/Unlimited	36/36	1626	Good
Volvo[3]	48/50[1]	48/50	144/Unlimited	60/Unlimited	1930	Very Good

[1] Free Scheduled Maintenance 60/60
[2] Scheduled Maintenance 60/50
[3] Wear Items 60/60
[4] Wear Items 60/50
[5] Lifetime fully transferable
[6] Wear Items 48/50S
[7] Scheduled inspections, oil changes 48/50
[8] Scheduled Maintenance 36/36
[9] Wear items 36/36
[10] Scheduled Maintenance 24/25
[11] Wear Items 12/12 wiper blades 6/6
[12] Wear Items 12/12
[13] Roadside assistance for parts covered under powertrain warranty 50/100
[14] Hybrid components 96/100

*In descending order of improvement value.

SECRET WARRANTIES

If dealers report a number of complaints about a certain part and the manufacturer determines that the problem is due to faulty design or assembly, the manufacturer may permit dealers to repair the problem at no charge to the customer even though the warranty is expired. In the past, this practice was often reserved for customers who made a big fuss. The availability of the free repair was never publicized, which is why we call these "secret warranties."

Manufacturers deny the existence of secret warranties. They call these free repairs "policy adjustments" or "goodwill service." Whatever they are called, most consumers never hear about them.

Many secret warranties are disclosed in service bulletins that the manufacturers send to dealers. These bulletins outline free repair or reimbursement programs, as well as other problems and their possible causes and solutions.

Service bulletins from many manufacturers may be on file at the National Highway Traffic Safety Administration. You can visit www.nhtsa.gov to access NHTSA's Service Bulletin database.

If you find that a secret warranty is in effect and repairs are being made at no charge after the warranty has expired, contact the Center for Auto Safety, 1825 Connecticut Ave. NW, #330, Washington, DC 20009. They will publish the information so others can benefit.

Disclosure Laws: Spurred by the proliferation of secret warranties and the failure of the FTC to take action, California, Connecticut, Virginia, Wisconsin, and Maryland have passed legislation that requires consumers to be notified of secret warranties on their cars. Several other states have introduced similar warranty bills.

Typically, the laws require the following: direct notice to consumers within a specified time after the adoption of a warranty adjustment policy; notice of the disclosure law to new car buyers; reimbursement within a number of years after payment to owners who paid for covered repairs before they learned of the extended warranty service; and dealers must inform consumers who complain about a covered defect that it is eligible for repair under warranty.

If you live in a state with a secret warranty law already in effect, write your state attorney general's office (in care of your state capital) for information. To encourage passage of such a bill, contact your state representative (in care of your state capital).

Some state lemon laws require dealers and manufacturers to give you copies of Technical Service Bulletins on problems affecting your vehicle. These bulletins may alert you to a secret warranty on your vehicle or help you make the case for a free repair if there isn't a secret warranty. See page 59 for an overview of your state's lemon law. If you would like to see the complete law, go to www.autosafety.org to view your state's lemon laws.

LITTLE SECRETS OF THE AUTO INDUSTRY

TIP

Every auto company makes mistakes building cars. When they do, they often issue technical service bulletins telling dealers how to fix the problem. Rarely do they publicize these fixes, many of which are offered for free, called secret warranties. The Center for Auto Safety has published a book called *Little Secrets of the Auto Industry*, a consumer guide to secret warranties. This book explains how to find out about secret warranties, offers tips for going to small claims court and getting federal and state assistance, and lists information on state secret warranty laws. To order a copy, send $17.50 to: Center for Auto Safety, Pub. Dept. CB, 1825 Connecticut Ave. NW, Suite 330, Washington, DC 20009.

KEEPING IT GOING

Comparing maintenance costs before you buy can help decide which car to purchase. These costs include preventive maintenance servicing—such as changing the oil and filters—as well as the cost of repairs after your warranty expires. Following, we enable you to compare the costs of preventive maintenance and nine likely repairs for the 2012 models.

Preventive Maintenance: The first column in the table is the periodic servicing, specified by the manufacturer, that keeps your car running properly. For example, regularly changing the oil and oil filter. Every owner's manual specifies a schedule of recommended servicing for at least the first 60,000 miles and many now go to 100,000 miles. The tables on the following pages estimate the labor cost of following this preventive maintenance schedule for 60,000 miles, the length of a typical warranty. Service parts are not included in this total.

Repairs Costs: The tables also list the costs for nine repairs that typically occur during the first 100,000 miles. There is no precise way to predict exactly when a repair will be needed. But if you keep a car for 75,000 to 100,000 miles, it is likely that you will experience most of these repairs at least once. The last column provides a relative indication of how expensive these nine repairs are for many cars. Repair cost is rated as Very Good if the total for nine repairs is in the lower fifth of all the cars rated, and Very Poor if the total is in the highest fifth.

Most repair shops use "flat-rate manuals" to estimate repair costs. These manuals list the approximate time required for repairing many items. Each automobile manufacturer publishes its own manual and there are several independent manuals as well. For many repairs, the time varies from one manual to another. Some repair shops even use different manuals for different repairs. To determine a repair bill, a shop multiplies the time listed in its manual by its hourly labor rate and then adds the cost of parts.

Some dealers and repair shops create their own maintenance schedules which call for more frequent (and thus more expensive) servicing than the manufacturer's recommendations. If the servicing recommended by your dealer or repair shop don't match what the manufacturer recommends, make sure you understand and agree to the extra items. Our cost estimates are based on published repair times multiplied by a nationwide average labor rate of $70 per hour and include the cost of replaced parts and related adjustments.

Prices in the following tables may not predict the exact costs of these repairs. For example, labor rates for your area may be more or less than the national average. However, the prices will provide you with a relative comparison of costs for various automobiles.

	PM Costs to 60,000 Miles	REPAIR COSTS									Relative Repair Cost*
		Front Brake Pads	Starter	Fuel Injector	Fuel Pump	Struts/ Shocks	Timing Belt/Chain	Water Pump	Muffler	Headlamps	
Subcompact											
BMW Z4	189	227	269	316	484	874	706	670	1,280	1,278	Vry. Pr.
Honda Fit	441	131	688	177	422	531	442	226	240	405	Good
Honda Insight	315	128	666	233	349	533	413	265	238	474	Good
Hyundai Accent	616	103	487	118	217	383	271	448	267	250	Vry. Gd.
Kia Rio	630	97	332	181	284	502	295	470	364	282	Vry. Gd.
Kia Soul	742	126	401	190	346	506	317	269	524	357	Vry. Gd.
Mazda MX-5 Miata	672	129	272	191	397	400	380	231	613	687	Good
Mini Cooper	1,463	170	384	175	346	484	818	363	470	615	Average
Nissan 370Z	462	144	387	319	380	794	1,287	551	524	1,119	Vry. Pr.
Nissan Versa	952	117	336	242	409	391	349	175	474	378	Vry. Gd.
Scion xB	588	119	364	268	409	558	653	333	229	383	Good
Scion xD	259	119	446	233	409	508	900	650	261	231	Average
Suzuki SX4	1,302	191	682	236	862	635	659	329	405	406	Poor
Toyota Yaris	231	111	375	212	404	523	429	218	236	204	Vry. Gd.
Volkswagen Beetle	-	153	376	296	408	501	299	398	347	628	Good
Compact											
Audi A3	616	140	523	222	390	512	367	563	493	421	Good
Audi A4	756	400	621	929	388	706	584	595	437	606	Vry. Pr.
BMW 1 Series	189	200	269	330	380	575	704	670	870	438	Poor
BMW 3 Series	189	227	269	190	422	863	755	670	532	571	Poor
Dodge Caliber	756	167	247	103	322	360	418	214	443	305	Vry. Gd.
Ford Focus	679	123	380	109	510	258	448	188	336	277	Vry. Gd.
Ford Mustang	637	207	283	179	471	313	787	319	389	347	Good
Honda Civic	224	121	328	177	424	601	513	251	203	362	Vry. Gd.
Honda Civic Coupe	224	121	328	177	424	501	513	251	203	327	Vry. Gd.
Hyundai Elantra	756	131	303	130	210	354	246	277	273	243	Vry. Gd.
Kia Forte	455	146	323	171	305	531	421	225	316	264	Vry. Gd.
Mazda 3	665	144	279	191	498	453	381	231	392	330	Vry. Gd.
Mercedes-Benz C-Class	826	163	762	253	437	789	529	559	906	585	Poor
Mitsubishi Lancer	392	178	277	324	546	534	455	473	386	441	Good
Nissan Altima Coupe	462	131	364	277	402	452	545	210	189	371	Vry. Gd.
Nissan Sentra	546	138	336	298	444	421	328	187	277	378	Vry. Gd.
Subaru Impreza	784	137	503	179	356	538	244	350	342	394	Vry. Gd.
Suzuki Kizashi	742	224	611	293	827	660	1,009	297	417	593	Poor
Toyota Corolla	280	104	432	289	388	417	536	230	342	319	Vry. Gd.
Toyota Matrix	280	139	439	289	409	417	536	188	414	299	Good
Volkswagen Golf	560	160	340	209	384	688	780	378	523	354	Average
Volkswagen Jetta	434	160	523	342	400	619	293	422	543	366	Good
Volvo C70	0	175	423	291	631	552	355	366	544	399	Average
Intermediate											
Acura TL	700	147	497	166	378	375	374	408	699	805	Average
Acura TSX	287	131	542	131	487	426	403	226	730	701	Average
Audi A5	756	173	568	258	508	630	334	675	521	438	Average
BMW 5 Series	105	248	262	218	567	940	968	684	711	624	Vry. Pr.
Buick LaCrosse	994	286	387	339	640	500	799	379	655	509	Poor
AVERAGE OF ALL VEHICLES	**$677**	**$177**	**$420**	**$253**	**$471**	**$574**	**$707**	**$420**	**$568**	**$507**	

*A comparison of the cost of 9 listed repair items.

| | PM Costs to 60,000 Miles | REPAIR COSTS | | | | | | | | |
		Front Brake Pads	Starter	Fuel Injector	Fuel Pump	Struts/ Shocks	Timing Belt/Chain	Water Pump	Muffler	Headlamps	Relative Repair Cost*
Buick Regal	973	259	326	301	580	337	449	612	742	481	Average
Cadillac CTS	994	439	254	654	423	737	610	396	1,199	518	Vry. Pr.
Chevrolet Camaro	994	275	247	337	619	425	960	310	1,155	325	Poor
Chevrolet Corvette	826	413	659	238	1,335	352	888	410	748	1,064	Vry. Pr.
Chevrolet Impala	994	236	541	249	653	816	536	385	718	336	Poor
Chevrolet Malibu	973	172	319	261	677	510	438	528	572	430	Average
Dodge Avenger	532	167	198	96	506	368	418	228	471	260	Vry. Gd.
Ford Fusion	665	153	290	88	356	298	461	211	514	411	Vry. Gd.
Honda Accord	721	131	542	124	522	254	354	248	484	392	Vry. Gd.
Honda Accord Coupe	462	121	508	114	451	324	405	180	469	414	Vry. Gd.
Hyundai Genesis	812	167	409	200	439	551	702	243	565	806	Average
Hyundai Sonata	756	103	303	151	266	414	432	273	436	352	Vry. Gd.
Infiniti EX	462	129	396	305	460	576	629	475	654	527	Average
Infiniti G	462	145	373	319	418	519	809	551	741	1,005	Poor
Kia Optima	483	137	323	194	291	331	421	239	671	414	Vry. Gd.
Lexus ES	847	123	362	408	432	551	2,000	1,376	475	422	Vry. Pr.
Lexus GS	602	138	471	331	413	602	2,133	330	787	1,117	Vry. Pr.
Lexus IS	588	145	623	581	435	616	1,867	467	801	682	Vry. Pr.
Lincoln MKZ	896	153	298	193	454	278	913	975	902	548	Poor
Mazda 6	616	152	271	165	447	398	494	156	286	798	Good
Mercedes-Benz E-Class	889	170	855	211	390	1,087	1,096	508	962	591	Vry. Pr.
Mitsubishi Galant	392	151	303	233	378	232	244	433	326	332	Vry. Gd.
Nissan Altima	462	152	297	302	425	543	895	203	230	371	Good
Nissan Maxima	644	131	349	304	402	503	734	295	333	364	Good
Subaru Legacy	1,029	144	370	179	356	638	244	350	347	526	Good
Subaru Outback	1,029	144	370	179	356	538	244	350	347	526	Vry. Gd.
Toyota Avalon	259	139	379	317	432	474	1,552	326	311	391	Poor
Toyota Camry	245	123	467	303	409	446	985	253	366	439	Average
Volkswagen CC	581	160	405	463	421	530	598	563	405	720	Average
Volkswagen Passat	476	160	320	299	398	620	444	590	398	391	Good
Volvo S60	0	185	393	499	466	301	243	355	515	517	Good
Large											
Audi A6	756	193	721	304	493	545	1,200	244	533	472	Poor
Audi A8	980	261	815	257	301	2,911	2,390	629	643	962	Vry. Pr.
BMW 7 Series	126	388	480	345	441	2,285	2,455	478	875	1,406	Vry. Pr.
Chrysler 300	945	175	137	184	203	348	463	484	678	361	Vry. Gd.
Dodge Challenger	1,218	232	219	167	264	224	487	438	724	298	Vry. Gd.
Dodge Charger	945	242	219	146	284	362	589	420	879	278	Good
Ford Taurus	812	159	401	179	360	458	913	989	621	679	Poor
Infiniti M	462	152	382	267	423	619	583	261	647	518	Average
Jaguar XF	147	201	801	280	540	478	939	217	491	602	Poor
Jaguar XJ	133	164	693	340	796	489	793	513	300	366	Poor
Lexus LS	763	145	1,071	735	452	751	1,122	383	571	830	Vry. Pr.
Lincoln MKS	644	137	401	179	344	465	913	975	1,001	1,038	Vry. Pr.
Mercedes-Benz S-Class	1,141	184	740	288	550	3,089	557	576	852	1,595	Vry. Pr.
Volvo S80	0	182	420	307	678	590	417	356	563	484	Average
AVERAGE OF ALL VEHICLES	**$677**	**$177**	**$420**	**$253**	**$471**	**$574**	**$707**	**$420**	**$568**	**$507**	

*A comparison of the cost of 9 listed repair items.

	PM Costs to 60,000 Miles	REPAIR COSTS								
		Front Brake Pads	Starter	Fuel Injector	Fuel Pump	Struts/ Shocks	Timing Belt/Chain	Water Pump	Muffler	Headlamps	Relative Repair Cost*
Minivan											
Chrysler Town and Country	889	190	160	162	564	404	394	497	467	332	Good
Dodge Grand Caravan	889	190	160	162	506	404	394	497	467	291	Good
Honda Odyssey	581	147	822	152	436	599	374	477	766	344	Average
Kia Sedona	770	146	418	184	347	597	1,297	343	339	314	Average
Mazda 5	672	145	358	200	323	516	427	212	455	811	Good
Toyota Sienna	637	153	393	331	391	480	404	1,347	408	359	Average
Volkswagen Routan	434	270	160	162	524	414	392	500	461	377	Good
Small SUV											
Acura RDX	371	147	467	131	444	404	392	264	448	868	Good
Ford Escape	966	137	426	109	322	250	395	211	324	282	Vry. Gd.
Honda CR-V	574	136	873	128	326	655	464	228	355	367	Good
Hyundai Tucson	756	117	324	137	418	448	243	357	519	242	Vry. Gd.
Jeep Compass	756	167	247	103	322	332	418	179	420	269	Vry. Gd.
Jeep Liberty	679	199	239	146	544	296	755	236	392	345	Good
Jeep Patriot	756	167	247	103	322	332	418	179	420	269	Vry. Gd.
Jeep Wrangler	770	199	165	183	299	284	338	168	295	203	Vry. Gd.
Kia Sportage	735	138	220	172	291	458	256	363	551	252	Vry. Gd.
Mitsubishi Outlander	763	177	242	227	750	318	546	494	355	690	Average
Subaru Forester	784	137	503	179	406	638	244	350	356	429	Good
Suzuki Grand Vitara	1,470	196	503	377	697	672	932	276	527	361	Poor
Toyota RAV4	252	133	364	212	507	418	1,409	272	988	195	Poor
Volkswagen Tiguan	532	160	348	437	421	494	640	591	419	314	Average
Mid-Size SUV											
Acura MDX	644	136	398	237	402	529	301	399	587	841	Average
Acura ZDX	665	147	467	166	413	470	276	387	1,029	831	Average
Audi Q5	756	173	648	304	482	545	1,648	414	521	379	Vry. Pr.
BMW X3	196	227	290	232	513	877	629	677	992	577	Vry. Pr.
BMW X5	161	265	270	183	434	742	629	726	1,077	1,537	Vry. Pr.
Buick Enclave	938	246	383	358	598	523	785	396	938	1,098	Vry. Pr.
Cadillac SRX	973	200	288	297	450	1,127	771	508	779	453	Poor
Chevrolet Equinox	994	272	340	258	778	789	449	528	711	452	Poor
Dodge Journey	532	165	219	124	459	341	418	228	564	280	Vry. Gd.
Ford Edge	602	208	304	186	444	359	804	948	792	249	Average
Ford Explorer	861	184	351	184	491	472	596	304	360	228	Good
GMC Terrain	994	284	380	421	778	485	554	455	731	906	Poor
Honda Pilot	861	147	497	194	485	574	339	449	631	418	Average
Hyundai Santa Fe	756	138	317	172	475	457	485	233	534	343	Good
Hyundai Veracruz	756	167	384	249	314	420	1,206	305	459	366	Average
Infiniti FX	546	129	403	270	425	697	622	503	648	1,785	Vry. Pr.
Kia Sorento	-	155	351	174	390	615	443	311	713	412	Good
Lexus GX	637	167	978	387	560	721	1,038	493	306	550	Vry. Pr.
Lexus RX	532	126	679	333	427	588	1,489	1,138	680	555	Vry. Pr.
Lincoln MKX	973	137	394	214	464	411	689	975	896	429	Poor
Mazda CX-7	616	169	343	372	349	403	430	177	810	696	Average
Mazda CX-9	602	179	366	176	332	387	829	895	469	519	Average
Mercedes-Benz GLK-Class	1,505	172	862	253	439	794	529	559	830	589	Vry. Pr.
Mercedes-Benz M-Class	1,050	229	715	289	434	874	1,404	750	613	448	Vry. Pr.
AVERAGE OF ALL VEHICLES	**$677**	**$177**	**$420**	**$253**	**$471**	**$574**	**$707**	**$420**	**$568**	**$507**	

*A comparison of the cost of 9 listed repair items.

	PM Costs to 60,000 Miles	REPAIR COSTS									Relative Repair Cost*
		Front Brake Pads	Starter	Fuel Injector	Fuel Pump	Struts/ Shocks	Timing Belt/Chain	Water Pump	Muffler	Headlamps	
Nissan Murano	546	124	324	333	437	488	1,276	373	505	395	Average
Nissan Pathfinder	840	138	374	298	493	315	898	261	362	394	Good
Nissan Rogue	546	138	340	298	315	613	881	255	598	377	Average
Nissan Xterra	840	138	360	298	472	288	898	261	362	357	Good
Porsche Cayenne	406	123	350	212	383	431	653	272	386	246	Vry. Gd.
Toyota 4Runner	273	167	327	289	567	482	1,549	319	253	382	Poor
Toyota Highlander	504	133	523	261	668	521	1,535	267	708	401	Vry. Pr.
Toyota Venza	868	133	486	373	462	604	1,478	253	650	440	Poor
Volvo XC60	0	173	373	321	638	649	484	320	497	470	Average
Volvo XC90	0	185	413	300	566	574	341	354	739	487	Average
Large SUV											
Audi Q7	840	233	646	287	404	1,000	1,097	414	856	349	Vry. Pr.
Cadillac Escalade	994	236	465	244	591	450	587	447	572	324	Average
Cadillac Escalade EXT	994	236	465	244	585	1,065	587	468	1,082	950	Vry. Pr.
Chevrolet Suburban	994	236	465	244	606	1,065	587	447	1,082	324	Vry. Pr.
Chevrolet Tahoe	994	236	465	244	591	450	587	447	572	324	Average
Chevrolet Traverse	938	246	383	358	598	402	806	396	860	463	Poor
Dodge Durango	854	257	312	185	672	351	659	249	536	284	Good
Ford Expedition	1,015	205	276	136	437	435	711	290	553	334	Good
Ford Flex	777	137	401	182	372	472	724	975	679	501	Poor
GMC Acadia	938	246	383	358	598	402	806	396	937	1,135	Vry. Pr.
GMC Yukon	994	237	288	147	606	1,054	671	458	572	310	Poor
GMC Yukon XL	994	237	288	147	606	1,054	573	458	1,115	410	Poor
Infiniti QX56	840	145	450	249	472	336	1,170	246	483	861	Poor
Jeep Grand Cherokee	1,232	214	169	132	483	400	749	257	515	198	Good
Land Rover LR4	805	225	745	533	545	828	1,142	790	416	1,024	Vry. Pr.
Land Rover Range Rover	749	317	794	350	473	2,473	834	762	785	1,035	Vry. Pr.
Lincoln MKT	707	130	297	286	395	422	734	906	1,270	1,400	Vry. Pr.
Mercedes-Benz GL-Class	1,505	250	740	232	560	1,963	386	639	660	598	Vry. Pr.
Nissan Armada	840	145	471	249	472	436	1,212	246	483	441	Average
Toyota FJ Cruiser	357	146	382	317	500	463	1,461	387	341	319	Poor
Toyota Sequoia	343	148	712	387	791	427	970	494	457	391	Poor
Compact Pickup											
Chevrolet Colorado	994	260	664	527	513	337	1,154	317	612	217	Poor
Nissan Frontier	840	138	357	277	493	278	573	210	439	394	Good
Toyota Tacoma	231	133	410	352	791	409	1,174	373	481	370	Poor
Standard Pickup											
Cadillac Escalade ESV	994	236	506	244	606	369	587	447	1,082	950	Vry. Pr.
Chevrolet Avalanche	994	236	465	244	585	415	587	468	1,115	324	Poor
Chevrolet Silverado	994	236	95	244	492	450	587	426	553	338	Good
Dodge Ram Pickup	1,463	152	258	132	504	235	615	236	375	234	Vry. Gd.
Ford F-150	742	181	304	96	466	317	556	241	416	255	Vry. Gd.
GMC Sierra	994	237	288	147	617	439	671	431	981	525	Poor
Honda Ridgeline	651	136	532	149	423	435	301	420	416	306	Good
Nissan Titan	840	204	471	249	472	293	1,212	246	353	441	Average
Toyota Tundra	357	148	364	289	791	406	850	415	457	391	Average
AVERAGE OF ALL VEHICLES	**$677**	**$177**	**$420**	**$253**	**$471**	**$574**	**$707**	**$420**	**$568**	**$507**	

*A comparison of the cost of 9 listed repair items.

SERVICE CONTRACTS

Service contracts are one of the most expensive options you can buy. In fact, service contracts are a major profit source for many dealers.

A service contract is not a warranty. It is more like an insurance plan that, in theory, covers repairs that are not covered by your warranty or that occur after the warranty runs out. They are often inaccurately referred to as "extended warranties."

Service contracts are generally a poor value. The companies who sell contracts are very sure that, on average, your repairs will cost considerably less that what you pay for the contract—if not, they wouldn't be in business.

Here are some important questions to ask before buying a service contract:

How reputable is the company responsible for the contract? If the company offering the contract goes out of business, you will be out of luck. The company may be required to be insured but they may not. Find out if they are insured and by whom. Check with your Better Business Bureau or office of consumer affairs if you are not sure of a company's reputation. Service contracts from car and insurance companies are more likely to remain in effect than those from independent companies.

Exactly what does the contract cover and for how long? Service contracts vary considerably—different items are covered and different time limits are offered. This is true even among service contracts offered by the same company. For example, one company has plans that range from 4 years/36,000 miles maximum coverage to 6 years/100,000 miles maximum coverage, with other options for only power train coverage. Make sure you know what components are covered because if a breakdown occurs on a part that is not covered, you are responsible for the repairs.

If you plan to resell your car in a few years, you won't want to purchase a long-running service contract. Some service contracts automatically cancel when you resell the car, while others require a hefty transfer fee before extending privileges to the new owner.

Some automakers offer a "menu" format, which lets you pick the items you want covered in your service contract. Find out if the contract pays for preventive maintenance, towing, and rental car expenses. If not written into the contract, assume they are not covered.

Make sure the contract clearly specifies how you can reach the company. Knowing this before you purchase a service contract can save you time and aggravation in the future.

How will the repair bills be paid? It is best to have the service contractor pay bills directly. Some contracts require you to pay the repair bill, and reimburse you later.

Where can the car be serviced? Can you take the car to any mechanic if you have trouble on the road? What if you move?

What other costs can be expected? Most service contracts will have a deductible expense. Compare deductibles on various plans. Also, some companies charge the deductible for each individual repair while other companies pay per visit, regardless of the number of repairs being made.

What are your responsibilities? Make sure you know what you have to do to uphold the contract. For example if you have to follow the manufacturer's recommended maintenance, keep detailed records or the contract could void. You will find your specific responsibilities in the contact. Be sure to have the seller point them out.

One alternative to buying a service contract is to deposit the cost of the contract into a savings account. If the car needs a major repair not covered by your warranty, the money in your account will cover the cost. Most likely, you'll be building up your down payment for your next car!

TIPS FOR DEALING WITH A MECHANIC

Call around. Don't choose a shop simply because it's nearby. Calling a few shops may turn up estimates cheaper by half.

Don't necessarily go for the lowest price. A good rule is to eliminate the highest and lowest estimates; the mechanic with the highest estimate is probably charging too much, and the lowest may be cutting too many corners.

Check the shop's reputation. Call your local consumer affairs agency and the Better Business Bureau. They don't have records on every shop, but unfavorable reports on a shop should disqualify it.

Look for certification. Mechanics can be certified by the National Institute for Automotive Service Excellence, an industry-wide yardstick for competence. Certification is offered in eight areas of repair and shops with certified mechanics are allowed to advertise this fact. However, make sure the mechanic working on your car is certified for the repair you need.

Take a look around. A well-kept shop reflects pride in workmanship. A skilled and efficient mechanic would probably not work in a messy shop.

Don't sign a blank check. The service order you sign should have specific instructions or describe your vehicle's symptoms. Avoid signing a vague work order. Be sure you are called for final approval before the shop does extra work. Many states require a written estimate signed by you and require that the shop get your permission for repairs that exceed the estimate by 10%.

Show interest. Ask about the repair. But don't act like an expert if you don't really understand what's wrong. Express your satisfaction. If you're happy with the work, compliment the mechanic and ask for him or her the next time you come in. You will get to know each other and the mechanic will get to know your vehicle.

Take a test-drive. Before you pay for a major repair, you should take the car for a test-drive. The few extra minutes you spend checking out the repair could save you a trip back to the mechanic. If you find that the problem still exists, there will be no question that the repair wasn't properly completed.

REPAIR PROTECTION BY CREDIT CARD

TIP

Paying your auto repair bills by credit card can provide a much needed recourse if you are having problems with an auto mechanic. According to federal law, you have the right to withhold payment for sloppy or incorrect repairs. Of course, you may withhold no more than the amount of the repair in dispute.

In order to use this right, you must first try to work out the problem with the mechanic. Also, unless the credit card company owns the repair shop (this might be the case with gasoline credit cards used at gas stations), two other conditions must be met. First, the repair shop must be in your home state (or within 100 miles of your current address), and second, the cost of repairs must be over $50. Until the problem is settled or resolved in court, the credit card company cannot charge you interest or penalties on the amount in dispute.

If you decide to take action, send a letter to the credit card company and a copy to the repair shop, explaining the details of the problem and what you want as settlement. Send the letter by certified mail with a return receipt requested.

Sometimes the credit card company or repair shop will attempt to put a "bad mark" on your credit record if you use this tactic. Legally, you can't be reported as delinquent if you've given the credit card company notice of your dispute, but a creditor can report that you are disputing your bill, which goes in your record. However, you have the right to challenge any incorrect information and add your side of the story to your file.

For more information, write to the Federal Trade Commission, Credit Practices Division, 601 Pennsylvania Avenue, NW, Washington, DC 20580.

TIRE RATINGS

Buying tires has become an infrequent task because today's radial tires last much longer than the tires of the past. Surprisingly, a tire has to perform more functions simultaneously than any other part of the car (steering, bearing the load, cushioning the ride, and stopping).

Because comparing tires is difficult, many consumers mistakenly use price and brand name to determine quality. Because there are hundreds of tire lines to choose from, and only a few tire manufacturers, the difference in many tires may only be the brand name.

But there is help. The U.S. government requires tires to be rated according to their safety and expected mileage.

Treadwear, traction, and heat resistance grades are printed on the sidewall and are attached to the tire on a paper label. Ask the dealer for the grades of the tires they sell. Using this rating system, a sampling of top rated tires follows on page 48.

Treadwear: The treadwear grade gives you an idea of the mileage you can expect from a tire. It is shown in numbers–720, 700, 680, 660, and so forth. Higher numbers mean longer tire life. A tire with a grade of 600 should give you twice as much mileage as one rated 300. Use the treadwear grade as a relative basis of comparison.

Traction: Traction grades of AA, A, B, and C describe the tire's ability to stop on wet surfaces. Tires graded AA will stop on a wet road in a shorter distance than tires graded B or C. Tires rated C have poor traction.

Heat Resistance: Heat resistance is graded A, B, and C. An A rating means the tire will run cooler than one rated B or C and be less likely to fail if driven over long distances at highway speeds. Tires that run cooler tend to be more fuel-efficient. Hot-running tires can result in blowouts or tread separation.

TIRE CARE

Pump 'em Up: An estimated one-third of us are driving on underinflated tires. Because even good tires lose air, it is important to check your tire pressure monthly. Underinflated tires can be dangerous, use more fuel and cause premature tire failure. When checking your tires, be sure to use an accurate gauge and inflate to the pressure indicated in your owner's manual, not the maximum pressure printed on your tire.

When to Replace: If any part of Lincoln's head is visible when you insert the top of a penny into a tread groove, it's time to replace the tire. While this old rule of thumb is still valid, today's tires also have a built-in wear indicator. A series of horizontal bars appear across the surface when the tread depth reaches the danger zone.

GETTING THE BEST PRICE

The price of the same tire can vary depending on where you shop so shopping around is vital to finding a good buy. Most tire ads appear in the sports section of your Wednesday and Saturday daily newspaper. You are most likely to find the best prices at independent tire dealers who carry a variety of tire brands.

The price of a tire is based on its size, and tires come in as many as nine sizes. For example, the list price of the same tire can range from $74.20 to $134.35, depending on its size.

To get the best buy:

1. Check to see which manufacturer makes the least expensive "off brand." Only a few manufacturers produce the over 1,800 types of tires sold in the U.S.

2. Don't forget to compare balancing and mounting costs. These extra charges can add up to more than $25 or be offered at no cost.

3. Never pay list price for a tire. A good rule of thumb is to pay at least 30-40 percent off the suggested list price.

4. Use the treadwear grade the same way you would the "unit price" in a supermarket. The tire with the lowest cost per grade point is the best value. For example, if tire A costs $100 and has a treadwear grade of 600, and tire B costs $80 and has a treadwear grade of 300, tire A is the better buy, even though its initial cost is more.

Tire A: $100÷600=$0.17 per point
Tire B: $80÷300=$0.27 per point

Where you live is a key factor in how long your tires will last. In addition to construction and design, tire wear is affected by the level of abrasive material in the road surface. Generally, the road surfaces of the West Coast, Great Lakes region, and northern New England are easiest on tires. The Appalachian and Rocky Mountain areas are usually hardest on tires.

HOW TO READ A TIRE

Tire Type and Size: The most important information on a tire are the letters and the numbers indicating its type and size.

1. Tire Type: The P at the beginning of the tire size indicates that the tire is a passenger vehicle tire. LT indicates light truck tire, and T indicates a temporary or spare tire.

2. Tire Width is the first part of the number and is measured in millimeters, from sidewall to sidewall.

3. Tire Height is the next number and tells you the height of the tire from the bead to the tread. This is described as a percentage of the tire width. In our example, the tire's height is 65 percent of its width. The smaller the aspect ratio, the wider the tire in relation to its height.

4. Tire Construction designates how the tire was made. R indicates radial construction which is the most common type. Older tires were made using diagonal bias D or bias belted B construction, but these tire types are no longer used on passenger vehicles.

5. Wheel Diameter identifies the wheel rim diameter (in inches-15) needed for this tire.

6. Load Index: The load rating indicates the maximum load for that tire. A higher number indicates a higher load capacity. The rating 95, for example, corresponds to a load capacity of 1521 pounds. Larger vehicles, SUVs and pickups

4. Construction
5. Wheel Diameter
3. Height
6. Load Index
2. Width
7. Speed Rating
1. Tire Type
P215/65R15 95H
9. U.S. DOT Tire Identification Number
13. Max. Pressure
12. Max. Load
10. Tire ply composition and material
11. Treadwear, traction, and temperature grades

need tires with a higher load capacity.

7. Speed Rating indicates the maximum speed that the tire can sustain a ten minute endurance test without being in danger. All passenger car tires are rated at least S and pass the test at speeds up to 112 mph. Other ratings are as follows: T up to 118 mph, H up to 130 mph, V up to 149 mph and Z 150 mph or higher. Other types of tires, temporary spares and snow tires are lower on the rating scale.

8. Severe Conditions: M+S indicates the tire meets the Rubber Manu. Association's definition of a mud and snow tire. There are no performance tests for this standard. If the tire has an M+S and a "mountain and snowflake" symbol then the traction is at least 10% bestter than the regular version of the tire. These symbols are not in the above example.

9. Tire Identification Number
Example: DOT NJ HR 2AF 5203
The letters DOT certify compliance with all applicable safety standards established by the U.S. Department of Transportation. The next four characters is a code where the first two characters indicate the manufacturer and the second two

characters indicate the plant where the tire was made.

Next you may see an optional string of three to four characters. Most manufacturers use these to record company specific information they use to identify their products or that can be used to identify tires in the market for recall purposes.

The last four digits determine the week and year the tire was made. The digits 5203 would signify that the tire was made during the 52nd week of 2003. Don't buy tires more than two years old. Tires naturally degrade with age, so you want the newest possible tires for the longest life (and safe operation.)

10. Tire Ply Composition and Material indicates the type of cord (polyester or steel) and number of plies in the tire, 4-ply, 6-ply, 8-ply, for both the tread and the sidewall.

11. Treadwear, Traction and Temperature Grades are three performance grades assigned to the tire are are the best way to truly evaluate the tires expected performance in these three critical areas. See page 46 for more information.

12. Max Load Limit tells you the cold inflation load limit in lbs. (pounds) and in kg (kilograms). The number corresponds to the load index.

13. Max Pressure is the maximum recommended pressure in psi (pounds per square inch) and in kPa (kilopascals). However, this is not the tire pressure for your car. You must check your owner's manual for the proper tire pressure for the tires on your car.

A Sampling of Top Rated Tires

Brand Name	Model	Description	Traction	Heat	Treadwear
Michelin	Hydroedge	ALL	A	B	760
Goodyear	Assurance Tripletred	ALL	A	B	740
Vogue	Wide Trac Touring LI	S-Rated	A	B	720
Cooper	Lifeliner STE	ALL	A	B	700
Cordovan	Grand Spirit Touring LS	ALL	A	B	700
Mastercraft	Touring LX	ALL	A	B	700
Toyo	800 Ultra	ALL	A	B	700
Michelin	X One With Durablack	ALL	A	B	700
Michelin	Cross Terrain Suv S-SP Rated	ALL	A	B	700
Big O	Legacy Tour Plus	P185,195,205 & 215/70R14 T	A	B	700
Big O	Legacy Tour Plus	P205,215/65R15 T	A	B	700
Big O	Legacy Tour Plus	P205,215,225 & 235/70R15 T	A	B	700
Big O	Legacy Tour Plus	P255 & 215/60R16 T	A	B	700
Big O	Legacy Tour Plus	P215/65R16 T	A	B	700
Big O	Legacy Tour Plus	P195/65R14 T	A	B	700
Big O	Legacy Tour Plus	P195/65R15 T	A	B	700
Mentor	Vantage Touring LE	ALL	A	B	700
Co-op	Goldenmark Luxury Touring (T)	ALL	A	B	700
Multi-Mile	Excel	ALL	A	B	700
Cordovan	Century	ALL	A	B	700
Bridgestone	Turanza LS "T"	ALL	A	B	700
Monarch	Ultra Tour LS	ALL	A	B	700
Lee	Ultra Tour LS	ALL	A	B	700
Kelly	Navigator Platinum TE	ALL Except	A	B	700
Republic	Ultra Tour LS	ALL	A	B	700
National	Ovation	P235/75R15	A	B	700
Delta	Esteem XLE	P235/75R15	A	B	700
Laramie	Grandeur Touring GT 60/65/70 Series	14-16	A	B	700
Jetzon	Grandeur Touring GT 60/65/70 Series	14-16	A	B	700
Telstar	Grandeur Touring GT 60/65/70 Series	14-16	A	B	700
Neutral	Touring LST	ALL Others	A	B	700
Goodyear	Assurance Comfortred	ALL	A	B	700
Bridgestone	Dueler HL Alenza T-Rated	ALL	A	B	700
Michelin	X Radial	ALL	A	B	680
National	Ovation	ALL 15 Except	A	B	680
Delta	Esteem XLE 70 & 75 Series	ALL 15 Except	A	B	680
Michelin	Harmony	ALL	A	B	680
Michelin	Destiny	ALL	A	B	680
Michelin	Agility	ALL	A	B	680
Big O	Legacy Tour Plus 60/65/70 Series	14-16	A	B	660
Riken	Raptor Touring Edition 70/75 Series	P205+	A	B	660
American	Gold Tour Plus 70/75 Series	P205+	A	B	660
Cavalier	Primera 70/75 Series	P205+	A	B	660
Trivant	Primera 70/75 Series	P205+	A	B	660
Co-op	Goldenmark Luxury Touring (S)	ALL	A	B	660
National	Ovation 70 & 75 Series	ALL 14	A	B	660
Delta	Esteem XLE 70 & 75 Series	ALL 14	A	B	660
Neutral	Touring LST 75 Series	ALL	A	B	660
Mastercraft	Touring LX	13 Only	A	B	640
Goodyear	Aquatred 3	ALL Others	AA	B	640
BFGoodrich	The Advantage Plus 70/75 Series	ALL	A	B	640
Hallmark	Ultra Touring GT	ALL	A	B	640
Lee	Ultra Touring GT	ALL	A	B	640
Riken	Raptor Touring Edition 70/75 Series	Thru P195	A	B	640
Cooper	Lifeliner STE	13	A	B	640
Sigma	Supreme Touring S-Series	ALL Others	A	B	640

For a complete listing of all the tires on the market, you can call the Auto Safety Hot Line toll free, at 888-327-4236 or 800-424-9153 (TTY). Or, go to www.safercar.gov

WARNING

As tires age, they naturally dry out and can become potentially dangerous. Some experts recommend getting rid of a six-year-old tire no matter what condition it is in. Recently, a national news organization went undercover and found 12 year old tires for sale, so be sure to check your tire date before purchasing. Ask for tires that are less than one year old.

INSURANCE

Insurance is a big part of ownership expenses, yet it's often forgotten in the showroom. As you shop, remember that the car's design and accident history may affect your insurance rates. Some cars cost less to insure because experience has shown that they are damaged less, less expensive to fix after a collision, or stolen less.

Shop Around: You can save hundreds of dollars by shopping around for insurance.

There are a number of factors that determine what coverage will cost you. A car's design can affect both the chances and severity of an accident. For example, a well-designed bumper may escape damage in a low-speed crash. Some cars are easier to repair than others or may have less expensive parts. Cars with four doors tend to be damaged less than cars with two doors.

Other factors that effect your insurance costs include:

Your Annual Mileage: The more you drive, the more your vehicle will be "exposed" to a potential accident. Driving less than 7,500 miles per year often gets a discount. Ask your insurer if they offer this option.

Where You Drive: If you regularly drive and park in the city, you will most likely pay more than if you drive in rural areas.

Youthful Drivers: Usually the highest premiums are paid by male drivers under the age of 25. Whether or not the under-25-year-old male is married also affects insurance rates. (Married males pay less.) As the driver gets older, rates are lowered.

Insurance discounts and surcharges depend upon the way a vehicle is traditionally driven. Sports cars, for example, are usually surcharged due, in part, to the typical driving habits of their owners. Four-door sedans and station wagons generally merit discounts.

Not all companies offer discounts or surcharges, and many cars receive neither. Some companies offer a discount or impose a surcharge on collision premiums only. Others apply discounts and surcharges on both collision and comprehensive coverage. Discounts and surcharges usually range from 10–30 percent. Remember that one company may offer a discount on a particular car while another may not.

TYPES OF COVERAGE

TIP

Collision Insurance: This pays for the damage to your car after an accident.

Comprehensive Physical Damage Insurance: This pays for damages when your car is stolen or damaged by fire, flood, or other perils.

Property Damage Liability: This pays claims and defense costs if your car damages someone else's property.

Medical Payments Insurance: This pays for your car's occupants' medical expenses resulting from an accident.

Bodily Injury Liability: This provides money to pay claims against you and to pay for the cost of your legal defense if your car injures or kills someone.

Uninsured Motorists Protection: This pays for injuries caused by an uninsured or a hit-and-run driver.

REDUCING INSURANCE COSTS

Get Your Discounts: After you have shopped around and found the best deal by comparing the costs of different coverages, be sure you get all the discounts you are entitled to.

Most insurance companies offer discounts of 5 to 30 percent on various parts of your insurance bill. Ask your insurance company for a complete list of the discounts that it offers. These can vary by company and from state to state.

Here are some of the most common insurance discounts:

Driver Education/Defensive Driving Courses: Discounts for completing a state-approved driver education course can mean a $40 reduction in the cost of coverage. Discounts of 5–15 percent are available in some states to those who complete a defensive driving course.

Good Student Discounts of up to 25 percent for full-time high school or college students who are in the upper 20 percent of their class, on the dean's list, or have a B or better grade point average.

Good Driver Discounts are available to drivers with an accident and violation-free record, (or no incidents in 3 years).

Mature Driver Credit: Drivers ages 50 and older may qualify for up to a 10 percent discount or a lower price bracket.

Sole Female Driver: Some companies offer discounts of 10 percent for females, ages 30 to 64, who are the only driver in a household.

Non-Drinkers and Non-Smokers: A limited number of companies offer incentives ranging from 10–25 percent to those who abstain.

Farmer Discounts: Many companies offer farmers either a discount of 10–30 percent or a lower price bracket.

Car Pooling: Commuters sharing driving may qualify for discounts of 5–25 percent or a lower price bracket.

Children away at school don't drive the family car very often, so if they're on your policy and they're at school, let your company know. If you insure them separately, discounts of 10–40 percent or a lower price bracket are available.

Desirable Cars: Premiums are usually much higher for cars with high collision rates or that are the favorite target of thieves.

Anti-Theft Device Credits: Discounts of 5 to 15 percent are offered in some states for cars equipped with a hood lock and an alarm or a disabling device (active or passive) that prevents the car from being started.

Multipolicy and Multicar Policy Discount: Some companies offer discounts of up to 10–20 percent for insuring your home and auto with the same company, or more than one car.

First Accident Allowance: Some insurers offer a "first accident allowance," which guarantees that if a customer achieves five accident-free years, his or her rates won't go up after the first at-fault accident.

Deductibles: Opting for the largest reasonable deductible is the obvious first step in reducing premiums. Increasing your deductible to $500 from $200 could cut your collision premium

---

! DON'T SPEED !

Besides endangering the lives of your passengers and other drivers, speeding tickets will increase your insurance premium. It only takes one speeding ticket to lose your "preferred" or "good driver" discount, which requires a clean driving record. Two or more speeding tickets or accidents can increase your premium by 40% to 200%. Some insurers may simply drop your coverage. According to the Insurance Institute for Highway Safety (IIHS), you are 17% more likely to be in an accident if you have just one speeding ticket. Insurance companies know this and will charge you for it.

about 20 percent. Raising the deductible to $1,000 from $200 could lower your premium about 45 percent. The discounts may vary by company.

Collision Coverage: The older the car, the less the need for collision insurance. Consider dropping collision insurance entirely on an older car. Regardless of how much coverage you carry, the insurance company will only pay up to the car's "book value." For example, if your car requires $1,000 in repairs, but its "book value" is only $500, the insurance company is required to pay only $500.

Organizations: If you are a member of AARP, AAA, the military, a union, a professional group, an alumni association, or similar organization, you may be able to get a discount. Often insurance companies will enter joint ventures with organizations.

YOUNG DRIVERS

Each year, teenagers account for about 15 percent of highway deaths. According to the Insurance Institute for Highway Safety (IIHS), the highest driver death rate per 100,000 people is among 18-year-olds. Parents need to make sure their children are fully prepared to be competent, safe drivers before letting them out on the road. All states issue learner's permits. However, only 35 states and the District of Columbia require permits before getting a driver's license. It isn't difficult for teenagers to get a license and only 14 states prohibit teenagers from driving during night and early morning. Call your state's MVA for young driver laws.

AUTO THEFT

The Highway Loss Data Institute (HLDI) regularly compiles statistics on motor vehicle thefts. Using the frequency of theft claims per 1,000 insured vehicle, the HLDI lists the following as the most and least stolen vehicles among the 2008-2010 models.

Most Stolen	Claim Frequency*
Cadillac Escalade	10.8
Ford F-250 Crew 4WD	9.7
Chevrolet Silverado 1500 Crew	9.2
Ford F-450 Crew 4WD	7.9
GMC Sierra 1500 Crew	7.3
Chrysler 300	7.1
Ford F-350 Crew 4WD	7.0
Chevrolet Avalanche 1500	6.4
GMC Yukon	6.4
Chrysler 300 HEMI	6.3

Least Stolen	
Audi A6 4WD	0.5
Mercury Mariner	0.5
Chevrolet Equinox	0.6
Volkswagen CC	0.6
Chevrolet Equinox 4WD	0.6
Lexus RX 350	0.6
Saturn VUE	0.6
Chevrolet Aveo	0.6
BMW 5 Series 4WD	0.7
Mini Cooper Clubman	0.7
Average All Passenger Vehicles	**1.7**

*Claim Frequency means the number of vehicles stolen per 1000 insured vehicles, for example about 11 Cadillac Escalades are stolen or broken into for every 1,000 insured.
Source: Highway Loss Data Institute (www.iihs.org)

BUMPERS

The main purpose of the bumper is to protect your car in low-speed collisions. Despite this intention, many of us have been victims of a $500-$3500 repair bill resulting from a seemingly minor impact. The federal government used to require that automakers equip cars with bumpers capable of withstanding up to 5 mph crashes with no damage. Unfortunately, in the early eighties, under pressure from car companies, the government rolled back this requirement. Now, the federal law only requires car companies to build bumpers to protect only cars in 2.5 mph collisions-about the speed at which we walk. This rollback enables the car companies to sell lots of expensive parts, and has cost consumers millions of dollars in increased insurance premiums and repair costs.

The good news is that Canada has a 5 mph (8k) standard and many car companies use the same designs in models sold in the U.S. In addition, the state of California requires that companies disclose which bumpers meet the old 5 mph standard which has motivated some companies to build better bumper systems.

In order to see how well bumpers actually protect our vehicles, the Insurance Institute for Highway Safety conducts a variety of bumper tests. In their low speed (6 mph) tests, it's shocking how poorly bumpers protect vehicles. In these tests, it can easily cost $2-$3,700 after a low speed fender bender.

Unfortunately, we can't simply look at a bumper and determine how good it will be at doing its job-protecting a car from inevitable bumps. The solution to this problem is quite simple—require carmakers to tell the consumer the highest speed at which their car could be crashed with no damage.

Federal standards *do* require that car bumpers be designed to match up to each other in a collision. This is an attempt to enable the bumpers to hit each other and absorb the energy of the crash rather than other parts of the car. Unfortunately there is a big hole in this federal requirement because SUVs, pickups, and minivans don't have to meet the same bumper height rules as cars. With such a high percentage of SUVs, pickups and minivans on the road, huge bumper mismatches in crashes are quite common. This mismatching between cars and SUVs results in excessive damage and pricey repairs.

In order to see how well bumpers actually function in car and SUV collisions, the Insurance Institute for Highway Safety conducted two types of tests at 10 mph; one with an SUV hitting the rear of a car and one with a car traveling at 10 mph and crashing into the rear of an SUV. For more results, visit the Insurance Institute for Highway Safety at www.iihs.org.

DAMAGE REPAIR COSTS IN 10 MPH FRONT-INTO-REAR CRASH TESTS

Source: Insurance Institute for Highway Safety

SUV INTO CAR	SUV Damage	Car Damage	Total Damage
Honda CR-V into Honda Civic	$1,721	$1,274	$2,995
Toyota RAV4 into Toyota Corolla	$1,434	$2,327	$3,761
Hyundai Tucson into Kia Forte	$850	$3,223	$4,073
Volkswagen Tiguan into Volkswagen Golf	$2,329	$2,058	$4,387
Jeep Patriot into Dodge Caliber	$1,415	$3,095	$4,510
Ford Escape into Ford Focus	$1,470	$3,386	$4,856
Nissan Rogue into Nissan Sentra	$2,884	$4,560	$7,444

CAR INTO SUV	Car Damage	SUV Damage	Total Damage
Kia Forte into Hyundai Tucson	$1,510	$2,091	$3,601
Dodge Caliber into Jeep Patriot	$2,559	$1,338	$3,897
Honda Civic into Honda CR-V	$4,921	$1,053	$5,974
Volkswagen Golf into Volkswagen Tiguan	$4,555	$1,872	$6,427
Nissan Sentra into Nissan Rogue	$5,114	$1,428	$6,542
Ford Focus into Ford Escape	$5,203	$2,208	$7,411
Toyota Corolla into Toyota RAV4	$3,852	$6,015	$9,867

See www.IIHS.org

COMPLAINTS

Americans spend billions of dollars on vehicle repairs every year. While many of those repairs are satisfactory, there are times when getting your vehicle fixed can be a very difficult process. In fact, vehicle defects and repairs are the number one cause of consumer complaints, according to the Federal Trade Commission. This chapter is designed to help you resolve your complaint, whether it's for a new vehicle still under warranty or for one you've had for years. In addition, we offer a guide to arbitration, the names and addresses of consumer groups, federal agencies, and the manufacturers themselves. Finally, we tell you how to take the important step of registering your complaint with the U.S. Department of Transportation.

No matter what your complaint, keep accurate records. Copies of the following items are indispensable in helping to resolve your problems:

☑ your service invoices

☑ bills you have paid

☑ letters you have written to the manufacturer or the repair facility owner

☑ written repair estimates from your independent mechanic.

☑ notes on discussion with company representatives including names and dates.

RESOLVING COMPLAINTS

Here are some basic steps to help you resolve your problem:

1 First, return your vehicle to the repair facility that did the work. Bring a written list of the problems and make sure that you keep a copy of the list. Give the repair facility a reasonable opportunity to examine your vehicle and attempt to fix it. Speak directly to the service manager (not to the service writer who wrote up your repair order), and ask him or her to test drive the vehicle with you so that you can point out the problem.

2 If that doesn't resolve the problem, take the vehicle to a diagnostic center for an independent examination. This may cost $45 to $60. Get a written statement defining the problem and outlining how it may be fixed. Give your repair shop a copy. If your vehicle is under warranty, do not allow any warranty repair by an independent mechanic; you may not be reimbursed by the manufacturer.

3 If your repair shop does not respond to the independent assessment, present your problem to a mediation panel. These panels hear both sides of the story and try to come to a resolution.

If the problem is with a new vehicle dealer, or if you feel that the manufacturer is responsible, you may be able to use one of the manufacturer's mediation programs.

If the problem is solely with an independent dealer, a local Better Business Bureau (BBB) may be able to mediate your complaint. It may also offer an arbitration hearing. In any case, the BBB should enter your complaint into its files on that establishment.

When contacting any mediation program, determine how long the process takes, who makes the final decision, whether you are bound by that decision, and whether the program handles all problems or only warranty complaints.

4 If there are no mediation programs in your area, contact private consumer groups, local government agencies, or your local "action line" newspaper columnist, newspaper editor, or radio or TV broadcaster. A phone call or letter from them may persuade a repair facility to take action. Send a copy of your letter to the repair shop.

5 One of your last resorts is to bring a lawsuit against the dealer, manufacturer, or repair facility in small claims court. The fee for filing such an action is usually small, and you generally act as your own attorney, saving attorney's fees. There is a monetary limit on the amount you can claim, which varies from state to state. Your local consumer affairs office, state attorney general's office, or the clerk of the court can tell you how to file such a suit.

6 Finally, talk with an attorney. It's best to select an attorney who is familiar with handling automotive problems. Call the lawyer referral service listed in the telephone directory and ask for the names of attorneys who deal with automobile problems. If you can't afford an attorney, contact the Legal Aid Society.

WARRANTY COMPLAINTS
If your vehicle is under warranty or you are having problems with a factory-authorized dealership, here are some special guidelines:

1 Have the warranty available to show the dealer. Make sure you call the problem to the dealer's attention before the end of the warranty period.

2 If you are still dissatisfied after giving the dealer a reasonable opportunity to fix your vehicle, contact the manufacturer's representative (also called the zone representative) in your area. This person can authorize the dealer to make repairs or take other steps to resolve the dispute. Your dealer will have your zone representative's name and telephone number. Explain the problem and ask for a meeting and a personal inspection of your vehicle.

3 If you can't get satisfaction from the zone representative, call or write the manufacturer's owner relations department. Your owner's manual contains this phone number and address. In each case, as you move up the chain, indicate the steps you have already taken and keep careful records of your efforts.

4 Your next option is to present your problem to a complaint handling panel or to the arbitration program in which the manufacturer of your vehicle participates.

If you complain of a problem during the warranty period,

you have a right to have the problem fixed even after the warranty runs out. If your warranty has not been honored, you may be able to "revoke acceptance," which means that you return the vehicle to the dealer. If you are successful, you may be entitled to a replacement

vehicle or to a full refund of the purchase price and reimbursement of legal fees under the Magnuson-Moss Warranty Act. Or, if you are covered by one of the state lemon laws, you may be able to return the vehicle and receive a refund or replacement from the manufacturer.

NEED HELP?

TIP

If you need legal assistance with your repair problem, the Center for Auto Safety has a list of lawyers who specialize in helping consumers with auto repair problems. For the names of attorneys in your area, send a stamped, self-addressed envelope to: Center for Auto Safety, 1825 Connecticut Ave. NW, Suite 330, Washington, DC 20009. Check their website at www.autosafety.org for a shorter list of lemon law attorneys.

In addition, the Center has published *The Lemon Book*, a detailed 368-page guide to resolving automobile complaints. The book is available for $17.50 directly from the Center.

Attorneys Take Note: For information on litigation assistance provided by the Center for Auto Safety, including *The Lemon Law Litigation Manual*, please contact the Center for Auto Safety at the above address.

AUTO SAFETY HOT LINE
800-424-9393
IN WASHINGTON, DC: 202-366-0123
TTY FOR HEARING IMPAIRED:
800-424-9153 OR DC: 202-366-7800

TIP

The toll-free Auto Safety Hot Line can provide information on recalls, record information about safety problems, and refer you to the appropriate government experts on other vehicle related problems. You can even have recall information mailed to you within 24 hours of your call at no charge. Most importantly, you can call the hot line to report safety problems which will become part of the National Highway Traffic Safety Administration's complaint database.

COMPLAINT INDEX

Thanks to the efforts of the Center for Auto Safety, we are able to provide you with the vehicle complaints on file with the National Highway Traffic Safety Administration (NHTSA). Each year, thousands of Americans file online or call the government in order to register complaints about their vehicles. The federal government collects this information but has never released it to the public.

The complaint index is the result of our analysis of these complaints. It is based on a ratio of the number of complaints for each vehicle to the sales of that vehicle. In order to predict the expected complaint performance of the 2012 models, we have examined the complaint history of that car's series. The term series refers to the fact that when a manufacturer introduces a new model, that vehicle remains essentially unchanged, on average, for four to six years. For example, the Cadillac Escalade was redesigned in 2002 and remains essentially the same car for 2012. As such, we have compiled the complaint experience for that series in order to give you some information to use in deciding which car to buy. For vehicles introduced or significantly changed in 2012, we do not yet have enough data to develop a complaint index.

The following table presents the projected best and worst complaint ratings for the 2012 models for which we can develop ratings. Higher index numbers mean the vehicle generated a greater number of complaints. Lower numbers indicate fewer complaints.

2012 PROJECTED COMPLAINT INDEX

THE BEST	INDEX*
Dodge Durango	391
Land Rover LR4	637
Lincoln MKZ	691
Mazda 2	727
Volvo C70	741
Chevrolet Silverado	757
Ford F-150	771
Nissan Altima Coupe	825
GMC Sierra	861
Acura RDX	864
Mitsubishi Galant	869
Mazda MX-5 Miata	891
Mazda CX-9	918
Volvo S60	948
Mercedes-Benz C-Class	993
Nissan Cube	999
Acura MDX	1,004
Chevrolet Colorado	1,026
Acura TL	1,032
Lexus LS	1,076

THE WORST	INDEX*
Toyota Prius	30,929
Hyundai Sonata	21,486
BMW 5 Series	17,702
Kia Sorento	14,106
Lexus HS	13,183
Dodge Journey	12,354
Jaguar XF	10,036
Jeep Wrangler	9,065
Volkswagen Routan	8,618
Jaguar XJ	7,558
Ford Fiesta	7,486
Nissan Leaf	7,358
Volkswagen Golf	7,137
Volkswagen Jetta	6,863
Porsche Cayenne	6,791
Mini Cooper	6,759
BMW Z4	6,614
Audi A3	6,198
Honda CR-Z	5,960
Mercedes-Benz GLK-Class	5,845

*IMPORTANT NOTE: The numbers represent relative index scores, not the number of complaints received. The complaint index score considers sales volume and years on the road. Lower index numbers are better.

CENTER FOR AUTO SAFETY

Every year automobile manufacturers spend millions of dollars making their voices heard in government decision making. For example, General Motors and Ford have large staffs in Detroit and Washington that work solely to influence government activity. But who looks out for the consumer?

For over 30 years, the non-profit Center for Auto Safety (CAS) has told the consumer's story to government agencies, to Congress, and to the courts. Its efforts focus on all consumers rather than only those with individual complaints.

CAS was established in 1970 by Ralph Nader and Consumers Union. As consumer concerns about auto safety issues expanded, so did the work of CAS. It became independent of its founders in 1972. CAS' activities include:

Initiating Safety Recalls: CAS analyzes over 50,000 consumer complaints each year. By following problems as they develop, CAS requests government investigations and recalls of defective vehicles. CAS was responsible for the Ford Pinto faulty gas tank recall, the Firestone 500 steel-belted radial tire recall, and the record recall of over three million Evenflo One Step child seats.

Representing the Consumer in Washington: CAS follows the activities of federal agencies and Congress to ensure that they carry out their responsibilities to the American taxpayer. CAS brings a consumer's point of view to vehicle safety policies and rule-making. Since 1970, CAS has submitted more than 500 petitions and comments on federal safety standards.

One major effort on safety standards has been the successful fight to get airbags in every car. After opposing airbags for decades, the auto industry now can't get enough lifesaving airbags in cars with some models having eight airbags. With airbags to protect consumers in front and side crashes, CAS is now working to strengthen weak roofs that cannot support a vehicle's own weight and crush in rollovers that result in 27,000 deaths and serious injuries each year.

In 1992, CAS uncovered a fire defect that dwarfed the highly publicized flammability of the Ford Pinto. It had to do with the side saddle gas tanks on full size 1973–87 GM pickups and 1988–90 crew cabs that can explode on impact. Over 2,000 people have been killed in fire crashes involving these trucks. After mounting a national campaign to warn consumers to steer clear of these GM fire hazards, the U.S. Department of Transportation granted CAS' petition and conducted one of its biggest defect investigations in history. The result—GM was asked to recall its pickups. GM, sadly, denied this request.

Exposing Secret Warranties: CAS played a prominent role in the disclosure of secret warranties, "policy adjustments," as they are called by manufacturers. These occur when an automaker agrees to pay for repair of certain defects beyond the warranty period but refuses to notify consumers.

Lemon Laws: CAS' work on Lemon Laws aided in the enactment of state laws which make it easier to return a defective new automobile and get money back.

Tire Ratings: After a suspension between 1982 and 1984, consumers have reliable treadwear ratings to help them get the most miles for their dollar. CAS' lawsuit overturned DOT's revocation of this valuable tire information program.

Initiating Legal Action: When CAS has exhausted other means of obtaining relief for consumer problems, it will initiate legal action. For example, in 1978 when the Department of Energy attempted to raise the price of unleaded gasoline four cents per gallon without notice or comment, CAS succeeded in stopping this illegal move through a lawsuit, thus saving consumers $2 billion for the 3-year period that the decision was in effect.

CENTER FOR AUTO SAFETY ONLINE

The Center for Auto Safety has a website at www.autosafety.org to provide information to consumers and to organize consumer campaigns against auto companies on safety defects. Detailed packages of information and advice on defects in specific makes and models are on CAS' website. Consumers with lemons and safety defects can file electronic complaints with CAS and get referred to lemon lawyers.

www.autosafety.org

A 1985 CAS lawsuit against the Environmental Protection Agency (EPA) forced the EPA to recall polluting cars, rather than let companies promise to make cleaner cars in the future. As part of the settlement, GM (which was responsible for the polluting cars) funded a $7 million methanol bus demonstration program in New York City.

In 2003, a CAS lawsuit forced the Department of Transportation (DOT) to require auto companies to use more accurate direct tire pressure monitors on the vehicle dash that identified which tire had low pressure versus an indirect system that only told consumers they had low tire pressure on some tire.

CAS also challenges class actions settlements that don't deliver for consumers. We have knocked off coupon settlement after coupon settlement where consumers got useless coupons to buy a new car while trial lawyers got cold cash. In 2010 we challenged a Honda Civic Hybrid gas mileage settlement that gave consumers a DVD on how to drive better. In 2009, we challenged a Ford Explorer rollover settlement that gave consumers a restricted $500 coupon toward a new $30,000 Explorer or $300 for a different Ford model that only 148 out of 1,000,000 class members redeemed for about $50,000 total while attorneys got $25 million in fees and costs.

CAS is your safety and lemon insurance. CAS depends on public support to do all its good work. Annual membership is $25. All contributions are tax-deductible. To contribute by credit card, go to the CAS website at: www.autosafety.org/make-donation-cas.

Consumer Groups and Government

Below are the names of additional consumer groups you may find helpful:

Advocates for Highway and Auto Safety
750 First St., NE, Suite 901
Washington, DC 20002
(202) 408-1711/408-1699 fax
www.saferoads.org
An alliance of consumer, health and safety groups and insurance companies.

Consumer Action
P.O. Box 70037
Washington, DC 20024
(202) 544-3088
(415) 777-9635 (Complaint Hotline)
www.consumer-action.org
Complaint handling and advocacy related to consumer rights.

Consumers for Auto Reliability and Safety
1303 J St., Suite 270
Sacramento, CA 95814
(530) 759-9440/www.carconsumers.com
Auto safety, airbags, and lemon laws.

KIDS AND CARS
2913 West 113th St.
Leawood, KS 66211
(913) 327-0013/327-0014 fax
www.kidsandcars.org
Safety and advocacy related to protecting children in and around motor vehicles.

Public Health Advocacy Institute
Motor Vehicle Hazard Archives Project
www.AutoHazardInfo.org
mvhap_phai@yahoo.com
The Project's mission is to preserve and broaden access to historical and current information about motor vehicle hazards and injury control. The website offers free information about vehicle safety and motor vehicle hazard control.

SafetyBelt Safe, U.S.A.
P.O. Box 553
Altadena, CA 91003
(800) 745-SAFE, stombrella@carseat.org
www.carseat.org
Excellent information and training on child safety seats and safety belt usage.

S.A.N.E., Inc.
2490 N. Park Road, #209 South
Hollywood, FL 33021
(954) 989-1251/www.saferautos.org
namrissam@bellsouth.net
Advocates and distributes information for better driving behavior and vehicle safety.

Several federal agencies conduct automobile- related programs. Following is each agency with a description of the type of work it performs and how to contact them.

National Highway Traffic Safety Administration
1200 New Jersey Ave., SE, West Bldg.
Washington, DC 20590
(888) DASH-2-DOT/www.nhtsa.dot.gov
www.safercar.gov
NHTSA issues safety and fuel economy standards for new motor vehicles; investigates safety defects and enforces recall of defective vehicles and equipment; conducts research and demonstration programs on vehicle safety, fuel economy, driver safety, and automobile inspection and repair; provides grants for state highway safety programs in areas such as police traffic services, driver education and licensing, emergency medical services, pedestrian safety, and alcohol abuse.

Environmental Protection Agency
1200 Pennsylvania Ave., NW
Washington, DC 20460
(202) 272-0167/www.epa.gov
www.fueleconomy.gov
EPA's responsibilities include setting and enforcing air and noise emission standards for motor vehicles and measuring fuel economy in new vehicles (EPA Fuel Economy Guide).

Federal Trade Commission
600 Pennsylvania Ave., NW
Washington, DC 20580
(877) FTC-HELP/www.ftc.gov
The FTC regulates advertising, credit practices, marketing abuses, and professional services and ensures that products are properly labeled (as in fuel economy ratings). The commission covers unfair or deceptive trade practices in motor vehicle sales and repairs, as well as non-safety defects.

U.S. Department of Justice
Office of Consumer Litigation
950 Pennsylvania Ave., NW
Washington, DC 20503
(800) 869-4499 or 202-514-2000
www.usdoj.gov/askdoj@usdoj.gov
The DOJ enforces federal law that requires manufacturers to label new automobiles and forbids removal or alteration of labels before delivery to consumers. Labels must contain make, model, vehicle identification number, dealer's name, suggested base price, manufacturer option costs, and manufacturer's suggested retail price.

AUTOMOBILE MANUFACTURERS

Acura (Division of Honda)
See Honda for address and executive
Customer Relations: 800-382-2238

Audi (See Volkswagen for address)
Johan de Nysschen, President
Customer Relations: 800-822-2834
E-mail: auditalk@audi.com

BMW
Ludwig Willisch, President
300 Chestnut Ridge Road
Woodcliff Lake, NJ 07677-7731
Customer Relations: 800-831-1117

Buick (Division of General Motors)
PO Box 33136
Detroit, MI 48232-5136
Customer Relations: 800-521-7300

Cadillac (Division of General Motors)
PO Box 33169
Detroit, MI 48232-5169
Customer Relations: 800-458-8006

Chevrolet (Division of General Motors)
PO Box 33170
Detroit, MI 48232-5170
Customer Relations: 800-222-1020
Fax: 313-556-5108

Chrysler (Chrysler, Dodge, Jeep)
Sergio Marchionne, CEO
1000 Chrysler Drive
Auburn Hills, MI 48321-8004
Customer Relations: 800-992-1997

Dodge (See Chrysler)

Ford (Ford, Lincoln)
Alan Mulally, President and CEO
P.O. Box 6248
Dearborn, MI 48121
Customer Relations: 800-392-3673
www.customersaskford.com

General Motors
(Buick, Cadillac, Chev., GMC)
Daniel Akerson, Chairman and CEO
300 Renaissance Center
Detroit, MI 48243

GMC (Division of General Motors)
PO Box 33172
Detroit, MI 48232
Customer Relations: 800-462-8782

Honda (Honda, Acura)
Tetsuo Iwamura, President and CEO
1919 Torrance Blvd.
Torrance, CA 90501
Customer Relations: 800-999-1009

Hyundai
John Krafcik, President and CEO
PO Box 20850
Fountain Valley, CA 92728-0850
Customer Relations: 800-633-5151
E-mail: consumeraffairs@hmausa.com

Infiniti (Division of Nissan)
See Nissan for address and executive
Customer Relations: 800-662-6200

Jaguar, Land Rover
Andy Goss, President
555 MacArthur Blvd.
Mahwah, NJ 07430
Jag Customer Relations: 800-452-4827

Jeep (See Chrysler)

Kia
Byung Mo Ahn, President and CEO
PO Box 52410
Irvine, CA 92619-2410
Customer Relations: 800-333-4542

Land Rover (See Jaguar)
Customer Relations: 800-637-6837
Fax: 201-760-8514

Lexus (Division of Toyota)
Mark Templin, VP and General Mgr.
PO Box 2991, Mail Drop L201
Torrance, CA 90501-2732
Customer Relations: 800-255-3987

Lincoln (Division of Ford)
PO Box 6128
Dearborn, MI 48121
Customer Relations: 800-521-4140

Mazda
Jim O' Sullivan, President and CEO
PO Box 19734
Irvine, CA 92623-9734
Customer Relations: 800-222-5500

Mercedes-Benz
Ernst Lieb, President and CEO
Three Mercedes Dr.
Montvale, NJ 07645
Customer Relations: 800-367-6372

Mini (Division of BMW)
Jim McDowell, Vice President
PO Box 1227
Westwood, NJ 07675-1227
Customer Relations: 866-275-6464

Mitsubishi
Seiei Ono, President and CEO
PO Box 6014, Cypress, CA 90630-0014
Customer Relations: 888-648-7820

Nissan
Carlos Ghosn, President and CEO
PO Box 685003
Franklin, TN 37068-5003
Customer Relations: 800-647-7261

Porsche
Detlev von Platen, President and CEO
980 Hammond Dr., Suite 1000
Atlanta, GA 30328
Customer Relations: 800-767-7243

Saab
Timothy Colbeck, President and COO
4327 Delemere Ct
Royal Oak, MI 48073
Customer Relations: 800-955-9007

Scion (Division of Toyota)
Jack Hollis, Vice President
D102 PO Box 2742
Torrence, CA 90509-2742
Customer Relations: 866-707-2466

Smart
Jill Lajdziak, President
2555 Telegraph Rd.
Bloomfield Hills, MI 48302
Customer Relations: 800-762-7887

Subaru
Takeshi Tachimori, Chairman,
President and CEO
Subaru Plaza, P.O. Box 6000
Cherry Hill, NJ 08034-6000
Customer Relations: 800-782-2783

Suzuki
Kevin Saito, President
PO Box 1100, Brea, CA 92822-1100
Customer Relations: 800-934-0934

Toyota (Toyota, Lexus, Scion)
Jim Lentz, President and COO
19001 S. Western Ave.
Torrance, CA 90501
Customer Relations: 800-331-4331

Volkswagen
Jonathan Browning, President and CEO
2200 Ferdinand Porsche Drive
Herndon, VA 20171
Customer Relations: 800-822-8987

Volvo
Stefan Jacoby, President and CEO
One Volvo Dr., PO Box 914
Rockleigh, NJ 07647
Customer Relations: 800-458-1552

LEMON LAWS

Sometimes, despite our best efforts, we buy a vehicle that just doesn't work right. There may be little problem after little problem, or perhaps one big problem that never seems to be fixed. Because of the "sour" taste that such vehicles leave in the mouths of consumers who buy them, these vehicles are known as "lemons."

In the past, it's been difficult to obtain a refund or replacement if a vehicle was a lemon. The burden of proof was left to the consumer. Because it is hard to define exactly what constitutes a lemon, many lemon owners were unable to win a case against a manufacturer. And when they won, consumers had to pay for their attorneys giving them less than if they had traded in their lemon.

Thanks to "Lemon Laws" passed by all states, lemon-aide is available when consumers get stuck with a lemon. Although there are some important state-to-state variations, all of the laws have similarities: They establish a period of coverage, usually two years from delivery or the written warranty period, whichever is shorter; they may require some form of noncourt arbitration; and most importantly they define a lemon. In most states a new car, truck, or van is "presume" to be a lemon when it has been taken back to the shop 3 to 4 times for the same problem or is out of service for a total of 30 days during the covered period. This time does not mean consecutive days and can be for different problems. 15 states have safety lemon provisions which presume a vehicle is a lemon after only 1 to 2 repairs of a defect likely to cause death or serious injury. Be sure to keep careful records of your repairs since some states now require only one of the repairs to be within the specified time period. 33 states provide for the award of attorney fees with the other 17 relying on the Federal lemon law for fees. A vehicle may be covered by the lemon law even though it doesn't meet the "presumption."

Specific information about your state's law can be obtained from your state attorney general's office or at the Center for Auto Safety's website. The following table offers a general description of the Lemon Law in your state and what you need to do to set it in motion (Notification/Trigger). We indicate where state-run arbitration programs are available. State-run programs are the best type of arbitration. Be aware a few state lemon laws are so bad consumers should only rely on the Federal lemon law and state contract law. We have marked these bad laws with a ☒ while the best laws have a ☑.

| ☑ **The Best Lemon Laws** |
| ☒ **The Worst Lemon Laws** |

Alabama	Qualification: 3 unsuccessful repairs or 30 calendar days within shorter of 24 months or 24,000 miles, provided 1 repair attempt or 1 day out of service is within shorter of 1 year or 12,000 miles. Notice/Trigger: Certified mail to manufacturer + opportunity for final repair attempt within 14 calendar days.
Alaska	Qualification: 3 unsuccessful repairs or 30 business days out of service within shorter of 1 year or warranty. Notice/Trigger: Certified mail to manufacturer + dealer (or repair agent) that problem has not been corrected in reasonable number of attempts + refund or replacement demanded within 60 days. Manufacturer has 30 calendar days for final repair attempt.
Arizona	Qualification: 4 unsuccessful repairs or 30 calendar days out of service within warranty period or shorter of 2 years or 24,000 miles. Notice/Trigger: Written notice + opportunity to repair to manufacturer.
Arkansas ☑ BEST	Qualification: 3 unsuccessful repairs, 5 total repairs of any nonconformity, or 1 unsuccessful repair of problem likely to cause death or serious bodily injury within longer of 24 months or 24,000 miles. Notice/Trigger: Certified or registered mail to manufacturer who has 10 days to notify consumer of repair facility. Facility has 10 days to repair.

L—Law specifically applies to leased vehicles; S-C—State has certified guidelines for arbitration; S-R—State-run arbitration mechanism available

State	Details
California ☑ BEST	Qualification: 4 repair attempts or 30 calendar days out of service or 2 repair attempts for defect likely to cause death or serious bodily injury within shorter of 18 months or 18,000 miles, or "reasonable" number of attempts during entire express warranty period. Notice/Trigger: Direct written notice to manufacturer at address clearly specified in owner's manual. Covers small businesses with up to 5 vehicles under 10,000 pounds GVWR.
Colorado ☒ WORST	Qualification: 4 unsuccessful repairs or 30 business days out of service within shorter of 1 year or warranty. Notice/Trigger: Prior certified mail notice + opportunity to repair for manufacturer.
Connecticut	Qualification: 4 unsuccessful repairs or 30 calendar days out of service within shorter of 2 years or 24,000 miles, or 2 unsuccessful repairs of problem likely to cause death or serious bodily injury within warranty period or 1 year. Notice/Trigger: Report to manufacturer, agent, or dealer. Written notice to manufacturer only if required in owner's manual or warranty. S-R
Delaware	Qualification: 4 unsuccessful repairs or 30 calendar days out of service within shorter of 1 year or warranty. Notice/Trigger: Written notice + opportunity to repair to manufacturer.
D.C.	Qualification: 4 unsuccessful repairs or 30 calendar days out of service or 1 unsuccessful repair of safety-related defect, within shorter of 2 years or 18,000 miles. Notice/Trigger: Report to manufacturer, agent, or dealer.
Florida	Qualification: 3 unsuccessful repairs or 15 calendar days within 24 months from delivery. Notice/Trigger: Certified or express mail notice to manufacturer who has 10 days to notify consumer of repair facility plus 10 more calendar days for final repair attempt after delivery to designated dealer. S-R
Georgia	Qualification: 1 unsuccessful repair of serious safety defect or 3 unsuccessful repair attempts or 30 calendar days out of service within shorter of 24,000 miles or 24 months. Notification/Trigger: Overnight or certified mail notice return receipt requested. Manufacturer has 7 days to notify consumer of repair facility & consumer has 14 days from manufacturer receipt of original notice to deliver vehicle to repair facility. Facility has 28 calendar days from manufacturer receipt of original notice to repair. State-run arbitration mechanism available. Law specifically applies to leased vehicles.
Hawaii	Qualification: 3 unsuccessful repair attempts, or 1 unsuccessful repair attempt of defect likely to cause death or serious bodily injury, or out of service for total of 30 days within shorter of 2 years or 24,000 miles. Notice/Trigger: Written notice + opportunity to repair to manufacturer. S-R
Idaho	Qualification: 4 repair attempts or 30 business days out of service within shorter of 2 years or 24,000 miles, or 1 repair of complete failure of braking or steering likely to cause death or serious bodily injury. Notice/Trigger: Written notice to manufacturer or dealer + one opportunity to repair to manufacturer. S-R.
Illinois	Qualification: 4 unsuccessful repairs or 30 business days out of service within shorter of 1 year or 12,000 miles. Notice/Trigger: Written notice + opportunity to repair to manufacturer.
Indiana ☒ WORST	Qualification: 4 unsuccessful repairs or 30 business days out of service within shorter of 18 months or 18,000 miles. Notice/Trigger: Written notice to manufacturer only if required in the warranty.

L—Law specifically applies to leased vehicles; S-C—State has certified guidelines for arbitration; S-R—State-run arbitration mechanism available

Iowa	Qualification: 3 unsuccessful repairs, or 1 unsuccessful repair of nonconformity likely to cause death or serious bodily injury, or 30 calendar days out of service within shorter of 2 years or 24,000 miles. Notice/Trigger: Certified registered mail + final opportunity to repair within 10 calendar days of receipt of notice to manufacturer.
Kansas	Qualification: 4 unsuccessful repairs or 30 calendar days out of service or 10 total repairs within shorter of 1 year or warranty. Notice/Trigger: Actual notice to manufacturer.
Kentucky	Qualification: 4 unsuccessful repairs or 30 calendar days out of service within shorter of 1 year or 12,000 miles. Notice/Trigger: Written notice to manufacturer.
Louisiana	Qualification: 4 unsuccessful repairs or 90 calendar days out of service within shorter of 1 year or warranty. Notice/Trigger: Report to manufacturer or dealer.
Maine	Qualification: 3 unsuccessful repairs (or 1 unsuccessful repair of serious failure of brakes or steering) or 15 business days out of service within shorter of warranty or 3 years or 18,000 miles. Applies to vehicles within first 18,000 miles or 3 years regardless of whether claimant is original owner. Notice/Trigger: Written notice to manufacturer or dealer. Manufacturer has 7 business days after receipt for final repair attempt. S-R
Maryland	Qualification: 4 unsuccessful repairs, 30 calendar days out of service or 1 unsuccessful repair of braking or steering system within shorter of 15 months or 15,000 miles. Notice/Trigger: Certified mail return receipt requested + opportunity to repair within 30 calendar days of receipt of notice to manufacturer or factory branch.
Massachusetts	Qualification: 3 unsuccessful repairs or 10 business days out of service within shorter of 1 year or 15,000 miles. Notice/Trigger: Notice to manufacturer or dealer who has 7 business days to attempt final repair. S-R
Michigan	Qualification: 4 unsuccessful repairs within 2 years from date of first unsuccessful repair or 30 calendar days within shorter of 1 year or warranty. Notice/Trigger: Certified mail return receipt requested to manufacturer who has 5 business days to repair after delivery. Consumer may notify manufacturer after third repair attempt.
Minnesota	Qualification: 4 unsuccessful repairs or 30 business days or 1 unsuccessful repair of total braking or steering loss likely to cause death or serious bodily injury within shorter of 2 years or warranty. Notice/Trigger: Written notice + opportunity to repair to manufacturer, agent, or dealer.
Mississippi	Qualification: 3 unsuccessful repairs or 15 business days out of service within shorter of 1 year or warranty. Notice/Trigger: Written notice to manufacturer who has 10 business days to repair after delivery to designated dealer.
Missouri	Qualification: 4 unsuccessful repairs or 30 business days out of service within shorter of 1 year or warranty. Notice/Trigger: Written notice to manufacturer who has 10 calendar days to repair after delivery to designated dealer.
Montana	Qualification: 4 unsuccessful repairs or 30 business days out of service after notice within shorter of 2 years or 18,000 miles. Notice/Trigger: Written notice + opportunity to repair to manufacturer. S-R
Nebraska	Qualification: 4 unsuccessful repairs or 40 calendar days out of service within shorter of 1 year or warranty. Notice/Trigger: Certified mail + opportunity to repair to manufacturer.

L—Law specifically applies to leased vehicles; S-C—State has certified guidelines for arbitration; S-R—State-run arbitration mechanism available

Nevada	Qualification: 4 unsuccessful repairs or 30 calendar days out of service within shorter of 1 year or warranty. Notice/Trigger: Written notice to manufacturer.
New Hampshire	Qualification: 3 unsuccessful repairs by same dealer or 30 business days out of service within warranty. Notice/Trigger: Report to manufacturer, distributor, agent, or dealer (on forms provided by manufacturer) + final opportunity to repair before arbitration. S-R
New Jersey ☑ BEST	Qualification: 3 Unsuccessful repairs or 20 calendar days out of service within shorter of 2 years or 24,000 miles; or 1 unsuccessful repair of a serious safety defect likely to cause death or serious bodily injury. Notice/Trigger: Certified mail notice, return receipt requested to manufacturer who has 10 days to repair. Consumer may notify manufacturer at any time after the second repair attempt, or after the first repair attempt in the case of a serious safety defect.
New Mexico ☒ WORST	Qualification: 4 unsuccessful repairs or 30 business days out of service within shorter of 1 year or warranty. Notice/Trigger: Written notice + opportunity to repair to manufacturer, agent, or dealer.
New York	Qualification: 4 unsuccessful repairs or 30 calendar days out of service within shorter of 2 years or 18,000 miles. Notice/Trigger: Notice to manufacturer, agent, or dealer.
North Carolina	Qualification: 4 unsuccessful repairs within shorter of 24 months, 24,000 miles or warranty or 20 business days out of service during any 12 month period of warranty. Notice/Trigger: Written notice to manufacturer + opportunity to repair within 15 calendar days of receipt only if required in warranty or owner's manual.
North Dakota ☒ WORST	Qualification: 3 unsuccessful repairs or 30 business days out of service within shorter of 1 year or warranty. Notice/Trigger: Direct written notice + opportunity to repair to manufacturer. (Manufacturer's informal arbitration process serves as prerequisite to consumer refund or replacement.)
Ohio ☑ BEST	Qualification: 3 unsuccessful repairs of same nonconformity, 30 calendar days out of service, 8 total repairs of any nonconformity, or 1 unsuccessful repair of problem likely to cause death or serious bodily injury within shorter of 1 year or 18,000 miles. Notice/Trigger: Report to manufacturer, its agent, or dealer.
Oklahoma	Qualification: 4 unsuccessful repairs or 30 calendar days out of service within shorter of 1 year or warranty. Notice/Trigger: Written notice + opportunity to repair to manufacturer.
Oregon	Qualification: 4 unsuccessful repairs or 30 business days within shorter of 1 year or 12,000 miles. Notice/Trigger: Direct written notice + opportunity to repair to manufacturer.
Pennsylvania	Qualification: 3 unsuccessful repairs or 30 calendar days within shorter of 1 year, 12,000 miles, or warranty. Notice/Trigger: Delivery to authorized service + repair facility. If delivery impossible, written notice to manufacturer or its repair facility obligates them to pay for delivery.
Rhode Island	Qualification: 4 unsuccessful repairs or 30 calendar days out of service within shorter of 1 year or 15,000 miles. Notice/Trigger: Report to dealer or manufacturer who has 7 days for final repair opportunity.

L—Law specifically applies to leased vehicles; S-C—State has certified guidelines for arbitration; S-R—State-run arbitration mechanism available

South Carolina	Qualification: 3 unsuccessful repairs or 30 calendar days out of service within shorter of 1 year or 12,000 miles. Notice/Trigger: Certified mail + opportunity to repair (not more than 10 business days) to manufacturer only if manufacturer informed consumer of such at time of sale.
South Dakota	Qualification: 4 unsuccessful repairs, 1 of which occurred during shorter of 1 year or 12,000 miles, or 30 calendar days out of service during shorter of 24 months or 24,000 miles. Notice/Trigger: Certified mail to manufacturer + final opportunity to repair + 7 calendar days to notify consumer of repair facility.
Tennessee	Qualification: 4 unsuccessful repairs or 30 calendar days out of service within shorter of 1 year or warranty. Notice/Trigger: Certified mail notice to manufacturer + final opportunity to repair within 10 calendar days.
Texas	Qualification: 4 unsuccessful repairs when 2 occurred within shorter of 1 year or 12,000 miles, + other 2 occur within shorter of 1 year or 12,000 miles immediately following second repair attempt; or 2 unsuccessful repairs of serious safety defect when 1 occurred within shorter of 1 year or 12,000 miles + other occurred within shorter of 1 year or 12,000 miles immediately following first repair; or 30 calendar days out of service within shorter of 2 years or 24,000 miles + at least 2 attempts were made within shorter of 1 year or 12,000 miles. Notice/Trigger: Written notice to manufacturer. S-R
Utah	Qualification: 4 unsuccessful repairs or 30 business days out of service within shorter of 1 year or warranty. Notice/Trigger: Report to manufacturer, agent, or dealer.
Vermont	Qualification: 3 unsuccessful repairs when at least first repair was within warranty, or 30 calendar days out of service within warranty. Notice/Trigger: Written notice to manufacturer (on provided forms) after third repair attempt, or 30 days. Arbitration must be held within 45 days after notice, during which time manufacturer has 1 final repair. S-R Note: Repairs must been done by same authorized agent or dealer, unless consumer shows good cause for taking vehicle to different agent or dealer.
Virginia	Qualification: 3 unsuccessful repairs, or 1 repair attempt of serious safety defect, or 30 calendar days out of service within 18 months. Notice/Trigger: Written notice to manufacturer. If 3 unsuccessful repairs or 30 days already exhausted before notice, manufacturer has 1 more repair attempt not to exceed 15 days.
Washington	Qualification: 4 unsuccessful repairs, 30 calendar days out of service (15 during warranty period), or 2 repairs of serious safety defect, first reported within shorter of warranty or 24 months or 24,000 miles. One repair attempt + 15 of 30 days must fall within manufacturer's express warranty of at least 1 year of 12,000 miles. Notice/Trigger: Written notice to manufacturer. S-R Note: Consumer should receive replacement or refund within 40 calendar days of request.
West Virginia ☑ BEST	Qualification: 3 unsuccessful repairs or 30 calendar days out of service or 1 unsuccessful repair of problem likely to cause death or serious bodily injury within shorter of 1 year or warranty. Notice/Trigger: Written notice + opportunity to repair to manufacturer.
Wisconsin	Qualification: 4 unsuccessful repairs or 30 calendar days out of service within shorter of 1 year or warranty. Notice/Trigger: Report to manufacturer or dealer. Note: Consumer should receive replacement or refund within 30 calendar days after offer to return title.
Wyoming	Qualification: 3 unsuccessful repairs or 30 business days out of service within 1 year. Notice/Trigger: Direct written notice + opportunity to repair to manufacturer. S-R State-run arbitration mechanism available.

L—Law specifically applies to leased vehicles; S-C—State has certified guidelines for arbitration; S-R—State-run arbitration mechanism available

5 BASIC STEPS TO CAR BUYING

Buying a car means matching wits with a seasoned professional. But if you know what to expect, you'll have a much better chance of getting a really good deal!

There's no question that buying a car can be an intimidating experience. But it doesn't have to be. First of all, you have in your hands all of the information you need to make an informed choice. Secondly, if you approach the purchase logically, you'll always maintain control of the decision. Start with the following basic steps:

1 Narrow your choice down to a particular class of car—sports, station wagon, minivan, sedan, large luxury, or economy car. These are general classifications and some cars may fit into more than one category. In most cases, *The Car Book* presents the vehicles by size class.

2 Determine what features are really important to you. Most buyers consider safety on the top of their list, which is why the "Safety" chapter is right up front in *The Car Book*. Airbags, power options, ABS, and the number of passengers, as well as "hidden" elements such as maintenance and insurance costs, should be considered at this stage in your selection process.

3 Find three or four cars that meet the needs you outlined above and your pocketbook. It's important not to narrow your choice down to one car because then you lose all your bargaining power in the showroom. (Why? Because you might lose the psychological ability to walk away from a bad deal!) In fact, because cars today are more similar than dissimilar, it's not hard to keep three or four choices in mind. In the car rating pages in the back of the book, we suggest some competitive choices for your consideration. For example, if you are interested in the Honda Accord, you should also consider the Toyota Camry and Ford Fusion.

4 Make sure you take a good, long test drive. The biggest car buying mistake most of us make is to overlook those nagging problems that seem to surface only after we've brought the car home. Spend at least an hour driving the car without a salesperson preferably. If a dealership won't allow you to test-drive a car without a salesperson, go somewhere else. The test-drive should include time on the highway, parking, taking the car in and out of your driveway or garage, sitting in the back seat, and using the trunk or storage area.

TIP: Whatever you do, don't talk price until you're ready to buy!

5 This is the stage most of us dread—negotiating the price. While price negotiation is a car buying tradition, a few carmakers and dealers are trying to break tradition by offering so-called "no-haggle pricing." Since they're still in the minority and because it's very hard for an individual to establish true competition between dealers, we offer a great means to avoid negotiating altogether by using the non-profit CarBargains pricing service described on page 68.

THE 180-DEGREE TURN

TIP

When buying a car, remember that you have the most important weapon in the bargaining process: the 180-degree turn. Be prepared to walk away from a deal, even at the risk of losing the "very best deal" your salesperson has ever offered, and you will be in the best position to get a real "best deal." Remember: Dealerships need you, the buyer, to survive.

IN THE SHOWROOM

Being prepared is the best way to turn a potentially intimidating showroom experience into a profitable one. Here's some advice on handling what you'll find in the showroom.

Beware of silence. Silence is often used to intimidate, so be prepared for long periods of time when the salesperson is "talking with the manager." This tactic is designed to make you want to "just get the negotiation over with." Instead of becoming a victim, do something that indicates you are serious about looking elsewhere. Bring the classified section of the newspaper and begin circling other cars or review brochures from other manufacturers. By sending the message that you have other options, you increase your bargaining power and speed up the process.

Don't fall in love with a car. Never look too interested in any particular car. Advise family members who go with you against being too enthusiastic about any one car. Tip: Beat the dealers at their own game—bring along a friend who tells you that the price is "too much compared to the other deal."

Keep your wallet in your pocket. Don't leave a deposit, even if it's refundable. You'll feel pressure to rush your shopping, and you'll have to return and face the salesperson again before you are ready.

Shop at the end of the month. Salespeople anxious to meet sales goals are more willing to negotiate a lower price at this time.

Buy last year's model. The majority of new cars are the same as the previous year, with minor cosmetic changes. You can save considerably by buying in early fall when dealers are clearing space for "new" models. The important trade-off you make using this technique is that the carmaker may have added a new safety feature to an otherwise unchanged vehicle.

Buying from stock. You can often get a better deal on a car that the dealer has on the lot. However, these cars often have expensive options you may not want or need. Do not hesitate to ask the dealer to remove an option (and its accompanying charge) or sell you the car without charging for the option. The longer the car sits there, the more interest the dealer pays on the car, which increases the dealer's incentive to sell.

Ordering a car. Cars can be ordered from the manufacturer with exactly the options you want. Simply offering a fixed amount over invoice may be attractive because it's a sure sale and the dealership has not invested in the car. All the salesperson has to do is take your order.

If you do order a car, make sure when it arrives that it includes only the options you requested. Don't fall for the trick where the dealer offers you unordered options at a "special price," because it was their mistake. If you didn't order an option, don't pay for it.

! BEWARE OF MANDATORY ARBITRATION AGREEMENTS

More and more dealers are adding mandatory binding arbitration agreements, which they often call "dispute resolution mechanisms," to your purchase contract. What this means is that you wave the right to sue or appeal any problem you have with the vehicle. Before you start negotiating the price, ask if the dealer requires Mandatory Binding Arbitration. If so, and they won't remove that requirement, you should buy elsewhere. Many dealers do not have this requirement.

GETTING THE BEST PRICE

One of the most difficult aspects of buying a new car is getting the best price. Most of us are at a disadvantage negotiating because we don't know how much the car actually cost the dealer. The difference between what the dealer paid and the sticker price represents the negotiable amount.

Beware, now that most savvy consumers know to check the so-called "dealer invoice," the industry has camouflaged this number. Special incentives, rebates, and kickbacks can account for $500 to $2,000 worth of extra profit to a dealer selling a car at "dealer invoice." The non-profit Center for the Study of Services recently discovered that in 37 percent of cases when dealers are forced to bid against each other for the sale, they offered the buyer a price below the "dealer invoice"—an unlikely event if the dealer was actually losing money. The bottom line is that "dealer invoice" doesn't really mean dealer cost.

You can't really negotiate with only one dealer, you need to get two or three bidding against each other. Introducing competition is the best way to get the lowest price on a new car. To do this you have to convince two or three dealers that you are, in fact, prepared to buy a car; that you have decided on the make, model, and features; and that your decision now rests solely on which dealer will give you the best price. You can try to do this by phone, but often dealers will not give you the best price, or will quote you a price over the phone that they will not honor

later. Instead, you should try to do this in person. As anyone knows who has ventured into an auto showroom simply to get the best price, the process can be lengthy as well as terribly arduous. Nevertheless, if you can convince the dealer that you are serious and are willing to take the time to go to a number of dealers, it will pay off. Otherwise, we suggest you use the CarBargains service described on page 68.

Here are some other showroom strategies:

Shop away from home. If you find a big savings at a dealership far from your home or on the Internet, call a local dealer with the price. They may very well match it. If not, pick up the car from the distant dealer, knowing your trip has saved you hundreds of dollars. You can still bring it to your local dealer for warranty work and repairs.

Beware of misleading advertising. New car ads are meant to get you into the showroom. They usually promise low prices, big rebates, high trade-in, and spotless integrity—don't be deceived. Advertised prices are rarely the true selling price. They usually exclude transportation charges, service fees, or document fees. And always look out for the asterisk, both in advertisements and on invoices. It can be a signal that the advertiser has something to hide.

Don't talk price until you're ready to buy. On your

first few trips to the showroom, simply look over the cars, decide what options you want, and do your test-driving.

Shop the corporate twins. Page 75 contains a list of corporate twins—nearly identical cars that carry different name plates. Check the price and options of the twins of the car you like. A higher-priced twin may have more options, so it may be a better deal than the lower-priced car without the options you want.

Watch out for dealer preparation overcharges. Before paying the dealer to clean your car, make sure that preparation is not included in the basic price. The price sticker will state: "Manufacturer's suggested retail price of this model includes dealer preparation."

If you must negotiate . . . negotiate up from the "invoice" price rather than down from the sticker price. Simply make an offer close to or at the "invoice" price. If the salesperson says that your offer is too low to make a profit, ask to see the factory invoice.

Don't trade in. Although it is more work, you can usually do better by selling your old car yourself than by trading it in. To determine what you'll gain by selling the car yourself, check the NADA Official Used Car Guide at your credit union or library. On the web, the Kelly Blue Book website at kbb.com is a good source for invoice pricing. The difference between the trade-in price (what the dealer will give you) and the retail price (what you typically can sell it for) is your extra payment for selling the car yourself.

If you do decide to trade your car in at the dealership, keep the buying and selling separate. First, negotiate the best price for your new car, then find out how much the dealer will give you for your old car. Keeping the two deals separate ensures that you know what you're paying for your new car and simplifies the entire transaction.

Question everything the dealer writes down. Nothing is etched in stone. Because things are written down, we tend not to question them. This is wrong—always assume that anything written down is negotiable.

BUYING FOR SAFETY

So how do you buy for safety? Many consumers mistakenly believe that handling and performance are the key elements in the safety of a car. While an extremely unresponsive car could cause an accident, most new cars meet basic handling requirements. In fact, many people actually feel uncomfortable driving high performance cars because the highly responsive steering, acceleration, and suspension systems can be difficult to get used to. But the main reason handling is overrated as a safety measure is that automobile collisions are, by nature, accidents. Once they've begun, they are beyond human capacity to prevent, no matter how well your car handles. So the key to protecting yourself is to purchase a car that offers a high degree of crash protection.

AVOIDING LEMONS

One way to avoid the sour taste of a lemon after you've bought your car is to protect yourself before you sign on the dotted line. These tips will help you avoid problems down the road.

1 **Avoid new models.** Any new car in its very first year of production often turns out to have a lot of defects. Sometimes the manufacturer isn't able to remedy the defects until the second, third, or even fourth year of production. If the manufacturer has not worked out problems by the third model year, the car will likely be a lemon forever.

2 **Avoid the first cars off the line.** Most companies close down their assembly lines every year to make annual changes. In addition to adding hundreds of dollars to the price of a new car, these changes can introduce new defects. It can take a few months to iron out these bugs. Ask the dealer when the vehicle you are interested in was manufactured, or look on the metal tag found on the inside of the driver-side door frame to find the date of manufacture.

3 **Avoid delicate options.** Delicate options have the highest frequency-of-repair records. Power seats, power windows, power antennas, and special roofs are nice conveniences—until they break down. Of all the items on the vehicles, they tend to be the most expensive to repair.

4 **Inspect the dealer's checklist.** Request a copy of the dealer's pre-delivery service and adjustment checklist (also called a "make-ready list") at the time your new vehicle is delivered. Write the request directly on the new vehicle order. This request informs the dealer that you are aware of the dealer's responsibility to check your new car for defects.

5 **Examine the car on delivery.** Most of us are very excited to take the vehicle home. A few minutes of careful inspection can save hours of misery later. Look over the body for any damage; check for the spare tire and jack equipment; make sure all electrical items work, and all the hubcaps and body molding are on. You may want to take a short test-drive. Finally, make sure you have the owner's manual, warranty forms, and all the legal documents.

CarBargains' Best Price Service

Even with the information that we provide you in this chapter of *The Car Book*, many of us still will not be comfortable negotiating for a fair price. In fact, as we indicated on the previous page, we believe it's really very difficult to negotiate the best price with a single dealer. The key to getting the best price is to get dealers to compete with each other.

CarBargains is a service of the non-profit Consumers' CHECKBOOK, a consumer group that provides comparative price and quality information for many products and services.

CarBargains will "shop" the dealerships in your area and obtain at least five price quotes for the make and model of the car that you want to buy. The dealers who submit quotes know that they are competing with other area dealerships and have agreed to honor the prices that they submit. It is important to note that CarBargains is not an auto broker or "car buying" service; they have no affiliation with dealers.

Here's how the service works:

1. You provide CarBargains with the make, model, and style of car you wish to buy (Toyota Camry XLE, for example) by phone or mail.

2. Within two weeks, CarBargains will send you dealer quote sheets from at least five local dealers who have bid against one another to sell you that car. Each dealer's offer is actually a commitment to a dollar amount above (or below) "factory invoice cost" for that model. You get the name and phone number of the manager responsible for handling the quote.

You will also receive a print-out that enables you to figure the exact cost for each available option you might want on the vehicle.

3. Determine which dealer offers the best price using the dealer quote sheets. Add up the cost including the specific options you want. Contact the sales manager of that dealership and arrange to purchase the car.

If a car with the options you want is not available on the dealer's lot, you can, in many cases, have the dealer order the car from the factory or from another dealer at the agreed price.

When you receive your quotes, you will also get some suggestions on low-cost sources of financing and a valuation of your used car (trade-in).

The price for this service ($200) may seem expensive, but when you consider the savings that will result by having dealers bid against each other, as well as the time and effort of trying to get these bids yourself, we believe it's a great value. The dealers know they have a bona fide buyer (you've paid for the service); they know they are bidding against five to seven of their competitors; and, you have Car-Bargains' experts on your side.

To obtain CarBargains' competitive price quotes, call them at 800-475-7283 or visit their website at www.carbargains.org. Or, you can send a check for $200 to CarBargains, 1625 K St., NW, 8th Floor, Washington, DC 20006. Be sure to include your complete mailing address, phone number, and e-mail address (in case of questions), and the exact make, model, style, and year of the car you want to buy. You should receive your report within two weeks.

! AUTO BROKERS !

While CarBargains is a non-profit organization created to help you find the best price for the car you want to purchase, auto brokers are typically in the business to make money. As such, whatever price you end up paying for the car will include additional profit for the broker. There have been cases where the auto broker makes certain promises, takes your money, and you never hear from him or her again. While many brokers are legitimately trying to get their customers the best price, others have developed special relationships with certain dealers and may not do much shopping for you. As a consumer, it is difficult to tell which are which. This is why we recommend CarBargains. If CarBargains is not for you, then we suggest you consider using a buying service associated with your credit union or auto club, which can arrange for the purchase of a car at some fixed price over "dealer invoice."

FINANCING

You've done your test-drive, researched prices, studied crash tests, determined the options you want, and haggled to get the best price. Now you have to decide how to pay for the car.

If you have the cash, pay for the car right away. You avoid finance charges, you won't have a large debt haunting you, and the full value of the car is yours. You can then make the monthly payments to yourself to save up for your next car.

However, most of us cannot afford to pay cash for a car, which leaves two options: financing or leasing. While leasing may seem more affordable, financing will actually cost you less. When you finance a car, you own it after you finish your payments. At the end of a lease, you have nothing. We don't recommend leasing, but if you want more information, see page 71.

Here are some tips when financing your car:

Shop around for interest rates. Most banks and credit unions will knock off at least a quarter of a percent for their customers. Have these quotes handy when you talk financing with the dealer.

The higher your down payment, the less you'll have to finance. This will not only reduce your overall interest charges, but often qualifies you for a lower interest rate. Down payments are typically 10–20 percent of the final price.

Avoid long car loans. The monthly payments are lower, but you'll pay far more in overall interest charges. For example, a two-year, $20,000 loan at 7 percent will cost you $1,491 in interest; the same amount at five years will cost you $3,761—over twice as much!

Check out manufacturer promotional rates—the 0.9–2.9 percent rates you see advertised. These low rates are usually only valid on two- to three-year loans.

Read everything you are asked to sign and ask questions about anything you don't fully understand.

Make sure that an extended warranty has not been added to the purchase price. Dealers will sometimes add this cost without informing the consumer. Extended warranties are generally a bad value. See the "Warranties" chapter for more information.

Credit Unions vs. Banks: Credit unions generally charge fewer and lower fees and offer better rates than banks. In addition, credit unions offer counseling services where consumers can find pricing information on

DON'T BE TONGUE-TIED

Beware of high-pressure phrases like "I've talked to the manager and this is really the best we can do. As it is, we're losing money on this deal." Rarely is this true. Dealers are in the business to make money and most do very well. Don't tolerate a take-it-or-leave-it attitude. Simply repeat that you will only buy when you see the deal you want and that you don't appreciate the dealer pressuring you. Threaten to leave if the dealer continues to pressure you to buy today.

Don't let the dealer answer your questions with a question. If you ask, "Can I get air conditioning with this car?" and the salesperson answers, "If I get you air conditioning in this car, will you buy today?" this response tries to force you to decide to buy before you are ready. Ask the dealer to just answer your question and say that you'll buy when you're ready. It's the dealer's job to answer questions, not yours.

If you are having a difficult time getting what you want, ask the dealer: "Why won't you let me buy a car today?" Most salespeople will be thrown off by this phrase as they are often too busy trying to use it on you. If they respond in frustration, "OK, what do you want?" then you can make straightforward answers to simple questions.

Get a price; don't settle for: "If you're shopping price, go to the other dealers first and then come back." This technique ensures that they don't have to truly negotiate. Your best response is: "I only plan to come back if your price is the lowest, so that's what I need today, your lowest price."

cars or compare monthly payments for financing. You can join a credit union either through your employer, an organization or club, or if you have a relative who is part of a credit union.

Low Rate or Cash Back? Sometimes auto manufacturers offer a choice of below market financing or cash back. The table below will tell you if it is better to take the lower rate or the cash back rebate. For example, say you want to finance $18,000. Your credit union or bank offers you 6.5 percent for an auto loan and the dealer offers either a 4 percent loan or a $1,500 rebate. Which is better? Find your bank or credit union's rate (6.5 percent in the square) on the left and the dealer's low rate (4 percent in the square) on the top of the table. Find where the two intersect on the table and you will find the difference per thousand dollars between the two interest rates (48 in the square). When you multiply this number (48) by the number of thousands you're financing (18 for $18,000), you get $864. Since the dealer's $1,500 rebate is more than the $864 savings if you went with the 4% rate over the 6.5%. So taking your bank's rate (6.5 percent) and the rebate is a better deal than taking the dealer's low rate (4 percent). If the answer had been more than $1,500, then the dealer's rate would have been the better deal. An asterisk (*) in the table means that the bank or credit union's rate is the better deal regardless of dealer discount.

TYPICAL OPERATING COSTS

The table below shows the annual operating costs for some popular vehicles. Costs include operating expenses (fuel, oil, maintenance, and tires) and ownership expenses (insurance, depreciation, financing, taxes, and licensing) and are based on keeping the vehicle for 3 years and driving 20,000 miles per year. This information is from Runzheimer International. Runzheimer evaluated thirty 2012 model cars, vans, SUVs, and light trucks and determined the most and least expensive to operate among those vehicles. (Source: Runzheimer International, www.runzheimer.com)

Projected Ownership and Operating Costs for Selected 2012 Cars

Most Expensive

BMW 550I 8-cyl. 4.4L	$22,403
Mercedes-Benz E350 6-cyl. 3.5L	$20,773
Cadillac CTS Premium 6-cyl. 3.6L	$19,889

Least Expensive

Ford Focus SE 4-cyl. 2L	$10,088
Honda Civic LX 4-cyl. 1.8L	$9,402
Chevrolet Sonic 2LT 4-cyl. 1.8L	$9,150

Projected Ownership and Operating Costs for Selected 2012 Light Trucks, Vans, and SUVs

Most Expensive

Ford E350 SD XL Passenger Van 8-cyl. 5.4L	$17,956
Chevrolet Tahoe LS 4x4 8-cyl. 5.3L	$17,080
Chevrolet Silverado 1500 LT 4x2 8ft 8-cyl. 4.8L	$14,792

Least Expensive

Toyota Sienna Passenger Van 6-cyl. 3.5L	$12,672
Ford Escape XLS 4x4 4-cyl. 2.5L	$11,666
Chevrolet Colorado LT 4x2 6ft 4-cyl. 2.9L	$10,847

Runzheimer International is a global leader in workforce mobility programs including business vehicle, logistics, business travel, corporate aircraft, employee relocation and compensation, and virtual office.

REBATE VS. LOW RATES (FOUR YEAR LOAN)

Credit Union or Bank Rate	Dealer Rate						
	1%	**2%**	**3%**	**4%**	**5%**	**6%**	**7%**
6%	95	76	58	39	19	*	*
6.5%	103	85	67	48	29	10	*
7%	112	94	76	57	38	19	*
7.5%	121	103	85	66	48	29	10

Based on data from *Home and Family Finances*, a publication of the Credit Union National Association.

LEASING VS. BUYING

Because the unpredictibility of the value of a vehicle at the end of a lease, more and more companies are getting out of the leasing business. That's good news because, in general, leasing costs more than buying outright or financing. When you pay cash or finance a car, you own an asset; leasing leaves you with nothing except all the headaches and responsibilities of ownership with none of the benefits. When you lease you pay a monthly fee for a predetermined time in exchange for the use of a car. However, you also pay for maintenance, insurance, and repairs as if you owned the car. Finally, when it comes time to turn in the car, it has to be in top shape—otherwise, you'll have to pay for repairs or body work.

If you are considering a lease, here are some leasing terms you need to know and some tips to get you through the process:

Capitalized Cost is the price of the car on which the lease is based. Negotiate this as if you were buying the car. Capitalized Cost Reduction is your down payment.

Know the make and model of the vehicle you want. Tell the agent exactly how you want the car equipped. You don't have to pay for options you don't request. Decide in advance how long you will keep the car.

Find out the price of the options on which the lease is based. Typically, they will be full retail price. Their cost can be negotiated (albeit with some difficulty) before you settle on the monthly payment.

Make sure options like a sunroof or stereo are added to the Capitalized Cost. When you purchase dealer-added options, be sure they add the full cost of the option to the Capitalized Cost so that you only pay for the depreciated value of the option, not the full cost.

Find out how much you are required to pay at delivery. Most leases require at least the first month's payment. Others have a security deposit, registration fees, or other "hidden costs." When shopping around, make sure price quotes include security deposit and taxes—sales tax, monthly use tax, or gross receipt tax. Ask how the length of the lease affects your monthly cost.

Find out how the lease price was determined. Lease prices are generally based on the manufacturer's suggested retail price, less the predetermined residual value. The best values are cars with a high expected residual value. To protect themselves, leasers tend to underestimate residual value, but you can do little about this estimate.

Find out the annual mileage limit. Don't accept a contract with a lower limit than you need. Most standard contracts allow 15,000 to 18,000 miles per year. If you go under the allowance one year, you can go over it the next. Watch out for Excess Mileage fees. If you go over, you'll get charged per mile.

Avoid "capitalized cost reduction" or "equity leases." Here the leaser offers to lower the monthly payment by asking you for more money up front—in other words, a down payment.

Ask about early termination. Between 30 and 40 percent of two-year leases are terminated early and 40–60 percent of four-year leases terminate early—this means expensive early termination fees. If you terminate the lease before it is up, what are the financial penalties? Typically, they are very high so watch out. Ask the dealer exactly what you would owe at the end of each year if you wanted out of the lease. Remember, if your car is stolen, the lease will typically be terminated. While your

---

LEASEWISE

TIP

If you must lease, why haggle when you can let someone else do it for you? LeaseWise, a service from the non-profit Center for the Study of Services, makes dealers bid for your lease. First, they get leasing bids from dealers on the vehicles you're interested in. Next, you'll receive a detailed report with all the bids, the dealer and invoice cost of the vehicle, and a complete explanation of the various bids. Then, you can lease from the lowest bidder or use the report as leverage with another dealer. The service costs $335. For more information, call 800-475-7283, or visit www.check-book.org.

insurance should cover the value of the car, you still may owe additional amounts per your lease contract.

Avoid maintenance contracts. Getting work done privately is cheaper in the long run. And don't forget, this is a new car with a standard warranty.

Arrange for your own insurance. By shopping around, you can generally find less expensive insurance than what's offered by the leaser.

Ask how quickly you can expect delivery. If your agent can't deliver in a reasonable time, maybe he or she can't meet the price quoted.

Retain your option to buy the car at the end of the lease at a predetermined price. The price should equal the residual value; if it is more then the leaser is trying to make an additional profit. Regardless of how the end-of-lease value is determined, if you want the car, make an offer based on the current "Blue Book" value of the car at the end of the lease.

Residual Value is the value of your car at the end of the lease.

Here's what Automotive Lease Guide estimates the residual value after five years will be for a few 2011 vehicles:

Hyundai Elantra	44%
Toyota Prius	40%
Acura MDX	38%
Jeep Liberty	23%
Nissan Titan	19%

LEASING VS. BUYING

The following table compares the costs of leasing vs. buying the same car over three and six years. Your actual costs may vary, but you can use this format to compare the cars you are considering. Our example assumes the residual value to be 68 percent after three years and 43 percent after six years.

3 Years

	Lease	Finance
MSRP	$29,000.00	$29,000.00
Purchase Cost of Car	$26,100.00	$26,100.00
Down Payment	$2,436.00[5]	$2,900.00
Monthly Payment	$273.00[5]	$432.00
Total Payments	$9,828.00	$15,552.00[1]
Amount left on loan		$9,909.00
Value of vehicle at 3 yrs.		$19,720.00
Excess miles & disposition[7]	$825.00	
Overall Cost, first 3 yrs.	$13,089.00	$8,641.00
Savings over Leasing		**$4,448.00**

If you choose to keep the car you financed for six years, the savings over leasing becomes huge!

6 Years

	Lease[2]	Finance[3]
MSRP	$30,450.00	$29,000.00
Cost of Car	$27,405.00	$26,100.00
Down Payment	$2,740.50[5]	$2,900.00
Monthly Payment	$273.00[5]	$432.00
Total Payments	$9,828.00	$25,920.00
Amount Left on Loan		–
Value of vehicle at 6 yrs.[8]		$12,470.00
Excess miles & disposition[7]	$825.00	
Overall Cost, 6 yrs.	$23,742.00[4]	$16,350.00
Savings over Leasing		**$7,392.00**

[1] First 3 years of 5-year loan with 4.5 percent annual percentage rate.
[2] These are the second 3 year lease costs which assume a 5% increase for a similar vehicle.
[3] Five year loan with 4.5 percent annual percentage rate, no monthly payments in sixth year.
[4] Two 3-year leases.
[5] Initial lease and monthly payments based on lease deals for January 2012 offered by major manufacturers on US News and World Report.
[6] 68% based on average actual 36-month residual value for the top 100 selling vehicles for model year 2006, 07 and 08.
[7] Total average excess miles fee of $475 based on 12000 miles limit and 25% of consumers driving over the mile limit unexpectedly for 1500 miles with charges of $0.17/mile, 50% pre-paying for expected mile overages of 1500 miles at $0.12/mile, and 25% not exceeding the mileage limit. Disposition fee based on average of $350.
[8] 43% based on average actual 36-month residual value for the top 100 selling vehicles for model year 2003, 04 and 05.

USING THE INTERNET

The Internet is changing the way car buyers research and shop for cars. But the Internet should be used with caution. Remember that anyone—and we mean *anyone*—can publish a website with no guarantee concerning the accuracy of the information on it. We advise that you only visit websites that have a familiar non-web counterpart. A good example is the Center for Auto Safety's website at www.autosafety.org where you'll find information on auto safety, including publications and newsletters which are typically mailed out to subscribers.

Use the Internet as an information resource. Unfortunately, most automaker websites are nothing more than sophisticated ads with little comparative information.

Good information, like pricing and features, *can* be found online. We've listed some useful websites on this page.

There are also several online car shopping services that have launched. We view most of them with skepticism. Many online car shopping services are tied to a limited, often non-competitive, group of dealers. They may claim the lowest price, but you'll most likely have a dealer calling you with a price that is not much better than what you'd get if you went into a dealership to haggle.

Auto insurance and financing sites are sometimes no better. Don't rely solely on these online services; getting quotes from other sources is the only way to make sure you truly have the best deal.

Finally, clicking a mouse is no substitute for going out and test-driving a car. If you are shopping for a used car, you must check out the actual car before signing on the dotted line. Do not rely on online photos. In fact, online classifieds for cars are no more reliable than looking in a newspaper.

If you do use an online car shopping service, be sure to shop around on your own. Visit dealerships, get quotes from several car shopping services, and research the value of your used car (see www.nadaguides.com). Beware that if you give anyone online your phone number, or email address, you are opening yourself up to unwanted email, junk mail, and even sales calls.

ON THE WEB

autosafety.org
The Center for Auto Safety (CAS) provides consumers with a voice for auto safety and quality in Washington and to help lemon owners fight back across the country.

carfax.com
Used car buyers will want to visit Carfax. Carfax collects information from numerous sources to provide a vehicle history on a specific vehicle, based on the Vehicle Identification Number (VIN). Carfax can help uncover costly and potentially dangerous hidden problems or confirm the clean history of a vehicle.

checkbook.org
The Center for the Study of Services (CSS) is an independent, nonprofit consumer organization and the creator of Consumers' CHECKBOOK. One of the few car buying services worth using, CHECKBOOK's CarBargains service pits dealers against each other, keeping you from haggling, and using the power of competitive bidding to get you a great price.

nhtsa.gov
The National Highway Traffic Safety Administration (NHTSA) website contains useful information on safety standards, crash tests, recalls, technical service bulletins, child seats, and safety advisories.

fueleconomy.gov
This joint effort by the Department of Energy and the Environmental Protection Agency contains EPA fuel economy ratings for passenger cars and trucks from 1985 to the present, gas saving tips, greenhouse gas and air pollution ratings, energy impact scores, a downloadable Fuel Economy Guide, and a variety of other useful information in a very user-friendly format.

DEPRECIATION

Over the past 20 years, new vehicle depreciation costs have steadily increased. A study conducted by Runzheimer International shows that depreciation and interest now account for just over 50 percent of the costs of owning and operating a vehicle. Recently, however, the increasing cost of depreciation has slowed down. This is due to the relatively stable prices of new vehicles and to the slow increase in finance rates. The higher cost of gasoline consumes a larger percentage of the automotive dollar than ever before. Other costs, including insurance, maintenance, and tires, have remained at relatively steady shares of the automotive dollar.

While there is no foolproof method for predicting retained vehicle value, your best bet is to purchase a popular vehicle model. Chances are it will also be a popular used vehicle model, meaning that the retained value may be higher when you go to sell it.

Most new cars are traded in within four years and are then available on the used car market. The priciest used cars may not be the highest quality. Supply and demand, as well as appearance, are important factors in determining used car prices.

The following table indicates which of the top-selling 2008 cars held their value the best and which did not.

2008 VEHICLES WITH THE BEST AND WORST RESALE VALUE

THE BEST				THE WORST			
Model	2008 Price	2011 Price	Retain. Value	Model	2008 Price	2011 Price	Retain. Value
Jeep Wrangler	$18,660	$19,250	103.2%	Chevrolet Uplander	$22,620	$10,500	46.4%
Toyota Tacoma	$14,280	$14,375	100.7%	Ford Crown Victoria	$25,570	$13,075	51.1%
Toyota Yaris	$11,300	$11,250	99.6%	Dodge Grand Caravan	$21,100	$11,375	53.9%
Mazda 3	$13,895	$13,800	99.3%	Dodge Charger	$27,765	$16,075	57.9%
Mini Cooper	$18,050	$17,650	97.8%	Buick Lucerne	$26,245	$15,550	59.2%
Scion tC	$15,300	$14,225	93.0%	Ford Taurus	$23,245	$13,950	60.0%
Honda Fit	$13,950	$12,900	92.5%	Buick LaCrosse	$23,310	$14,150	60.7%
Scion xB	$15,650	$14,450	92.3%	Jeep Grand Cherokee	$28,520	$17,500	61.4%
Nissan Frontier	$16,150	$14,875	92.1%	Dodge Ram Pickup	$21,155	$13,200	62.4%
Nissan Versa	$12,650	$11,500	90.9%	GMC Sierra	$24,570	$15,475	63.0%
Jeep Patriot	$15,475	$13,925	90.0%	Chevrolet Impala	$21,225	$13,400	63.1%
Subaru Impreza	$16,995	$14,875	87.5%	Chrysler 300	$24,595	$15,550	63.2%
Ford Ranger	$13,995	$12,225	87.4%	Chrysler Sebring	$18,690	$11,875	63.5%
Toyota 4Runner	$28,015	$24,425	87.2%	Acura TL	$33,725	$21,700	64.3%
Nissan Rogue	$19,250	$16,625	86.4%	Chevrolet Silverado	$24,030	$15,475	64.4%
Hyundai Elantra	$13,525	$11,625	86.0%	Chrys. Town & Country	$22,460	$14,500	64.6%
Chevrolet Colorado	$14,785	$12,650	85.6%	Chevrolet Trail Blazer	$25,480	$16,450	64.6%
Lexus IS	$30,455	$25,950	85.2%	Dodge Avenger	$18,220	$11,775	64.6%
Toyota Corolla	$14,405	$12,100	84.0%	Pontiac G6	$22,345	$14,475	64.8%
Toyota RAV4	$21,100	$17,550	83.2%	BMW 5 Series	$44,300	$29,200	65.9%
Toyota Prius	$20,950	$17,350	82.8%	Merc.-Benz E-Class	$51,900	$34,325	66.1%
Honda CR-V	$20,700	$17,050	82.4%	Honda Odyssey	$25,860	$17,125	66.2%
Ford Mustang	$19,250	$15,725	81.7%	Chrysler PT Cruiser	$15,015	$10,150	67.6%
Hyundai Accent	$10,775	$8,800	81.7%	Honda Pilot	$27,595	$18,725	67.9%
Volkswagen Jetta	$16,690	$13,550	81.2%	Saturn Aura	$19,745	$13,400	67.9%

CORPORATE TWINS

"Corporate twins" refers to vehicles that have different names but share the same mechanics, drivetrain, and chassis. In most cases the vehicles are identical. Sometimes the difference is in body style, price, or options as with the Chevrolet Tahoe and the Cadillac Escalade. Traditionally, corporate twins have been limited mainly to domestic car companies. Today, due to the many car company mergers, corporate twins include cars that were once considered European or Asian coupled with a domestic model name.

CORPORATE TWINS

Chrysler Corp.
Chrysler 300
Dodge Charger

Chrysler 200
Dodge Avenger

Chrysler Town & Country
Dodge Grand Caravan

Ford Motor Co.
Ford Edge
Lincoln MKX

Ford Expedition
Lincoln Navigator

Ford Fusion
Lincoln MKZ

General Motors
Buick Regal
Chevrolet Malibu

General Motors (cont.)
Buick Verano
Chevrolet Cruze

Cadillac Escalade
Chevrolet Tahoe
GMC Yukon

Cadillac Escalade ESV
Chevrolet Suburban
GMC Yukon XL

Cadillac Escalade EXT
Chevrolet Avalanche

Chevrolet Colorado
GMC Canyon

Chevrolet Equinox
GMC Terrain

Chevrolet Silverado
GMC Sierra

General Motors (cont.)
Chevrolet Traverse
GMC Acadia

Hyundai-Kia
Hyundai Accent
Kia Rio

Hyundai Santa Fe
Kia Sorento

Toyota
Lexus ES
Toyota Camry

Lexus GX
Toyota 4Runner

Lexus LX
Toyota Land Cruiser

Volkswagen
Porsche Cayenne
Volkswagen Touareg

Cadillac Escalade

Chevrolet Tahoe

GMC Yukon

T his section provides an overview of the most important features of this year's new models. Nearly all the information you'll need to make a smart choice is concisely presented on one page. (The data are collected for the model expected to be the most popular.) Here's what you'll find and how to interpret the data we've provided:

The Ratings

These are the ratings in nine important categories, as well as an overall comparative rating. We have adopted the Olympic rating system with "10" being the best.

Overall Rating: This is the "bottom line." Using a combination of all of the key ratings, this tells how this vehicle stacks up against the others on a scale of 1 to 10. Due to the importance of safety, the combined crash test rating is 20 percent of the overall rating while the other eight ratings are 10 percent each. Vehicles with no front or side crash test results, as of our publication date, cannot be given an overall rating. In other categories, if information is unavailable, an "average" is included in order to develop an overall rating.

Overall Crash Test: This rating represents a combination of the front and side crash test ratings and provides a relative comparison of how this year's models did against each other. We give the best performers a 10 and the worst a 1. Remember to compare crash test results relative to other cars in the same size class. For details, see page 18.

Safety Features: This is an evaluation of how much extra safety is built into the car. We give credit for head, torso and pelvis side airbags, roll-sensing side airbags, knee bolster bag, crash imminent braking, daytime running lamps, adjustable upper seat belt anchorages, and frontal collision warning. We also include dynamic head restraint and blind spot detection among other important safety features. See the "Safety Checklist" box on each page for more details.

Rollover: Many consumers are aware that vehicles with higher centers of gravity could be more likely to roll over. Comparing the tendency of a vehicle to roll over is very difficult, as there is no agreed upon comparative rating system. The U.S. government adopted the rating system that we have been using called the static stability formula (SSF). The government provides the SSF rating for some vehicles. For those vehicles not on the government list, we use the SSF formula to provide a rating. The details behind the SSF appear on page 30.

Preventive Maintenance: Each manufacturer suggests a preventive maintenance schedule designed to keep the car in good shape and to protect your rights under the warranty. Those with the lowest estimated PM costs get a 10 and the highest a 1. See pages 39-43 for the estimated costs and more information.

Repair Costs: It is virtually impossible to predict exactly what any new car will cost you in repairs. As such, we take nine typical repairs that you are likely to experience after your warranty expires and compare those costs among this year's models. Those with the lowest cost get a 10 and the highest a 1. See pages 39-43 for specific part repair cost and more information.

Warranty: This is an overall assessment of the manufacturer's basic, powertrain, corrosion, and roadside assistance warranties when compared to all other manufacturer warranties. We give the highest-rated warranties a 10 and the lowest a 1. For details, see the Warranty section.

Fuel Economy: Here we compare the EPA mileage ratings of each car. The misers get a 10 and the guzzlers get a 1. For the purposes of the overall rating we pick the fuel economy rating of what is expected to be the most popular engine and drive train configuration. See page 33 for more information.

Complaints: This is where you'll find how each vehicle stacks up against hundreds of others on the road, based on the U.S. government complaint data for that vehicle. If the car has not been around long enough to have developed a complaint history, it is given a 5 (average). The least complained about cars get a 10 and the most problematic a 1. See the "Complaints Chapter" for details.

Insurance Costs: Insurance companies rate vehicles to determine how much they plan to charge for insurance. Here, you'll find whether you can expect to pay higher or lower insurance premium for what we expect to be the most popular model. We looked at data from the insurance rating program of the largest insurer in America. Vehicles with a low rating (1 or 3) are more expensive to insure, vehicles with a high rating (8 or 10) are less expensive to insure and those receiving a 5 are typical. This rating will give you a basic idea of the cost to insure the vehicle. Because insurance companies may rate vehicles differently, it's best to compare prices between companies.

At-a-Glance

Status: Here we tell you if a vehicle is all-new, unchanged, or has received appearance change. All-new vehicles (the minority) are brand new from the ground up. Unchanged vehicles are essentially the same, but could have some different color or feature options. Vehicles with an appearance change are those whose internal workings stayed essentially the same, but have updated body panels.

Year Series Started: We generally recommend against buying a car during its first model year of production. Each year the model is made, the production usually improves and as a result there are fewer defects. Therefore, the longer a car has been made, the less likely you are to be plagued with manufacturing and design defects. On the other hand, the newer a car is, the more likely it is to have the latest in features and safety.

Twins: These are cars with different make and model names but share the same mechanics, drive train, and chassis. In some cases the vehicles are identical, in other cases the body style, pricing or options are different.

Body Styles: This is a listing of the various body styles available such as coupe, sedan, wagon, etc. SUVs and minivans are only offered in one body style. Data on the page are for the first style listed.

Seating: This is the number of seating positions in the most popular model. When more than one number is listed (for example, 5/6) it means that different seat configurations are available.

Anti-theft Device: This lists the anti-theft devices standard for the vehicle. An immobilizer is an electronic device fitted to an automobile which prevents the engine from running unless the correct key (or other token) is present. This prevents the car from being "hot-wired" and driven away. A car alarm is an electronic device that emits high-volume sound and can sometimes flash the vehicles headlights in an attempt to discourage theft of the vehicle itself, its contents, or both. Passive devices automatically enter an armed state after the ignition is turned off and doors are closed. Active devices require the user to perform some action like pressing a button to arm and disarm the system.

Parking Index Rating: Using the car's length, wheelbase, and turning circle, we have calculated how easy it will be to maneuver this car in tight spots. This rating of "very easy" to "very hard" is an indicator of

how much difficulty you may have parking.

Where Made: Here we tell you where the car was assembled. You'll find that traditional domestic companies often build their vehicles in other countries. Also, many foreign companies build their cars in the U.S.

Fuel Factor

MPG Rating (city/hwy): This is the EPA-rated fuel economy for city and highway driving measured in miles per gallon. Most models have a variety of fuel economy ratings because of different engine and transmission options. We've selected the combination expected to be most popular.

Driving Range: Given the car's expected fuel economy and gas tank size, this value gives you an idea of the number of miles you can expect go on one tank of gas.

Fuel: The type of fuel specified by the manufacturer: regular, premium, E85.

Annual Fuel Cost: This is an estimate based on driving 15,000 miles per year at $3.23/gallon for regular and $3.50/gallon for premium. If the vehicle takes E85 (85% ethanol and 15% gasoline) or gasoline we calculated the annual cost using gasoline.

Gas Guzzler Tax: Auto companies are required to pay a gas guzzler tax on the sale of cars with exceptionally low fuel economy. This tax does not apply to light trucks.

Greenhouse Gas Emissions: This shows the amount (in tons) of greenhouse gases (carbon dioxide, nitrous oxide, and methane) that a vehicle emits per year along with the

CO_2 emitted in producing and distributing the fuel.

Barrels of Oil Used Per Year: This is the number of barrels of petroleum the vehicle will likely use each year. One barrel, once refined, makes about 19.5 gallons of gas.

Competition

Here we tell you how the car stacks up with some of its key competitors. Use this information to broaden your choice of new car possibilities. This list is only a guideline, not an all-inclusive list of every possible alternative.

Price Range

This box contains information on the MSRP. When available, we offer a variety of prices between the base and the most luxurious version of the car. The difference is often substantial. Usually the more expensive versions have fancy trim, larger engines, and lots of automatic equipment. The least expensive versions usually have manual transmissions and few extra features. In addition to the price range, we provide the estimated dealer markup. Be prepared for higher retail prices when you get to the showroom. Manufacturers like to load their cars with factory options, and dealers like to add their own items such as fabric protection and paint sealant. Remember, prices and dealer costs can change during the year. Use these figures for general reference and comparisons,

not as a precise indication of exactly how much the car you are interested in will cost. See page 68 for a buying service designed to ensure that you get the very best price.

Safety Checklist

Crash Tests

Frontal and Side Crash Test Ratings: : Here's where we tell you if the front or side crash test index was very good, good, average, poor or very poor when compared to 2012 cars tested to date. To provide this rating we use the crash test for the vehicles with the best available

safety equipment among the models when multiple models were tested. In 2011, the government developed a new crash test program. Because only about half the vehicles have been tested under the new program, many will not have a rating. For details about the crash test programs, see page 18.

Airbags

Head Side Airbag: This side airbag protects the head area from impacting the roof, door, and window and can offer extra rollover protection.

Torso Side Airbag: This type of side airbag protects the

TYPES OF AIRBAGS

Airbags were introduced over 30 years ago and have been so successful in saving lives that car makers now include a variety of types. Here's a rundown of the basic types of airbags available. Manufacturers have varying marketing names for these airbags.

Front: These deploy toward the front occupants and are now standard in all vehicles.

Side: These deploy from the side of the seat or door and protect both the front and rear passengers in a side impact. Bags mounted in seats offer protection in a wider range of seating positions.

Head: These deploy from above the doors and are often called curtain airbags. They can reduce head injuries, shield from spraying glass, and provide protection in rollovers.

Rollover Protection: These head curtain airbags remain inflated for five seconds to protect in a sustained rollover.

Knee Bolster: These fill space between the front occupant's knees and instrument panel protecting the knees and legs.

chest from serious injury in a side impact crash.

Pelvis Side Airbag: Provides extra protection around the pelvis and hip area, as this portion of the body is usually closest to the vehicles interior.

Rollover Sensing Airbags: Some companies offer a special side airbag system which keeps the side airbags inflated longer in the event of a rollover. This can reduce the likelihood of injury when a vehicle flips.

Knee Bolster Airbag: The airbag is inflated to fill space between the knees of the front occupant and the instrument panel.

Crash Avoidance

Frontal Collision Warning: This feature use radar or laser sensors to detect an imminent crash in front of the vehicle. Systems may warn the driver with a light and/or audible alert, retract the seat belts removing excess slack, and automatically apply partial or full braking to minimize the crash severity.

Blind Spot Detection: This is a blind spot monitor that uses radar or other technologies to detect objects in the driver's blind spot. When switching lanes a visible and/or audible alert warns if a vehicle has entered your blind spot.

Crash Imminent Braking (CIB): This technology is intended to mitigate crashes by automatically applying the vehicle's brakes just prior to impact.

Lane Departure Warning: This mechanism warns a driver when the vehicle begins to move out of its lane (unless a turn signal is on in that direction). The warning may be a light, audible chime, or a vibrating steering wheel.

General

Automatic Crash Notification: Using cellular technology and global positioning systems, some vehicles have the ability to send a call for help in the event of airbag deployment or accident. You'll have to pay extra for this feature.

Daytime Running Lights: Some cars offer daytime running lights that can reduce your chances of being in a crash by up to 40 percent by increasing the visibility of your vehicle. We indicate whether daytime running lights are standard, optional, or not available.

Safety Belts/Restraints

Dynamic Head Restraints: Many people position their seat and head restraint according to their own body and comfort requirements. This may not be the best position to protect you in a crash. These adjustors, sensing a crash, will automatically move the seat and headrest to the optimal position to help reduce injury during a rear-end crash.

Pretensioners: How snugly your seat belt fits is a critical factor in crash protection. Some manufacturers offer special devices that, sensing a potential crash, tighten up and/or lock the safety belt.

Adjustable Front Belts: Proper positioning of the safety belt across your chest is critical to obtaining the benefits of buckling up. Some systems allow you to adjust the height of the belt so it crosses your chest properly.

Specifications

Drive: This indicates the type of drive the manufacturer offers. This could be two wheel drive in the front (FWD) or rear (RWD) or all or four wheel drive (AWD/4WD).

Engine: This is the engine size (liters) and type that is expected to be the most popular. The engine types specify V6 or V8 for six or eight cylinders and I4 for four in-line.

Transmission: This is the type of transmission expected to be the most popular. Most drivers today prefer automatic transmissions. The number listed with the transmission (5-sp.) is the number of gears or speeds. Then we list whether it's automatic or manual and if the transmission is a continuously variable transmission (CVT). CVT changes smoothly and efficiently between gears. This can provide better fuel economy than other transmissions by enabling the engine to run at its most efficient speed.

Tow Rating: Ratings of very low, low, average, high, and very high indicate the vehicle's relative ability to tow trailers or other loads. Some manufacturers do not provide a tow rating.

Head/Leg Room: This tells how roomy the front seat is. The values are given in inches and rated in comparison to all other vehicles.

Interior Space: This tells how roomy the car's passenger area should feel. This value is given in cubic feet and rated in comparison to all other vehicles. Many SUVs do not provide interior space specifications.

Cargo Space: This gives you the cubic feet available for cargo. For minivans, the volume is behind the last row of seats. In cars, it's the trunk space. We rate the roominess of the cargo space compared to all SUVs and cars. For trucks we list the Truck Bed Volume and rate it, small, medium, or large, compared to other truck bed volumes available.

Wheelbase/Length: The wheelbase is the distance between the centers of the front and rear wheels and the length is the distance from front bumper to rear bumper. Wheelbase can affect the ride and length affects how big the car "feels."

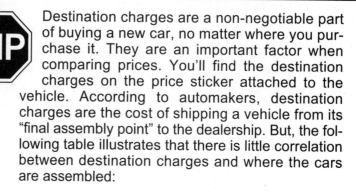

DESTINATION CHARGES

Destination charges are a non-negotiable part of buying a new car, no matter where you purchase it. They are an important factor when comparing prices. You'll find the destination charges on the price sticker attached to the vehicle. According to automakers, destination charges are the cost of shipping a vehicle from its "final assembly point" to the dealership. But, the following table illustrates that there is little correlation between destination charges and where the cars are assembled:

Vehicle	Destination Charge*	Assembly Country
Chevrolet Silverado	$995	U.S.A.
BMW 5 Series	$875	Germany
Kia Sedona	$800	South Korea
Jeep Liberty	$795	U.S.A.

*Data based on 2012 model year cars.

Ratings—10 Best, 1 Worst

Combo Crash Tests	6
Safety Features	9
Rollover	5
Preventative Maintenance	6
Repair Costs	6
Warranty	5
Fuel Economy	2
Complaints	10
Insurance Costs	10
OVERALL RATING	**8**

Acura MDX

Acura MDX

At-a-Glance

Status/Year Series Started Unchanged/2007
Twins . . . . –
Body Styles. . . . . SUV
Seating. 5
Anti-Theft Device. . . . . . . Std. Pass. Immobil. & Alarm
Parking Index Rating . . . . Average
Where Made. . . . . Alliston, Ontario
Fuel Factor
  MPG Rating (city/hwy). . . . . Very Poor-16/21
  Driving Range (mi.). Short-376.3
  Fuel Type. . . . . Premium
  Annual Fuel Cost. . . . . Very High-$2930
  Gas Guzzler Tax . . . . No
  Greenhouse Gas Emissions (tons/yr.) High-10.4
  Barrels of Oil Used per year . . . . Very High-19.0

How the Competition Rates

Competitors	Rating	Pg.
BMW X5	–	99
Lexus GX	–	189
Volvo XC90	–	270

Price Range	Retail	Markup
Base	$42,930	9%
Technology Package	$46,605	9%
Advance Package	$52,555	9%
Advance & Entertain. Package	$56,570	9%

Safety Checklist

Crash Tests:
  Frontal. . . . . Average
  Side. . . . . Average
Airbags:
  Head . . . . Fr. & Rr. Roof Curtain
  Torso . . . . Front Pelvis/Torso from Seat
  Pelvis . . . . Front Pelvis/Torso from Seat
  Roll Sensing. . . . . Yes
  Knee Bolster . . . . None
Crash Avoidance:
  Frontal Collision Warning . . . . Optional
  Blind Spot Detection . . . . Optional
  Crash Imminent Braking . . . . Optional
  Lane Departure Warning . . . . None
General:
  Auto. Crash Notification. . . . . None
  Day Running Lamps . . . . Standard
Safety Belt/Restraint:
  Dynamic Head Restraints. . . . . . Standard Front
  Adjustable Belt . . . . Standard Front
  Pretensioners . . . . Standard Front

Acura MDX

Specifications

Drive . . . . AWD
Engine 3.7-liter V6
Transmission . . . . 6-sp. Automatic
Tow Rating (lbs.). Average-5000
Head/Leg Room (in.) Cramped-39.2/41.2
Interior Space (cu. ft.) . . . . Very Roomy-145.2
Cargo Space (cu. ft.). Cramped-15
Wheelbase/Length (in.) 108.3/191.6

Ratings—10 Best, 1 Worst

Combo Crash Tests	–
Safety Features	7
Rollover	4
Preventative Maintenance	9
Repair Costs	7
Warranty	5
Fuel Economy	3
Complaints	10
Insurance Costs	10
OVERALL RATING	**–**

Acura RDX

Acura RDX

At-a-Glance

Status/Year Series Started	Unchanged/2007
Twins	–
Body Styles	SUV
Seating	5
Anti-Theft Device	Std. Pass. Immobil. & Alarm
Parking Index Rating	Hard
Where Made	Marysville, OH
Fuel Factor	
MPG Rating (city/hwy)	Poor-19/24
Driving Range (mi.)	Short-377.4
Fuel Type	Premium
Annual Fuel Cost	High-$2504
Gas Guzzler Tax	No
Greenhouse Gas Emissions (tons/yr.)	High-8.9
Barrels of Oil Used per year	High-16.3

How the Competition Rates

Competitors	Rating	Pg.
Infiniti FX	–	166
Lexus RX	4	193
Volkswagen Tiguan	–	265

Price Range

Price Range	Retail	Markup
Base	$32,895	7%
SH-AWD	$34,895	7%
Tech. Package	$35,995	7%
SH-AWD w/ Tech. Package	$37,995	8%

Safety Checklist

Crash Tests:
Frontal .... –
Side .... –

Airbags:
Head .... Fr. & Rr. Roof Curtain
Torso. .... Front Torso from Seat
Pelvis .... None
Roll Sensing .... Yes
Knee Bolster .... None

Crash Avoidance:
Frontal Collision Warning. .... None
Blind Spot Detection .... None
Crash Imminent Braking .... None
Lane Departure Warning .... None

General:
Auto. Crash Notification. .... None
Day Running Lamps .... Standard

Safety Belt/Restraint:
Dynamic Head Restraints. ..... Standard Front
Adjustable Belt .... Standard Front
Pretensioners .... Standard Front

Acura RDX

Specifications

Drive	FWD
Engine	2.3-liter I4
Transmission	5-sp. Automatic
Tow Rating (lbs.)	Very Low-1500
Head/Leg Room (in.)	Cramped-38.7/41.8
Interior Space (cu. ft.)	Average-101.4
Cargo Space (cu. ft.)	Roomy-27.8
Wheelbase/Length (in.)	104.3/182.5

Ratings—10 Best, 1 Worst

Combo Crash Tests	–
Safety Features	4
Rollover	9
Preventative Maintenance	5
Repair Costs	6
Warranty	5
Fuel Economy	5
Complaints	9
Insurance Costs	8
OVERALL RATING	–

Acura TL

Acura TL

At-a-Glance

Status/Year Series Started	Unchanged/2009
Twins	–
Body Styles	Sedan
Seating	5
Anti-Theft Device	Std. Pass. Immobil. & Alarm
Parking Index Rating	Hard
Where Made	Marysville, OH

Fuel Factor

MPG Rating (city/hwy)	Average-20/29
Driving Range (mi.)	Long-430.1
Fuel Type	Premium
Annual Fuel Cost	Average-$2258
Gas Guzzler Tax	No
Greenhouse Gas Emissions (tons/yr.)	Average-8.1
Barrels of Oil Used per year	High-14.9

How the Competition Rates

Competitors	Rating	Pg.
Cadillac CTS	7	105
Infiniti G	–	167
Lexus ES	–	187

Price Range

Price Range	Retail	Markup
Base	$35,605	7%
SH-AWD	$39,155	8%
Tech. Package	$42,885	8%
SH-AWD 6MT w/ Advance Pkg.	$45,085	8%

Safety Checklist

Crash Tests:
Frontal	–
Side	–

Airbags:
Head	Fr. & Rr. Roof Curtain
Torso	Front Pelvis/Torso from Seat
Pelvis	Front Pelvis/Torso from Seat
Roll Sensing	No
Knee Bolster	None

Crash Avoidance:
Frontal Collision Warning	None
Blind Spot Detection	None
Crash Imminent Braking	None
Lane Departure Warning	None

General:
Auto. Crash Notification	None
Day Running Lamps	Standard

Safety Belt/Restraint:
Dynamic Head Restraints	Standard Front
Adjustable Belt	Standard Front
Pretensioners	Standard Front

Acura TL

Specifications

Drive	FWD
Engine	3.5-liter V6
Transmission	6-sp. Automatic
Tow Rating (lbs.)	–
Head/Leg Room (in.)	Average-38.4/42.5
Interior Space (cu. ft.)	Average-98.2
Cargo Space (cu. ft.)	Cramped-13.1
Wheelbase/Length (in.)	109.3/194

Ratings—10 Best, 1 Worst

Combo Crash Tests	–
Safety Features	4
Rollover	8
Preventative Maintenance	9
Repair Costs	6
Warranty	5
Fuel Economy	6
Complaints	3
Insurance Costs	5
OVERALL RATING	**–**

Acura TSX

Acura TSX

At-a-Glance

Status/Year Series Started Unchanged/2009
Twins . . . . –
Body Styles. . . . . Sedan, Wagon
Seating. 5
Anti-Theft Device. . . . . . . Std. Pass. Immobil. & Alarm
Parking Index Rating . . . . Easy
Where Made . . . . Sayama, Japan
Fuel Factor
  MPG Rating (city/hwy) Average-22/31
  Driving Range (mi.). . . . . Very Long-468.2
  Fuel Type. . . . . Premium
  Annual Fuel Cost. . . . . Average-$2075
  Gas Guzzler Tax . . . . No
  Greenhouse Gas Emissions (tons/yr.) . . Average-7.2
  Barrels of Oil Used per year. Average-13.2

How the Competition Rates

Competitors	Rating	Pg.
Chrysler 200	3	121
Hyundai Sonata	10	161
Lexus IS	–	191

Price Range

Price Range	Retail	Markup
Base	$29,810	7%
Sport Wagon	$31,160	8%
Tech. Package	$32,910	7%
V6 w/ Tech. Package	$38,450	8%

Safety Checklist

Crash Tests:
  Frontal . . . . –
  Side . . . . –
Airbags:
  Head . . . . Fr. & Rr. Roof Curtain
  Torso . . . . Front Pelvis/Torso from Seat
  Pelvis . . . . Front Pelvis/Torso from Seat
  Roll Sensing. . . . . No
  Knee Bolster . . . . None
Crash Avoidance:
  Frontal Collision Warning. . . . . None
  Blind Spot Detection . . . . None
  Crash Imminent Braking . . . . None
  Lane Departure Warning . . . . None
General:
  Auto. Crash Notification. . . . . None
  Day Running Lamps . . . . Standard
Safety Belt/Restraint:
  Dynamic Head Restraints. . . . . . Standard Front
  Adjustable Belt . . . . Standard Front
  Pretensioners . . . . Standard Front

Acura TSX

Specifications

Drive . . . . FWD
Engine. 2.4-liter I4
Transmission . . . . 5-sp. Automatic
Tow Rating (lbs.) . . . . –
Head/Leg Room (in.) Cramped-37.6/42.4
Interior Space (cu. ft.). Cramped-94.5
Cargo Space (cu. ft.). Cramped-14
Wheelbase/Length (in.) 106.4/185.6

Ratings—10 Best, 1 Worst	
Combo Crash Tests	8
Safety Features	9
Rollover	6
Preventative Maintenance	6
Repair Costs	5
Warranty	5
Fuel Economy	2
Complaints	–
Insurance Costs	8
OVERALL RATING	8

Acura ZDX

Acura ZDX

At-a-Glance

Status/Year Series Started	Unchanged/2010
Twins	–
Body Styles	SUV
Seating	5
Anti-Theft Device	Std. Pass. Immobil. & Alarm
Parking Index Rating	Hard
Where Made	Alliston, Ontario

Fuel Factor

MPG Rating (city/hwy)	Very Poor-16/23
Driving Range (mi.)	Average-389.3
Fuel Type	Premium
Annual Fuel Cost	Very High-$2832
Gas Guzzler Tax	No
Greenhouse Gas Emissions (tons/yr.)	High-9.8
Barrels of Oil Used per year	High-18.0

How the Competition Rates

Competitors	Rating	Pg.
Lexus RX	4	193
Mazda CX-7	–	200
Volvo XC60	10	269

Price Range	Retail	Markup
Base	$46,020	8%
Tech. Package	$50,520	8%
Advance Package	$56,570	8%

Safety Checklist

Crash Tests:

Frontal	Good
Side	Average

Airbags:

Head	Fr. & Rr. Roof Curtain
Torso	Front Pelvis/Torso from Seat
Pelvis	Front Pelvis/Torso from Seat
Roll Sensing	Yes
Knee Bolster	None

Crash Avoidance:

Frontal Collision Warning	Optional
Blind Spot Detection	Optional
Crash Imminent Braking	Optional
Lane Departure Warning	None

General:

Auto. Crash Notification	None
Day Running Lamps	Standard

Safety Belt/Restraint:

Dynamic Head Restraints	Standard Front
Adjustable Belt	Standard Front
Pretensioners	Standard Front

Acura ZDX

Specifications

Drive	AWD
Engine	3.7-liter V6
Transmission	6-sp. Automatic
Tow Rating (lbs.)	Very Low-1500
Head/Leg Room (in.)	Cramped-38/42.6
Interior Space (cu. ft.)	Cramped-91.2
Cargo Space (cu. ft.)	Roomy-26.3
Wheelbase/Length (in.)	108.3/192.4

Ratings—10 Best, 1 Worst

Combo Crash Tests	–
Safety Features	4
Rollover	8
Preventative Maintenance	6
Repair Costs	7
Warranty	8
Fuel Economy	5
Complaints	1
Insurance Costs	5
OVERALL RATING	–

Audi A3

Audi A3

At-a-Glance

Status/Year Series Started Unchanged/2006
Twins . . . . –
Body Styles . . . . Hatchback
Seating 5
Anti-Theft Device . . . . Std. Pass. Immobil. & Alarm
Parking Index Rating . . . . Very Easy
Where Made . . . . Ingolstadt, Germany

Fuel Factor
MPG Rating (city/hwy) Average-21/30
Driving Range (mi.) . . . . Very Short-352.0
Fuel Type . . . . Premium
Annual Fuel Cost . . . . Average-$2163
Gas Guzzler Tax . . . . No
Greenhouse Gas Emissions (tons/yr.) . . Average-7.8
Barrels of Oil Used per year High-14.3

How the Competition Rates

Competitors	Rating	Pg.
BMW 1 Series	–	94
Lexus HS	–	190
Volkswagen Golf	–	261

Price Range	Retail	Markup
2.0T Premium	$27,270	8%
2.0T Premium TDI	$30,250	8%
2.0T Premium Plus	$30,750	8%
2.0T Premium Plus TDI	$32,250	8%

Safety Checklist

Crash Tests:
Frontal . . . . –
Side . . . . –
Airbags:
Head . . . . Fr. & Rr. Roof Curtain
Torso . . . . Fr. & Opt. Rr. Pelvis/Torso from Seat
Pelvis . . . Fr. & Opt. Rr. Pelvis/Torso from Seat
Roll Sensing . . . . No
Knee Bolster . . . . None
Crash Avoidance:
Frontal Collision Warning . . . . –
Blind Spot Detection . . . . None
Crash Imminent Braking . . . . None
Lane Departure Warning . . . . –
General:
Auto. Crash Notification . . . . None
Day Running Lamps . . . . Standard
Safety Belt/Restraint:
Dynamic Head Restraints . . . . –
Adjustable Belt . . . . Standard Front
Pretensioners . . . . Standard Front & Rear

Audi A3

Specifications

Drive . . . . FWD
Engine 2.0-liter I4
Transmission . . . . 6 sp. Automatic
Tow Rating (lbs.) . . . . –
Head/Leg Room (in.) Cramped-39.3/41.2
Interior Space (cu. ft.) . . . . Very Cramped-89
Cargo Space (cu. ft.) Average-19.5
Wheelbase/Length (in.) 101.5/107

Audi A4

Ratings—10 Best, 1 Worst

Combo Crash Tests	5
Safety Features	5
Rollover	8
Preventative Maintenance	4
Repair Costs	2
Warranty	8
Fuel Economy	6
Complaints	7
Insurance Costs	5
OVERALL RATING	**6**

Audi A4

At-a-Glance

Status/Year Series Started Unchanged/2009
Twins . . . . –
Body Styles. Sedan, Wagon
Seating 5
Anti-Theft Device . . . . Std. Pass. Immobil. & Alarm
Parking Index Rating . . . . Average
Where Made . . . . Germany
Fuel Factor
  MPG Rating (city/hwy) Average-22/30
  Driving Range (mi.) Long-422.5
  Fuel Type. . . . . Premium
  Annual Fuel Cost. . . . . Average-$2100
  Gas Guzzler Tax . . . . No
  Greenhouse Gas Emissions (tons/yr.) . . Average-7.5
  Barrels of Oil Used per year. Average-13.7

How the Competition Rates

Competitors	Rating	Pg.
BMW 3 Series	–	95
Cadillac CTS	7	105
Mercedes-Benz C-Class	3	203

Price Range	Retail	Markup
2.0T Premium	$32,500	8%
2.0T Premium Plus	$37,600	8%
2.0T Prestige	$42,800	8%
2.0T Prestige S-Line Avant	$47,550	8%

Safety Checklist

Crash Tests:
  Frontal. . . . . Poor
  Side . . . . Good
Airbags:
  Head . . . . Fr. & Rr. Roof Curtain
  Torso . . . . Fr. & Opt. Rr. Pelvis/Torso from Seat
  Pelvis . . . Fr. & Opt. Rr. Pelvis/Torso from Seat
  Roll Sensing. . . . . No
  Knee Bolster . . . . None
Crash Avoidance:
  Frontal Collision Warning . . . . –
  Blind Spot Detection . . . . Optional
  Crash Imminent Braking . . . . None
  Lane Departure Warning . . . . –
General:
  Auto. Crash Notification . . . . None
  Day Running Lamps . . . . Standard
Safety Belt/Restraint:
  Dynamic Head Restraints . . . . –
  Adjustable Belt . . . . Standard Front
  Pretensioners . . . . Standard Front & Rear

Audi A4

Specifications

Drive . . . . FWD
Engine. 2.0-liter I4
Transmission . . . . 8-sp. Automatic
Tow Rating (lbs.) . . . . –
Head/Leg Room (in.) Average-40/41.3
Interior Space (cu. ft.) Cramped-91
Cargo Space (cu. ft.) Cramped-12.4
Wheelbase/Length (in.) 110.6/185.2

Ratings—10 Best, 1 Worst

Combo Crash Tests	–
Safety Features	5
Rollover	10
Preventative Maintenance	4
Repair Costs	5
Warranty	8
Fuel Economy	6
Complaints	8
Insurance Costs	3
OVERALL RATING	**–**

Audi A5

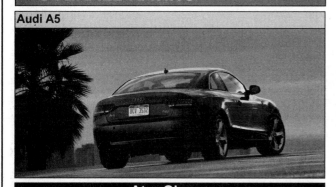

At-a-Glance

Status/Year Series Started Unchanged/2008
Twins . . . . –
Body Styles . . . . Coupe, Convertible
Seating 4
Anti-Theft Device . . . . Std. Pass. Immobil. & Alarm
Parking Index Rating . . . . Average
Where Made . . . . Neckarsulm, Germany
Fuel Factor
  MPG Rating (city/hwy) Average-22/30
  Driving Range (mi.) Long-422.5
  Fuel Type . . . . Premium
  Annual Fuel Cost . . . . Average-$2100
  Gas Guzzler Tax . . . . No
  Greenhouse Gas Emissions (tons/yr.) . . Average-7.5
  Barrels of Oil Used per year Average-13.7

How the Competition Rates

Competitors	Rating	Pg.
BMW 3 Series	–	95
Infiniti G	–	167
Lexus GS	–	188

Price Range	Retail	Markup
2.0T Premium	$37,100	8%
2.0T Premium Plus	$41,000	8%
2.0T Prestige	$46,300	8%
2.0T Prestige S-Line	$55,400	8%

Audi A5

Safety Checklist

Crash Tests:
  Frontal . . . . –
  Side . . . . –
Airbags:
  Head . . . . Fr. & Rr. Roof Curtain
  Torso . . . . Front Pelvis/Torso from Seat
  Pelvis . . . . Front Pelvis/Torso from Seat
  Roll Sensing . . . . No
  Knee Bolster . . . . Standard Front
Crash Avoidance:
  Frontal Collision Warning . . . . –
  Blind Spot Detection . . . . Optional
  Crash Imminent Braking . . . . None
  Lane Departure Warning . . . . –
General:
  Auto. Crash Notification . . . . None
  Day Running Lamps . . . . Standard
Safety Belt/Restraint:
  Dynamic Head Restraints . . . . –
  Adjustable Belt . . . . None
  Pretensioners . . . . Standard Front & Rear

Audi A5

Specifications

Drive . . . . FWD
Engine 2.0-liter I4
Transmission . . . . 8-sp. Automatic
Tow Rating (lbs.) . . . . –
Head/Leg Room (in.) Cramped-39.1/41.3
Interior Space (cu. ft.) . . . . . . Very Cramped-81
Cargo Space (cu. ft.) Cramped-12.4
Wheelbase/Length (in.) 108.3/182.1

Ratings—10 Best, 1 Worst

Combo Crash Tests	–
Safety Features	9
Rollover	9
Preventative Maintenance	4
Repair Costs	3
Warranty	8
Fuel Economy	8
Complaints	–
Insurance Costs	5
OVERALL RATING	**–**

Audi A6

Audi A6

At-a-Glance

Status/Year Series Started . . . . All New/2012
Twins . . . . –
Body Styles. Sedan, Wagon
Seating 5
Anti-Theft Device. . . . . . . Std. Pass. Immobil. & Alarm
Parking Index Rating . . . . Hard
Where Made. . . . . Guajarat, India
Fuel Factor
  MPG Rating (city/hwy) Good-25/33
  Driving Range (mi.). . . . . Very Long-555.6
  Fuel Type. . . . . Premium
  Annual Fuel Cost . . . . Low-$1871
  Gas Guzzler Tax . . . . No
  Greenhouse Gas Emissions (tons/yr.) . . Average-6.7
  Barrels of Oil Used per year. Average-12.2

How the Competition Rates

Competitors	Rating	Pg.
BMW 7 Series	–	97
Lexus LS	–	192
Volvo S80	–	268

Price Range

	Retail	Markup
2.0T Premium	$41,700	8%
3.0T Premium	$49,900	8%

Safety Checklist

Crash Tests:
  Frontal . . . . –
  Side . . . . –
Airbags:
  Head . . . . Fr. & Rr. Roof Curtain
  Torso . . . . Fr. & Opt. Rr. Pelvis/Torso from Seat
  Pelvis . . . Fr. & Opt. Rr. Pelvis/Torso from Seat
  Roll Sensing . . . . Yes
  Knee Bolster. . . . . Standard Front
Crash Avoidance:
  Frontal Collision Warning . . . . –
  Blind Spot Detection . . . . Optional
  Crash Imminent Braking . . . . Optional
  Lane Departure Warning . . . . –
General:
  Auto. Crash Notification. . . . . None
  Day Running Lamps . . . . Standard
Safety Belt/Restraint:
  Dynamic Head Restraints . . . . –
  Adjustable Belt . . . . Standard Front
  Pretensioners. . . . . Standard Front & Rear

Audi A6

Specifications

Drive . . . . FWD
Engine 3.0-liter V6
Transmission . . . . 6-sp. Automatic
Tow Rating (lbs.) . . . . –
Head/Leg Room (in.) . . . . . Very Cramped-37.2/41.3
Interior Space (cu. ft.). Cramped-97.2
Cargo Space (cu. ft.) Cramped-14.1
Wheelbase/Length (in.) 114.7/193.9

Ratings—10 Best, 1 Worst

Combo Crash Tests	–
Safety Features	9
Rollover	10
Preventative Maintenance	–
Repair Costs	–
Warranty	8
Fuel Economy	4
Complaints	–
Insurance Costs	5
OVERALL RATING	–

Audi A7

Audi A7

At-a-Glance

Status/Year Series Started . . . . All New/2012
Twins . . . . –
Body Styles . . . . Sedan
Seating 4
Anti-Theft Device . . . . Std. Pass. Immobil. & Alarm
Parking Index Rating . . . . Hard
Where Made . . . . Neckarsulm, Germany
Fuel Factor
  MPG Rating (city/hwy) Poor-18/28
  Driving Range (mi.) Long-424.6
  Fuel Type . . . . Premium
  Annual Fuel Cost . . . . High-$2448
  Gas Guzzler Tax . . . . No
  Greenhouse Gas Emissions (tons/yr.) High-8.5
  Barrels of Oil Used per year High-15.6

How the Competition Rates

Competitors	Rating	Pg.
BMW 5 Series	9	96
Jaguar XF	–	170
Infiniti G	–	167

Price Range	Retail	Markup
Premium	$59,250	8%
Premium Plus	$62,870	8%
Prestige	$65,580	8%

Safety Checklist

Crash Tests:
  Frontal . . . . –
  Side . . . . –
Airbags:
  Head . . . . Fr. & Rr. Roof Curtain
  Torso . . . . Fr. & Opt. Rr. Pelvis/Torso from Seat
  Pelvis . . . Fr. & Opt. Rr. Pelvis/Torso from Seat
  Roll Sensing . . . . Yes
  Knee Bolster . . . . Standard Front
Crash Avoidance:
  Frontal Collision Warning . . . . –
  Blind Spot Detection . . . . Optional
  Crash Imminent Braking . . . . Optional
  Lane Departure Warning . . . . –
General:
  Auto. Crash Notification . . . . None
  Day Running Lamps . . . . Standard
Safety Belt/Restraint:
  Dynamic Head Restraints . . . . –
  Adjustable Belt . . . . Standard Front
  Pretensioners . . . . Standard Front & Rear

Audi A7

Specifications

Drive . . . . FWD
Engine 3.0-liter V6
Transmission . . . . 8-sp. Automatic
Tow Rating (lbs.) . . . . –
Head/Leg Room (in.) . . . . . Very Cramped-36.9/41.3
Interior Space (cu. ft.) Cramped-94.3
Cargo Space (cu. ft.) Roomy-24.5
Wheelbase/Length (in.) 114.7/195.6

Ratings—10 Best, 1 Worst

Combo Crash Tests	–
Safety Features	10
Rollover	9
Preventative Maintenance	2
Repair Costs	1
Warranty	8
Fuel Economy	4
Complaints	–
Insurance Costs	5
OVERALL RATING	**–**

Audi A8

Audi A8

At-a-Glance

Status/Year Series Started	Unchanged/2011
Twins	–
Body Styles	Sedan
Seating	5
Anti-Theft Device	Std. Pass. Immobil. & Alarm
Parking Index Rating	Very Hard
Where Made	Neckarsulm, Germany

Fuel Factor

MPG Rating (city/hwy)	Poor-18/28
Driving Range (mi.)	Very Long-510.4
Fuel Type	Premium
Annual Fuel Cost	High-$2448
Gas Guzzler Tax	No
Greenhouse Gas Emissions (tons/yr.)	High-8.9
Barrels of Oil Used per year	High-16.3

How the Competition Rates

Competitors	Rating	Pg.
BMW 7 Series	–	97
Jaguar XJ	–	171
Mercedes-Benz S-Class	–	208

Price Range	Retail	Markup
Base	$78,750	8%
Convenience Package	$81,650	8%
Sport Package	$84,650	8%

Safety Checklist

Crash Tests:
- Frontal ... –
- Side ... –

Airbags:
- Head ... Fr. & Rr. Roof Curtain
- Torso ... Fr. & Rr. Pelvis/Torso from Seat
- Pelvis ... Fr. & Rr. Pelvis/Torso from Seat
- Roll Sensing ... Yes
- Knee Bolster ... Standard Front

Crash Avoidance:
- Frontal Collision Warning ... –
- Blind Spot Detection ... Optional
- Crash Imminent Braking ... Optional
- Lane Departure Warning ... –

General:
- Auto. Crash Notification ... None
- Day Running Lamps ... Standard

Safety Belt/Restraint:
- Dynamic Head Restraints ... Standard Front
- Adjustable Belt ... Standard Front
- Pretensioners ... Standard Front & Rear

Audi A8

Specifications

Drive	AWD
Engine	4.2-liter V8
Transmission	8-sp. Automatic
Tow Rating (lbs.)	–
Head/Leg Room (in.)	Very Cramped-37.2/41.4
Interior Space (cu. ft.)	Roomy-115.1
Cargo Space (cu. ft.)	Cramped-13.2
Wheelbase/Length (in.)	117.8/202.2

Ratings—10 Best, 1 Worst

Combo Crash Tests	–
Safety Features	7
Rollover	5
Preventative Maintenance	4
Repair Costs	2
Warranty	8
Fuel Economy	3
Complaints	9
Insurance Costs	8
OVERALL RATING	**–**

Audi Q5

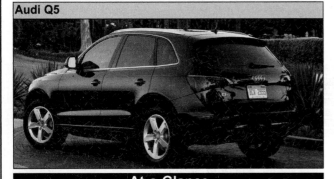
Audi Q5

At-a-Glance

Status/Year Series Started Unchanged/2009
Twins . . . . –
Body Styles . . . . SUV
Seating 5
Anti-Theft Device . . . . Std. Pass. Immobil. & Alarm
Parking Index Rating . . . . Average
Where Made . . . . Ingolstadt, Germany

Fuel Factor
  MPG Rating (city/hwy) Poor-18/23
  Driving Range (mi.) Average-395.0
  Fuel Type . . . . Premium
  Annual Fuel Cost . . . . High-$2631
  Gas Guzzler Tax . . . . No
  Greenhouse Gas Emissions (tons/yr.) High-9.3
  Barrels of Oil Used per year High-17.1

How the Competition Rates

Competitors	Rating	Pg.
Cadillac SRX	–	106
Lexus RX	4	193
Volvo XC60	10	269

Price Range	Retail	Markup
Premium	$35,600	8%
Premium Plus	$39,900	8%

Safety Checklist

Crash Tests:
  Frontal . . . . –
  Side . . . . –
Airbags:
  Head . . . . Fr. & Rr. Roof Curtain
  Torso . . . . Fr. & Opt. Rr. Pelvis/Torso from Seat
  Pelvis . . . Fr. & Opt. Rr. Pelvis/Torso from Seat
  Roll Sensing . . . . Yes
  Knee Bolster . . . . None
Crash Avoidance:
  Frontal Collision Warning . . . . –
  Blind Spot Detection . . . . Optional
  Crash Imminent Braking . . . . None
  Lane Departure Warning . . . . –
General:
  Auto. Crash Notification . . . . None
  Day Running Lamps . . . . Standard
Safety Belt/Restraint:
  Dynamic Head Restraints . . . . –
  Adjustable Belt . . . . Standard Front
  Pretensioners . . . . Standard Front & Rear

Audi Q5

Specifications

Drive 4WD
Engine 3.2-liter V6
Transmission . . . . 6-sp. Automatic
Tow Rating (lbs.) Low-4400
Head/Leg Room (in.) Cramped-39.4/41
Interior Space (cu. ft.) Average-101.5
Cargo Space (cu. ft.) Roomy-29.1
Wheelbase/Length (in.) 110.5/182.2

Ratings—10 Best, 1 Worst

Combo Crash Tests	–
Safety Features	7
Rollover	4
Preventative Maintenance	3
Repair Costs	2
Warranty	8
Fuel Economy	2
Complaints	8
Insurance Costs	8
OVERALL RATING	**–**

Audi Q7

At-a-Glance

Status/Year Series Started Unchanged/2007
Twins . . . . –
Body Styles . . . . SUV
Seating 7
Anti-Theft Device . . . . Std. Pass. Immobil. & Alarm
Parking Index Rating . . . . Very Hard
Where Made . . . . Bratislava, Slovakia
Fuel Factor
  MPG Rating (city/hwy) . . . . Very Poor-16/22
  Driving Range (mi.) . . . . Very Long-481.5
  Fuel Type . . . . Premium
  Annual Fuel Cost . . . . Very High-$2879
  Gas Guzzler Tax . . . . No
  Greenhouse Gas Emissions (tons/yr.) High-10.4
  Barrels of Oil Used per year . . . . Very High-19.0

How the Competition Rates

Competitors	Rating	Pg.
BMW X5	–	99
Land Rover Range Rover	–	185
Lexus GS	–	188

Price Range

	Retail	Markup
Premium	$46,250	8%
Premium Plus	$52,550	8%
S Line Prestige	$59,950	8%

Audi Q7

Safety Checklist

Crash Tests:
  Frontal . . . . –
  Side . . . . –
Airbags:
  Head . . . . Fr. & Rr. Roof Curtain
  Torso . . . . Fr. & Opt. Rr. Pelvis/Torso from Seat
  Pelvis . . . Fr. & Opt. Rr. Pelvis/Torso from Seat
  Roll Sensing . . . . Yes
  Knee Bolster . . . . None
Crash Avoidance:
  Frontal Collision Warning . . . . –
  Blind Spot Detection . . . . Optional
  Crash Imminent Braking . . . . None
  Lane Departure Warning . . . . –
General:
  Auto. Crash Notification . . . . None
  Day Running Lamps . . . . Standard
Safety Belt/Restraint:
  Dynamic Head Restraints . . . . –
  Adjustable Belt . . . . . . Standard Front and Rear
  Pretensioners . . . . Standard Front & Rear

Audi Q7

Specifications

Drive . . . . AWD
Engine 3.0-liter V6
Transmission . . . . 8-sp. Automatic
Tow Rating (lbs.) Average-5500
Head/Leg Room (in.) Cramped-39.5/41.3
Interior Space (cu. ft.) . . . . Very Roomy-133.2
Cargo Space (cu. ft.) . . . . Very Cramped-10.9
Wheelbase/Length (in.) 118.2/200.3

Ratings—10 Best, 1 Worst

Combo Crash Tests	–
Safety Features	2
Rollover	7
Preventative Maintenance	10
Repair Costs	4
Warranty	10
Fuel Economy	4
Complaints	2
Insurance Costs	5
OVERALL RATING	**–**

BMW 1 Series

BMW 1 Series

At-a-Glance

Status/Year Series Started	Unchanged/2008
Twins	–
Body Styles	Coupe, Convertible
Seating	4
Anti-Theft Device	Std. Pass. Immobil.
Parking Index Rating	Easy
Where Made	Leipzig, Germany

Fuel Factor

MPG Rating (city/hwy)	Poor-18/28
Driving Range (mi.)	Very Short-300.3
Fuel Type	Premium
Annual Fuel Cost	High-$2448
Gas Guzzler Tax	No
Greenhouse Gas Emissions (tons/yr.)	High-8.9
Barrels of Oil Used per year	High-16.3

How the Competition Rates

Competitors	Rating	Pg.
Lexus CT	–	186
Mercedes-Benz C-Class	3	203
Volvo C70	–	266

Price Range

Price Range	Retail	Markup
128i Coupe	$30,950	9%
128i Convertible	$36,600	9%
135i Coupe	$39,050	9%
135i Convertible	$43,800	9%

Safety Checklist

Crash Tests:

Frontal	–
Side	–

Airbags:

Head	Fr. & Rr. Roof Curtain
Torso	Front Torso from Seat
Pelvis	None
Roll Sensing	No
Knee Bolster	None

Crash Avoidance:

Frontal Collision Warning	None
Blind Spot Detection	None
Crash Imminent Braking	None
Lane Departure Warning	None

General:

Auto. Crash Notification	Optional
Day Running Lamps	Standard

Safety Belt/Restraint:

Dynamic Head Restraints	None
Adjustable Belt	None
Pretensioners	Standard Front

BMW 1 Series

Specifications

Drive	RWD
Engine	3.0-liter I6
Transmission	6-sp. Automatic
Tow Rating (lbs.)	–
Head/Leg Room (in.)	Very Cramped-37.9/41.4
Interior Space (cu. ft.)	Very Cramped-86
Cargo Space (cu. ft.)	Very Cramped-10
Wheelbase/Length (in.)	104.7/172.2

Ratings—10 Best, 1 Worst

Combo Crash Tests	–
Safety Features	4
Rollover	8
Preventative Maintenance	10
Repair Costs	4
Warranty	10
Fuel Economy	4
Complaints	5
Insurance Costs	5
OVERALL RATING	–

BMW 3 Series

At-a-Glance

Status/Year Series Started Unchanged/2006
Twins . . . . –
Body Styles. . . . . Sedan, Coupe, Convertible
Seating 5
Anti-Theft Device. . . . . Std. Pass. Immobil.
Parking Index Rating . . . . Easy
Where Made . . . . Munich, Germany

Fuel Factor
  MPG Rating (city/hwy) Poor-18/28
  Driving Range (mi.). . . . . Very Short-345.3
  Fuel Type. . . . . Premium
  Annual Fuel Cost. . . . . High-$2448
  Gas Guzzler Tax . . . . No
  Greenhouse Gas Emissions (tons/yr.) High-8.9
  Barrels of Oil Used per year. High-16.3

How the Competition Rates

Competitors	Rating	Pg.
Audi A4	5	87
Lexus IS	–	191
Mercedes-Benz C-Class	3	203

Price Range

Price Range	Retail	Markup
328i	$38,500	9%
328i xDrive	$40,200	9%
335i	$44,900	9%
335is HP	$51,900	9%

BMW 3 Series

Safety Checklist

Crash Tests:
  Frontal . . . . –
  Side . . . . –
Airbags:
  Head . . . . Fr. & Rr. Roof Curtain
  Torso. . . . . Front Torso from Seat
  Pelvis . . . . None
  Roll Sensing. . . . . No
  Knee Bolster . . . . None
Crash Avoidance:
  Frontal Collision Warning. . . . . None
  Blind Spot Detection . . . . None
  Crash Imminent Braking . . . . None
  Lane Departure Warning . . . . None
General:
  Auto. Crash Notification . . . . Optional
  Day Running Lamps . . . . Standard
Safety Belt/Restraint:
  Dynamic Head Restraints. . . . . . Standard Front
  Adjustable Belt. None
  Pretensioners . . . . Standard Front

BMW 3 Series

Specifications

Drive . . . . RWD
Engine. 3.0-liter I6
Transmission . . . . 6 sp. Automatic
Tow Rating (lbs.) . . . . –
Head/Leg Room (in.) Cramped-38.4/41.8
Interior Space (cu. ft.) . . . . Very Cramped-88
Cargo Space (cu. ft.). . . . . Very Cramped-11
Wheelbase/Length (in.) 108.7/181.9

Ratings—10 Best, 1 Worst	
Combo Crash Tests	8
Safety Features	9
Rollover	9
Preventative Maintenance	10
Repair Costs	2
Warranty	10
Fuel Economy	5
Complaints	1
Insurance Costs	5
OVERALL RATING	**9**

BMW 5 Series

BMW 5 Series

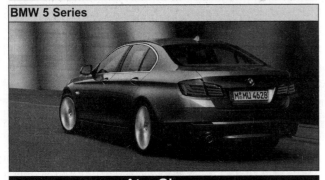

BMW 5 Series

At-a-Glance

Status/Year Series Started	Unchanged/2011
Twins	–
Body Styles	Sedan
Seating	5
Anti-Theft Device	Std. Pass. Immobil.
Parking Index Rating	Hard
Where Made	Dingolfing, Germany

Fuel Factor

MPG Rating (city/hwy)	Average-20/30
Driving Range (mi.)	Long-435.3
Fuel Type	Premium
Annual Fuel Cost	Average-$2231
Gas Guzzler Tax	No
Greenhouse Gas Emissions (tons/yr.)	Average-7.8
Barrels of Oil Used per year	High-14.3

How the Competition Rates

Competitors	Rating	Pg.
Infiniti G	–	167
Lexus GS	–	188
Mercedes-Benz E-Class	–	204

Price Range	Retail	Markup
528i	$46,700	9%
535i	$52,250	9%
550i	$61,700	9%
550xi	$64,000	9%

Safety Checklist

Crash Tests:

Frontal	Average
Side	Very Good

Airbags:

Head	Fr. & Rr. Roof Curtain
Torso	Front Torso from Seat
Pelvis	None
Roll Sensing	No
Knee Bolster	Standard Front

Crash Avoidance:

Frontal Collision Warning	Optional
Blind Spot Detection	Optional
Crash Imminent Braking	Optional
Lane Departure Warning	Optional

General:

Auto. Crash Notification	Standard
Day Running Lamps	Standard

Safety Belt/Restraint:

Dynamic Head Restraints	Standard Front
Adjustable Belt	None
Pretensioners	Standard Front

BMW 5 Series

Specifications

Drive	RWD
Engine	2.0-liter I4
Transmission	8-sp. Automatic
Tow Rating (lbs.)	–
Head/Leg Room (in.)	Average-40.5/41.4
Interior Space (cu. ft.)	Roomy-116
Cargo Space (cu. ft.)	Cramped-14
Wheelbase/Length (in.)	116.9/193.1

Ratings—10 Best, 1 Worst	
Combo Crash Tests	–
Safety Features	10
Rollover	9
Preventative Maintenance	10
Repair Costs	1
Warranty	10
Fuel Economy	2
Complaints	5
Insurance Costs	5
OVERALL RATING	–

BMW 7 Series

BMW 7 Series

At-a-Glance

Status/Year Series Started	Unchanged/2011
Twins	–
Body Styles	Sedan
Seating	5
Anti-Theft Device	Std. Pass. Immobil.
Parking Index Rating	Very Hard
Where Made	Dingolfing, Germany
Fuel Factor	
MPG Rating (city/hwy)	Very Poor-15/22
Driving Range (mi.)	Short-379.9
Fuel Type	Premium
Annual Fuel Cost	Very High-$2999
Gas Guzzler Tax	Yes
Greenhouse Gas Emissions (tons/yr.)	Very High-11.0
Barrels of Oil Used per year	Very High-20.1

How the Competition Rates

Competitors	Rating	Pg.
Jaguar XF	–	170
Lexus LS	–	192
Mercedes-Benz S-Class	–	208

Price Range	Retail	Markup
740i	$71,000	9%
750i	$84,300	9%
750Li	$88,200	9%
750Lxi	$91,200	9%

Safety Checklist

Crash Tests:
Frontal . . . . –
Side . . . . –
Airbags:
Head . . . . Fr. & Rr. Roof Curtain
Torso . . . . Front Torso from Seat
Pelvis . . . . None
Roll Sensing . . . . Yes
Knee Bolster . . . . Standard Front
Crash Avoidance:
Frontal Collision Warning . . . . Optional
Blind Spot Detection . . . . Optional
Crash Imminent Braking . . . . Optional
Lane Departure Warning . . . . Optional
General:
Auto. Crash Notification . . . . Standard
Day Running Lamps . . . . Standard
Safety Belt/Restraint:
Dynamic Head Restraints . . . . . . Standard Front
Adjustable Belt . . . . None
Pretensioners . . . . Standard Front

BMW 7 Series

Specifications

Drive	RWD
Engine	4.4-liter V8
Transmission	6-sp. Automatic
Tow Rating (lbs.)	–
Head/Leg Room (in.)	Average-40.6/41.3
Interior Space (cu. ft.)	Roomy-106
Cargo Space (cu. ft.)	Cramped-14
Wheelbase/Length (in.)	120.9/199.8

Ratings—10 Best, 1 Worst

Combo Crash Tests	–
Safety Features	9
Rollover	5
Preventative Maintenance	10
Repair Costs	2
Warranty	10
Fuel Economy	4
Complaints	2
Insurance Costs	8
OVERALL RATING	**–**

BMW X3

BMW X3

BMW X3

At-a-Glance

Status/Year Series Started	Unchanged/2011
Twins	–
Body Styles	SUV
Seating	5
Anti-Theft Device	Std. Pass. Immobil.
Parking Index Rating	Hard
Where Made	Spartanburg, SC

Fuel Factor

MPG Rating (city/hwy)	Poor-19/26
Driving Range (mi.)	Short-382.7
Fuel Type	Premium
Annual Fuel Cost	High-$2428
Gas Guzzler Tax	No
Greenhouse Gas Emissions (tons/yr.)	High-8.9
Barrels of Oil Used per year	High-16.3

How the Competition Rates

Competitors	Rating	Pg.
Audi Q5	–	92
Infiniti FX	–	166
Porsche Cayenne	–	230

Price Range	Retail	Markup
xDrive28i	$36,850	9%
xDrive35i	$42,400	9%

Safety Checklist

Crash Tests:
Frontal . . . . –
Side . . . . –
Airbags:
Head . . . . Fr. & Rr. Roof Curtain
Torso. . . . . Front Torso from Seat
Pelvis . . . . None
Roll Sensing . . . . Yes
Knee Bolster . . . . Standard Driver
Crash Avoidance:
Frontal Collision Warning . . . . Optional
Blind Spot Detection . . . . None
Crash Imminent Braking . . . . None
Lane Departure Warning. . . . . Optional
General:
Auto. Crash Notification . . . . Optional
Day Running Lamps . . . . Standard
Safety Belt/Restraint:
Dynamic Head Restraints. . . . . . . Standard Front
Adjustable Belt . . . . None
Pretensioners . . . . Standard Front

BMW X3

Specifications

Drive	4WD
Engine	3.0-liter I6
Transmission	8-sp. Automatic
Tow Rating (lbs.)	Average-5291
Head/Leg Room (in.)	Cramped-40.7/39.9
Interior Space (cu. ft.)	Very Cramped-90.1
Cargo Space (cu. ft.)	Roomy-27.6
Wheelbase/Length (in.)	110.6/183

Ratings—10 Best, 1 Worst

Combo Crash Tests	–
Safety Features	8
Rollover	3
Preventative Maintenance	10
Repair Costs	1
Warranty	10
Fuel Economy	2
Complaints	8
Insurance Costs	8
OVERALL RATING	**–**

BMW X5

BMW X5

At-a-Glance

Status/Year Series Started Unchanged/2007
Twins . . . . –
Body Styles. . . . . SUV
Seating 5/7
Anti-Theft Device. . . . . Std. Pass. Immobil.
Parking Index Rating . . . . Very Hard
Where Made . . . . Spartanburg, SC

Fuel Factor
MPG Rating (city/hwy). . . . . Very Poor-16/23
Driving Range (mi.) Long-417.1
Fuel Type. . . . . Premium
Annual Fuel Cost. . . . . Very High-$2832
Gas Guzzler Tax . . . . No
Greenhouse Gas Emissions (tons/yr.) High-9.8
Barrels of Oil Used per year. High-18.0

How the Competition Rates

Competitors	Rating	Pg.
Audi Q7	–	93
Cadillac SRX	–	106
Volvo XC90	–	270

Price Range	Retail	Markup
xDrive35i	$47,500	9%
xDrive35d	$56,700	9%
xDrive50i	$84,200	9%

Safety Checklist

Crash Tests:
Frontal . . . . –
Side . . . . –
Airbags:
Head . . . . Fr. & Rr. Roof Curtain
Torso. . . . . Front Torso from Seat
Pelvis . . . . None
Roll Sensing . . . . Yes
Knee Bolster . . . . None
Crash Avoidance:
Frontal Collision Warning. . . . . None
Blind Spot Detection . . . . None
Crash Imminent Braking . . . . None
Lane Departure Warning. . . . . Optional
General:
Auto. Crash Notification . . . . Standard
Day Running Lamps . . . . Standard
Safety Belt/Restraint:
Dynamic Head Restraints. . . . . . Standard Front
Adjustable Belt. . . . . None
Pretensioners . . . . Standard Front

BMW X5

Specifications

Drive 4WD
Engine. 3.0-liter I6
Transmission . . . . 8-sp. Automatic
Tow Rating (lbs.). Average-6000
Head/Leg Room (in.) . . . . . . Very Cramped-39.3/40
Interior Space (cu. ft.) Average-102.4
Cargo Space (cu. ft.) Roomy-23.2
Wheelbase/Length (in.) 115.5/191.2

Ratings—10 Best, 1 Worst

Combo Crash Tests	–
Safety Features	5
Rollover	10
Preventative Maintenance	10
Repair Costs	1
Warranty	10
Fuel Economy	3
Complaints	1
Insurance Costs	8
OVERALL RATING	–

BMW Z4

BMW Z4

Safety Checklist

Crash Tests:
Frontal . . . . −
Side . . . . −
Airbags:
Head . . . . Front Head from Seat
Torso . . . . Front Head/Torso from Seat
Pelvis . . . . None
Roll Sensing . . . . Yes
Knee Bolster . . . . Standard Front
Crash Avoidance:
Frontal Collision Warning . . . . None
Blind Spot Detection . . . . None
Crash Imminent Braking . . . . None
Lane Departure Warning . . . . None
General:
Auto. Crash Notification . . . . Optional
Day Running Lamps . . . . Standard
Safety Belt/Restraint:
Dynamic Head Restraints . . . . None
Adjustable Belt . . . . None
Pretensioners . . . . Standard Front

At-a-Glance

Status/Year Series Started Unchanged/2003
Twins . . . . −
Body Styles . . . . Convertible
Seating 2
Anti-Theft Device . . . . Std. Pass. Immobil.
Parking Index Rating . . . . Very Easy
Where Made . . . . Regensburg, Germany
Fuel Factor
MPG Rating (city/hwy) Poor-17/24
Driving Range (mi.) . . . . Very Short-283.7
Fuel Type . . . . Premium
Annual Fuel Cost . . . . Very High-$2683
Gas Guzzler Tax . . . . No
Greenhouse Gas Emissions (tons/yr.) High-9.8
Barrels of Oil Used per year High-18.0

BMW Z4

How the Competition Rates

Competitors	Rating	Pg.
Chevrolet Corvette	–	110
Nissan 370Z	–	214

Specifications

Drive . . . . RWD
Engine 3.6-liter I6
Transmission . . . . 7-sp. Automatic
Tow Rating (lbs.) . . . . −
Head/Leg Room (in.) Average-39.1/42.2
Interior Space (cu. ft.) . . . . Very Cramped-47.6
Cargo Space (cu. ft.) . . . . Very Cramped-8
Wheelbase/Length (in.) 98.3/166.9

Price Range

Price Range	Retail	Markup
2.8is	$48,650	9%
3.5i	$55,150	9%
3.5is	$64,200	9%

#Additional injury potential in side test see footnote (8) on page 23.

Ratings—10 Best, 1 Worst

Combo Crash Tests	9
Safety Features	7
Rollover	4
Preventative Maintenance	3
Repair Costs	2
Warranty	7
Fuel Economy	3
Complaints	5
Insurance Costs	10
OVERALL RATING	**7**

Buick Enclave

Buick Enclave

At-a-Glance

Status/Year Series Started Unchanged/2008
Twins . . . . –
Body Styles. . . . . SUV
Seating 7/8
Anti-Theft Device. . . . . . . Std. Pass. Immobil. & Alarm
Parking Index Rating . . . . Very Hard
Where Made . . . . Lansing, MI
Fuel Factor
  MPG Rating (city/hwy) Poor-17/24
  Driving Range (mi.) Long-430.5
  Fuel Type. . . . . Regular
  Annual Fuel Cost. . . . . High-$2476
  Gas Guzzler Tax . . . . No
  Greenhouse Gas Emissions (tons/yr.) High-9.8
  Barrels of Oil Used per year. High-18.0

How the Competition Rates

Competitors	Rating	Pg.
Acura MDX	9	81
Lexus RX	4	193
Volvo XC90	–	270

Price Range

	Retail	Markup
Base	$36,600	5%
Convenience	$37,520	5%
Leather	$39,715	5%
Premium	$43,080	5%

Safety Checklist

Crash Tests:
  Frontal . . . . Good
  Side . . . . Very Good
Airbags:
  Head . . . . Fr. & Rr. Roof Curtain
  Torso . . . . Front Pelvis/Torso from Seat
  Pelvis . . . . Front Pelvis/Torso from Seat
  Roll Sensing . . . . Yes
  Knee Bolster . . . . None
Crash Avoidance:
  Frontal Collision Warning. . . . . None
  Blind Spot Detection . . . . None
  Crash Imminent Braking . . . . None
  Lane Departure Warning . . . . None
General:
  Auto. Crash Notification . . . . Standard
  Day Running Lamps . . . . Standard
Safety Belt/Restraint:
  Dynamic Head Restraints . . . . None
  Adjustable Belt . . . . . . Standard Front and Rear
  Pretensioners . . . . Standard Front

Buick Enclave

Specifications

Drive . . . . FWD
Engine 3.6-liter V6
Transmission . . . . 6-sp. Automatic
Tow Rating (lbs.). Low-4500
Head/Leg Room (in.) Average-40.4/41.3
Interior Space (cu. ft.). . . . . Very Roomy-153
Cargo Space (cu. ft.). Roomy-23.2
Wheelbase/Length (in.). 119/201.5

Buick LaCrosse

Ratings—10 Best, 1 Worst	
Combo Crash Tests	10
Safety Features	7
Rollover	7
Preventative Maintenance	2
Repair Costs	4
Warranty	7
Fuel Economy	8
Complaints	3
Insurance Costs	10
OVERALL RATING	9

Buick LaCrosse

Buick LaCrosse

At-a-Glance

Status/Year Series Started Unchanged/2010
Twins . . . . –
Body Styles . . . . Sedan
Seating 5
Anti-Theft Device . . . . Std. Pass. Immobil. & Alarm
Parking Index Rating . . . . Hard
Where Made . . . . Kansas City, KS

Fuel Factor
MPG Rating (city/hwy) Good-25/36
Driving Range (mi.) . . . . Very Long-533.3
Fuel Type Regular/E85
Annual Fuel Cost . . . . Very Low-$1672
Gas Guzzler Tax . . . . No
Greenhouse Gas Emissions (tons/yr.) High-8.9
Barrels of Oil Used per year High-16.3

How the Competition Rates

Competitors	Rating	Pg.
Acura TL	–	83
Lexus ES	–	187
Volvo S60	–	267

Price Range	Retail	Markup
Base	$29,960	4%
Leather	$31,895	4%
Premium II	$33,865	4%
Touring	$38,270	4%

Safety Checklist

Crash Tests:
Frontal . . . . Very Good
Side . . . . Good
Airbags:
Head . . . . Fr. & Rr. Roof Curtain
Torso . . . . Front Pelvis/Torso from Seat
Pelvis . . . . Front Pelvis/Torso from Seat
Roll Sensing . . . . Yes
Knee Bolster . . . . None
Crash Avoidance:
Frontal Collision Warning . . . . None
Blind Spot Detection . . . . Optional
Crash Imminent Braking . . . . None
Lane Departure Warning . . . . None
General:
Auto. Crash Notification . . . . Standard
Day Running Lamps . . . . Standard
Safety Belt/Restraint:
Dynamic Head Restraints . . . . None
Adjustable Belt . . . . . . Standard Front and Rear
Pretensioners . . . . Standard Front

Buick LaCrosse

Specifications

Drive . . . . FWD
Engine 2.4-liter I4
Transmission . . . . 6-sp. Automatic
Tow Rating (lbs.) . . . . Very Low-1000
Head/Leg Room (in.) Cramped-38/41.7
Interior Space (cu. ft.) Average-101.7
Cargo Space (cu. ft.) Cramped-13.3
Wheelbase/Length (in.) 111.7/197

Ratings—10 Best, 1 Worst

Combo Crash Tests	–
Safety Features	7
Rollover	8
Preventative Maintenance	2
Repair Costs	5
Warranty	7
Fuel Economy	4
Complaints	3
Insurance Costs	5
OVERALL RATING	**–**

Buick Regal

Safety Checklist

Crash Tests:
Frontal . . . . –
Side . . . . –
Airbags:
Head . . . . Fr. & Rr. Roof Curtain
Torso . . . . Front Pelvis/Torso from Seat
Pelvis . . . . Front Pelvis/Torso from Seat
Roll Sensing . . . . Yes
Knee Bolster . . . . None
Crash Avoidance:
Frontal Collision Warning. . . . . None
Blind Spot Detection . . . . None
Crash Imminent Braking . . . . None
Lane Departure Warning . . . . None
General:
Auto. Crash Notification . . . . Standard
Day Running Lamps . . . . Standard
Safety Belt/Restraint:
Dynamic Head Restraints . . . . None
Adjustable Belt . . . . . . Standard Front and Rear
Pretensioners . . . . Standard Front

Buick Regal

At-a-Glance

Status/Year Series Started Unchanged/2011
Twins. . . . . Chevrolet Malibu
Body Styles . . . . Sedan
Seating. 5
Anti-Theft Device. . . . . . . Std. Pass. Immobil. & Alarm
Parking Index Rating . . . . Average
Where Made . . . . Ontario, Canada
Fuel Factor
MPG Rating (city/hwy). Poor-19/31
Driving Range (mi.) Long-425.6
Fuel Type. Regular/E85
Annual Fuel Cost. . . . . Average-$2106
Gas Guzzler Tax . . . . No
Greenhouse Gas Emissions (tons/yr.) . . Average-8.1
Barrels of Oil Used per year. High-14.9

How the Competition Rates

Competitors	Rating	Pg.
Dodge Avenger	3	124
Lincoln MKZ	3	140
Hyundai Azera	–	156

Price Range

	Retail	Markup
2.4L	$26,670	4%
Premium 2.4L	$29,515	4%
Prem 2 Turbo	$31,285	4%
GS	$34,450	4%

Buick Regal

Specifications

Drive . . . . FWD
Engine. 2.4-liter I4
Transmission . . . . 6-sp. Automatic
Tow Rating (lbs.) . . . . –
Head/Leg Room (in.) Average-38.8/42.1
Interior Space (cu. ft.). Cramped-96.81
Cargo Space (cu. ft.) Cramped-14.2
Wheelbase/Length (in.) 107.8/190.2

Ratings—10 Best, 1 Worst

Combo Crash Tests	–
Safety Features	10
Rollover	7
Preventative Maintenance	–
Repair Costs	–
Warranty	7
Fuel Economy	6
Complaints	–
Insurance Costs	5
OVERALL RATING	–

Buick Verano

At-a-Glance

Status/Year Series Started . . . . All New/2012
Twins . . . . Chevrolet Cruze
Body Styles . . . . Sedan
Seating 5
Anti-Theft Device . . . . Std. Pass. Immobil. & Alarm
Parking Index Rating . . . . Easy
Where Made . . . . Orion Township, MI
Fuel Factor
MPG Rating (city/hwy) Average-22/31
Driving Range (mi.) Short-379.6
Fuel Type . . . . Regular
Annual Fuel Cost . . . . Low-$1915
Gas Guzzler Tax . . . . No
Greenhouse Gas Emissions (tons/yr.) Low-5.9
Barrels of Oil Used per year Average-13.7

How the Competition Rates

Competitors	Rating	Pg.
Audi A3	–	86
Ford Fusion	5	140
Lexus IS	–	191

Price Range

Price Range	Retail	Markup
Base	$22,585	4%
Convenience	$23,785	4%
Leather	$25,965	4%

Buick Verano

Safety Checklist

Crash Tests:
Frontal . . . . –
Side . . . . –
Airbags:
Head . . . . Fr. & Rr. Roof Curtain
Torso . . . . Fr. & Rr. Pelvis/Torso from Seat
Pelvis . . . . Fr. & Rr. Pelvis/Torso from Seat
Roll Sensing . . . . Yes
Knee Bolster . . . . Standard Front
Crash Avoidance:
Frontal Collision Warning . . . . None
Blind Spot Detection . . . . None
Crash Imminent Braking . . . . None
Lane Departure Warning . . . . None
General:
Auto. Crash Notification . . . . Standard
Day Running Lamps . . . . Standard
Safety Belt/Restraint:
Dynamic Head Restraints . . . . None
Adjustable Belt . . . . . . Standard Front and Rear
Pretensioners . . . . Standard Front

Buick Verano

Specifications

Drive . . . . FWD
Engine 2.4-liter I4
Transmission . . . . 6-sp. Automatic
Tow Rating (lbs.) . . . . Very Low-1000
Head/Leg Room (in.) Cramped-38.3/42
Interior Space (cu. ft.) Cramped-95
Cargo Space (cu. ft.) Cramped-15.2
Wheelbase/Length (in.) 105.7/183.9

Ratings—10 Best, 1 Worst

Combo Crash Tests	10
Safety Features	8
Rollover	8
Preventative Maintenance	2
Repair Costs	2
Warranty	7
Fuel Economy	3
Complaints	5
Insurance Costs	5
OVERALL RATING	**7**

Cadillac CTS

Cadillac CTS

At-a-Glance

Status/Year Series Started	Unchanged/2003
Twins	–
Body Styles	Sedan, Coupe, Wagon
Seating	4
Anti-Theft Device	Std. Pass. Immobil.
Parking Index Rating	Easy
Where Made	Lansing, MI

Fuel Factor

MPG Rating (city/hwy)	Poor-18/27
Driving Range (mi.)	Short-381.2
Fuel Type	Regular
Annual Fuel Cost	High-$2288
Gas Guzzler Tax	No
Greenhouse Gas Emissions (tons/yr.)	High-8.9
Barrels of Oil Used per year	High-16.3

How the Competition Rates

Competitors	Rating	Pg.
Acura TL	–	83
Infiniti G	–	167
Lexus ES	–	187

Price Range	Retail	Markup
Base	$38,715	6%
Performance	$43,950	6%
Premium	$48,150	6%
V	$63,215	7%

Safety Checklist

Crash Tests:

Frontal	Very Good
Side	Good

Airbags:

Head	Fr. & Rr. Roof Curtain
Torso	Front Pelvis/Torso from Seat
Pelvis	Front Pelvis/Torso from Seat
Roll Sensing	Yes
Knee Bolster	None

Crash Avoidance:

Frontal Collision Warning	None
Blind Spot Detection	None
Crash Imminent Braking	None
Lane Departure Warning	None

General:

Auto. Crash Notification	Standard
Day Running Lamps	Standard

Safety Belt/Restraint:

Dynamic Head Restraints	Standard Front
Adjustable Belt	Standard Rear
Pretensioners	Standard Front

Cadillac CTS

Specifications

Drive	RWD
Engine	3.6-liter V6
Transmission	6-sp. Automatic
Tow Rating (lbs.)	–
Head/Leg Room (in.)	Very Cramped-36.9/42.4
Interior Space (cu. ft.)	Very Cramped-86.6
Cargo Space (cu. ft.)	Very Cramped-10.5
Wheelbase/Length (in.)	113.4/188.5

Cadillac SRX

Ratings—10 Best, 1 Worst

Combo Crash Tests	9
Safety Features	7
Rollover	4
Preventative Maintenance	2
Repair Costs	3
Warranty	7
Fuel Economy	3
Complaints	4
Insurance Costs	10
OVERALL RATING	**7**

Cadillac SRX

Cadillac SRX

At-a-Glance

Status/Year Series Started Unchanged/2010
Twins . . . . –
Body Styles . . . . SUV
Seating 5
Anti-Theft Device . . . . . . Std. Pass. Immobil. & Alarm
Parking Index Rating . . . . Hard
Where Made . . . . Ramos Arizpe, Mexico
Fuel Factor
MPG Rating (city/hwy) Poor-17/24
Driving Range (mi.) Average-410.9
Fuel Type Regular/E85
Annual Fuel Cost . . . . High-$2476
Gas Guzzler Tax . . . . No
Greenhouse Gas Emissions (tons/yr.) High-9.8
Barrels of Oil Used per year High-18.0

How the Competition Rates

Competitors	Rating	Pg.
Acura MDX	9	81
Lexus RX	4	193
Volvo XC90	–	270

Price Range	Retail	Markup
Base	$35,185	6%
Luxury	$39,715	6%
Performance	$43,530	6%
Premium	$45,975	6%

Safety Checklist

Crash Tests:
Frontal . . . . Very Good
Side . . . . Good
Airbags:
Head . . . . Fr. & Rr. Roof Curtain
Torso . . . . Front Pelvis/Torso from Seat
Pelvis . . . . Front Pelvis/Torso from Seat
Roll Sensing . . . . Yes
Knee Bolster . . . . None
Crash Avoidance:
Frontal Collision Warning . . . . None
Blind Spot Detection . . . . None
Crash Imminent Braking . . . . None
Lane Departure Warning . . . . None
General:
Auto. Crash Notification . . . . Standard
Day Running Lamps . . . . Standard
Safety Belt/Restraint:
Dynamic Head Restraints . . . . None
Adjustable Belt . . . . . . Standard Front and Rear
Pretensioners . . . . Standard Front

Cadillac SRX

Specifications

Drive . . . . FWD
Engine 3.6-liter V6
Transmission . . . . 6-sp. Automatic
Tow Rating (lbs.) Low-3500
Head/Leg Room (in.) Average-39.7/41.2
Interior Space (cu. ft.) Average-100.6
Cargo Space (cu. ft.) Roomy-29.2
Wheelbase/Length (in.) 110.5/190.3

Ratings—10 Best, 1 Worst	Avalanche	Escalade EXT
Combo Crash Tests	–	–
Safety Features	7	7
Rollover	2	3
Preventative Maintenance	2	2
Repair Costs	4	2
Warranty	5	7
Fuel Economy	1	1
Complaints	6	9
Insurance Costs	10	5
OVERALL RATING	–	–

Chevrolet Avalanche

Cadillac Escalade EXT

At-a-Glance

Status/Year Series Started Unchanged/2002
Twins . . . . Cadillac Escalade EXT
Body Styles . . . . SUV, Crew Cab Pickup
Seating 5
Anti-Theft Device . . . . Std. Pass. Immobil. & Alarm
Parking Index Rating . . . . Very Hard
Where Made . . . . Silao, Mexico
Fuel Factor
  MPG Rating (city/hwy) . . . . Very Poor-15/21
  Driving Range (mi.) . . . . Very Long-542.2
  Fuel Type Regular/E85
  Annual Fuel Cost . . . . Very High-$2815
  Gas Guzzler Tax . . . . No
  Greenhouse Gas Emissions (tons/yr.) Very High-11.0
  Barrels of Oil Used per year . . . . Very High-20.1

How the Competition Rates

Competitors	Rating	Pg.
Ram 1500 Quad Cab	2	231
Ford F-150 Super Cab	4	136
Honda Ridgeline	–	154

Price Range	Retail	Markup
LS 2WD	$36,720	8%
LT 2WD	$40,115	8%
LT 4WD	$43,165	8%
LTZ 4WD	$50,225	8%

Safety Checklist

Crash Tests:
  Frontal . . . . –
  Side . . . . –
Airbags:
  Head . . . . Fr. & Rr. Roof Curtain
  Torso . . . . Front Pelvis/Torso from Seat
  Pelvis . . . . Front Pelvis/Torso from Seat
  Roll Sensing . . . . Yes
  Knee Bolster . . . . None
Crash Avoidance:
  Frontal Collision Warning . . . . None
  Blind Spot Detection . . . . Optional
  Crash Imminent Braking . . . . None
  Lane Departure Warning . . . . None
General:
  Auto. Crash Notification . . . . Standard
  Day Running Lamps . . . . Standard
Safety Belt/Restraint:
  Dynamic Head Restraints . . . . None
  Adjustable Belt . . . . . . Standard Front and Rear
  Pretensioners . . . . Standard Front

Specifications

Drive . . . . RWD
Engine 5.3-liter V8
Transmission . . . . 6-sp. Automatic
Tow Rating (lbs.) . . . . Very High-8100
Head/Leg Room (in.) Roomy-41.1/41.3
Interior Space (cu. ft.) Roomy-120.2
Cargo Space (cu. ft.) . . . . Very Roomy-45.5
Wheelbase/Length (in.) 130/221.3

Ratings—10 Best, 1 Worst	
Combo Crash Tests	10
Safety Features	6
Rollover	9
Preventative Maintenance	2
Repair Costs	3
Warranty	5
Fuel Economy	4
Complaints	3
Insurance Costs	3
OVERALL RATING	**6**

Chevrolet Camaro

Chevrolet Camaro

At-a-Glance

Status/Year Series Started Unchanged/2010
Twins . . . . —
Body Styles . . . . Coupe
Seating 4
Anti-Theft Device . . . . Std. Pass. Immobil. & Alarm
Parking Index Rating . . . . Average
Where Made . . . . Ontario, Canada
Fuel Factor
  MPG Rating (city/hwy) Poor-18/29
  Driving Range (mi.) Long-412.4
  Fuel Type. . . . . Regular
  Annual Fuel Cost. . . . . Average-$2232
  Gas Guzzler Tax . . . . No
  Greenhouse Gas Emissions (tons/yr.) High-8.5
  Barrels of Oil Used per year. High-15.6

How the Competition Rates

Competitors	Rating	Pg.
Dodge Challenger	–	126
Ford Mustang	2	141
Nissan 370Z	–	214

Price Range	Retail	Markup
LS	$23,200	4%
LT	$25,200	4%
SS	$31,850	4%

Safety Checklist

Crash Tests:
  Frontal . . . . Very Good
  Side . . . . Very Good
Airbags:
  Head . . . . Fr. & Rr. Roof Curtain
  Torso . . . . Front Pelvis/Torso from Seat
  Pelvis . . . . Front Pelvis/Torso from Seat
  Roll Sensing . . . . Yes
  Knee Bolster . . . . None
Crash Avoidance:
  Frontal Collision Warning. . . . . None
  Blind Spot Detection . . . . None
  Crash Imminent Braking . . . . None
  Lane Departure Warning . . . . None
General:
  Auto. Crash Notification . . . . Standard
  Day Running Lamps . . . . Standard
Safety Belt/Restraint:
  Dynamic Head Restraints . . . . None
  Adjustable Belt . . . . Standard Rear
  Pretensioners . . . . Standard Front

Chevrolet Camaro

Specifications

Drive . . . . RWD
Engine 3.6-liter V6
Transmission . . . . 6-sp. Automatic
Tow Rating (lbs.). . . . . Very Low-1000
Head/Leg Room (in.) Cramped-37.4/42.4
Interior Space (cu. ft.) Cramped-93
Cargo Space (cu. ft.) . . . . Very Cramped-11.3
Wheelbase/Length (in.) 112.3/190.4

Ratings—10 Best, 1 Worst	Colorado	Canyon
Combo Crash Tests	–	–
Safety Features	2	2
Rollover	2	2
Preventative Maintenance	2	2
Repair Costs	3	3
Warranty	5	5
Fuel Economy	3	3
Complaints	9	7
Insurance Costs	5	8
OVERALL RATING	–	–

Chevrolet Colorado

GMC Canyon

At-a-Glance

Status/Year Series Started	Unchanged/2007
Twins	GMC Canyon
Body Styles	Quad, Regular, Crew Cabs
Seating	4/5
Anti-Theft Device	Std. Pass. Immobil.
Parking Index Rating	Very Hard
Where Made	Shreveport, LA

Fuel Factor

MPG Rating (city/hwy)	Poor-18/25
Driving Range (mi.)	Average-403.7
Fuel Type	Regular
Annual Fuel Cost	High-$2353
Gas Guzzler Tax	No
Greenhouse Gas Emissions (tons/yr.)	High-8.9
Barrels of Oil Used per year	High-16.3

How the Competition Rates

Competitors	Rating	Pg.
Honda Ridgeline	–	154
Nissan Frontier	–	219
Toyota Tacoma	1	255

Price Range	Retail	Markup
W/T Regular Cab	$17,395	4%
LT Regular Cab 4WD Z85	$23,265	5%
LT Ext Cab 2WD Z71	$26,080	5%
LT Crew Cab 4WD Z71	$30,240	5%

Safety Checklist

Crash Tests:

Frontal	–
Side	–

Airbags:

Head	Front Roof Curtain
Torso	None
Pelvis	None
Roll Sensing	No
Knee Bolster	None

Crash Avoidance:

Frontal Collision Warning	None
Blind Spot Detection	None
Crash Imminent Braking	None
Lane Departure Warning	None

General:

Auto. Crash Notification	Standard
Day Running Lamps	Standard

Safety Belt/Restraint:

Dynamic Head Restraints	None
Adjustable Belt	Standard Front and Rear
Pretensioners	Standard Front

Chevrolet Colorado

Specifications

Drive	RWD
Engine	2.9-liter I4
Transmission	4-sp. Automatic
Tow Rating (lbs.)	Low-3200
Head/Leg Room (in.)	Very Roomy-39.6/44
Interior Space (cu. ft.)	–
Cargo Space (cu. ft.)	Very Roomy-44
Wheelbase/Length (in.)	126/207.1

Chevrolet Corvette Intermediate

Ratings—10 Best, 1 Worst

Combo Crash Tests	–
Safety Features	2
Rollover	10
Preventative Maintenance	4
Repair Costs	1
Warranty	5
Fuel Economy	2
Complaints	3
Insurance Costs	10
OVERALL RATING	**–**

Chevrolet Corvette

Chevrolet Corvette

At-a-Glance

Status/Year Series Started Unchanged/2005
Twins . . . . –
Body Styles . . . . Coupe, Convertible
Seating 2
Anti-Theft Device . . . . Std. Pass. Immobil. & Alarm
Parking Index Rating . . . . Average
Where Made . . . . Bowling Green, KY
Fuel Factor
MPG Rating (city/hwy) . . . . Very Poor-15/25
Driving Range (mi.) . . . . Very Short-329.3
Fuel Type . . . . Regular
Annual Fuel Cost . . . . Very High-$2649
Gas Guzzler Tax . . . . No
Greenhouse Gas Emissions (tons/yr.) High-10.4
Barrels of Oil Used per year . . . . Very High-19.0

How the Competition Rates

Competitors	Rating	Pg.
Audi A5	–	88
Dodge Avenger	3	124
Ford Mustang	2	141

Price Range	Retail	Markup
Base Coupe	$49,525	10%
GS Convertible	$59,525	10%
Z06 Coupe	$75,525	10%
ZR1 Coupe	$111,525	7%

Safety Checklist

Crash Tests:
Frontal . . . . –
Side . . . . –
Airbags:
Head . . . . Front Head from Seat
Torso . . . . Front Head/Torso from Seat
Pelvis . . . . None
Roll Sensing . . . . No
Knee Bolster . . . . None
Crash Avoidance:
Frontal Collision Warning . . . . None
Blind Spot Detection . . . . None
Crash Imminent Braking . . . . None
Lane Departure Warning . . . . None
General:
Auto. Crash Notification . . . . Standard
Day Running Lamps . . . . Standard
Safety Belt/Restraint:
Dynamic Head Restraints . . . . None
Adjustable Belt . . . . None
Pretensioners . . . . Standard Front

Chevrolet Corvette

Specifications

Drive . . . . RWD
Engine 6.2-liter V8
Transmission . . . . 6-sp. Automatic
Tow Rating (lbs.) . . . . –
Head/Leg Room (in.) Average-38/43
Interior Space (cu. ft.) . . . . Very Cramped-52
Cargo Space (cu. ft.) Average-22
Wheelbase/Length (in.) 105.7/174.6

Ratings—10 Best, 1 Worst	
Combo Crash Tests	10
Safety Features	10
Rollover	7
Preventative Maintenance	–
Repair Costs	–
Warranty	5
Fuel Economy	9
Complaints	5
Insurance Costs	1
OVERALL RATING	9

Chevrolet Cruze

Chevrolet Cruze

At-a-Glance

Status/Year Series Started Unchanged/2010
Twins. . . . . Buick Verano
Body Styles . . . . Sedan
Seating. 5
Anti-Theft Device. . . . . . . Std. Pass. Immobil. & Alarm
Parking Index Rating . . . . Very Easy
Where Made . . . . Lordstown, OH
Fuel Factor
  MPG Rating (city/hwy) . . . . Very Good-26/38
  Driving Range (mi.). . . . . Very Long-472.8
  Fuel Type. . . . . Regular
  Annual Fuel Cost . . . . Very Low-$1599
  Gas Guzzler Tax . . . . No
  Greenhouse Gas Emissions (tons/yr.) Low-6.2
  Barrels of Oil Used per year Low-11.4

How the Competition Rates

Competitors	Rating	Pg.
Ford Focus	6	139
Honda Civic	–	146
Toyota Corolla	4	247

Price Range	Retail	Markup
2LS	$16,720	4%
1LT	$18,475	4%
2LT	$20,605	4%
LTZ	$23,110	5%

Safety Checklist

Crash Tests:
  Frontal . . . . Very Good
  Side . . . . Very Good
Airbags:
  Head . . . . Fr. & Rr. Roof Curtain
  Torso . . . . Fr. & Rr. Pelvis/Torso from Seat
  Pelvis . . . . Fr. & Rr. Pelvis/Torso from Seat
  Roll Sensing . . . . Yes
  Knee Bolster. . . . . Standard Front
Crash Avoidance:
  Frontal Collision Warning. . . . . None
  Blind Spot Detection . . . . None
  Crash Imminent Braking . . . . None
  Lane Departure Warning . . . . None
General:
  Auto. Crash Notification . . . . Standard
  Day Running Lamps . . . . Standard
Safety Belt/Restraint:
  Dynamic Head Restraints . . . . None
  Adjustable Belt . . . . . . Standard Front and Rear
  Pretensioners . . . . Standard Front

Chevrolet Cruze

Specifications

Drive . . . . FWD
Engine. 1.8-liter I4
Transmission . . . . 6-sp. Automatic
Tow Rating (lbs.). . . . . Very Low-1000
Head/Leg Room (in.) Average-39.3/42.3
Interior Space (cu. ft.) Cramped-95
Cargo Space (cu. ft.) Cramped-15.4
Wheelbase/Length (in.) 105.7/181

Ratings—10 Best, 1 Worst

	Equinox	Terrain
Combo Crash Tests	6	6
Safety Features	8	8
Rollover	3	3
Preventative Maintenance	2	2
Repair Costs	3	3
Warranty	5	5
Fuel Economy	3	3
Complaints	4	3
Insurance Costs	8	8
OVERALL RATING	**3**	**4**

Chevrolet Equinox

GMC Terrain

At-a-Glance

Status/Year Series Started Unchanged/2005
Twins . . . . GMC Terrain
Body Styles . . . . SUV
Seating 5
Anti-Theft Device . . . . Std. Pass. Immobil. & Alarm
Parking Index Rating . . . . Hard
Where Made . . . . Ontario, Canada
Fuel Factor
MPG Rating (city/hwy) Poor-17/24
Driving Range (mi.) Short-367.9
Fuel Type Regular/E85
Annual Fuel Cost . . . . High-$2476
Gas Guzzler Tax . . . . No
Greenhouse Gas Emissions (tons/yr.) . . Average-7.2
Barrels of Oil Used per year Average-13.2

How the Competition Rates

Competitors	Rating	Pg.
Dodge Journey	5	130
Ford Escape	2	133
Hyundai Santa Fe	–	160

Price Range

	Retail	Markup
LS	$23,450	5%
LT	$24,970	5%
2LT	$26,790	5%
LTZ	$30,890	5%

Safety Checklist

Crash Tests:
Frontal . . . . Average
Side . . . . Average
Airbags:
Head . . . . Fr. & Rr. Roof Curtain
Torso . . . . Front Pelvis/Torso from Seat
Pelvis . . . . Front Pelvis/Torso from Seat
Roll Sensing . . . . Yes
Knee Bolster . . . . None
Crash Avoidance:
Frontal Collision Warning . . . . Optional
Blind Spot Detection . . . . None
Crash Imminent Braking . . . . None
Lane Departure Warning . . . . Optional
General:
Auto. Crash Notification . . . . Standard
Day Running Lamps . . . . Standard
Safety Belt/Restraint:
Dynamic Head Restraints . . . . None
Adjustable Belt . . . . . . Standard Front and Rear
Pretensioners . . . . Standard Front

Chevrolet Equinox

Specifications

Drive . . . . FWD
Engine 2.4-liter I4
Transmission . . . . 6-sp. Automatic
Tow Rating (lbs.) Low-3500
Head/Leg Room (in.) Roomy-40.9/41.2
Interior Space (cu. ft.) Average-99.7
Cargo Space (cu. ft.) Roomy-31.4
Wheelbase/Length (in.) 112.5/187.8

Ratings—10 Best, 1 Worst

Combo Crash Tests	7
Safety Features	4
Rollover	7
Preventative Maintenance	2
Repair Costs	4
Warranty	5
Fuel Economy	4
Complaints	6
Insurance Costs	5
OVERALL RATING	**4**

Chevrolet Impala

Chevrolet Impala

At-a-Glance

Status/Year Series Started	Unchanged/1999
Twins	–
Body Styles	Sedan
Seating	5
Anti-Theft Device	Std. Pass. Immobil.
Parking Index Rating	Hard
Where Made	Ontario, Canada

Fuel Factor

MPG Rating (city/hwy)	Poor-19/29
Driving Range (mi.)	Average-393.6
Fuel Type	Regular
Annual Fuel Cost	Average-$2154
Gas Guzzler Tax	No
Greenhouse Gas Emissions (tons/yr.)	High-8.5
Barrels of Oil Used per year	High-15.6

How the Competition Rates

Competitors	Rating	Pg.
Dodge Charger	–	127
Ford Taurus	4	142
Toyota Avalon	–	245

Price Range

	Retail	Markup
LS	$25,645	4%
LT	$27,170	4%
LTZ	$30,185	4%

Safety Checklist

Crash Tests:
Frontal . . . . Good
Side . . . . Poor

Airbags:
Head . . . . Fr. & Rr. Roof Curtain
Torso . . . . Front Torso from Seat
Pelvis . . . . None
Roll Sensing . . . . No
Knee Bolster . . . . None

Crash Avoidance:
Frontal Collision Warning . . . . None
Blind Spot Detection . . . . None
Crash Imminent Braking . . . . None
Lane Departure Warning . . . . None

General:
Auto. Crash Notification . . . . Standard
Day Running Lamps . . . . Standard

Safety Belt/Restraint:
Dynamic Head Restraints . . . . None
Adjustable Belt . . . . . . Standard Front and Rear
Pretensioners . . . . Standard Front

Chevrolet Impala

Specifications

Drive	FWD
Engine	3.6-liter V6
Transmission	6-sp. Automatic
Tow Rating (lbs.)	Very Low-1000
Head/Leg Room (in.)	Average-39.4/42.3
Interior Space (cu. ft.)	Roomy-104.5
Cargo Space (cu. ft.)	Average-18.6
Wheelbase/Length (in.)	110.5/200.4

Ratings—10 Best, 1 Worst

Combo Crash Tests	5
Safety Features	4
Rollover	7
Preventative Maintenance	2
Repair Costs	6
Warranty	5
Fuel Economy	6
Complaints	7
Insurance Costs	5
OVERALL RATING	**5**

Chevrolet Malibu

Chevrolet Malibu

At-a-Glance

Status/Year Series Started Unchanged/2012
Twins. . . . . Buick Regal
Body Styles . . . . Sedan
Seating. 5
Anti-Theft Device . . . . Std. Pass. Immobil. & Alarm
Parking Index Rating . . . . Average
Where Made. . . . . Kansas City, KS
Fuel Factor
  MPG Rating (city/hwy) Average-22/33
  Driving Range (mi.) . . . . Very Long-424
  Fuel Type. . . . . Regular
  Annual Fuel Cost . . . . Low-$1872
  Gas Guzzler Tax . . . . No
  Greenhouse Gas Emissions (tons/yr.) . . Average-7.2
  Barrels of Oil Used per year. Average-13.2

How the Competition Rates

Competitors	Rating	Pg.
Ford Fusion	5	140
Honda Accord	8	144
Toyota Camry	10	246

Price Range	Retail	Markup
LS	$21,995	5%
LT	$23,355	5%
3LT	$28,185	5%
2LTZ	$30,085	6%

Safety Checklist

Crash Tests:
  Frontal. . . . . Average
  Side. . . . . Average
Airbags:
  Head . . . . Fr. & Rr. Roof Curtain
  Torso . . . . Front Pelvis/Torso from Seat
  Pelvis . . . . Front Pelvis/Torso from Seat
  Roll Sensing. . . . . No
  Knee Bolster . . . . None
Crash Avoidance:
  Frontal Collision Warning. . . . . None
  Blind Spot Detection . . . . None
  Crash Imminent Braking . . . . None
  Lane Departure Warning . . . . None
General:
  Auto. Crash Notification . . . . Standard
  Day Running Lamps . . . . Standard
Safety Belt/Restraint:
  Dynamic Head Restraints . . . . None
  Adjustable Belt . . . . . . Standard Front and Rear
  Pretensioners . . . . Standard Front

Chevrolet Malibu

Specifications

Drive . . . . FWD
Engine. 2.4-liter I4
Transmission . . . . 6-sp. Automatic
Tow Rating (lbs.) . . . . Very Low-1000
Head/Leg Room (in.) Average-39.4/42.2
Interior Space (cu. ft.). Cramped-97.7
Cargo Space (cu. ft.) Cramped-15.1
Wheelbase/Length (in.) 112.3/191.8

Ratings—10 Best, 1 Worst

	Silverado	Sierra
Combo Crash Tests	7	8
Safety Features	4	4
Rollover	3	3
Preventative Maintenance	2	2
Repair Costs	7	7
Warranty	5	5
Fuel Economy	1	1
Complaints	10	10
Insurance Costs	8	8
OVERALL RATING	**5**	**6**

Chevrolet Silverado

GMC Sierra

At-a-Glance

Status/Year Series Started Unchanged/2007
Twins . . . . GMC Sierra
Body Styles . . . . Pickup
Seating 5/6
Anti-Theft Device . Std. Pass. Immobil. & Opt. Pass. Alarm
Parking Index Rating . . . . Very Hard
Where Made . . . . Mexico / Fort Wayne, IN
Fuel Factor
  MPG Rating (city/hwy) . . . . Very Poor-15/21
  Driving Range (mi.) . . . . Very Long-447.5
  Fuel Type Regular/E85
  Annual Fuel Cost. . . . . Very High-$2815
  Gas Guzzler Tax . . . . No
  Greenhouse Gas Emissions (tons/yr.) Very High-11.0
  Barrels of Oil Used per year . . . . Very High-20.1

How the Competition Rates

Competitors	Rating	Pg.
Ram 1500 Quad Cab	2	231
Ford F-150 Super Cab	4	136
Toyota Tundra	3	256

Price Range

Price Range	Retail	Markup
W/T	$21,945	4%
LS	$29,530	8%
LT	$32,395	8%
Hybrid	$42,415	6%

Safety Checklist

Crash Tests:
  Frontal . . . . Average
  Side . . . . Very Good
Airbags:
  Head . . . . Front Roof Curtain
  Torso . . . . Front Pelvis/Torso from Seat
  Pelvis . . . . Front Pelvis/Torso from Seat
  Roll Sensing . . . . Yes
  Knee Bolster . . . . None
Crash Avoidance:
  Frontal Collision Warning. . . . . None
  Blind Spot Detection . . . . None
  Crash Imminent Braking . . . . None
  Lane Departure Warning . . . . None
General:
  Auto. Crash Notification . . . . Standard
  Day Running Lamps . . . . Standard
Safety Belt/Restraint:
  Dynamic Head Restraints . . . . None
  Adjustable Belt . . . . Standard Front
  Pretensioners . . . . Standard Front

Chevrolet Silverado

Specifications

Drive 4WD
Engine 5.3-liter V8
Transmission . . . . 6-sp. Automatic
Tow Rating (lbs.) . . . . Very High-9500
Head/Leg Room (in.). Roomy-41.2/41.3
Interior Space (cu. ft.) . . . . –
Cargo Space (cu. ft.) . . . . Very Roomy-60.7
Wheelbase/Length (in.). 143.5/230

Ratings—10 Best, 1 Worst

Combo Crash Tests	10
Safety Features	9
Rollover	6
Preventative Maintenance	–
Repair Costs	–
Warranty	5
Fuel Economy	8
Complaints	–
Insurance Costs	5
OVERALL RATING	**9**

Chevrolet Sonic

Chevrolet Sonic

At-a-Glance

Status/Year Series Started . . . . All New/2012
Twins . . . . –
Body Styles. . . . . Hatchback, Sedan
Seating 5
Anti-Theft Device. . . . . . . Std. Pass. Immobil. & Alarm
Parking Index Rating . . . . Very Easy
Where Made . . . . Orion Township, MI
Fuel Factor
  MPG Rating (city/hwy) Good-25/35
  Driving Range (mi.). . . . . Very Short-350.0
  Fuel Type. . . . . Regular
  Annual Fuel Cost . . . . Low-$1679
  Gas Guzzler Tax . . . . No
  Greenhouse Gas Emissions (tons/yr.) . . Average-6.7
  Barrels of Oil Used per year. Average-12.2

How the Competition Rates

Competitors	Rating	Pg.
Ford Fiesta	5	137
Honda Fit	–	150
Mazda 2	–	196

Price Range	Retail	Markup
LS	$13,735	3%
2LS	$14,805	3%
LTZ	$16,535	5%
2LTZ	$18,495	5%

Safety Checklist

Crash Tests:
  Frontal . . . . Very Good
  Side . . . . Very Good
Airbags:
  Head . . . . Fr. & Rr. Roof Curtain
  Torso . . . . Fr. & Rr. Pelvis/Torso from Seat
  Pelvis . . . . Fr. & Rr. Pelvis/Torso from Seat
  Roll Sensing . . . . Yes
  Knee Bolster . . . . Standard Front
Crash Avoidance:
  Frontal Collision Warning. . . . . None
  Blind Spot Detection . . . . None
  Crash Imminent Braking . . . . None
  Lane Departure Warning . . . . None
General:
  Auto. Crash Notification . . . . Standard
  Day Running Lamps . . . . Standard
Safety Belt/Restraint:
  Dynamic Head Restraints . . . . None
  Adjustable Belt . . . . . . Std. Front and Opt. Rear
  Pretensioners . . . . Standard Front

Chevrolet Sonic

Specifications

Drive . . . . FWD
Engine. 1.8-liter I4
Transmission . . . . 6-sp. Automatic
Tow Rating (lbs.) . . . . –
Head/Leg Room (in.) Cramped-38.7/41.8
Interior Space (cu. ft.) Cramped-90.4
Cargo Space (cu. ft.) Cramped-14
Wheelbase/Length (in.) 99.4/173.1

Ratings—10 Best, 1 Worst	Suburban	Escalade ESV	Yukon XL
Combo Crash Tests	10	10	10
Safety Features	7	7	7
Rollover	2	2	2
Preventative Maintenance	2	2	2
Repair Costs	2	2	3
Warranty	5	7	5
Fuel Economy	1	1	1
Complaints	8	8	8
Insurance Costs	10	8	10
OVERALL RATING	6	6	7

Chevrolet Suburban

Safety Checklist

Crash Tests:
Frontal . . . . Very Good
Side . . . . Very Good
Airbags:
Head . . . . Fr. & Rr. Roof Curtain
Torso . . . . Front Pelvis/Torso from Seat
Pelvis . . . . Front Pelvis/Torso from Seat
Roll Sensing . . . . Yes
Knee Bolster . . . . None
Crash Avoidance:
Frontal Collision Warning. . . . . None
Blind Spot Detection . . . . Optional
Crash Imminent Braking . . . . None
Lane Departure Warning . . . . None
General:
Auto. Crash Notification . . . . Standard
Day Running Lamps . . . . Standard
Safety Belt/Restraint:
Dynamic Head Restraints . . . . None
Adjustable Belt . . . . . . Standard Front and Rear
Pretensioners . . . . Standard Front

Cadillac Escalade ESV

At-a-Glance

Status/Year Series Started Unchanged/2007
Twins . . . . . . Cadillac Escalade ESV, GMC Yukon XL
Body Styles. . . . . SUV
Seating 6/9
Anti-Theft Device. . . . . . . Std. Pass. Immobil. & Alarm
Parking Index Rating . . . . Very Hard
Where Made . . . . Arlington, TX
Fuel Factor
MPG Rating (city/hwy). . . . . Very Poor-15/21
Driving Range (mi.) . . . . Very Long-542.2
Fuel Type. Regular/E85
Annual Fuel Cost. . . . . Very High-$2815
Gas Guzzler Tax . . . . No
Greenhouse Gas Emissions (tons/yr.) Very High-11.0
Barrels of Oil Used per year . . . . Very High-20.1

How the Competition Rates

Competitors	Rating	Pg.
Dodge Durango	4	128
Ford Expedition	–	134
Nissan Armada	–	217

Price Range	Retail	Markup
1500 LS	$41,915	8%
1500 LT	$45,675	8%
2500 LT	$47,265	8%
1500 LTZ	$57,810	8%

GMC Yukon XL

Specifications

Drive . . . . RWD
Engine 5.3-liter V8
Transmission . . . . 6-sp. Automatic
Tow Rating (lbs.) . . . . Very High-8100
Head/Leg Room (in.). Roomy-41.1/41.3
Interior Space (cu. ft.) . . . . Very Roomy-137.4
Cargo Space (cu. ft.). . . . . Very Roomy-45.8
Wheelbase/Length (in.) 130/222.4

Ratings—10 Best, 1 Worst	Tahoe	Escalade	Yukon
Combo Crash Tests	9	9	9
Safety Features	7	7	7
Rollover	1	1	1
Preventative Maintenance	2	2	2
Repair Costs	6	6	6
Warranty	5	7	5
Fuel Economy	1	1	1
Complaints	8	8	8
Insurance Costs	10	8	10
OVERALL RATING	7	7	6

Chevrolet Tahoe

Safety Checklist

Crash Tests:
Frontal . . . . Very Good
Side . . . . Good
Airbags:
Head . . . . Fr. & Rr. Roof Curtain
Torso . . . . Front Pelvis/Torso from Seat
Pelvis . . . . Front Pelvis/Torso from Seat
Roll Sensing . . . . Yes
Knee Bolster . . . . None
Crash Avoidance:
Frontal Collision Warning. . . . . None
Blind Spot Detection . . . . Optional
Crash Imminent Braking . . . . None
Lane Departure Warning . . . . None
General:
Auto. Crash Notification . . . . Standard
Day Running Lamps . . . . Standard
Safety Belt/Restraint:
Dynamic Head Restraints . . . . None
Adjustable Belt . . . . . . Standard Front and Rear
Pretensioners . . . . Standard Front

Cadillac Escalade

At-a-Glance

Status/Year Series Started Unchanged/2007
Twins . . . . Cadillac Escalade, GMC Yukon
Body Styles . . . . SUV
Seating 6/9
Anti-Theft Device . . . . Std. Pass. Immobil. & Alarm
Parking Index Rating . . . . Very Hard
Where Made . . . . Arlington, TX
Fuel Factor
MPG Rating (city/hwy) . . . . Very Poor-15/21
Driving Range (mi.) . . . . Very Long-447.5
Fuel Type Regular/E85
Annual Fuel Cost. . . . . Very High-$2815
Gas Guzzler Tax . . . . No
Greenhouse Gas Emissions (tons/yr.) Very High-11.0
Barrels of Oil Used per year . . . . Very High-20.1

How the Competition Rates

Competitors	Rating	Pg.
Ford Expedition	–	134
Nissan Armada	–	217
Toyota Sequoia	–	253

Price Range	Retail	Markup
LS	$38,450	8%
LT	$43,600	8%
LTZ	$52,665	8%
Hybrid	$54,470	6%

GMC Yukon

Specifications

Drive . . . . RWD
Engine 5.3-liter V8
Transmission . . . . 6-sp. Automatic
Tow Rating (lbs.) . . . . Very High-8500
Head/Leg Room (in.) Roomy-41.1/41.3
Interior Space (cu. ft.) Roomy-108.9
Cargo Space (cu. ft.) Average-16.9
Wheelbase/Length (in.) 116/205

Ratings—10 Best, 1 Worst	
Combo Crash Tests	9
Safety Features	7
Rollover	4
Preventative Maintenance	3
Repair Costs	4
Warranty	5
Fuel Economy	3
Complaints	9
Insurance Costs	10
OVERALL RATING	**8**

Chevrolet Traverse

Chevrolet Traverse

At-a-Glance

Status/Year Series Started	Unchanged/2009
Twins	GMC Acadia
Body Styles	SUV
Seating	7/8
Anti-Theft Device	Std. Pass. Immobil. & Alarm
Parking Index Rating	Very Hard
Where Made	Lansing, MI
Fuel Factor	
MPG Rating (city/hwy)	Poor-17/24
Driving Range (mi.)	Long-430.5
Fuel Type	Regular
Annual Fuel Cost	High-$2476
Gas Guzzler Tax	No
Greenhouse Gas Emissions (tons/yr.)	High-9.8
Barrels of Oil Used per year	High-18.0

How the Competition Rates

Competitors	Rating	Pg.
Ford Flex	–	138
Honda Pilot	4	153
Toyota Highlander	4	249

Price Range	Retail	Markup
LS	$29,430	5%
LT	$32,530	5%
2LT	$35,675	5%
LTZ	$38,805	5%

Safety Checklist

Crash Tests:
Frontal . . . . Good
Side . . . . Very Good

Airbags:
Head . . . . Fr. & Rr. Roof Curtain
Torso . . . . Front Pelvis/Torso from Seat
Pelvis . . . . Front Pelvis/Torso from Seat
Roll Sensing . . . . Yes
Knee Bolster . . . . None

Crash Avoidance:
Frontal Collision Warning . . . . None
Blind Spot Detection . . . . None
Crash Imminent Braking . . . . None
Lane Departure Warning . . . . None

General:
Auto. Crash Notification . . . . Standard
Day Running Lamps . . . . Standard

Safety Belt/Restraint:
Dynamic Head Restraints . . . . None
Adjustable Belt . . . . . . Standard Front and Rear
Pretensioners . . . . Standard Front

Chevrolet Traverse

Specifications

Drive	FWD
Engine	3.6-liter V6
Transmission	6-sp. Automatic
Tow Rating (lbs.)	Average-5200
Head/Leg Room (in.)	Average-40.4/41.3
Interior Space (cu. ft.)	Very Roomy-153.1
Cargo Space (cu. ft.)	Roomy-24.4
Wheelbase/Length (in.)	118.9/205

Ratings—10 Best, 1 Worst

Combo Crash Tests**	8
Safety Features	8
Rollover	9
Preventative Maintenance	–
Repair Costs	–
Warranty	5
Fuel Economy	10
Complaints	2
Insurance Costs	5
OVERALL RATING	**8**

Chevrolet Volt

At-a-Glance

Status/Year Series Started Unchanged/2011
Twins . . . . –
Body Styles . . . . Hatchback
Seating 4
Anti-Theft Device . . . . Std. Pass. Immobil. & Alarm
Parking Index Rating . . . . Easy
Where Made . . . . Hamtramck, MI

Fuel Factor

  MPG Rating (city/hwy) . Very Good-35/40 (Gas Only)
  Driving Range (mi.) . . . . Very Short-352.3
  Fuel Type . . . . Premium
  Annual Fuel Cost . . . . Very Low-$1416
  Gas Guzzler Tax . . . . No
  Greenhouse Gas Emissions (tons/yr.) . Very Low-5.1
  Barrels of Oil Used per year . . . . Very Low-9.3

How the Competition Rates

Competitors	Rating	Pg.
Nissan Leaf	5	221
Toyota Prius	7	251
Volkswagen Jetta	5	262

Price Range	Retail	Markup
4D Hatchback	$39,145	4%

Chevrolet Volt

Safety Checklist*

Crash Tests:**
  Frontal . . . . Good
  Side . . . . Good
Airbags:
  Head . . . . Fr. & Rr. Roof Curtain
  Torso . . . . Front Pelvis/Torso from Seat
  Pelvis . . . . Front Pelvis/Torso from Seat
  Roll Sensing . . . . Yes
  Knee Bolster . . . . Standard Front
Crash Avoidance:
  Frontal Collision Warning . . . . None
  Blind Spot Detection . . . . None
  Crash Imminent Braking . . . . None
  Lane Departure Warning . . . . None
General:
  Auto. Crash Notification . . . . Standard
  Day Running Lamps . . . . Standard
Safety Belt/Restraint:
  Dynamic Head Restraints . . . . None
  Adjustable Belt . . . . . . Standard Front and Rear
  Pretensioners . . . . Standard Front

Chevrolet Volt

Specifications

Drive . . . . FWD
Engine 1.4-liter I4
Transmission . . . . Automatic
Tow Rating (lbs.) . . . . –
Head/Leg Room (in.) Cramped-37.8/42
Interior Space (cu. ft.) . . . . Very Cramped-90
Cargo Space (cu. ft.) . . . . Very Cramped-10.6
Wheelbase/Length (in.) 105.7/177.1

*Best Bet designation is for Volts produced after January 2012. Chevrolet upgraded the steel structure surrounding the battery to prevent the electrical fire hazard reported by NHTSA after their crash test.**See page 20 for further details.

Ratings—10 Best, 1 Worst	
Combo Crash Tests	3
Safety Features	4
Rollover	7
Preventative Maintenance	–
Repair Costs	–
Warranty	4
Fuel Economy	5
Complaints	8
Insurance Costs	3
OVERALL RATING	**3**

Chrysler 200

Chrysler 200

At-a-Glance

Status/Year Series Started Unchanged/2011
Twins . . . . Dodge Avenger
Body Styles . . . . Sedan
Seating 5
Anti-Theft Device . . . . Std. Pass. Immobil. & Alarm
Parking Index Rating . . . . Average
Where Made . . . . Sterling Heights, MI
Fuel Factor
  MPG Rating (city/hwy) Average-20/31
  Driving Range (mi.) Average-402.2
  Fuel Type . . . . Regular
  Annual Fuel Cost . . . . Average-$2036
  Gas Guzzler Tax . . . . No
  Greenhouse Gas Emissions (tons/yr.) . . Average-7.8
  Barrels of Oil Used per year High-14.3

How the Competition Rates

Competitors	Rating	Pg.
Chevrolet Malibu	4	114
Ford Fusion	5	140
Nissan Maxima	4	222

Price Range	Retail	Markup
LX	$18,995	1%
Touring	$21,370	4%
Limited	$24,070	4%
S	$26,365	5%

Chrysler 200

Safety Checklist

Crash Tests:
  Frontal . . . . Poor
  Side . . . . Very Poor
Airbags:
  Head . . . . Fr. & Rr. Roof Curtain
  Torso . . . . Front Torso from Seat
  Pelvis . . . . None
  Roll Sensing . . . . No
  Knee Bolster . . . . None
Crash Avoidance:
  Frontal Collision Warning . . . . None
  Blind Spot Detection . . . . None
  Crash Imminent Braking . . . . None
  Lane Departure Warning . . . . None
General:
  Auto. Crash Notification . . . . None
  Day Running Lamps . . . . Optional
Safety Belt/Restraint:
  Dynamic Head Restraints . . . . . . Standard Front
  Adjustable Belt . . . . Standard Front
  Pretensioners . . . . Standard Front

Chrysler 200

Specifications

Drive . . . . FWD
Engine 2.4-liter I4
Transmission . . . . 6-sp. Auto. w/ Overdrive
Tow Rating (lbs.) . . . . Very Low-1000
Head/Leg Room (in.) Roomy-40.1/42.4
Interior Space (cu. ft.) Average-100.3
Cargo Space (cu. ft.) Cramped-13.6
Wheelbase/Length (in.) 108.9/191.7

Ratings—10 Best, 1 Worst

Combo Crash Tests	–
Safety Features	7
Rollover	8
Preventative Maintenance	3
Repair Costs	9
Warranty	4
Fuel Economy	3
Complaints	5
Insurance Costs	5
OVERALL RATING	–

Chrysler 300

Chrysler 300

At-a-Glance

Status/Year Series Started	Unchanged/2011
Twins	Dodge Charger
Body Styles	Sedan
Seating	5
Anti-Theft Device	Std. Pass. Immobil. & Alarm
Parking Index Rating	Hard
Where Made	Brampton, Ontario

Fuel Factor

MPG Rating (city/hwy)	Poor-18/27
Driving Range (mi.)	Average-404.5
Fuel Type	Regular
Annual Fuel Cost	High-$2288
Gas Guzzler Tax	No
Greenhouse Gas Emissions (tons/yr.)	High-8.9
Barrels of Oil Used per year	High-16.3

How the Competition Rates

Competitors	Rating	Pg.
Buick LaCrosse	9	102
Chevrolet Impala	4	113
Lincoln MKS	–	194

Price Range	Retail	Markup
Base	$27,170	3%
Limited	$34,320	5%
S	$39,170	5%
SRT8	$47,170	3%

Safety Checklist

Crash Tests:

Frontal	–
Side	–

Airbags:

Head	Fr. & Rr. Roof Curtain
Torso	Front Pelvis/Torso from Seat
Pelvis	Front Pelvis/Torso from Seat
Roll Sensing	No
Knee Bolster	Standard Driver

Crash Avoidance:

Frontal Collision Warning	Optional
Blind Spot Detection	Optional
Crash Imminent Braking	None
Lane Departure Warning	None

General:

Auto. Crash Notification	None
Day Running Lamps	Optional

Safety Belt/Restraint:

Dynamic Head Restraints	Standard Front
Adjustable Belt	Standard Front
Pretensioners	Standard Front

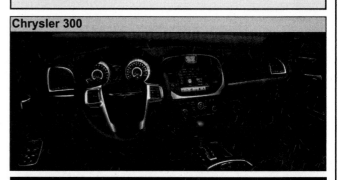

Chrysler 300

Specifications

Drive	RWD
Engine	3.6-liter V6
Transmission	5-sp. Auto. w/Overdrive
Tow Rating (lbs.)	Very Low-1000
Head/Leg Room (in.)	Cramped-38.6/41.8
Interior Space (cu. ft.)	Roomy-106.3
Cargo Space (cu. ft.)	Average-16.3
Wheelbase/Length (in.)	120.2/198.6

Ratings—10 Best, 1 Worst

Combo Crash Tests	6
Safety Features	8
Rollover	4
Preventative Maintenance	3
Repair Costs	8
Warranty	4
Fuel Economy	3
Complaints	2
Insurance Costs	10
OVERALL RATING	**5**

Chrysler Town and Country

Chrysler Town and Country

Chrysler Town and Country

At-a-Glance

Status/Year Series Started Unchanged/2008
Twins . . . . Dodge Grand Caravan
Body Styles . . . . Minivan
Seating. 7
Anti-Theft Device. . . . . . . Std. Pass. Immobil. & Alarm
Parking Index Rating . . . . Very Hard
Where Made . . . . Windsor, Ontario
Fuel Factor
  MPG Rating (city/hwy). Poor-17/25
  Driving Range (mi.) Average-397.2
  Fuel Type. Regular/E85
  Annual Fuel Cost. . . . . High-$2440
  Gas Guzzler Tax . . . . No
  Greenhouse Gas Emissions (tons/yr.) High-9.3
  Barrels of Oil Used per year. High-17.1

How the Competition Rates

Competitors	Rating	Pg.
Honda Odyssey	7	152
Kia Sedona	–	180
Volkswagen Routan	–	264

Price Range	Retail	Markup
Touring	$30,360	5%
Touring L	$32,835	6%
Limited	$39,300	6%

Safety Checklist

Crash Tests:
  Frontal . . . . Good
  Side. . . . . Poor
Airbags:
  Head . . . . Fr. & Rr. Roof Curtain
  Torso . . . . Front Pelvis/Torso from Seat
  Pelvis . . . . Front Pelvis/Torso from Seat
  Roll Sensing . . . . Yes
  Knee Bolster . . . . Standard Driver
Crash Avoidance:
  Frontal Collision Warning. . . . . None
  Blind Spot Detection . . . . Optional
  Crash Imminent Braking . . . . None
  Lane Departure Warning . . . . None
General:
  Auto. Crash Notification. . . . . None
  Day Running Lamps. . . . . Optional
Safety Belt/Restraint:
  Dynamic Head Restraints. . . . . . Standard Front
  Adjustable Belt . . . . . . Standard Front and Rear
  Pretensioners . . . . Standard Front

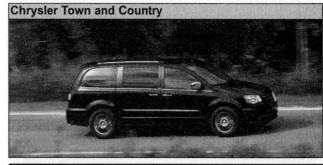

Chrysler Town and Country

Specifications

Drive . . . . FWD
Engine 3.6-liter V6
Transmission . . . . 6-sp. Auto. w/ Overdrive
Tow Rating (lbs.) Low-3600
Head/Leg Room (in.) Cramped-39.8/40.7
Interior Space (cu. ft.) . . . . Very Roomy-163.5
Cargo Space (cu. ft.) . . . . Very Roomy-33
Wheelbase/Length (in.) 121.2/202.8

Dodge Avenger

Ratings—10 Best, 1 Worst

Combo Crash Tests	3
Safety Features	4
Rollover	7
Preventative Maintenance	7
Repair Costs	10
Warranty	4
Fuel Economy	5
Complaints	3
Insurance Costs	1
OVERALL RATING	**3**

Dodge Avenger

Dodge Avenger

Dodge Avenger

At-a-Glance

Status/Year Series Started Unchanged/2008
Twins . . . . Chrysler 200
Body Styles . . . . Sedan
Seating 5
Anti-Theft Device . . . . Std. Pass. Immobil. & Alarm
Parking Index Rating . . . . Average
Where Made . . . . Sterling Heights, MI
Fuel Factor
  MPG Rating (city/hwy) Average-21/30
  Driving Range (mi.) Average-410.3
  Fuel Type . . . . Regular
  Annual Fuel Cost . . . . Average-$1996
  Gas Guzzler Tax . . . . No
  Greenhouse Gas Emissions (tons/yr.) . . Average-7.8
  Barrels of Oil Used per year High-14.3

How the Competition Rates

Competitors	Rating	Pg.
Chevrolet Impala	4	113
Ford Fusion	5	140
Nissan Maxima	4	222

Price Range	Retail	Markup
SE	$18,995	1%
SXT	$21,495	4%
SXT Plus	$23,995	5%
R/T	$25,995	5%

Safety Checklist

Crash Tests:
  Frontal . . . . Poor
  Side . . . . Poor
Airbags:
  Head . . . . Fr. & Rr. Roof Curtain
  Torso . . . . Front Torso from Seat
  Pelvis . . . . None
  Roll Sensing . . . . No
  Knee Bolster . . . . None
Crash Avoidance:
  Frontal Collision Warning . . . . None
  Blind Spot Detection . . . . None
  Crash Imminent Braking . . . . None
  Lane Departure Warning . . . . None
General:
  Auto. Crash Notification . . . . None
  Day Running Lamps . . . . Optional
Safety Belt/Restraint:
  Dynamic Head Restraints . . . . . . Standard Front
  Adjustable Belt . . . . Standard Front
  Pretensioners . . . . Standard Front

Dodge Avenger

Specifications

Drive . . . . FWD
Engine 2.4-liter I4
Transmission . . . . 4-sp. Auto. w/Overdrive
Tow Rating (lbs.) . . . . Very Low-1000
Head/Leg Room (in.) Roomy-40/42.4
Interior Space (cu. ft.) Average-100.2
Cargo Space (cu. ft.) Cramped-13.5
Wheelbase/Length (in.) 108.9/192.6

Ratings—10 Best, 1 Worst

Combo Crash Tests	3
Safety Features	5
Rollover	4
Preventative Maintenance	4
Repair Costs	10
Warranty	4
Fuel Economy	6
Complaints	4
Insurance Costs	3
OVERALL RATING	**3**

Dodge Caliber

Dodge Caliber

At-a-Glance

Status/Year Series Started Unchanged/2006
Twins . . . . –
Body Styles . . . . Hatchback
Seating 5
Anti-Theft Device . . . . Std. Pass. Immobil.
Parking Index Rating . . . . Easy
Where Made . . . . Belvedere, IL
Fuel Factor
  MPG Rating (city/hwy) Average-23/27
  Driving Range (mi.) . . . . Very Short-335.1
  Fuel Type . . . . Regular
  Annual Fuel Cost . . . . Low-$1966
  Gas Guzzler Tax . . . . No
  Greenhouse Gas Emissions (tons/yr.) . . Average-7.8
  Barrels of Oil Used per year High-14.3

How the Competition Rates

Competitors	Rating	Pg.
Ford Focus	6	139
Subaru Impreza	–	238
Toyota Matrix	–	250

Price Range	Retail	Markup
SE	$17,380	3%
SXT Plus	$18,730	3%
SXT	$18,765	3%

Safety Checklist

Crash Tests:
  Frontal . . . . Poor
  Side . . . . Very Poor
Airbags:
  Head . . . . Fr. & Rr. Roof Curtain
  Torso . . . . Opt. Front Pelvis/Torso from Seat
  Pelvis . . . . None
  Roll Sensing . . . . No
  Knee Bolster . . . . Standard Driver
Crash Avoidance:
  Frontal Collision Warning . . . . None
  Blind Spot Detection . . . . None
  Crash Imminent Braking . . . . None
  Lane Departure Warning . . . . None
General:
  Auto. Crash Notification . . . . None
  Day Running Lamps . . . . Optional
Safety Belt/Restraint:
  Dynamic Head Restraints . . . . . . Standard Front
  Adjustable Belt . . . . Standard Front
  Pretensioners . . . . Standard Front

Dodge Caliber

Specifications

Drive . . . . FWD
Engine 2.0-liter I4
Transmission . . . . CVT
Tow Rating (lbs.) . . . . Very Low-1000
Head/Leg Room (in.) Average-39.8/41.8
Interior Space (cu. ft.) Cramped-96.2
Cargo Space (cu. ft.) Average-18.4
Wheelbase/Length (in.) 103.7/173.8

Ratings—10 Best, 1 Worst

Combo Crash Tests	–
Safety Features	3
Rollover	9
Preventative Maintenance	1
Repair Costs	9
Warranty	4
Fuel Economy	3
Complaints	2
Insurance Costs	3
OVERALL RATING	–

Dodge Challenger

At-a-Glance

Status/Year Series Started Unchanged/2009
Twins . . . . –
Body Styles . . . . Coupe
Seating 5
Anti-Theft Device . . . . Std. Pass. Immobil. & Alarm
Parking Index Rating . . . . Hard
Where Made . . . . Brampton, Ontario
Fuel Factor
MPG Rating (city/hwy) Poor-18/27
Driving Range (mi.) Average-404.5
Fuel Type . . . . Regular
Annual Fuel Cost . . . . High-$2288
Gas Guzzler Tax . . . . No
Greenhouse Gas Emissions (tons/yr.) High-8.9
Barrels of Oil Used per year High-16.3

How the Competition Rates

Competitors	Rating	Pg.
Chevrolet Camaro	5	108
Ford Mustang	2	141
Hyundai Equus	–	158

Price Range	Retail	Markup
SXT	$24,995	3%
R/T	$29,995	4%
SRT8	$43,995	3%

Dodge Challenger

Safety Checklist

Crash Tests:
Frontal . . . . –
Side . . . . –
Airbags:
Head . . . . Fr. & Rr. Roof Curtain
Torso . . . . Front Pelvis/Torso from Seat
Pelvis . . . . Front Pelvis/Torso from Seat
Roll Sensing . . . . No
Knee Bolster . . . . None
Crash Avoidance:
Frontal Collision Warning . . . . None
Blind Spot Detection . . . . None
Crash Imminent Braking . . . . None
Lane Departure Warning . . . . None
General:
Auto. Crash Notification . . . . None
Day Running Lamps . . . . Optional
Safety Belt/Restraint:
Dynamic Head Restraints . . . . . . Standard Front
Adjustable Belt . . . . None
Pretensioners . . . . Standard Front

Dodge Challenger

Specifications

Drive . . . . RWD
Engine 3.6-liter V6
Transmission . . . . 5-sp. Auto. w/Overdrive
Tow Rating (lbs.) . . . . Very Low-1000
Head/Leg Room (in.) Average-39.3/42
Interior Space (cu. ft.) Cramped-91.5
Cargo Space (cu. ft.) Average-16.2
Wheelbase/Length (in.) 116/197.7

Ratings—10 Best, 1 Worst

Combo Crash Tests	–
Safety Features	7
Rollover	8
Preventative Maintenance	3
Repair Costs	7
Warranty	4
Fuel Economy	3
Complaints	6
Insurance Costs	3
OVERALL RATING	–

Dodge Charger

At-a-Glance

Status/Year Series Started Unchanged/2006
Twins . . . . Chrysler 300
Body Styles . . . . Sedan
Seating 5
Anti-Theft Device . . . . Std. Pass. Immobil. & Alarm
Parking Index Rating . . . . Hard
Where Made . . . . Brampton, Ontario
Fuel Factor
MPG Rating (city/hwy) Poor-18/27
Driving Range (mi.) Average-404.5
Fuel Type . . . . Regular
Annual Fuel Cost . . . . High-$2288
Gas Guzzler Tax . . . . No
Greenhouse Gas Emissions (tons/yr.) High-8.9
Barrels of Oil Used per year High-16.3

How the Competition Rates

Competitors	Rating	Pg.
Chrysler 300	–	122
Ford Taurus	4	142
Lincoln MKS	–	194

Price Range	Retail	Markup
SE	$25,495	4%
SXT	$28,495	4%
R/T	$29,995	4%
SRT8	$45,795	4%

Dodge Charger

Safety Checklist

Crash Tests:
Frontal . . . . –
Side . . . . –
Airbags:
Head . . . . Fr. & Rr. Roof Curtain
Torso . . . . Front Pelvis/Torso from Seat
Pelvis . . . . Front Pelvis/Torso from Seat
Roll Sensing . . . . No
Knee Bolster . . . . Standard Driver
Crash Avoidance:
Frontal Collision Warning . . . . Optional
Blind Spot Detection . . . . Optional
Crash Imminent Braking . . . . None
Lane Departure Warning . . . . None
General:
Auto. Crash Notification . . . . None
Day Running Lamps . . . . Optional
Safety Belt/Restraint:
Dynamic Head Restraints . . . . . . Standard Front
Adjustable Belt . . . . Standard Front
Pretensioners . . . . Standard Front

Dodge Charger

Specifications

Drive . . . . RWD
Engine 3.6-liter V6
Transmission . . . . 5-sp. Auto. w/Overdrive
Tow Rating (lbs.) . . . . Very Low-1000
Head/Leg Room (in.) Cramped-38.6/41.8
Interior Space (cu. ft.) Roomy-104.7
Cargo Space (cu. ft.) Average-16.5
Wheelbase/Length (in.) 120.2/199.9

Ratings—10 Best, 1 Worst

Combo Crash Tests	2
Safety Features	8
Rollover	2
Preventative Maintenance	3
Repair Costs	7
Warranty	4
Fuel Economy	2
Complaints	10
Insurance Costs	10
OVERALL RATING	**4**

Dodge Durango

Dodge Durango

At-a-Glance

Status/Year Series Started Unchanged/2011
Twins . . . . –
Body Styles . . . . SUV
Seating 7
Anti-Theft Device . . . . Std. Pass. Immobil. & Alarm
Parking Index Rating . . . . Hard
Where Made . . . . Detroit, MI
Fuel Factor
  MPG Rating (city/hwy) . . . . Very Poor-16/23
  Driving Range (mi.) . . . . Very Long-456.1
  Fuel Type Regular/E85
  Annual Fuel Cost . . . . High-$2613
  Gas Guzzler Tax . . . . No
  Greenhouse Gas Emissions (tons/yr.) High-9.8
  Barrels of Oil Used per year High-18.0

How the Competition Rates

Competitors	Rating	Pg.
Chevrolet Tahoe	6	118
Ford Expedition	–	134
Toyota 4Runner	–	244

Price Range	Retail	Markup
SXT	$28,995	5%
Crew	$33,695	6%
R/T	$35,795	6%
Citadel	$40,995	6%

Safety Checklist

Crash Tests:
  Frontal . . . . Poor
  Side . . . . Very Poor
Airbags:
  Head . . . . Fr. & Rr. Roof Curtain
  Torso . . . . Front Pelvis/Torso from Seat
  Pelvis . . . . Front Pelvis/Torso from Seat
  Roll Sensing . . . . Yes
  Knee Bolster . . . . None
Crash Avoidance:
  Frontal Collision Warning . . . . Optional
  Blind Spot Detection . . . . Optional
  Crash Imminent Braking . . . . Optional
  Lane Departure Warning . . . . None
General:
  Auto. Crash Notification . . . . None
  Day Running Lamps . . . . Optional
Safety Belt/Restraint:
  Dynamic Head Restraints . . . . . . Standard Front
  Adjustable Belt . . . . Standard Front
  Pretensioners . . . . Standard Front

Dodge Durango

Specifications

Drive . . . . AWD
Engine 3.6-liter V6
Transmission . . . . 5-sp. Auto. w/Overdrive
Tow Rating (lbs.) Average-6200
Head/Leg Room (in.) Cramped-39.9/40.3
Interior Space (cu. ft.) . . . . Very Roomy-141
Cargo Space (cu. ft.) Average-17.2
Wheelbase/Length (in.) 119.8/199.8

Dodge Grand Caravan   Minivan

Ratings—10 Best, 1 Worst

Combo Crash Tests	6
Safety Features	8
Rollover	4
Preventative Maintenance	3
Repair Costs	8
Warranty	4
Fuel Economy	3
Complaints	3
Insurance Costs	8
OVERALL RATING	**5**

Dodge Grand Caravan

Dodge Grand Caravan

Safety Checklist

Crash Tests:
Frontal . . . . Good
Side. . . . . Poor
Airbags:
Head . . . . Fr. & Rr. Roof Curtain
Torso . . . . Front Pelvis/Torso from Seat
Pelvis . . . . Front Pelvis/Torso from Seat
Roll Sensing . . . . Yes
Knee Bolster . . . . Standard Driver
Crash Avoidance:
Frontal Collision Warning. . . . . None
Blind Spot Detection . . . . Optional
Crash Imminent Braking . . . . None
Lane Departure Warning . . . . None
General:
Auto. Crash Notification. . . . . None
Day Running Lamps . . . . Optional
Safety Belt/Restraint:
Dynamic Head Restraints. . . . . . Standard Front
Adjustable Belt . . . . . . Standard Front and Rear
Pretensioners . . . . Standard Front

At-a-Glance

Status/Year Series Started Unchanged/2008
Twins . . . . Chrysler Town & Country
Body Styles . . . . Minivan
Seating. 7
Anti-Theft Device. . . . . Std. Pass. Immobil.
Parking Index Rating . . . . Very Hard
Where Made . . . . Windsor, Ontario
Fuel Factor
 MPG Rating (city/hwy). Poor-17/25
 Driving Range (mi.) Average-397.2
 Fuel Type. Regular/E85
 Annual Fuel Cost. . . . . High-$2440
 Gas Guzzler Tax . . . . No
 Greenhouse Gas Emissions (tons/yr.) High-9.3
 Barrels of Oil Used per year. High-17.1

How the Competition Rates

Competitors	Rating	Pg.
Honda Odyssey	7	152
Toyota Sienna	1	254
Volkswagen Routan	–	264

Price Range	Retail	Markup
SE	$22,995	2%
SXT	$26,495	4%
Crew	$28,495	4%
R/T	$29,995	5%

Dodge Grand Caravan

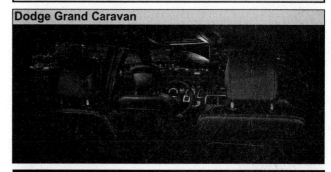

Specifications

Drive . . . . FWD
Engine 3.6-liter V6
Transmission . . . . 6-sp. Auto. w/ Overdrive
Tow Rating (lbs.). Low-3600
Head/Leg Room (in.) Cramped-39.8/40.7
Interior Space (cu. ft.) . . . . Very Roomy-163.5
Cargo Space (cu. ft.) . . . . Very Roomy-33
Wheelbase/Length (in.) 121.2/202.8

Ratings—10 Best, 1 Worst

Combo Crash Tests	5
Safety Features	6
Rollover	3
Preventative Maintenance	7
Repair Costs	10
Warranty	4
Fuel Economy	4
Complaints	1
Insurance Costs	8
OVERALL RATING	**5**

Dodge Journey

Dodge Journey

At-a-Glance

```
Status/Year Series Started . . . . . . . . Unchanged/2009
Twins . . . . . . . . . . . . . . . . . . . . . . . . . . . . . . . . . . . –
Body Styles. . . . . . . . . . . . . . . . . . . . . . . . . . . . . . SUV
Seating . . . . . . . . . . . . . . . . . . . . . . . . . . . . . . . . . 5/7
Anti-Theft Device. . . . . . . Std. Pass. Immobil. & Alarm
Parking Index Rating . . . . . . . . . . . . . . . . . . . . . Hard
Where Made. . . . . . . . . . . . . . . . . Toluca, Mexico
```

Fuel Factor
```
MPG Rating (city/hwy) . . . . . . . . . . . . . . Poor-19/26
Driving Range (mi.) . . . . . . . . . . . . Very Long-443.2
Fuel Type. . . . . . . . . . . . . . . . . . . . . . . . . . Regular
Annual Fuel Cost. . . . . . . . . . . . . . Average-$2241
Gas Guzzler Tax . . . . . . . . . . . . . . . . . . . . . . . . No
Greenhouse Gas Emissions (tons/yr.) . . . . . High-8.5
Barrels of Oil Used per year. . . . . . . . . . . High-15.6
```

How the Competition Rates

Competitors	Rating	Pg.
Chevrolet Equinox	3	112
Ford Edge	5	132
Nissan Murano	3	223

Price Range	Retail	Markup
SE	$20,995	2%
SXT	$24,495	4%
Crew	$28,495	5%
R/T	$29,995	5%

Safety Checklist

Crash Tests:
```
Frontal . . . . . . . . . . . . . . . . . . . . . . . . . Average
Side. . . . . . . . . . . . . . . . . . . . . . . . . . . . . . Poor
```
Airbags:
```
Head . . . . . . . . . . . . . . . Fr. & Rr. Roof Curtain
Torso. . . . . . . . . . . . . . . Front Torso from Seat
Pelvis . . . . . . . . . . . . . . . . . . . . . . . . . . . None
Roll Sensing. . . . . . . . . . . . . . . . . . . . . . . . No
Knee Bolster . . . . . . . . . . . . . Standard Driver
```
Crash Avoidance:
```
Frontal Collision Warning. . . . . . . . . . . . None
Blind Spot Detection . . . . . . . . . . . . Optional
Crash Imminent Braking . . . . . . . . . . . . None
Lane Departure Warning . . . . . . . . . . . . None
```
General:
```
Auto. Crash Notification. . . . . . . . . . . . . None
Day Running Lamps . . . . . . . . . . . . . Optional
```
Safety Belt/Restraint:
```
Dynamic Head Restraints. . . . . . Standard Front
Adjustable Belt . . . . . . . . . . . . . Standard Front
Pretensioners . . . . . . . . . . . . . Standard Front
```

Dodge Journey

Specifications

```
Drive . . . . . . . . . . . . . . . . . . . . . . . . . . . . . . . FWD
Engine . . . . . . . . . . . . . . . . . . . . . . . . . 3.6-liter V6
Transmission . . . . . . . . . . . . 4-sp. Auto. w/Overdrive
Tow Rating (lbs.). . . . . . . . . . . . . . Very Low-1000
Head/Leg Room (in.) . . . . . . . . . Average-40.8/40.8
Interior Space (cu. ft.) . . . . . . . . . . . . Roomy-123.7
Cargo Space (cu. ft.) . . . . . . . . Very Cramped-10.7
Wheelbase/Length (in.) . . . . . . . . . 113.8/192.4
```

Ratings—10 Best, 1 Worst	
Combo Crash Tests	2
Safety Features	5
Rollover	5
Preventative Maintenance	–
Repair Costs	–
Warranty	1
Fuel Economy	8
Complaints	–
Insurance Costs	5
OVERALL RATING	**2**

Fiat 500

Fiat 500

Safety Checklist

Crash Tests:
Frontal . . . . Poor
Side . . . . Very Poor
Airbags:
Head . . . . Fr. & Rr. Roof Curtain
Torso . . . . Front Pelvis/Torso from Seat
Pelvis . . . . Front Pelvis/Torso from Seat
Roll Sensing. . . . . No
Knee Bolster . . . . Standard Driver
Crash Avoidance:
Frontal Collision Warning. . . . . None
Blind Spot Detection . . . . None
Crash Imminent Braking . . . . None
Lane Departure Warning . . . . None
General:
Auto. Crash Notification . . . . None
Day Running Lamps . . . . Optional
Safety Belt/Restraint:
Dynamic Head Restraints. . . . . . Standard Front
Adjustable Belt. None
Pretensioners . . . . Standard Front

At-a-Glance

Status/Year Series Started . . . . All New/2012
Twins . . . . –
Body Styles . . . . Hatchback
Seating 4
Anti-Theft Device . . . . Std. Pass. Immobil. & Alarm
Parking Index Rating . . . . Very Easy
Where Made . . . . Toluca, Mexico
Fuel Factor
MPG Rating (city/hwy) Good-27/34
Driving Range (mi.) . . . . Very Short-312.4
Fuel Type . . . . Premium
Annual Fuel Cost . . . . Low-$1764
Gas Guzzler Tax . . . . No
Greenhouse Gas Emissions (tons/yr.) Low-6.2
Barrels of Oil Used per year Low-11.4

How the Competition Rates

Competitors	Rating	Pg.
Ford Fiesta	5	137
Mini Cooper	–	209
Nissan Cube	–	218

Price Range	Retail	Markup
Pop	$15,500	3%
Sport	$17,500	4%
Lounge	$19,500	4%

Fiat 500

Specifications

Drive . . . . FWD
Engine 1.4-liter I4
Transmission . . . . 6-sp. Automatic
Tow Rating (lbs.) . . . . –
Head/Leg Room (in.) . . . . . Very Cramped-38.9/40.7
Interior Space (cu. ft.) . . . . Very Cramped-85.1
Cargo Space (cu. ft.) . . . . Very Cramped-9.5
Wheelbase/Length (in.) 90.6/139.6

Ratings—10 Best, 1 Worst	Edge	MKX
Combo Crash Tests	3	–
Safety Features	7	7
Rollover	5	5
Preventative Maintenance	6	6
Repair Costs	5	3
Warranty	3	6
Fuel Economy	5	3
Complaints	7	8
Insurance Costs	10	10
OVERALL RATING	**5**	**3**

Ford Edge

Lincoln MKX

At-a-Glance

Status/Year Series Started Unchanged/2007
Twins . . . . Lincoln MKX
Body Styles . . . . SUV
Seating 5
Anti-Theft Device . . . . Std. Pass. Immobil. & Alarm
Parking Index Rating . . . . Hard
Where Made . . . . Oakville, Ontario

Fuel Factor
MPG Rating (city/hwy) Average-21/30
Driving Range (mi.) Long-437.0
Fuel Type . . . . Regular
Annual Fuel Cost . . . . Average-$1996
Gas Guzzler Tax . . . . No
Greenhouse Gas Emissions (tons/yr.) . . Average-7.8
Barrels of Oil Used per year High-14.3

How the Competition Rates

Competitors	Rating	Pg.
Dodge Journey	5	130
Hyundai Veracruz	–	164
Nissan Murano	3	223

Price Range	Retail	Markup
SE	$27,640	5%
SEL	$30,945	7%
Limited	$34,800	7%
Sport	$36,975	7%

Safety Checklist

Crash Tests:
Frontal . . . . Very Poor
Side . . . . Average
Airbags:
Head . . . . Fr. & Rr. Roof Curtain
Torso . . . . Front Torso from Seat
Pelvis . . . . None
Roll Sensing . . . . Yes
Knee Bolster . . . . None
Crash Avoidance:
Frontal Collision Warning . . . . Optional
Blind Spot Detection . . . . Optional
Crash Imminent Braking . . . . None
Lane Departure Warning . . . . None
General:
Auto. Crash Notification . . . . Optional
Day Running Lamps . . . . None
Safety Belt/Restraint:
Dynamic Head Restraints . . . . None
Adjustable Belt . . . . Standard Front
Pretensioners . . . . Standard Front

Ford Edge

Specifications

Drive . . . . FWD
Engine 3.5-liter V6
Transmission . . . . 6-sp. Automatic
Tow Rating (lbs.) Low-3500
Head/Leg Room (in.) Cramped-40/40.7
Interior Space (cu. ft.) Roomy-108.4
Cargo Space (cu. ft.) . . . . Very Roomy-32.2
Wheelbase/Length (in.) 111.2/184.2

Ratings—10 Best, 1 Worst	
Combo Crash Tests	1
Safety Features	5
Rollover	2
Preventative Maintenance	2
Repair Costs	10
Warranty	3
Fuel Economy	5
Complaints	6
Insurance Costs	8
OVERALL RATING	**2**

Ford Escape

Ford Escape

At-a-Glance

Status/Year Series Started	Unchanged/2005
Twins	–
Body Styles	SUV
Seating	5
Anti-Theft Device	Std. Pass. Immobil. & Alarm
Parking Index Rating	Easy
Where Made	Kansas City, MO

Fuel Factor

MPG Rating (city/hwy)	Average-21/28
Driving Range (mi.)	Long-414.1
Fuel Type	Regular
Annual Fuel Cost	Average-$2048
Gas Guzzler Tax	No
Greenhouse Gas Emissions (tons/yr.)	Average-8.1
Barrels of Oil Used per year	High-14.9

How the Competition Rates

Competitors	Rating	Pg.
Jeep Compass	–	172
Kia Sportage	–	183
Toyota RAV4	1	252

Price Range	Retail	Markup
XLS FWD	$21,240	6%
XLT 4WD	$26,420	7%
Hybrid FWD	$30,570	8%
Limited Hybrid 4WD	$34,830	8%

Safety Checklist

Crash Tests:

Frontal	Very Poor
Side	Very Poor

Airbags:

Head	Fr. & Rr. Roof Curtain
Torso	Front Torso from Seat
Pelvis	None
Roll Sensing	Yes
Knee Bolster	None

Crash Avoidance:

Frontal Collision Warning	None
Blind Spot Detection	None
Crash Imminent Braking	None
Lane Departure Warning	None

General:

Auto. Crash Notification	Optional
Day Running Lamps	None

Safety Belt/Restraint:

Dynamic Head Restraints	None
Adjustable Belt	Standard Front
Pretensioners	Standard Front

Ford Escape

Specifications

Drive	FWD
Engine	2.5-liter I4
Transmission	6-sp. Automatic
Tow Rating (lbs.)	Very Low-1500
Head/Leg Room (in.)	Average-40.4/41.6
Interior Space (cu. ft.)	Average-99.4
Cargo Space (cu. ft.)	Roomy-31.4
Wheelbase/Length (in.)	103.1/174.7

Ratings—10 Best, 1 Worst

Combo Crash Tests	–
Safety Features	7
Rollover	2
Preventative Maintenance	2
Repair Costs	7
Warranty	3
Fuel Economy	1
Complaints	6
Insurance Costs	10
OVERALL RATING	–

Ford Expedition

Ford Expedition

At-a-Glance

Status/Year Series Started Unchanged/2003
Twins . . . . Lincoln Navigator
Body Styles. . . . . SUV
Seating. 5/6/7
Anti-Theft Device. . . . . . . Std. Pass. Immobil. & Alarm
Parking Index Rating . . . . Very Hard
Where Made. . . . . Louisville, Kentucky
Fuel Factor
  MPG Rating (city/hwy). . . . . Very Poor-13/18
  Driving Range (mi.) Long-416.0
  Fuel Type Regular/E85
  Annual Fuel Cost. . . . . Very High-$3261
  Gas Guzzler Tax . . . . No
  Greenhouse Gas Emissions (tons/yr.) Very High-12.4
  Barrels of Oil Used per year . . . . Very High-22.8

How the Competition Rates

Competitors	Rating	Pg.
Chevrolet Suburban	6	117
Nissan Armada	–	217
Toyota Sequoia	–	253

Price Range	Retail	Markup
XL 2WD	$36,530	7%
XLT 4WD	$42,040	7%
Limited 4WD	$48,170	7%
King Ranch 4WD	$52,330	8%

Safety Checklist

Crash Tests:
  Frontal . . . . –
  Side . . . . –
Airbags:
  Head . . . . Fr. & Rr. Roof Curtain
  Torso. . . . . Front Torso from Seat
  Pelvis . . . . None
  Roll Sensing . . . . Yes
  Knee Bolster . . . . None
Crash Avoidance:
  Frontal Collision Warning. . . . . None
  Blind Spot Detection . . . . None
  Crash Imminent Braking . . . . None
  Lane Departure Warning . . . . None
General:
  Auto. Crash Notification . . . . Optional
  Day Running Lamps . . . . None
Safety Belt/Restraint:
  Dynamic Head Restraints. . . . . . Standard Front
  Adjustable Belt . . . . Standard Front
  Pretensioners . . . . Standard Front

Ford Expedition

Specifications

Drive 4WD
Engine 5.4-liter V8
Transmission . . . . 6-sp. Automatic
Tow Rating (lbs.) . . . . Very High-9200
Head/Leg Room (in.) Cramped-39.6/41.1
Interior Space (cu. ft.) . . . . Very Roomy-160.3
Cargo Space (cu. ft.) Average-18.6
Wheelbase/Length (in.). 119/206.5

Ratings—10 Best, 1 Worst

Combo Crash Tests	6
Safety Features	7
Rollover	4
Preventative Maintenance	3
Repair Costs	8
Warranty	3
Fuel Economy	3
Complaints	7
Insurance Costs	10
OVERALL RATING	**6**

Ford Explorer

Ford Explorer

At-a-Glance

Status/Year Series Started	Unchanged/2011
Twins	–
Body Styles	SUV
Seating	6/7
Anti-Theft Device	Std. Pass. Immobil. & Alarm
Parking Index Rating	Hard
Where Made	Chicago, IL
Fuel Factor	
MPG Rating (city/hwy)	Poor-17/23
Driving Range (mi.)	Very Short-358.3
Fuel Type	Regular
Annual Fuel Cost	High-$2515
Gas Guzzler Tax	No
Greenhouse Gas Emissions (tons/yr.)	High-9.3
Barrels of Oil Used per year	High-17.1

How the Competition Rates

Competitors	Rating	Pg.
Dodge Journey	5	130
Nissan Pathfinder	–	224
Toyota 4Runner	–	244

Price Range

Price Range	Retail	Markup
Base	$28,170	5%
XLT	$31,980	7%
Limited	$37,740	7%

Safety Checklist

Crash Tests:
Frontal . . . . Average
Side . . . . Good

Airbags:
Head . . . . Fr. & Rr. Roof Curtain
Torso . . . . Front Pelvis/Torso from Seat
Pelvis . . . . Front Pelvis/Torso from Seat
Roll Sensing . . . . Yes
Knee Bolster . . . . None

Crash Avoidance:
Frontal Collision Warning . . . . Optional
Blind Spot Detection . . . . Optional
Crash Imminent Braking . . . . None
Lane Departure Warning . . . . None

General:
Auto. Crash Notification . . . . Optional
Day Running Lamps . . . . None

Safety Belt/Restraint:
Dynamic Head Restraints . . . . None
Adjustable Belt . . . . Standard Front
Pretensioners . . . . Standard Front

Ford Explorer

Specifications

Drive 4WD
Engine 3.5-liter V6
Transmission . . . . 6-sp. Automatic
Tow Rating (lbs.) Average-5000
Head/Leg Room (in.) Cramped-39.1/40.6
Interior Space (cu. ft.) . . . . Very Roomy-151.7
Cargo Space (cu. ft.) . . . . Very Roomy-80.7
Wheelbase/Length (in.) 112.6/197.1

Ratings—10 Best, 1 Worst	Reg./Super	Crew
Combo Crash Tests	4	5
Safety Features	3	3
Rollover	3	3
Preventative Maintenance	5	5
Repair Costs	9	9
Warranty	3	3
Fuel Economy	1	1
Complaints	10	10
Insurance Costs	10	10
OVERALL RATING	**5**	**5**

Ford F-150

Ford F-150

At-a-Glance

Status/Year Series Started Unchanged/2009
Twins . . . . –
Body Styles . . . SuperCab, Regular, SuperCrew Cabs
Seating 5/6
Anti-Theft Device . . . . Std. Pass. Immobil. & Alarm
Parking Index Rating . . . . Very Hard
Where Made . . . . Dearborn, MI
Fuel Factor
  MPG Rating (city/hwy) . . . . Very Poor-14/19
  Driving Range (mi.) . . . . Very Long-571.7
  Fuel Type Regular/E85
  Annual Fuel Cost . . . . Very High-$3051
  Gas Guzzler Tax . . . . No
  Greenhouse Gas Emissions (tons/yr.) Very High-11.6
  Barrels of Oil Used per year . . . . Very High-21.4

How the Competition Rates

Competitors	Rating	Pg.
Chevrolet Silverado Ext.	5	115
Nissan Titan	–	227
Toyota Tundra	3	256

Price Range	Retail	Markup
XL Reg. Cab 126WB	$22,990	6%
STX SuperCab 145WB 4WD	$30,080	10%
Lariat 133WB 4WD	$38,285	10%
Harley-Davidson 4WD	$51,995	11%

Safety Checklist

Crash Tests:
  Frontal . . . . Very Poor
  Side . . . . Very Good
Airbags:
  Head . . . . Front Roof Curtain
  Torso . . . . Front Pelvis/Torso from Seat
  Pelvis . . . . Front Pelvis/Torso from Seat
  Roll Sensing . . . . Yes
  Knee Bolster . . . . None
Crash Avoidance:
  Frontal Collision Warning . . . . None
  Blind Spot Detection . . . . None
  Crash Imminent Braking . . . . None
  Lane Departure Warning . . . . None
General:
  Auto. Crash Notification . . . . Optional
  Day Running Lamps . . . . None
Safety Belt/Restraint:
  Dynamic Head Restraints . . . . None
  Adjustable Belt . . . . Standard Front
  Pretensioners . . . . Standard Front

Ford F-150

Specifications

Drive 4WD
Engine 5.0-liter V8
Transmission . . . . 6-sp. Automatic
Tow Rating (lbs.) . . . . Very High-7800
Head/Leg Room (in.) Roomy-41/41.4
Interior Space (cu. ft.) . . . . Very Roomy-130.9
Cargo Space (cu. ft.) . . . . Very Roomy-44.5
Wheelbase/Length (in.) 144.5/231.9

Ratings—10 Best, 1 Worst

Combo Crash Tests	9
Safety Features	4
Rollover	5
Preventative Maintenance	–
Repair Costs	–
Warranty	3
Fuel Economy	9
Complaints	1
Insurance Costs	3
OVERALL RATING	**5**

Ford Fiesta

Ford Fiesta

At-a-Glance

Status/Year Series Started Unchanged/2011
Twins . . . . –
Body Styles . . . . Sedan, Hatchback
Seating 5
Anti-Theft Device . . . . Std. Pass. Immobil. & Alarm
Parking Index Rating . . . . Very Easy
Where Made . . . . Cuautitlán, Mexico

Fuel Factor
  MPG Rating (city/hwy) . . . . Very Good-29/39
  Driving Range (mi.) Average-406.5
  Fuel Type . . . . Regular
  Annual Fuel Cost . . . . Very Low-$1478
  Gas Guzzler Tax . . . . No
  Greenhouse Gas Emissions (tons/yr.) Low-5.7
  Barrels of Oil Used per year Low-10.4

How the Competition Rates

Competitors	Rating	Pg.
Honda Fit	–	150
Hyundai Accent	9	155
Toyota Yaris	–	258

Price Range	Retail	Markup
S	$13,200	3%
SE	$14,500	3%
SEL	$16,600	4%
SES	$17,500	4%

Safety Checklist

Crash Tests:
  Frontal . . . . Good
  Side . . . . Good*
Airbags:
  Head . . . . Fr. & Rr. Roof Curtain
  Torso . . . . Front Pelvis/Torso from Seat
  Pelvis . . . . Front Pelvis/Torso from Seat
  Roll Sensing . . . . No
  Knee Bolster . . . . Standard Driver
Crash Avoidance:
  Frontal Collision Warning . . . . None
  Blind Spot Detection . . . . None
  Crash Imminent Braking . . . . None
  Lane Departure Warning . . . . None
General:
  Auto. Crash Notification . . . . Optional
  Day Running Lamps . . . . None
Safety Belt/Restraint:
  Dynamic Head Restraints . . . . None
  Adjustable Belt . . . . Standard Front
  Pretensioners . . . . Standard Front

Ford Fiesta

Specifications

Drive . . . . FWD
Engine 1.6-liter I4
Transmission . . . . 6-sp. Automatic
Tow Rating (lbs.) . . . . –
Head/Leg Room (in.) Average-39.1/42.2
Interior Space (cu. ft.) . . . . Very Cramped-85.1
Cargo Space (cu. ft.) Cramped-12.8
Wheelbase/Length (in.) 98/173.6

*Additional injury potential in side test see asterisked footnote on page 19.

Ratings—10 Best, 1 Worst

Combo Crash Tests	–
Safety Features	5
Rollover	4
Preventative Maintenance	4
Repair Costs	4
Warranty	3
Fuel Economy	3
Complaints	3
Insurance Costs	10
OVERALL RATING	**–**

Ford Flex

Ford Flex

Ford Flex

At-a-Glance

Status/Year Series Started Unchanged/2009
Twins . . . . –
Body Styles . . . . SUV
Seating 6/7
Anti-Theft Device . . . . Std. Pass. Immobil. & Alarm
Parking Index Rating . . . . Very Hard
Where Made . . . . Oakville, Ontario

Fuel Factor
MPG Rating (city/hwy) Poor-17/24
Driving Range (mi.) Short-364.0
Fuel Type . . . . Regular
Annual Fuel Cost . . . . High-$2476
Gas Guzzler Tax . . . . No
Greenhouse Gas Emissions (tons/yr.) High-9.8
Barrels of Oil Used per year High-18.0

How the Competition Rates

Competitors	Rating	Pg.
Chevrolet Traverse	8	119
GMC Acadia	6	143
Honda Pilot	4	153

Price Range

Price Range	Retail	Markup
SE	$29,355	6%
SEL	$31,985	7%
Limited	$37,500	7%
Titanium	$42,990	8%

Safety Checklist

Crash Tests:
Frontal . . . . –
Side . . . . –

Airbags:
Head . . . . Fr. & Rr. Roof Curtain
Torso . . . . Front Torso from Seat
Pelvis . . . . None
Roll Sensing . . . . Yes
Knee Bolster . . . . None

Crash Avoidance:
Frontal Collision Warning . . . . None
Blind Spot Detection . . . . None
Crash Imminent Braking . . . . None
Lane Departure Warning . . . . None

General:
Auto. Crash Notification . . . . Optional
Day Running Lamps . . . . None

Safety Belt/Restraint:
Dynamic Head Restraints . . . . None
Adjustable Belt . . . . Standard Front
Pretensioners . . . . Standard Front

Ford Flex

Specifications

Drive . . . . FWD
Engine 3.5-liter V6
Transmission . . . . 6-sp. Automatic
Tow Rating (lbs.) Low-4500
Head/Leg Room (in.) Roomy-41.8/40.8
Interior Space (cu. ft.) . . . . Very Roomy-155.8
Cargo Space (cu. ft.) Average-20
Wheelbase/Length (in.) 117.9/201.8

Ratings—10 Best, 1 Worst

Combo Crash Tests	6
Safety Features	2
Rollover	7
Preventative Maintenance	5
Repair Costs	10
Warranty	3
Fuel Economy	9
Complaints	–
Insurance Costs	3
OVERALL RATING	**6**

Ford Focus

At-a-Glance

Status/Year Series Started . . . . All New/2012
Twins . . . . –
Body Styles. . . . . Sedan, Hatchback
Seating. 5
Anti-Theft Device. . . . . . . Std. Pass. Immobil. & Alarm
Parking Index Rating . . . . Easy
Where Made . . . . Wayne, MI
Fuel Factor
  MPG Rating (city/hwy) . . . . Very Good-28/38
  Driving Range (mi.) Average-393.8
  Fuel Type. . . . . Regular
  Annual Fuel Cost . . . . Very Low-$1525
  Gas Guzzler Tax . . . . No
  Greenhouse Gas Emissions (tons/yr.) Low-6.0
  Barrels of Oil Used per year Low-11.0

How the Competition Rates

Competitors	Rating	Pg.
Honda Civic	–	146
Kia Forte	8	177
Toyota Corolla	4	247

Price Range	Retail	Markup
S	$16,500	6%
SE	$17,400	7%
SEL	$20,300	7%
Titanium	$22,200	7%

Ford Focus

Safety Checklist

Crash Tests:
  Frontal. . . . . Average
  Side. . . . . Average
Airbags:
  Head . . . . Fr. & Rr. Roof Curtain
  Torso . . . . Front Pelvis/Torso from Seat
  Pelvis . . . . Front Pelvis/Torso from Seat
  Roll Sensing. . . . . No
  Knee Bolster . . . . None
Crash Avoidance:
  Frontal Collision Warning. . . . . None
  Blind Spot Detection . . . . None
  Crash Imminent Braking . . . . None
  Lane Departure Warning . . . . None
General:
  Auto. Crash Notification . . . . Optional
  Day Running Lamps . . . . None
Safety Belt/Restraint:
  Dynamic Head Restraints . . . . None
  Adjustable Belt . . . . Standard Front
  Pretensioners . . . . Standard Front

Ford Focus

Specifications

Drive . . . . FWD
Engine. 2.0-liter I4
Transmission . . . . 6-sp. Automatic
Tow Rating (lbs.) . . . . –
Head/Leg Room (in.) Cramped-38.3/41.9
Interior Space (cu. ft.) . . . . Very Cramped-90
Cargo Space (cu. ft.) Cramped-13.2
Wheelbase/Length (in.) 104.3/178.5

Ratings—10 Best, 1 Worst

	Fusion	MKZ
Combo Crash Tests	3	3
Safety Features	3	3
Rollover	8	8
Preventative Maintenance	6	3
Repair Costs	10	3
Warranty	3	6
Fuel Economy	7	3
Complaints	7	10
Insurance Costs	3	5
OVERALL RATING	**5**	**3**

Ford Fusion

Lincoln MKZ

At-a-Glance

Status/Year Series Started Unchanged/2006
Twins . . . . Lincoln MKZ
Body Styles . . . . Sedan
Seating 5
Anti-Theft Device . . . . Std. Pass. Immobil. & Alarm
Parking Index Rating . . . . Average
Where Made . . . . Hermosillo, Mexico
Fuel Factor
MPG Rating (city/hwy) Good-23/33
Driving Range (mi.) . . . . Very Long-466.1
Fuel Type . . . . Regular
Annual Fuel Cost . . . . Low-$1819
Gas Guzzler Tax . . . . No
Greenhouse Gas Emissions (tons/yr.) . . Average-7.2
Barrels of Oil Used per year Average-13.2

How the Competition Rates

Competitors	Rating	Pg.
Chevrolet Malibu	4	114
Hyundai Sonata	10	161
Toyota Camry	10	246

Price Range	Retail	Markup
S	$19,850	7%
Sport	$27,150	9%
Hybrid	$28,600	9%
SEL AWD	$28,760	9%

Safety Checklist

Crash Tests:
　Frontal . . . . Poor
　Side . . . . Poor
Airbags:
　Head . . . . Fr. & Rr. Roof Curtain
　Torso . . . . Front Pelvis/Torso from Seat
　Pelvis . . . . Front Pelvis/Torso from Seat
　Roll Sensing . . . . No
　Knee Bolster . . . . None
Crash Avoidance:
　Frontal Collision Warning . . . . None
　Blind Spot Detection . . . . Optional
　Crash Imminent Braking . . . . None
　Lane Departure Warning . . . . None
General:
　Auto. Crash Notification . . . . Optional
　Day Running Lamps . . . . None
Safety Belt/Restraint:
　Dynamic Head Restraints . . . . None
　Adjustable Belt . . . . Standard Front
　Pretensioners . . . . Standard Front

Ford Fusion

Specifications

Drive . . . . FWD
Engine 2.5-liter I4
Transmission . . . . 6-sp. Automatic
Tow Rating (lbs.) . . . . –
Head/Leg Room (in.) Average-38.7/42.3
Interior Space (cu. ft.) Average-100.3
Cargo Space (cu. ft.) Average-16.5
Wheelbase/Length (in.) 107.4/190.6

Ratings—10 Best, 1 Worst

Combo Crash Tests	6
Safety Features	1
Rollover	9
Preventative Maintenance	6
Repair Costs	8
Warranty	3
Fuel Economy	4
Complaints	2
Insurance Costs	1
OVERALL RATING	**3**

Ford Mustang

Ford Mustang

At-a-Glance

Status/Year Series Started Unchanged/2005
Twins . . . . –
Body Styles . . . . Coupe, Convertible
Seating. 4
Anti-Theft Device. . . . . . . Std. Pass. Immobil. & Alarm
Parking Index Rating . . . . Very Easy
Where Made . . . . Flat Rock, MI

Fuel Factor
MPG Rating (city/hwy) Poor-19/31
Driving Range (mi.) Short-368.1
Fuel Type. . . . . Regular
Annual Fuel Cost. . . . . Average-$2106
Gas Guzzler Tax . . . . No
Greenhouse Gas Emissions (tons/yr.) . . Average-8.1
Barrels of Oil Used per year. High-14.9

How the Competition Rates

Competitors	Rating	Pg.
Chevrolet Camaro	5	108
Dodge Challenger	–	126
Hyundai Elantra	7	157

Price Range

Price Range	Retail	Markup
Base	$22,310	5%
GT	$29,310	8%
Boss 302	$40,310	9%
Shelby GT500	$48,810	11%

Safety Checklist

Crash Tests:
  Frontal . . . . Good
  Side. . . . . Poor
Airbags:
  Head. . . . . Front Head from Seat
  Torso. . . . . Front Head/Torso from Seat
  Pelvis . . . . None
  Roll Sensing . . . . –
  Knee Bolster . . . . None
Crash Avoidance:
  Frontal Collision Warning. . . . . None
  Blind Spot Detection . . . . None
  Crash Imminent Braking . . . . None
  Lane Departure Warning . . . . None
General:
  Auto. Crash Notification . . . . Optional
  Day Running Lamps . . . . None
Safety Belt/Restraint:
  Dynamic Head Restraints . . . . None
  Adjustable Belt. . . . . None
  Pretensioners . . . . Standard Front

Ford Mustang

Specifications

Drive . . . . RWD
Engine 3.7-liter V6
Transmission . . . . 6-sp. Automatic
Tow Rating (lbs.) . . . . Very Low-1000
Head/Leg Room (in.) Average-38.5/42.4
Interior Space (cu. ft.) . . . . Very Cramped-83.3
Cargo Space (cu. ft.) Cramped-13.4
Wheelbase/Length (in.) 107.1/188.1

*In side test, head of rear dummy struck convertible roof linkage resulting in a higher likelihood of serious injury.

Ratings—10 Best, 1 Worst

Combo Crash Tests	7
Safety Features	6
Rollover	7
Preventative Maintenance	4
Repair Costs	3
Warranty	3
Fuel Economy	4
Complaints	4
Insurance Costs	5
OVERALL RATING	**4**

Ford Taurus

At-a-Glance

Status/Year Series Started Unchanged/2008
Twins . . . . –
Body Styles . . . . Sedan
Seating 5
Anti-Theft Device . . . . . . Std. Pass. Immobil. & Alarm
Parking Index Rating . . . . Very Hard
Where Made . . . . Chicago, IL
Fuel Factor
  MPG Rating (city/hwy) Poor-18/28
  Driving Range (mi.) Average-407.5
  Fuel Type. . . . . Regular
  Annual Fuel Cost. . . . . High-$2259
  Gas Guzzler Tax . . . . No
  Greenhouse Gas Emissions (tons/yr.) High-8.5
  Barrels of Oil Used per year. High-15.6

How the Competition Rates

Competitors	Rating	Pg.
Chevrolet Malibu	4	114
Dodge Charger	–	127
Lincoln MKS	–	194

Price Range

Price Range	Retail	Markup
SE	$25,555	8%
SEL	$27,755	8%
Limited	$32,155	9%
SHO	$38,155	9%

Ford Taurus

Safety Checklist

Crash Tests:
  Frontal . . . . Average
  Side . . . . Good
Airbags:
  Head . . . . Fr. & Rr. Roof Curtain
  Torso. . . . . Front Torso from Seat
  Pelvis . . . . None
  Roll Sensing . . . . Yes
  Knee Bolster . . . . None
Crash Avoidance:
  Frontal Collision Warning. . . . . None
  Blind Spot Detection . . . . Optional
  Crash Imminent Braking . . . . None
  Lane Departure Warning . . . . None
General:
  Auto. Crash Notification . . . . Optional
  Day Running Lamps . . . . None
Safety Belt/Restraint:
  Dynamic Head Restraints . . . . None
  Adjustable Belt . . . . Standard Front
  Pretensioners . . . . Standard Front

Ford Taurus

Specifications

Drive . . . . FWD
Engine 3.5-liter V6
Transmission . . . . 6-sp. Automatic
Tow Rating (lbs.) . . . . Very Low-1000
Head/Leg Room (in.) Average-39/41.9
Interior Space (cu. ft.) Average-102.2
Cargo Space (cu. ft.) Average-20.1
Wheelbase/Length (in.) 112.9/202.9

Ratings—10 Best, 1 Worst

Combo Crash Tests	9
Safety Features	7
Rollover	4
Preventative Maintenance	3
Repair Costs	2
Warranty	5
Fuel Economy	3
Complaints	5
Insurance Costs	10
OVERALL RATING	**6**

GMC Acadia

At-a-Glance

Status/Year Series Started Unchanged/2007
Twins . . . . Chevrolet Traverse
Body Styles. . . . . SUV
Seating 7/8
Anti-Theft Device. . . . . . . Std. Pass. Immobil. & Alarm
Parking Index Rating . . . . Very Hard
Where Made . . . . Lansing, MI

Fuel Factor
MPG Rating (city/hwy). Poor-17/24
Driving Range (mi.) Long-430.5
Fuel Type. . . . . Regular
Annual Fuel Cost. . . . . High-$2476
Gas Guzzler Tax . . . . No
Greenhouse Gas Emissions (tons/yr.) High-9.8
Barrels of Oil Used per year. High-18.0

How the Competition Rates

Competitors	Rating	Pg.
Honda Pilot	4	153
Mazda CX-9	–	201
Toyota Highlander	4	249

Price Range	Retail	Markup
SL	$32,605	5%
SLE	$35,080	5%
SLT	$38,830	5%
Denali	$45,880	5%

GMC Acadia

Safety Checklist

Crash Tests:
Frontal . . . . Good
Side. . . . . Very Good
Airbags:
Head . . . . Fr. & Rr. Roof Curtain
Torso . . . . Front Pelvis/Torso from Seat
Pelvis . . . . Front Pelvis/Torso from Seat
Roll Sensing . . . . Yes
Knee Bolster . . . . None
Crash Avoidance:
Frontal Collision Warning. . . . . None
Blind Spot Detection . . . . None
Crash Imminent Braking . . . . None
Lane Departure Warning . . . . None
General:
Auto. Crash Notification . . . . Standard
Day Running Lamps . . . . Standard
Safety Belt/Restraint:
Dynamic Head Restraints . . . . None
Adjustable Belt . . . . . . Standard Front and Rear
Pretensioners . . . . Standard Front

GMC Acadia

Specifications

Drive . . . . FWD
Engine 3.6-liter V6
Transmission . . . . 6-sp. Automatic
Tow Rating (lbs.). Average-5200
Head/Leg Room (in.). Average-40.4/41.3
Interior Space (cu. ft.). . . . . Very Roomy-154
Cargo Space (cu. ft.) Roomy-24.1
Wheelbase/Length (in.) 118.9/201.1

Ratings—10 Best, 1 Worst	
Combo Crash Tests	8
Safety Features	4
Rollover	9
Preventative Maintenance	5
Repair Costs	9
Warranty	1
Fuel Economy	7
Complaints	4
Insurance Costs	8
OVERALL RATING	**8**

Honda Accord

Honda Accord

At-a-Glance

Status/Year Series Started	Unchanged/2008
Twins	—
Body Styles	Sedan
Seating	5
Anti-Theft Device	Std. Pass. Immobil. & Opt. Pass. Alarm
Parking Index Rating	Hard
Where Made	Marysville, OH

Fuel Factor

MPG Rating (city/hwy)	Good-23/34
Driving Range (mi.)	Very Long-498.0
Fuel Type	Regular
Annual Fuel Cost	Low-$1800
Gas Guzzler Tax	No
Greenhouse Gas Emissions (tons/yr.)	Average-6.9
Barrels of Oil Used per year	Average-12.7

How the Competition Rates

Competitors	Rating	Pg.
Ford Fusion	5	140
Nissan Altima	6	215
Toyota Camry	10	246

Price Range	Retail	Markup
LX	$21,380	10%
SE	$23,930	10%
EX	$25,105	10%
EX-L	$31,830	10%

Safety Checklist

Crash Tests:

Frontal	Very Good
Side	Average

Airbags:

Head	Fr. & Rr. Roof Curtain
Torso	Front Pelvis/Torso from Seat
Pelvis	Front Pelvis/Torso from Seat
Roll Sensing	No
Knee Bolster	None

Crash Avoidance:

Frontal Collision Warning	None
Blind Spot Detection	None
Crash Imminent Braking	None
Lane Departure Warning	None

General:

Auto. Crash Notification	None
Day Running Lamps	Standard

Safety Belt/Restraint:

Dynamic Head Restraints	Standard Front
Adjustable Belt	Standard Front
Pretensioners	Standard Front

Honda Accord

Specifications

Drive	FWD
Engine	2.4-liter I4
Transmission	5-sp. Automatic
Tow Rating (lbs.)	Very Low-1000
Head/Leg Room (in.)	Average-39/42.5
Interior Space (cu. ft.)	Average-101
Cargo Space (cu. ft.)	Cramped-14.7
Wheelbase/Length (in.)	110.2/194.9

Honda Accord Coupe

Ratings—10 Best, 1 Worst	
Combo Crash Tests	–
Safety Features	4
Rollover	9
Preventative Maintenance	8
Repair Costs	9
Warranty	1
Fuel Economy	6
Complaints	–
Insurance Costs	3
OVERALL RATING	–

Honda Accord Coupe

Honda Accord Coupe

Safety Checklist

Crash Tests:
Frontal . . . . –
Side . . . . –
Airbags:
Head . . . . Fr. & Rr. Roof Curtain
Torso . . . . Front Pelvis/Torso from Seat
Pelvis . . . . Front Pelvis/Torso from Seat
Roll Sensing . . . . No
Knee Bolster . . . . None
Crash Avoidance:
Frontal Collision Warning . . . . None
Blind Spot Detection . . . . None
Crash Imminent Braking . . . . None
Lane Departure Warning . . . . None
General:
Auto. Crash Notification . . . . None
Day Running Lamps . . . . Standard
Safety Belt/Restraint:
Dynamic Head Restraints . . . . . . Standard Front
Adjustable Belt . . . . None
Pretensioners . . . . Standard Front

At-a-Glance

Status/Year Series Started Unchanged/2008
Twins . . . . –
Body Styles . . . . Coupe
Seating 5
Anti-Theft Device . Std. Pass. Immobil. & Opt. Pass. Alarm
Parking Index Rating . . . . Average
Where Made . . . . Marysville, OH
Fuel Factor
  MPG Rating (city/hwy) Average-22/33
  Driving Range (mi.) . . . . Very Long-478.8
  Fuel Type . . . . Regular
  Annual Fuel Cost . . . . Low-$1872
  Gas Guzzler Tax . . . . No
  Greenhouse Gas Emissions (tons/yr.) . . Average-7.2
  Barrels of Oil Used per year Average-13.2

How the Competition Rates

Competitors	Rating	Pg.
Hyundai Genesis	–	159
Infiniti G	–	167
Volkswagen CC	–	260

Price Range	Retail	Markup
LX-S	$22,980	10%
EX	$25,455	10%
EX-L	$29,930	10%
EX-L w/Nav	$31,930	10%

Specifications

Drive . . . . FWD
Engine 2.4-liter I4
Transmission . . . . 5-sp. Automatic
Tow Rating (lbs.) . . . . Very Low-1000
Head/Leg Room (in.) Average-39.1/42.2
Interior Space (cu. ft.) Cramped-92.1
Cargo Space (cu. ft.) . . . . Very Cramped-11.9
Wheelbase/Length (in.) 107.9/191

Ratings—10 Best, 1 Worst

Combo Crash Tests	–
Safety Features	2
Rollover	7
Preventative Maintenance	10
Repair Costs	9
Warranty	1
Fuel Economy	9
Complaints	–
Insurance Costs	1
OVERALL RATING	–

Honda Civic

Honda Civic

At-a-Glance

Status/Year Series Started . . . . All New/2012
Twins . . . . –
Body Styles . . . . Sedan
Seating 5
Anti-Theft Device . Std. Pass. Immobil. & Opt. Pass. Alarm
Parking Index Rating . . . . Easy
Where Made . . . . . . Alliston, Ontario / Greensburg, IN
Fuel Factor
  MPG Rating (city/hwy) . . . . Very Good-28/39
  Driving Range (mi.) Long-423.3
  Fuel Type. . . . . Regular
  Annual Fuel Cost . . . . Very Low-$1511
  Gas Guzzler Tax . . . . No
  Greenhouse Gas Emissions (tons/yr.) Low-5.8
  Barrels of Oil Used per year Low-10.7

How the Competition Rates

Competitors	Rating	Pg.
Nissan Sentra	4	226
Suzuki Kizashi	–	242
Volkswagen Jetta	5	262

Price Range	Retail	Markup
DX	$15,805	8%
EX	$20,505	9%
EX-L	$21,955	9%
Hybrid-L	$26,750	9%

Safety Checklist

Crash Tests:
  Frontal . . . . –
  Side . . . . –
Airbags:
  Head. . . . . Fr. & Rr. Roof Curtain
  Torso . . . . Front Torso from Seat
  Pelvis . . . . None
  Roll Sensing. . . . . No
  Knee Bolster . . . . None
Crash Avoidance:
  Frontal Collision Warning. . . . . None
  Blind Spot Detection . . . . None
  Crash Imminent Braking . . . . None
  Lane Departure Warning . . . . None
General:
  Auto. Crash Notification . . . . None
  Day Running Lamps . . . . Standard
Safety Belt/Restraint:
  Dynamic Head Restraints . . . . None
  Adjustable Belt . . . . Standard Front
  Pretensioners . . . . Standard Front

Honda Civic

Specifications

Drive . . . . FWD
Engine. 1.8-liter I4
Transmission . . . . 5-sp. Automatic
Tow Rating (lbs.) . . . . –
Head/Leg Room (in.) Average-39/42
Interior Space (cu. ft.) Cramped-94.6
Cargo Space (cu. ft.) Cramped-12.5
Wheelbase/Length (in.) 105.1/177.3

Ratings—10 Best, 1 Worst

Combo Crash Tests	–
Safety Features	2
Rollover	8
Preventative Maintenance	10
Repair Costs	9
Warranty	1
Fuel Economy	9
Complaints	–
Insurance Costs	1
OVERALL RATING	–

Honda Civic Coupe

Honda Civic Coupe

At-a-Glance

Status/Year Series Started . . . . All New/2012
Twins . . . . –
Body Styles . . . . Coupe
Seating 5
Anti-Theft Device . Std. Pass. Immobil. & Opt. Pass. Alarm
Parking Index Rating . . . . Easy
Where Made . . . . . . Alliston, Ontario / Greensburg, IN
Fuel Factor
  MPG Rating (city/hwy) . . . . Very Good-28/39
  Driving Range (mi.) Long-423.3
  Fuel Type. . . . . Regular
  Annual Fuel Cost . . . . Very Low-$1511
  Gas Guzzler Tax . . . . No
  Greenhouse Gas Emissions (tons/yr.) Low-5.8
  Barrels of Oil Used per year Low-10.7

How the Competition Rates

Competitors	Rating	Pg.
Ford Focus	6	139
Mazda 3	6	197
Scion tC	7	233

Price Range	Retail	Markup
DX	$15,605	8%
LX	$18,455	9%
EX	$20,505	9%
EX-L	$23,455	9%

Safety Checklist

Crash Tests:
  Frontal . . . . –
  Side . . . . –
Airbags:
  Head . . . . Fr. & Rr. Roof Curtain
  Torso . . . . Front Torso from Seat
  Pelvis . . . . None
  Roll Sensing . . . . No
  Knee Bolster . . . . None
Crash Avoidance:
  Frontal Collision Warning . . . . None
  Blind Spot Detection . . . . None
  Crash Imminent Braking . . . . None
  Lane Departure Warning . . . . None
General:
  Auto. Crash Notification . . . . None
  Day Running Lamps . . . . Standard
Safety Belt/Restraint:
  Dynamic Head Restraints . . . . None
  Adjustable Belt . . . . Standard Front
  Pretensioners . . . . Standard Front

Honda Civic Coupe

Specifications

Drive . . . . FWD
Engine 1.8-liter I4
Transmission . . . . 5-sp. Automatic
Tow Rating (lbs.) . . . . –
Head/Leg Room (in.) Cramped-38.1/42.2
Interior Space (cu. ft.) . . . . Very Cramped-83.2
Cargo Space (cu. ft.) . . . . Very Cramped-11.7
Wheelbase/Length (in.) 103.2/175.5

Additional injury potential in side test see footnote (4) on page 21.

Ratings—10 Best, 1 Worst

Combo Crash Tests	2
Safety Features	5
Rollover	4
Preventative Maintenance	7
Repair Costs	7
Warranty	1
Fuel Economy	6
Complaints	–
Insurance Costs	10
OVERALL RATING	**4**

Honda CR-V

Honda CR-V

At-a-Glance

Status/Year Series Started . . . . All New/2012
Twins . . . . –
Body Styles. . . . . SUV
Seating. 5
Anti-Theft Device . . Std. Pass. Immob. & Opt. Pass. Alarm
Parking Index Rating . . . . Easy
Where Made . . . . East Liberty, OH / Mexico

Fuel Factor
MPG Rating (city/hwy) Average-23/31
Driving Range (mi.) Average-398.1
Fuel Type. . . . . Regular
Annual Fuel Cost . . . . Low-$1862
Gas Guzzler Tax . . . . No
Greenhouse Gas Emissions (tons/yr.) Low-5.7
Barrels of Oil Used per year. Average-13.2

How the Competition Rates

Competitors	Rating	Pg.
Ford Escape	2	133
Hyundai Tucson	8	162
Kia Sportage	–	183

Price Range

	Retail	Markup
LX	$21,895	7%
SE	$22,595	7%
EX	$25,445	7%
EX-L	$30,095	7%

Safety Checklist

Crash Tests:
Frontal. . . . . Poor
Side . . . . Very Poor
Airbags:
Head. . . . . Fr. & Rr. Roof Curtain
Torso . . . . Front Torso from Seat
Pelvis . . . . None
Roll Sensing . . . . Yes
Knee Bolster . . . . None
Crash Avoidance:
Frontal Collision Warning. . . . . None
Blind Spot Detection . . . . None
Crash Imminent Braking . . . . None
Lane Departure Warning . . . . None
General:
Auto. Crash Notification. . . . . None
Day Running Lamps . . . . Standard
Safety Belt/Restraint:
Dynamic Head Restraints . . . . None
Adjustable Belt . . . . Standard Front
Pretensioners . . . . Standard Front

Honda CR-V

Specifications

Drive . . . . FWD
Engine. 2.4-liter I4
Transmission . . . . 5-sp. Automatic
Tow Rating (lbs.). . . . . Very Low-1500
Head/Leg Room (in.) Average-39.9/41.3
Interior Space (cu. ft.) Roomy-104.1
Cargo Space (cu. ft.). . . . . Very Roomy-37.2
Wheelbase/Length (in.) 103.1/178.3

Ratings—10 Best, 1 Worst	
Combo Crash Tests	2
Safety Features	2
Rollover	9
Preventative Maintenance	–
Repair Costs	–
Warranty	1
Fuel Economy	10
Complaints	2
Insurance Costs	1
OVERALL RATING	**1**

Honda CR-Z

Honda CR-Z

At-a-Glance

Status/Year Series Started Unchanged/2011
Twins . . . . –
Body Styles . . . . Coupe
Seating 2
Anti-Theft Device . . . . Std. Pass. Immobil. & Alarm
Parking Index Rating . . . . Very Easy
Where Made . . . . Suzuka, Japan
Fuel Factor
MPG Rating (city/hwy) . . . . Very Good-35/39
Driving Range (mi.) Average-389.0
Fuel Type . . . . Regular
Annual Fuel Cost . . . . Very Low-$1320
Gas Guzzler Tax . . . . No
Greenhouse Gas Emissions (tons/yr.) . Very Low-5.1
Barrels of Oil Used per year . . . . Very Low-9.3

How the Competition Rates

Competitors	Rating	Pg.
Hyundai Veloster	–	163
Nissan Juke	–	220
Scion xB	–	234

Price Range	Retail	Markup
Base Manual	$19,545	6%
Base Automatic	$20,195	6%
EX	$21,755	6%
EX w/ Nav	$23,555	6%

Safety Checklist

Crash Tests:
  Frontal . . . . Very Poor
  Side . . . . Average
Airbags:
  Head . . . . Front Roof Curtain
  Torso . . . . Front Torso from Seat
  Pelvis . . . . None
  Roll Sensing . . . . No
  Knee Bolster . . . . None
Crash Avoidance:
  Frontal Collision Warning . . . . None
  Blind Spot Detection . . . . None
  Crash Imminent Braking . . . . None
  Lane Departure Warning . . . . None
General:
  Auto. Crash Notification . . . . None
  Day Running Lamps . . . . Standard
Safety Belt/Restraint:
  Dynamic Head Restraints . . . . . . Standard Front
  Adjustable Belt . . . . None
  Pretensioners . . . . Standard Front

Honda CR-Z

Specifications

Drive . . . . FWD
Engine 1.5-liter I4
Transmission . . . . CVT
Tow Rating (lbs.) . . . . –
Head/Leg Room (in.) . . . . . Very Cramped-36.9/42.7
Interior Space (cu. ft.) . . . . . Very Cramped-49.1
Cargo Space (cu. ft.) Roomy-25.1
Wheelbase/Length (in.) 95.9/160.6

Ratings—10 Best, 1 Worst	
Combo Crash Tests	–
Safety Features	4
Rollover	5
Preventative Maintenance	8
Repair Costs	8
Warranty	1
Fuel Economy	9
Complaints	7
Insurance Costs	1
OVERALL RATING	**–**

Honda Fit

Honda Fit

At-a-Glance

Status/Year Series Started Unchanged/2009
Twins . . . . –
Body Styles . . . . Hatchback
Seating 5
Anti-Theft Device . Std. Pass. Immobil. & Opt. Pass. Alarm
Parking Index Rating . . . . Very Easy
Where Made. . . . . Suzuka, Japan

Fuel Factor
MPG Rating (city/hwy) . . . . Very Good-28/35
Driving Range (mi.). . . . . Very Short-326.2
Fuel Type. . . . . Regular
Annual Fuel Cost . . . . Very Low-$1575
Gas Guzzler Tax . . . . No
Greenhouse Gas Emissions (tons/yr.) Low-6.0
Barrels of Oil Used per year Low-11.0

How the Competition Rates

Competitors	Rating	Pg.
Hyundai Accent	9	155
Nissan Versa	1	228
Toyota Yaris	–	258

Price Range	Retail	Markup
Base Manual	$15,175	4%
Base Automatic	$15,975	4%
Sport	$17,760	4%
Sport w/Nav	$19,540	4%

Safety Checklist

Crash Tests:
Frontal . . . . –
Side . . . . –
Airbags:
Head. . . . . Fr. & Rr. Roof Curtain
Torso . . . . Front Torso from Seat
Pelvis . . . . None
Roll Sensing. . . . . No
Knee Bolster . . . . None
Crash Avoidance:
Frontal Collision Warning. . . . . None
Blind Spot Detection . . . . None
Crash Imminent Braking . . . . None
Lane Departure Warning . . . . None
General:
Auto. Crash Notification . . . . None
Day Running Lamps . . . . Standard
Safety Belt/Restraint:
Dynamic Head Restraints . . . . . . Standard Front
Adjustable Belt . . . . Standard Front
Pretensioners . . . . Standard Front

Honda Fit

Specifications

Drive . . . . FWD
Engine. 1.5-liter I4
Transmission . . . . 5-sp. Automatic
Tow Rating (lbs.). . . . . –
Head/Leg Room (in.). Average-40.4/41.3
Interior Space (cu. ft.) Cramped-90.8
Cargo Space (cu. ft.) Average-20.6
Wheelbase/Length (in.) 98.4/161.6

Ratings—10 Best, 1 Worst

Combo Crash Tests	–
Safety Features	4
Rollover	7
Preventative Maintenance	9
Repair Costs	8
Warranty	1
Fuel Economy	10
Complaints	4
Insurance Costs	1
OVERALL RATING	**–**

Honda Insight

Honda Insight

At-a-Glance

Status/Year Series Started . Appearance Change/2010
Twins . . . . –
Body Styles . . . . Hatchback
Seating 5
Anti-Theft Device . Std. Pass. Immobil. & Opt. Pass. Alarm
Parking Index Rating . . . . Easy
Where Made . . . . Suzuka, Japan
Fuel Factor
MPG Rating (city/hwy) . . . . Very Good-40/43
Driving Range (mi.) Long-437.7
Fuel Type . . . . Regular
Annual Fuel Cost . . . . Very Low-$1173
Gas Guzzler Tax . . . . No
Greenhouse Gas Emissions (tons/yr.) . Very Low-4.6
Barrels of Oil Used per year . . . . Very Low-8.3

How the Competition Rates

Competitors	Rating	Pg.
Kia Soul	6	182
Scion xD	–	235
Toyota Prius	7	251

Price Range

Price Range	Retail	Markup
Base	$18,350	6%
LX	$20,125	6%
EX	$21,815	6%
EX w/Nav	$23,540	6%

Safety Checklist

Crash Tests:
  Frontal . . . . –
  Side . . . . –
Airbags:
  Head . . . . Fr. & Rr. Roof Curtain
  Torso . . . . Front Torso from Seat
  Pelvis . . . . None
  Roll Sensing . . . . No
  Knee Bolster . . . . None
Crash Avoidance:
  Frontal Collision Warning . . . . None
  Blind Spot Detection . . . . None
  Crash Imminent Braking . . . . None
  Lane Departure Warning . . . . None
General:
  Auto. Crash Notification . . . . None
  Day Running Lamps . . . . Standard
Safety Belt/Restraint:
  Dynamic Head Restraints . . . . . . Standard Front
  Adjustable Belt . . . . Standard Front
  Pretensioners . . . . Standard Front

Honda Insight

Specifications

Drive . . . . FWD
Engine 1.3-liter I4
Transmission . . . . CVT
Tow Rating (lbs.) . . . . –
Head/Leg Room (in.) Cramped-38.4/42.3
Interior Space (cu. ft.) . . . . Very Cramped-85
Cargo Space (cu. ft.) Average-15.9
Wheelbase/Length (in.) 100.4/172.3

Ratings—10 Best, 1 Worst

Combo Crash Tests	8
Safety Features	8
Rollover	6
Preventative Maintenance	7
Repair Costs	5
Warranty	1
Fuel Economy	4
Complaints	3
Insurance Costs	10
OVERALL RATING	**7**

Honda Odyssey

At-a-Glance

Status/Year Series Started Unchanged/2005
Twins . . . . −
Body Styles . . . . Minivan
Seating. 7
Anti-Theft Device . Std. Pass. Immobil. & Opt. Pass. Alarm
Parking Index Rating . . . . Hard
Where Made. . . . . Lincoln, AL

Fuel Factor
MPG Rating (city/hwy) Poor-18/28
Driving Range (mi.) . . . . Very Long-450.4
Fuel Type. . . . . Regular
Annual Fuel Cost. . . . . High-$2259
Gas Guzzler Tax . . . . No
Greenhouse Gas Emissions (tons/yr.) High-8.5
Barrels of Oil Used per year. High-15.6

How the Competition Rates

Competitors	Rating	Pg.
Chrysler Town and Country	5	123
Toyota Sienna	1	254
Volkswagen Routan	−	264

Price Range	Retail	Markup
LX	$28,225	10%
EX	$31,475	10%
Touring	$41,180	10%
Touring Elite	$43,675	10%

Honda Odyssey

Safety Checklist

Crash Tests:
Frontal . . . . Very Good
Side. . . . . Average
Airbags:
Head . . . . Fr. & Rr. Roof Curtain
Torso. . . . . Front Pelvis/Torso from Seat
Pelvis . . . . Front Pelvis/Torso from Seat
Roll Sensing . . . . Yes
Knee Bolster . . . . None
Crash Avoidance:
Frontal Collision Warning. . . . . None
Blind Spot Detection . . . . Optional
Crash Imminent Braking . . . . None
Lane Departure Warning . . . . None
General:
Auto. Crash Notification. . . . . None
Day Running Lamps . . . . Standard
Safety Belt/Restraint:
Dynamic Head Restraints. . . . . . Standard Front
Adjustable Belt . . . . . . Standard Front and Rear
Pretensioners . . . . Standard Front

Honda Odyssey

Specifications

Drive . . . . FWD
Engine 3.5-liter V6
Transmission . . . . 5-sp. Automatic
Tow Rating (lbs.) Low-3500
Head/Leg Room (in.) Cramped-39.7/40.9
Interior Space (cu. ft.) . . . . Very Roomy-172.5
Cargo Space (cu. ft.) . . . . Very Roomy-38.4
Wheelbase/Length (in.) 118.1/202.9

Honda Pilot

Ratings—10 Best, 1 Worst	
Combo Crash Tests	4
Safety Features	7
Rollover	4
Preventative Maintenance	3
Repair Costs	6
Warranty	1
Fuel Economy	3
Complaints	9
Insurance Costs	10
OVERALL RATING	**4**

Honda Pilot

Honda Pilot

At-a-Glance

Status/Year Series Started . Appearance Change/2009
Twins . . . . —
Body Styles. . . . . SUV
Seating. 8
Anti-Theft Device . . Std. Pass. Immob. & Opt. Pass. Alarm
Parking Index Rating . . . . Average
Where Made. . . . . Lincoln, AL

Fuel Factor
MPG Rating (city/hwy). Poor-17/24
Driving Range (mi.) Average-410.9
Fuel Type. . . . . Regular
Annual Fuel Cost. . . . . High-$2476
Gas Guzzler Tax . . . . No
Greenhouse Gas Emissions (tons/yr.) High-9.3
Barrels of Oil Used per year. High-17.1

How the Competition Rates

Competitors	Rating	Pg.
Ford Explorer	6	135
Nissan Pathfinder	–	224
Toyota 4Runner	–	244

Price Range	Retail	Markup
LX	$28,470	10%
EX	$31,320	10%
EX-L	$36,170	10%
Touring	$40,820	10%

Safety Checklist

Crash Tests:
Frontal. . . . . Average
Side . . . . Very Poor

Airbags:
Head. . . . . Fr. & Rr. Roof Curtain
Torso. . . . . Front Pelvis/Torso from Seat
Pelvis . . . . Front Pelvis/Torso from Seat
Roll Sensing . . . . Yes
Knee Bolster . . . . None

Crash Avoidance:
Frontal Collision Warning. . . . . None
Blind Spot Detection . . . . None
Crash Imminent Braking . . . . None
Lane Departure Warning . . . . None

General:
Auto. Crash Notification. . . . . None
Day Running Lamps . . . . Standard

Safety Belt/Restraint:
Dynamic Head Restraints. . . . . . Standard Front
Adjustable Belt . . . . . . Standard Front and Rear
Pretensioners . . . . Standard Front

Honda Pilot

Specifications

Drive 4WD
Engine. 3.5-liter V6
Transmission . . . . 5-sp. Automatic
Tow Rating (lbs.) Low-4500
Head/Leg Room (in.) Average-40/41.4
Interior Space (cu. ft.) . . . . Very Roomy-153.7
Cargo Space (cu. ft.) Average-18
Wheelbase/Length (in.) 109.2/191.4

Ratings—10 Best, 1 Worst

Combo Crash Tests	–
Safety Features	7
Rollover	4
Preventative Maintenance	6
Repair Costs	8
Warranty	1
Fuel Economy	1
Complaints	7
Insurance Costs	8
OVERALL RATING	–

Honda Ridgeline

Honda Ridgeline

Safety Checklist

Crash Tests:
Frontal . . . . –
Side . . . . –
Airbags:
Head . . . . Fr. & Rr. Roof Curtain
Torso . . . . Front Torso from Seat
Pelvis . . . . None
Roll Sensing . . . . Yes
Knee Bolster . . . . None
Crash Avoidance:
Frontal Collision Warning . . . . None
Blind Spot Detection . . . . None
Crash Imminent Braking . . . . None
Lane Departure Warning . . . . None
General:
Auto. Crash Notification . . . . None
Day Running Lamps . . . . Standard
Safety Belt/Restraint:
Dynamic Head Restraints . . . . . Standard Front
Adjustable Belt . . . . Standard Front
Pretensioners . . . . Standard Front

At-a-Glance

Status/Year Series Started . Appearance Change/2006
Twins . . . . –
Body Styles . . . . Pickup
Seating 5
Anti-Theft Device . . . Std. Pass. Immob. & Opt. Pass. Alarm
Parking Index Rating . . . . Very Hard
Where Made . . . . Alliston, Ontario
Fuel Factor
MPG Rating (city/hwy) . . . . Very Poor-15/20
Driving Range (mi.) Short-371.8
Fuel Type . . . . Regular
Annual Fuel Cost . . . . Very High-$2867
Gas Guzzler Tax . . . . No
Greenhouse Gas Emissions (tons/yr.) Very High-11.0
Barrels of Oil Used per year . . . . . . Very High-20.1

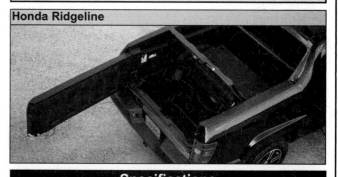

Honda Ridgeline

How the Competition Rates

Competitors	Rating	Pg.
Chevrolet Avalanche	–	107
Nissan Titan	–	227
Toyota Tacoma	1	255

Price Range	Retail	Markup
RT	$29,250	10%
RTS	$31,955	10%
RTL	$34,830	10%
RTL w/Nav	$37,180	10%

Specifications

Drive 4WD
Engine 3.5-liter V6
Transmission . . . . 5-sp. Automatic
Tow Rating (lbs.) Average-5000
Head/Leg Room (in.) Average-40.7/40.8
Interior Space (cu. ft.) Roomy-112
Cargo Space (cu. ft.) . . . . . . Very Roomy-37.6
Wheelbase/Length (in.) 122/206.9

Ratings—10 Best, 1 Worst

Combo Crash Tests	6
Safety Features	4
Rollover	7
Preventative Maintenance	6
Repair Costs	10
Warranty	10
Fuel Economy	10
Complaints	–
Insurance Costs	1
OVERALL RATING	**8**

Hyundai Accent

Hyundai Accent

At-a-Glance

Status/Year Series Started . . . . All New/2012
Twins . . . . Kia Rio
Body Styles. . . . . Sedan, Hatchback
Seating. 5
Anti-Theft Device. . . . . None
Parking Index Rating . . . . Very Easy
Where Made . . . . Ulsan, South Korea
Fuel Factor
MPG Rating (city/hwy) . . . . Very Good-30/40
Driving Range (mi.). Short-385.4
Fuel Type. . . . . Regular
Annual Fuel Cost . . . . Very Low-$1433
Gas Guzzler Tax . . . . No
Greenhouse Gas Emissions (tons/yr.) Low-5.7
Barrels of Oil Used per year Low-10.4

How the Competition Rates

Competitors	Rating	Pg.
Ford Fiesta	5	137
Nissan Versa	1	228
Suzuki SX4	–	243

Price Range	Retail	Markup
GLS Manual Trans.	$12,445	2%
GL Manual Trans.	$14,595	3%
GLS Auto. Trans.	$15,195	3%
SE Auto Trans.	$16,795	3%

Safety Checklist

Crash Tests:
Frontal . . . . Good
Side. . . . . Poor
Airbags:
Head . . . . Fr. & Rr. Roof Curtain
Torso. . . . . Front Pelvis/Torso from Seat
Pelvis . . . . Front Pelvis/Torso from Seat
Roll Sensing. . . . . No
Knee Bolster . . . . None
Crash Avoidance:
Frontal Collision Warning. . . . . None
Blind Spot Detection . . . . None
Crash Imminent Braking . . . . None
Lane Departure Warning . . . . None
General:
Auto. Crash Notification . . . . None
Day Running Lamps . . . . None
Safety Belt/Restraint:
Dynamic Head Restraints. . . . . Standard Front
Adjustable Belt . . . . Standard Front
Pretensioners . . . . Standard Front

Hyundai Accent

Specifications

Drive . . . . FWD
Engine. 1.6-liter I4
Transmission . . . . 4-sp. Automatic
Tow Rating (lbs.). . . . . –
Head/Leg Room (in.). Average-39.9/41.8
Interior Space (cu. ft.) . . . . Very Cramped-90.1
Cargo Space (cu. ft.). Average-21.2
Wheelbase/Length (in.). 101.2/162

Ratings—10 Best, 1 Worst

Combo Crash Tests	–
Safety Features	7
Rollover	8
Preventative Maintenance	–
Repair Costs	–
Warranty	10
Fuel Economy	5
Complaints	–
Insurance Costs	5
OVERALL RATING	**–**

Hyundai Azera

At-a-Glance

Status/Year Series Started . . . . All New/2012
Twins . . . . –
Body Styles . . . . Sedan
Seating 5
Anti-Theft Device . Std. Pass. Immobil. & Active Alarm
Parking Index Rating . . . . Average
Where Made . . . . Ulsan, South Korea
Fuel Factor
MPG Rating (city/hwy) Average-20/29
Driving Range (mi.) Long-430.1
Fuel Type. . . . . Regular
Annual Fuel Cost. . . . . Average-$2084
Gas Guzzler Tax . . . . No
Greenhouse Gas Emissions (tons/yr.) Low-6.4
Barrels of Oil Used per year. High-14.9

How the Competition Rates

Competitors	Rating	Pg.
Lexus ES	–	187
Nissan Maxima	4	222
Toyota Avalon	–	245

Price Range	Retail	Markup

Hyundai Azera

Safety Checklist

Crash Tests:
Frontal . . . . –
Side . . . . –
Airbags:
Head. . . . . Fr. & Rr. Roof Curtain
Torso. . . . . Fr. & Rr. Pelvis/Torso from Seat
Pelvis . . . . Front Pelvis/Torso from Seat
Roll Sensing. . . . . No
Knee Bolster . . . . Standard Driver
Crash Avoidance:
Frontal Collision Warning. . . . . None
Blind Spot Detection . . . . None
Crash Imminent Braking . . . . None
Lane Departure Warning . . . . None
General:
Auto. Crash Notification . . . . Optional
Day Running Lamps . . . . Standard
Safety Belt/Restraint:
Dynamic Head Restraints . . . . None
Adjustable Belt . . . . Standard Front
Pretensioners . . . . Standard Front

Hyundai Azera

Specifications

Drive . . . . FWD
Engine 3.3-liter V6
Transmission . . . . 6-sp. Automatic
Tow Rating (lbs.). . . . . Very Low-1000
Head/Leg Room (in.) . . . . . . Very Roomy-40.3/45.5
Interior Space (cu. ft.). Roomy-107
Cargo Space (cu. ft.) Average-16.3
Wheelbase/Length (in.) 112/193.3

Hyundai Elantra

Ratings—10 Best, 1 Worst

Combo Crash Tests	3
Safety Features	4
Rollover	8
Preventative Maintenance	4
Repair Costs	10
Warranty	10
Fuel Economy	10
Complaints	8
Insurance Costs	1
OVERALL RATING	**7**

Hyundai Elantra

Hyundai Elantra

At-a-Glance

Status/Year Series Started	Unchanged/2011
Twins	–
Body Styles	Sedan, Wagon
Seating	5
Anti-Theft Device	Opt. Pass. Immobil. & Active Alarm
Parking Index Rating	Easy
Where Made	Montgomery, AL

Fuel Factor

MPG Rating (city/hwy)	Very Good-29/40
Driving Range (mi.)	Long-423.6
Fuel Type	Regular
Annual Fuel Cost	Very Low-$1464
Gas Guzzler Tax	No
Greenhouse Gas Emissions (tons/yr.)	Low-5.7
Barrels of Oil Used per year	Low-10.4

How the Competition Rates

Competitors	Rating	Pg.
Honda Civic	–	146
Nissan Sentra	4	226
Toyota Corolla	4	247

Price Range

Price Range	Retail	Markup
GLS	$15,195	3%
Touring GLS	$17,195	3%
Touring SE	$20,295	4%
Limited	$20,445	4%

Safety Checklist

Crash Tests:

Frontal	Very Poor
Side	Good

Airbags:

Head	Fr. & Rr. Roof Curtain
Torso	Front Pelvis/Torso from Seat
Pelvis	Front Pelvis/Torso from Seat
Roll Sensing	No
Knee Bolster	None

Crash Avoidance:

Frontal Collision Warning	None
Blind Spot Detection	None
Crash Imminent Braking	None
Lane Departure Warning	None

General:

Auto. Crash Notification	None
Day Running Lamps	Optional

Safety Belt/Restraint:

Dynamic Head Restraints	Standard Front
Adjustable Belt	Standard Front
Pretensioners	Standard Front

Hyundai Elantra

Specifications

Drive	FWD
Engine	1.6-liter I4
Transmission	4-sp. Automatic
Tow Rating (lbs.)	Very Low-1000
Head/Leg Room (in.)	Very Roomy-40/43.6
Interior Space (cu. ft.)	Cramped-95.6
Cargo Space (cu. ft.)	Cramped-14.8
Wheelbase/Length (in.)	106.3/178.3

Ratings—10 Best, 1 Worst

Combo Crash Tests	–
Safety Features	9
Rollover	8
Preventative Maintenance	–
Repair Costs	–
Warranty	10
Fuel Economy	2
Complaints	–
Insurance Costs	3
OVERALL RATING	–

Hyundai Equus

Hyundai Equus

At-a-Glance

Status/Year Series Started Unchanged/2011
Twins . . . . –
Body Styles . . . . Sedan
Seating 4
Anti-Theft Device . Std. Pass. Immobil. & Active Alarm
Parking Index Rating . . . . Very Hard
Where Made . . . . Ulsan, South Korea
Fuel Factor
  MPG Rating (city/hwy) . . . . Very Poor-15/23
  Driving Range (mi.) Short-361.0
  Fuel Type . . . . Premium
  Annual Fuel Cost . . . . Very High-$2952
  Gas Guzzler Tax . . . . No
  Greenhouse Gas Emissions (tons/yr.) High-10.4
  Barrels of Oil Used per year . . . . Very High-19.0

How the Competition Rates

Competitors	Rating	Pg.
Audi A8	–	91
Jaguar XF	–	170
Mercedes-Benz S-Class	–	208

Price Range

Price Range	Retail	Markup
Base Signature	$58,750	7%
Ultimate	$65,750	7%

Safety Checklist

Crash Tests:
  Frontal . . . . –
  Side . . . . –
Airbags:
  Head . . . . Fr. & Rr. Roof Curtain
  Torso . . . . Fr. & Rr. Pelvis/Torso from Seat
  Pelvis . . . . Front Pelvis/Torso from Seat
  Roll Sensing . . . . No
  Knee Bolster . . . . Standard Driver
Crash Avoidance:
  Frontal Collision Warning . . . . None
  Blind Spot Detection . . . . None
  Crash Imminent Braking . . . . Optional
  Lane Departure Warning . . . . Optional
General:
  Auto. Crash Notification . . . . None
  Day Running Lamps . . . . Standard
Safety Belt/Restraint:
  Dynamic Head Restraints . . . . . . Standard Front
  Adjustable Belt . . . . Standard Front
  Pretensioners . . . . Standard Front

Hyundai Equus

Specifications

Drive . . . . RWD
Engine 5.0-liter I-4
Transmission . . . . 6-sp. Electronic
Tow Rating (lbs.) . . . . –
Head/Leg Room (in.) . . . . . . Very Roomy-38.7/45.1
Interior Space (cu. ft.) Roomy-109.3
Cargo Space (cu. ft.) Average-16.7
Wheelbase/Length (in.) 119.9/203.1

Ratings—10 Best, 1 Worst

Combo Crash Tests	–
Safety Features	7
Rollover	9
Preventative Maintenance	4
Repair Costs	5
Warranty	10
Fuel Economy	4
Complaints	2
Insurance Costs	5
OVERALL RATING	–

Hyundai Genesis

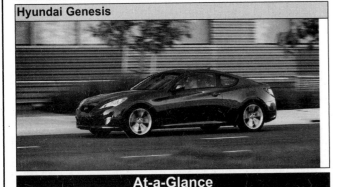
Hyundai Genesis

At-a-Glance

Status/Year Series Started . Appearance Change/2009
Twins . . . . –
Body Styles . . . . Sedan
Seating. 5
Anti-Theft Device . Std. Pass. Immobil. & Active Alarm
Parking Index Rating . . . . Average
Where Made . . . . Ulsan, South Korea
Fuel Factor
  MPG Rating (city/hwy) Poor-19/29
  Driving Range (mi.) Long-434.1
  Fuel Type. . . . . Regular
  Annual Fuel Cost. . . . . Average-$2154
  Gas Guzzler Tax . . . . No
  Greenhouse Gas Emissions (tons/yr.) High-8.5
  Barrels of Oil Used per year. High-15.6

How the Competition Rates

Competitors	Rating	Pg.
Acura TL	–	83
Lexus ES	–	187
Volkswagen CC	–	260

Price Range

Price Range	Retail	Markup
V6	$34,200	7%
V8	$44,500	8%
R-Spec	$46,500	8%

Safety Checklist

Crash Tests:
  Frontal . . . . –
  Side . . . . –
Airbags:
  Head. . . . . Fr. & Rr. Roof Curtain
  Torso. . . . . Fr. & Rr. Pelvis/Torso from Seat
  Pelvis . . . . Front Pelvis/Torso from Seat
  Roll Sensing. . . . . No
  Knee Bolster . . . . None
Crash Avoidance:
  Frontal Collision Warning. . . . . None
  Blind Spot Detection . . . . None
  Crash Imminent Braking . . . . None
  Lane Departure Warning. . . . . Optional
General:
  Auto. Crash Notification. . . . . None
  Day Running Lamps . . . . Optional
Safety Belt/Restraint:
  Dynamic Head Restraints. . . . . . Standard Front
  Adjustable Belt . . . . Standard Front
  Pretensioners . . . . Standard Front

Hyundai Genesis

Specifications

Drive . . . . FWD
Engine 3.8-liter V6
Transmission . . . . 6-sp. Automatic
Tow Rating (lbs.). . . . . –
Head/Leg Room (in.) . . . . . . Very Roomy-40.4/44.3
Interior Space (cu. ft.) Roomy-109.4
Cargo Space (cu. ft.) Average-15.9
Wheelbase/Length (in.) 115.6/196.3

Ratings—10 Best, 1 Worst

Combo Crash Tests	–
Safety Features	6
Rollover	4
Preventative Maintenance	4
Repair Costs	8
Warranty	10
Fuel Economy	4
Complaints	4
Insurance Costs	10
OVERALL RATING	**–**

Hyundai Santa Fe

Hyundai Santa Fe

At-a-Glance

Status/Year Series Started . Appearance Change/2007
Twins . . . . Kia Sorento
Body Styles . . . . SUV
Seating 5
Anti-Theft Device . . . . Std. Active Alarm
Parking Index Rating . . . . Easy
Where Made . . . . West Point, GA
Fuel Factor
  MPG Rating (city/hwy) Poor-20/28
  Driving Range (mi.) Long-413.1
  Fuel Type . . . . Regular
  Annual Fuel Cost . . . . Average-$2111
  Gas Guzzler Tax . . . . No
  Greenhouse Gas Emissions (tons/yr.) . . Average-8.1
  Barrels of Oil Used per year High-14.9

How the Competition Rates

Competitors	Rating	Pg.
Mazda CX-7	–	200
Nissan Rogue	5	225
Toyota RAV4	1	252

Price Range

	Retail	Markup
GLS	$23,225	4%
GLS V6	$25,125	4%
SE	$26,225	5%
Limited	$30,925	7%

Safety Checklist

Crash Tests:
  Frontal . . . . –
  Side . . . . –
Airbags:
  Head . . . . Fr. & Rr. Roof Curtain
  Torso . . . . Front Pelvis/Torso from Seat
  Pelvis . . . . Front Pelvis/Torso from Seat
  Roll Sensing . . . . Yes
  Knee Bolster . . . . None
Crash Avoidance:
  Frontal Collision Warning . . . . None
  Blind Spot Detection . . . . None
  Crash Imminent Braking . . . . None
  Lane Departure Warning . . . . None
General:
  Auto. Crash Notification . . . . None
  Day Running Lamps . . . . None
Safety Belt/Restraint:
  Dynamic Head Restraints . . . . . . Standard Front
  Adjustable Belt . . . . Standard Front
  Pretensioners . . . . Standard Front

Hyundai Santa Fe

Specifications

Drive . . . . FWD
Engine 2.4-liter I4
Transmission . . . . 6-sp. Automatic
Tow Rating (lbs.) . . . . Very Low-2000
Head/Leg Room (in.) Roomy-40.2/42.6
Interior Space (cu. ft.) Roomy-108.3
Cargo Space (cu. ft.) . . . . Very Roomy-34.2
Wheelbase/Length (in.) 106.3/184.1

Hyundai Sonata Intermediate

Ratings—10 Best, 1 Worst

Combo Crash Tests	9
Safety Features	6
Rollover	9
Preventative Maintenance	4
Repair Costs	10
Warranty	10
Fuel Economy	8
Complaints	1
Insurance Costs	3
OVERALL RATING	**9**

Hyundai Sonata

Hyundai Sonata

At-a-Glance

Status/Year Series Started	Unchanged/2011
Twins	–
Body Styles	Sedan
Seating	5
Anti-Theft Device	Std. Pass. Immobil. & Active Alarm
Parking Index Rating	Easy
Where Made	Montgomery, AL

Fuel Factor

MPG Rating (city/hwy)	Good-24/35
Driving Range (mi.)	Very Long-517.1
Fuel Type	Regular
Annual Fuel Cost	Low-$1733
Gas Guzzler Tax	No
Greenhouse Gas Emissions (tons/yr.)	Average-6.7
Barrels of Oil Used per year	Average-12.2

How the Competition Rates

Competitors	Rating	Pg.
Mazda 6	7	199
Toyota Camry	10	246
Volkswagen Passat	10	263

Price Range

Price Range	Retail	Markup
GLS Manual Trans.	$19,695	4%
GLS Auto. Trans.	$20,695	4%
SE	$23,095	6%
Limited	$26,345	7%

Safety Checklist

Crash Tests:

Frontal	Good
Side	Very Good

Airbags:

Head	Fr. & Rr. Roof Curtain
Torso	Front Pelvis/Torso from Seat
Pelvis	Front Pelvis/Torso from Seat
Roll Sensing	No
Knee Bolster	None

Crash Avoidance:

Frontal Collision Warning	None
Blind Spot Detection	None
Crash Imminent Braking	None
Lane Departure Warning	None

General:

Auto. Crash Notification	Standard
Day Running Lamps	Standard

Safety Belt/Restraint:

Dynamic Head Restraints	Standard Front
Adjustable Belt	Standard Front
Pretensioners	Standard Front

Hyundai Sonata

Specifications

Drive	FWD
Engine	2.4-liter I4
Transmission	6-sp. Automatic
Tow Rating (lbs.)	–
Head/Leg Room (in.)	Very Roomy-40/45.5
Interior Space (cu. ft.)	Roomy-103.8
Cargo Space (cu. ft.)	Average-16.4
Wheelbase/Length (in.)	110/189.8

Hyundai Tucson

Ratings—10 Best, 1 Worst

Combo Crash Tests	5
Safety Features	6
Rollover	4
Preventative Maintenance	4
Repair Costs	10
Warranty	10
Fuel Economy	6
Complaints	6
Insurance Costs	8
OVERALL RATING	**8**

Hyundai Tucson

Hyundai Tucson

At-a-Glance

Status/Year Series Started Unchanged/2010
Twins . . . . –
Body Styles. . . . . SUV
Seating. 5
Anti-Theft Device . . . . Opt. Active Alarm
Parking Index Rating . . . . Very Easy
Where Made . . . . Zilina, Slovakia
Fuel Factor
MPG Rating (city/hwy) Average-23/31
Driving Range (mi.) Average-398.1
Fuel Type. . . . . Regular
Annual Fuel Cost . . . . Low-$1862
Gas Guzzler Tax . . . . No
Greenhouse Gas Emissions (tons/yr.) . . Average-7.2
Barrels of Oil Used per year. Average-13.2

How the Competition Rates

Competitors	Rating	Pg.
Honda CR-V	3	148
Suzuki Grand Vitara	–	241
Toyota RAV4	1	252

Price Range	Retail	Markup
GL	$19,045	4%
GLS FWD	$22,195	4%
GLS AWD	$23,845	4%
Limited	$26,395	5%

Safety Checklist

Crash Tests:
Frontal . . . . Average
Side . . . . Average
Airbags:
Head . . . . Fr. & Rr. Roof Curtain
Torso . . . . Front Pelvis/Torso from Seat
Pelvis . . . . Front Pelvis/Torso from Seat
Roll Sensing . . . . Yes
Knee Bolster . . . . None
Crash Avoidance:
Frontal Collision Warning. . . . . None
Blind Spot Detection . . . . None
Crash Imminent Braking . . . . None
Lane Departure Warning . . . . None
General:
Auto. Crash Notification . . . . None
Day Running Lamps . . . . None
Safety Belt/Restraint:
Dynamic Head Restraints. . . . . . Standard Front
Adjustable Belt . . . . Standard Front
Pretensioners . . . . Standard Front

Hyundai Tucson

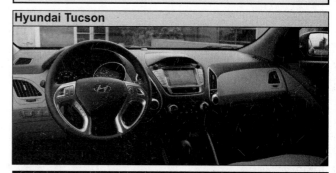

Specifications

Drive . . . . FWD
Engine. 2.0-liter I4
Transmission . . . . 6-sp. Automatic
Tow Rating (lbs.) . . . . Very Low-1000
Head/Leg Room (in.) Average-39.4/42.1
Interior Space (cu. ft.) Average-101.9
Cargo Space (cu. ft.) Roomy-25.7
Wheelbase/Length (in.) 103.9/173.2

Ratings—10 Best, 1 Worst

Combo Crash Tests	–
Safety Features	2
Rollover	9
Preventative Maintenance	–
Repair Costs	–
Warranty	10
Fuel Economy	9
Complaints	–
Insurance Costs	–
OVERALL RATING	–

Hyundai Veloster

Hyundai Veloster

At-a-Glance

Status/Year Series Started . . . . All New/2012
Twins . . . . –
Body Styles . . . . Hatchback
Seating 4
Anti-Theft Device . Std. Pass. Immobil. & Active Alarm
Parking Index Rating . . . . Very Easy
Where Made . . . . Ulsan, South Korea
Fuel Factor
  MPG Rating (city/hwy) . . . . Very Good-29/38
  Driving Range (mi.) Long-428.5
  Fuel Type. . . . . Regular
  Annual Fuel Cost . . . . Very Low-$1493
  Gas Guzzler Tax . . . . No
  Greenhouse Gas Emissions (tons/yr.) Low-5.8
  Barrels of Oil Used per year Low-10.7

How the Competition Rates

Competitors	Rating	Pg.
Honda CR-Z	1	149
Mini Cooper	–	209
Scion tC	7	233

Price Range	Retail	Markup
Manual	$17,300	4%
Automatic	$18,550	4%

Safety Checklist

Crash Tests:
  Frontal . . . . –
  Side . . . . –
Airbags:
  Head . . . . Fr. & Rr. Roof Curtain
  Torso. . . . . Front Pelvis/Torso from Seat
  Pelvis . . . . Front Pelvis/Torso from Seat
  Roll Sensing. . . . . No
  Knee Bolster . . . . None
Crash Avoidance:
  Frontal Collision Warning. . . . . None
  Blind Spot Detection . . . . None
  Crash Imminent Braking . . . . None
  Lane Departure Warning . . . . None
General:
  Auto. Crash Notification . . . . Standard
  Day Running Lamps . . . . None
Safety Belt/Restraint:
  Dynamic Head Restraints . . . . None
  Adjustable Belt. None
  Pretensioners . . . . Standard Front

Hyundai Veloster

Specifications

Drive . . . . FWD
Engine. 1.6-liter I4
Transmission . . . . 6-sp. Automatic
Tow Rating (lbs.) . . . . –
Head/Leg Room (in.) Roomy-39/43.9
Interior Space (cu. ft.) . . . . Very Cramped-89.8
Cargo Space (cu. ft.) Cramped-15.5
Wheelbase/Length (in.) 104.3/166.1

Ratings—10 Best, 1 Worst

Combo Crash Tests	–
Safety Features	4
Rollover	3
Preventative Maintenance	4
Repair Costs	6
Warranty	10
Fuel Economy	2
Complaints	5
Insurance Costs	10
OVERALL RATING	**–**

Hyundai Veracruz

Hyundai Veracruz

At-a-Glance

Status/Year Series Started Unchanged/2008
Twins . . . . –
Body Styles. . . . . SUV
Seating 7/8
Anti-Theft Device . Opt. Pass. Immobil. & Active Alarm
Parking Index Rating . . . . Average
Where Made. . . . . Ulsan, South Korea
Fuel Factor
. MPG Rating (city/hwy). . . . . Very Poor-17/22
Driving Range (mi.) Average-390.1
Fuel Type. . . . . Regular
Annual Fuel Cost. . . . . High-$2559
Gas Guzzler Tax . . . . No
Greenhouse Gas Emissions (tons/yr.) High-9.8
Barrels of Oil Used per year. High-18.0

How the Competition Rates

Competitors	Rating	Pg.
Acura MDX	9	81
Nissan Pathfinder	–	224
Toyota Highlander	4	249

Price Range

Price Range	Retail	Markup
GLS	$28,345	5%
Limited	$34,495	8%

Hyundai Veracruz

Safety Checklist

Crash Tests:
Frontal . . . . –
Side . . . . –
Airbags:
Head. . . . . Fr. & Rr. Roof Curtain
Torso. . . . . Front Pelvis/Torso from Seat
Pelvis . . . . Front Pelvis/Torso from Seat
Roll Sensing. . . . . No
Knee Bolster . . . . None
Crash Avoidance:
Frontal Collision Warning. . . . . None
Blind Spot Detection . . . . None
Crash Imminent Braking . . . . None
Lane Departure Warning . . . . None
General:
Auto. Crash Notification. . . . . None
Day Running Lamps . . . . None
Safety Belt/Restraint:
Dynamic Head Restraints. . . . . . Standard Front
Adjustable Belt . . . . Standard Front
Pretensioners . . . . Standard Front

Hyundai Veracruz

Specifications

Drive . . . . FWD
Engine. 3.8-liter V6
Transmission . . . . 6-sp. Automatic
Tow Rating (lbs.) Low-3500
Head/Leg Room (in.). Roomy-40.3/42.6
Interior Space (cu. ft.) . . . . Very Roomy-150.6
Cargo Space (cu. ft.) Cramped-13.4
Wheelbase/Length (in.) 110.4/190.6

Ratings—10 Best, 1 Worst

Combo Crash Tests	–
Safety Features	7
Rollover	6
Preventative Maintenance	8
Repair Costs	5
Warranty	7
Fuel Economy	3
Complaints	4
Insurance Costs	8
OVERALL RATING	**–**

Infiniti EX

Infiniti EX

At-a-Glance

Status/Year Series Started Unchanged/2008
Twins . . . . –
Body Styles . . . . Sedan
Seating 5
Anti-Theft Device . . . . Std. Pass. Immobil. & Alarm
Parking Index Rating . . . . Easy
Where Made . . . . Tochigi, Japan

Fuel Factor
  MPG Rating (city/hwy) Poor-17/24
  Driving Range (mi.) Average-391.4
  Fuel Type . . . . Premium
  Annual Fuel Cost . . . . Very High-$2683
  Gas Guzzler Tax . . . . No
  Greenhouse Gas Emissions (tons/yr.) High-9.3
  Barrels of Oil Used per year High-17.1

How the Competition Rates

Competitors	Rating	Pg.
Audi Q5	–	92
Subaru Legacy	2	239
Volkswagen Passat	10	263

Price Range

Price Range	Retail	Markup
Base RWD	$35,600	8%
Base AWD	$37,000	8%
Journey RWD	$37,900	8%
Journey AWD	$39,300	8%

Safety Checklist

Crash Tests:
  Frontal . . . . –
  Side . . . . –
Airbags:
  Head . . . . Fr. & Rr. Roof Curtain
  Torso . . . . Front Pelvis/Torso from Seat
  Pelvis . . . . Front Pelvis/Torso from Seat
  Roll Sensing . . . . No
  Knee Bolster . . . . None
Crash Avoidance:
  Frontal Collision Warning . . . . Optional
  Blind Spot Detection . . . . Optional
  Crash Imminent Braking . . . . Optional
  Lane Departure Warning . . . . Optional
General:
  Auto. Crash Notification . . . . None
  Day Running Lamps . . . . None
Safety Belt/Restraint:
  Dynamic Head Restraints . . . . . . Standard Front
  Adjustable Belt . . . . Standard Front
  Pretensioners . . . . Standard Front

Infiniti EX

Specifications

Drive . . . . AWD
Engine 3.5-liter V6
Transmission . . . . 7-sp. Auto. w/Overdrive
Tow Rating (lbs.) . . . . Very Low-1065
Head/Leg Room (in.) . . . . . . Very Roomy-40.5/44.3
Interior Space (cu. ft.) Roomy-107.1
Cargo Space (cu. ft.) Average-18.6
Wheelbase/Length (in.) 110.2/182.3

Ratings—10 Best, 1 Worst

Combo Crash Tests	–
Safety Features	8
Rollover	5
Preventative Maintenance	7
Repair Costs	2
Warranty	7
.Fuel Economy	2
Complaints	8
Insurance Costs	8
OVERALL RATING	–

Infiniti FX

Infiniti FX

Infiniti FX

At-a-Glance

Status/Year Series Started . Appearance Change/2009
Twins . . . . –
Body Styles. . . . . .SUV
Seating. 5
Anti-Theft Device. . . . . . . Std. Pass. Immobil. & Alarm
Parking Index Rating . . . . Average
Where Made . . . . Tochigi, Japan

Fuel Factor
MPG Rating (city/hwy). . . . . Very Poor-16/21
Driving Range (mi.) Long-426.5
Fuel Type. . . . . .Premium
Annual Fuel Cost. . . . . Very High-$2930
Gas Guzzler Tax . . . . .No
Greenhouse Gas Emissions (tons/yr.) High-10.4
Barrels of Oil Used per year . . . . Very High-19.0

How the Competition Rates

Competitors	Rating	Pg.
BMW X5	–	99
Lexus GX	–	189
Mercedes-Benz M-Class	–	207

Price Range	Retail	Markup
35 RWD	$43,450	8%
35 AWD	$44,900	8%
35 Limited Edition	$51,550	8%
50 AWD	$59,350	8%

Safety Checklist

Crash Tests:
Frontal . . . .–
Side . . . .–
Airbags:
Head. . . . . Fr. & Rr. Roof Curtain
Torso. . . . . Front Pelvis/Torso from Seat
Pelvis . . . . Front Pelvis/Torso from Seat
Roll Sensing . . . . Yes
Knee Bolster . . . . None
Crash Avoidance:
Frontal Collision Warning . . . . Optional
Blind Spot Detection . . . . None
Crash Imminent Braking . . . . Optional
Lane Departure Warning. . . . . Optional
General:
Auto. Crash Notification . . . . None
Day Running Lamps . . . . None
Safety Belt/Restraint:
Dynamic Head Restraints. . . . . . Standard Front
Adjustable Belt . . . . Standard Front
Pretensioners . . . . Standard Front

Infiniti FX

Specifications

Drive . . . . .AWD
Engine 3.5-liter V6
Transmission . . . . 7-sp. Auto. w/Overdrive
Tow Rating (lbs.) Low-3500
Head/Leg Room (in.) . . . . . . Very Roomy-39.3/44.7
Interior Space (cu. ft.) Average-102.5
Cargo Space (cu. ft.) Roomy-24.8
Wheelbase/Length (in.) 113.6/191.3

Ratings—10 Best, 1 Worst

Combo Crash Tests	–
Safety Features	4
Rollover	7
Preventative Maintenance	8
Repair Costs	3
Warranty	7
Fuel Economy	5
Complaints	7
Insurance Costs	3
OVERALL RATING	**–**

Infiniti G

Infiniti G

At-a-Glance

Status/Year Series Started	Unchanged/2003
Twins	–
Body Styles	Sedan, Coupe, Convertible
Seating	5
Anti-Theft Device	Std. Pass. Immobil. & Alarm
Parking Index Rating	Easy
Where Made	Tochigi, Japan

Fuel Factor

MPG Rating (city/hwy)	Average-20/29
Driving Range (mi.)	Very Long-464.9
Fuel Type	Premium
Annual Fuel Cost	Average-$2258
Gas Guzzler Tax	No
Greenhouse Gas Emissions (tons/yr.)	Average-8.1
Barrels of Oil Used per year	High-14.9

How the Competition Rates

Competitors	Rating	Pg.
Acura TL	–	83
Cadillac CTS	7	105
Lexus GS	–	188

Price Range	Retail	Markup
25	$32,400	8%
37 Journey	$36,200	8%
37 Sport	$40,600	8%
37x Limited Edition	$45,150	8%

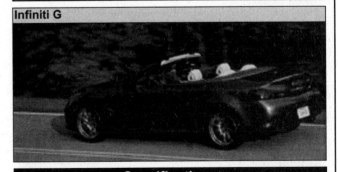
Infiniti G

Safety Checklist

Crash Tests:
Frontal . . . . –
Side . . . . –

Airbags:
Head . . . . Fr. & Rr. Roof Curtain
Torso . . . . Front Pelvis/Torso from Seat
Pelvis . . . . Front Pelvis/Torso from Seat
Roll Sensing . . . . No
Knee Bolster . . . . None

Crash Avoidance:
Frontal Collision Warning . . . . None
Blind Spot Detection . . . . None
Crash Imminent Braking . . . . None
Lane Departure Warning . . . . None

General:
Auto. Crash Notification . . . . None
Day Running Lamps . . . . None

Safety Belt/Restraint:
Dynamic Head Restraints . . . . . . Standard Front
Adjustable Belt . . . . Standard Front
Pretensioners . . . . Standard Front

Infiniti G

Specifications

Drive	RWD
Engine	2.5-liter V6
Transmission	7-sp. Automatic
Tow Rating (lbs.)	–
Head/Leg Room (in.)	Very Roomy-40.5/43.9
Interior Space (cu. ft.)	Average-99
Cargo Space (cu. ft.)	Cramped-13.5
Wheelbase/Length (in.)	112.2/187.9

Ratings—10 Best, 1 Worst	
Combo Crash Tests	5
Safety Features	7
Rollover	7
Preventative Maintenance	8
Repair Costs	6
Warranty	7
Fuel Economy	3
Complaints	4
Insurance Costs	5
OVERALL RATING	**6**

Infiniti M

Infiniti M

At-a-Glance

Status/Year Series Started Unchanged/2006
Twins . . . . –
Body Styles . . . . Sedan
Seating 5
Anti-Theft Device . . . . Std. Pass. Immobil. & Alarm
Parking Index Rating . . . . Average
Where Made . . . . Tochigi, Japan
Fuel Factor
  MPG Rating (city/hwy) Poor-18/26
  Driving Range (mi.) Long-417.9
  Fuel Type . . . . Premium
  Annual Fuel Cost . . . . High-$2513
  Gas Guzzler Tax . . . . No
  Greenhouse Gas Emissions (tons/yr.) High-8.9
  Barrels of Oil Used per year High-16.3

How the Competition Rates

Competitors	Rating	Pg.
BMW 7 Series	–	97
Jaguar XF	–	170
Volvo S80	–	268

Price Range	Retail	Markup
M37	$47,700	8%
M37x AWD	$49,850	8%
M56	$59,100	8%
M56x	$61,600	8%

Safety Checklist

Crash Tests:
  Frontal . . . . Poor
  Side . . . . Good
Airbags:
  Head . . . . Fr. & Rr. Roof Curtain
  Torso . . . . Front Pelvis/Torso from Seat
  Pelvis . . . . Front Pelvis/Torso from Seat
  Roll Sensing . . . . No
  Knee Bolster . . . . None
Crash Avoidance:
  Frontal Collision Warning . . . . Optional
  Blind Spot Detection . . . . Optional
  Crash Imminent Braking . . . . Optional
  Lane Departure Warning . . . . Optional
General:
  Auto. Crash Notification . . . . None
  Day Running Lamps . . . . None
Safety Belt/Restraint:
  Dynamic Head Restraints . . . . . . Standard Front
  Adjustable Belt . . . . Standard Front
  Pretensioners . . . . Standard Front

Infiniti M

Specifications

Drive . . . . RWD
Engine 3.7-liter V6
Transmission . . . . 7-sp. Automatic
Tow Rating (lbs.) . . . . –
Head/Leg Room (in.) Roomy-39.1/44
Interior Space (cu. ft.) Roomy-103.6
Cargo Space (cu. ft.) Cramped-14.9
Wheelbase/Length (in.) 114.2/194.7

Ratings—10 Best, 1 Worst

Combo Crash Tests	–
Safety Features	9
Rollover	2
Preventative Maintenance	3
Repair Costs	4
Warranty	7
Fuel Economy	1
Complaints	6
Insurance Costs	10
OVERALL RATING	–

Infiniti QX56

Infiniti QX56

At-a-Glance

Status/Year Series Started Unchanged/2011
Twins . . . . –
Body Styles. . . . . SUV
Seating 7/8
Anti-Theft Device. . . . . . . Std. Pass. Immobil. & Alarm
Parking Index Rating . . . . Very Hard
Where Made. Kyushu, Japan
Fuel Factor
MPG Rating (city/hwy). . . . . Very Poor-14/20
Driving Range (mi.) Long-420.8
Fuel Type. . . . . Premium
Annual Fuel Cost. . . . . Very High-$3244
Gas Guzzler Tax . . . . No
Greenhouse Gas Emissions (tons/yr.) Very High-11.6
Barrels of Oil Used per year . . . . Very High-21.4

How the Competition Rates

Competitors	Rating	Pg.
Audi Q7	–	93
Land Rover LR4	–	184
Mercedes-Benz GL-Class	–	205

Price Range	Retail	Markup
2WD	$58,700	8%
4WD	$61,800	8%

Safety Checklist

Crash Tests:
Frontal . . . . –
Side . . . . –
Airbags:
Head. . . . . Fr. & Rr. Roof Curtain
Torso. . . . . Front Pelvis/Torso from Seat
Pelvis . . . . Front Pelvis/Torso from Seat
Roll Sensing . . . . Yes
Knee Bolster . . . . None
Crash Avoidance:
Frontal Collision Warning . . . . Optional
Blind Spot Detection . . . . Optional
Crash Imminent Braking. . . . . Optional
Lane Departure Warning. . . . . Optional
General:
Auto. Crash Notification. . . . . None
Day Running Lamps . . . . None
Safety Belt/Restraint:
Dynamic Head Restraints. . . . . . Standard Front
Adjustable Belt . . . . . . Standard Front and Rear •
Pretensioners . . . . Standard Front

Infiniti QX56

Specifications

Drive. . . . . RWD
Engine 5.6-liter V8
Transmission . . . . 7-sp. Automatic
Tow Rating (lbs.) . . . . Very High-8500
Head/Leg Room (in.) . . . . . Very Cramped-39.9/39.6
Interior Space (cu. ft.) . . . . Very Roomy-151.3
Cargo Space (cu. ft.) Average-16.6
Wheelbase/Length (in.) . . . . 121.1/208.3 •

Ratings—10 Best, 1 Worst

Combo Crash Tests	–
Safety Features	5
Rollover	8
Preventative Maintenance	10
Repair Costs	3
Warranty	6
Fuel Economy	2
Complaints	1
Insurance Costs	5
OVERALL RATING	**–**

Jaguar XF

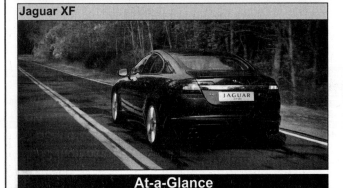
Jaguar XF

At-a-Glance

Status/Year Series Started . Appearance Change/2009
Twins . . . . –
Body Styles . . . . Sedan
Seating 5
Anti-Theft Device . Std. Pass. Immobil. & Active Alarm
Parking Index Rating . . . . Hard
Where Made . . . . Castle Bromwich, UK
Fuel Factor
 MPG Rating (city/hwy) . . . . Very Poor-16/24
 Driving Range (mi.) . . . . Very Short-288.0
 Fuel Type . . . . Premium
 Annual Fuel Cost . . . . Very High-$2789
 Gas Guzzler Tax . . . . No
 Greenhouse Gas Emissions (tons/yr.) High-9.8
 Barrels of Oil Used per year High-18.0

How the Competition Rates

Competitors	Rating	Pg.
BMW 7 Series	–	97
Lexus LS	–	192
Mercedes-Benz S-Class	–	208

Price Range

	Retail	Markup
Base	$53,000	9%
Portfolio	$59,000	9%
Supercharged	$68,100	9%
XFR	$82,000	9%

Safety Checklist

Crash Tests:
 Frontal . . . . –
 Side . . . . –
Airbags:
 Head . . . . Fr. & Rr. Roof Curtain
 Torso . . . . Front Pelvis/Torso from Seat
 Pelvis . . . . Front Pelvis/Torso from Seat
 Roll Sensing . . . . No
 Knee Bolster . . . . None
Crash Avoidance:
 Frontal Collision Warning . . . . None
 Blind Spot Detection . . . . Optional
 Crash Imminent Braking . . . . Optional
 Lane Departure Warning . . . . None
General:
 Auto. Crash Notification . . . . None
 Day Running Lamps . . . . Optional
Safety Belt/Restraint:
 Dynamic Head Restraints . . . . . . Standard Front
 Adjustable Belt . . . . Standard Front
 Pretensioners . . . . Standard Front

Jaguar XF

Specifications

Drive . . . . RWD
Engine 3.0-liter V6
Transmission . . . . 6-sp. Automatic
Tow Rating (lbs.) . . . . Very Low-1655
Head/Leg Room (in.) Cramped-39/41.5
Interior Space (cu. ft.) Cramped-95
Cargo Space (cu. ft.) Average-17
Wheelbase/Length (in.) 114.5/195.3

Ratings—10 Best, 1 Worst

Combo Crash Tests	–
Safety Features	5
Rollover	9
Preventative Maintenance	10
Repair Costs	4
Warranty	6
Fuel Economy	2
Complaints	–
Insurance Costs	5
OVERALL RATING	**–**

Jaguar XJ

Jaguar XJ

At-a-Glance

Status/Year Series Started Unchanged/2011
Twins . . . . –
Body Styles . . . . Sedan
Seating 5
Anti-Theft Device . Std. Pass. Immobil. & Active Alarm
Parking Index Rating . . . . Very Hard
Where Made . . . . Castle Bromwich, UK
Fuel Factor
  MPG Rating (city/hwy) . . . . Very Poor-16/23
  Driving Range (mi.) Average-402.3
  Fuel Type . . . . Premium
  Annual Fuel Cost . . . . Very High-$2832
  Gas Guzzler Tax . . . . No
  Greenhouse Gas Emissions (tons/yr.) High-9.8
  Barrels of Oil Used per year High-18.0

How the Competition Rates

Competitors	Rating	Pg.
Audi A8	–	91
BMW 7 Series	–	97
Lexus LS	–	192

Price Range	Retail	Markup
Base	$73,700	9%
XJL	$80,700	9%
XJL Supercharged	$91,600	9%
XJL Supersport	$117,700	9%

Safety Checklist

Crash Tests:
  Frontal . . . . –
  Side . . . . –
Airbags:
  Head . . . . Fr. & Rr. Roof Curtain
  Torso . . . . Front Pelvis/Torso from Seat
  Pelvis . . . . Front Pelvis/Torso from Seat
  Roll Sensing . . . . No
  Knee Bolster . . . . None
Crash Avoidance:
  Frontal Collision Warning . . . . None
  Blind Spot Detection . . . . Optional
  Crash Imminent Braking . . . . None
  Lane Departure Warning . . . . None
General:
  Auto. Crash Notification . . . . None
  Day Running Lamps . . . . Optional
Safety Belt/Restraint:
  Dynamic Head Restraints . . . . . . Standard Front
  Adjustable Belt . . . . Standard Front
  Pretensioners . . . . Standard Front

Jaguar XJ

Specifications

Drive . . . . RWD
Engine 5.0-liter V8
Transmission . . . . 6-sp. Automatic
Tow Rating (lbs.) . . . . –
Head/Leg Room (in.) Average-39.5/41.5
Interior Space (cu. ft.) Roomy-120
Cargo Space (cu. ft.) Cramped-15.2
Wheelbase/Length (in.) 119.4/201.7

Ratings—10 Best, 1 Worst

Combo Crash Tests	–
Safety Features	6
Rollover	3
Preventative Maintenance	4
Repair Costs	10
Warranty	4
Fuel Economy	4
Complaints	3
Insurance Costs	8
OVERALL RATING	**–**

Jeep Compass

Jeep Compass

At-a-Glance

Status/Year Series Started Unchanged/2007
Twins . . . . –
Body Styles . . . . SUV
Seating 5
Anti-Theft Device . . . . Std. Pass. Immobil.
Parking Index Rating . . . . Easy
Where Made . . . . Belvedere, IL

Fuel Factor
MPG Rating (city/hwy) Poor-21/26
Driving Range (mi.) . . . . Very Short-310.4
Fuel Type . . . . Regular
Annual Fuel Cost . . . . Average-$2107
Gas Guzzler Tax . . . . No
Greenhouse Gas Emissions (tons/yr.) . . Average-8.1
Barrels of Oil Used per year High-14.9

How the Competition Rates

Competitors	Rating	Pg.
Acura RDX	–	82
Honda CR-V	3	148
Subaru Forester	5	237

Price Range	Retail	Markup
Sport FWD	$19,295	2%
Sport 4WD	$21,045	2%
Latitude	$23,445	4%
Limited	$26,045	4%

Safety Checklist

Crash Tests:
  Frontal . . . . –
  Side . . . . –
Airbags:
  Head . . . . Fr. & Rr. Roof Curtain
  Torso . . . . Opt. Front Pelvis/Torso from Seat
  Pelvis . . . . None
  Roll Sensing . . . . Yes
  Knee Bolster . . . . None
Crash Avoidance:
  Frontal Collision Warning . . . . None
  Blind Spot Detection . . . . None
  Crash Imminent Braking . . . . None
  Lane Departure Warning . . . . None
General:
  Auto. Crash Notification . . . . None
  Day Running Lamps . . . . Optional
Safety Belt/Restraint:
  Dynamic Head Restraints . . . . . Standard Front
  Adjustable Belt . . . . Standard Front
  Pretensioners . . . . Standard Front

Jeep Compass

Specifications

Drive 4WD
Engine 2.4-liter I4
Transmission . . . . CVT
Tow Rating (lbs.) . . . . Very Low-2000
Head/Leg Room (in.) Average-40.7/40.6
Interior Space (cu. ft.) Average-101.3
Cargo Space (cu. ft.) Roomy-22.7
Wheelbase/Length (in.) 103.7/175.1

Ratings—10 Best, 1 Worst

Combo Crash Tests	7
Safety Features	8
Rollover	4
Preventative Maintenance	1
Repair Costs	8
Warranty	4
Fuel Economy	2
Complaints	6
Insurance Costs	10
OVERALL RATING	**6**

Jeep Grand Cherokee

Jeep Grand Cherokee

At-a-Glance

Status/Year Series Started	Unchanged/2011
Twins	–
Body Styles	SUV
Seating	5
Anti-Theft Device	Std. Pass. Immobil. & Alarm
Parking Index Rating	Average
Where Made	Detroit, MI

Fuel Factor

MPG Rating (city/hwy)	Very Poor-16/23
Driving Range (mi.)	Very Long-456.1
Fuel Type	Regular/E85
Annual Fuel Cost	High-$2613
Gas Guzzler Tax	No
Greenhouse Gas Emissions (tons/yr.)	High-9.8
Barrels of Oil Used per year	High-18.0

How the Competition Rates

Competitors	Rating	Pg.
Chevrolet Tahoe	6	118
Ford Expedition	–	134
Lincoln MKT	–	195

Price Range

	Retail	Markup
Laredo	$26,995	1%
Limited	$36,795	6%
Overland	$39,495	6%
SRT8	$54,470	5%

Safety Checklist

Crash Tests:
Frontal . . . . Good
Side . . . . Average

Airbags:
Head . . . . Fr. & Rr. Roof Curtain
Torso . . . . Front Pelvis/Torso from Seat
Pelvis . . . . Front Pelvis/Torso from Seat
Roll Sensing . . . . Yes
Knee Bolster . . . . None

Crash Avoidance:
Frontal Collision Warning . . . . Optional
Blind Spot Detection . . . . Optional
Crash Imminent Braking . . . . Optional
Lane Departure Warning . . . . None

General:
Auto. Crash Notification . . . . None
Day Running Lamps . . . . Optional

Safety Belt/Restraint:
Dynamic Head Restraints . . . . . . Standard Front
Adjustable Belt . . . . Standard Front
Pretensioners . . . . Standard Front

Jeep Grand Cherokee

Specifications

Drive	4WD
Engine	3.6-liter V6
Transmission	5-sp. Automatic
Tow Rating (lbs.)	Average-5000
Head/Leg Room (in.)	Cramped-39.9/40.3
Interior Space (cu. ft.)	Roomy-105.4
Cargo Space (cu. ft.)	Very Roomy-35.1
Wheelbase/Length (in.)	114.8/189.8

Ratings—10 Best, 1 Worst

Combo Crash Tests	–
Safety Features	5
Rollover	1
Preventative Maintenance	5
Repair Costs	8
Warranty	4
Fuel Economy	1
Complaints	6
Insurance Costs	10
OVERALL RATING	–

Jeep Liberty

Jeep Liberty

At-a-Glance

Status/Year Series Started Unchanged/2008
Twins . . . . –
Body Styles. . . . . SUV
Seating. 5
Anti-Theft Device . . . . Std. Pass. Immobil. & Alarm
Parking Index Rating . . . . Easy
Where Made . . . . Toldeo, OH

Fuel Factor
MPG Rating (city/hwy). . . . . Very Poor-15/21
Driving Range (mi.). . . . . Very Short-335.7
Fuel Type. . . . . Regular
Annual Fuel Cost. . . . . Very High-$2815
Gas Guzzler Tax . . . . No
Greenhouse Gas Emissions (tons/yr.) Very High-11.0
Barrels of Oil Used per year . . . . Very High-20.1

How the Competition Rates

Competitors	Rating	Pg.
Ford Escape	2	133
Kia Sportage	–	183
Toyota RAV4	1	252

Price Range	Retail	Markup
Sport 2WD	$23,360	3%
Sport 4WD	$24,975	3%
Limited	$28,360	4%
Jet	$28,560	4%

Safety Checklist

Crash Tests:
Frontal . . . . –
Side . . . . –
Airbags:
Head. . . . . Fr. & Rr. Roof Curtain
Torso . . . . None
Pelvis . . . . None
Roll Sensing . . . . Yes
Knee Bolster . . . . None
Crash Avoidance:
Frontal Collision Warning. . . . . None
Blind Spot Detection . . . . None
Crash Imminent Braking . . . . None
Lane Departure Warning . . . . None
General:
Auto. Crash Notification. . . . . None
Day Running Lamps . . . . Optional
Safety Belt/Restraint:
Dynamic Head Restraints. . . . . . Standard Front
Adjustable Belt . . . . Standard Front
Pretensioners . . . . Standard Front

Jeep Liberty

Specifications

Drive 4WD
Engine. 3.7-liter V6
Transmission . . . . 4-sp. Auto. w/Overdrive
Tow Rating (lbs.) Average-5000
Head/Leg Room (in.) Average-40.4/40.8
Interior Space (cu. ft.) Roomy-104.7
Cargo Space (cu. ft.). Roomy-26.1
Wheelbase/Length (in.) 106.1/176.9

Ratings—10 Best, 1 Worst

Combo Crash Tests	–
Safety Features	6
Rollover	3
Preventative Maintenance	4
Repair Costs	10
Warranty	4
Fuel Economy	5
Complaints	3
Insurance Costs	5
OVERALL RATING	–

Jeep Patriot

Jeep Patriot

At-a-Glance

Status/Year Series Started Unchanged/2007
Twins . . . . –
Body Styles. . . . . SUV
Seating. 5
Anti-Theft Device. . . . . Std. Pass. Immobil.
Parking Index Rating . . . . Easy
Where Made . . . . Belvedere, IL
Fuel Factor
  MPG Rating (city/hwy) Average-21/27
  Driving Range (mi.). . . . . Very Short-317.3
  Fuel Type. . . . . Regular
  Annual Fuel Cost. . . . . Average-$2076
  Gas Guzzler Tax . . . . No
  Greenhouse Gas Emissions (tons/yr.) . . Average-7.8
  Barrels of Oil Used per year. High-14.3

How the Competition Rates

Competitors	Rating	Pg.
Ford Escape	2	133
Suzuki Grand Vitara	–	241
Kia Sportage	–	183

Price Range	Retail	Markup
Sport 2WD	$15,995	1%
Sport 4WD	$17,745	2%
Latitude	$22,780	4%
Limited	$25,330	4%

Safety Checklist

Crash Tests:
  Frontal . . . . –
  Side . . . . –
Airbags:
  Head. . . . . Fr. & Rr. Roof Curtain
  Torso . . . . Opt. Front Pelvis/Torso from Seat
  Pelvis . . . . None
  Roll Sensing . . . . Yes
  Knee Bolster . . . . None
Crash Avoidance:
  Frontal Collision Warning. . . . . None
  Blind Spot Detection . . . . None
  Crash Imminent Braking . . . . None
  Lane Departure Warning . . . . None
General:
  Auto. Crash Notification . . . . None
  Day Running Lamps . . . . Optional
Safety Belt/Restraint:
  Dynamic Head Restraints. . . . . . Standard Front
  Adjustable Belt . . . . Standard Front
  Pretensioners . . . . Standard Front

Jeep Patriot

Specifications

Drive . . . . FWD
Engine. 2.4-liter I4
Transmission . . . . CVT
Tow Rating (lbs.). . . . . Very Low-1000
Head/Leg Room (in.) Average-41/40.6
Interior Space (cu. ft.) Roomy-104.4
Cargo Space (cu. ft.) Roomy-23
Wheelbase/Length (in.) 103.7/173.8

Ratings—10 Best, 1 Worst

Combo Crash Tests	–
Safety Features	1
Rollover	2
Preventative Maintenance	4
Repair Costs	10
Warranty	4
Fuel Economy	2
Complaints	1
Insurance Costs	10
OVERALL RATING	**–**

Jeep Wrangler

At-a-Glance

Status/Year Series Started Unchanged/2007
Twins . . . . –
Body Styles . . . . SUV
Seating 4
Anti-Theft Device . . . . . . Std. Pass. Immobil. & Alarm
Parking Index Rating . . . . Very Easy
Where Made . . . . Toldeo, OH

Fuel Factor
MPG Rating (city/hwy) . . . . Very Poor-17/21
Driving Range (mi.) . . . . Very Short-345.8
Fuel Type . . . . Regular
Annual Fuel Cost . . . . High-$2606
Gas Guzzler Tax . . . . No
Greenhouse Gas Emissions (tons/yr.) High-10.4
Barrels of Oil Used per year . . . . Very High-19.0

How the Competition Rates

Competitors	Rating	Pg.
Nissan Xterra	–	229
Suzuki Grand Vitara	–	241
Toyota FJ Cruiser	–	248

Price Range	Retail	Markup
Sport	$22,045	3%
Unlimited Sport	$25,545	3%
Rubicon	$29,995	6%
Unlimited Rubicon	$33,570	6%

Jeep Wrangler

Safety Checklist

Crash Tests:
Frontal . . . . –
Side . . . . –
Airbags:
Head . . . . Opt. Front Head from Seat
Torso . . . . Opt. Front Pelvis/Torso from Seat
Pelvis . . . . None
Roll Sensing . . . . No
Knee Bolster . . . . None
Crash Avoidance:
Frontal Collision Warning . . . . None
Blind Spot Detection . . . . None
Crash Imminent Braking . . . . None
Lane Departure Warning . . . . None
General:
Auto. Crash Notification . . . . None
Day Running Lamps . . . . Optional
Safety Belt/Restraint:
Dynamic Head Restraints . . . . None
Adjustable Belt . . . . Standard Front
Pretensioners . . . . Standard Front

Jeep Wrangler

Specifications

Drive 4WD
Engine 3.6-liter V6
Transmission . . . . 4-sp. Auto. w/Overdrive
Tow Rating (lbs.) Low-3500
Head/Leg Room (in.) Roomy-41.3/41
Interior Space (cu. ft.) Average-102.9
Cargo Space (cu. ft.) Average-17.15
Wheelbase/Length (in.) 95.4/152.8

Ratings—10 Best, 1 Worst	
Combo Crash Tests	4
Safety Features	4
Rollover	8
Preventative Maintenance	8
Repair Costs	10
Warranty	8
Fuel Economy	8
Complaints	7
Insurance Costs	1
OVERALL RATING	**8**

Kia Forte

Kia Forte

At-a-Glance

Status/Year Series Started Unchanged/2010
Twins . . . . –
Body Styles . . . . Sedan, Coupe, Hatchback
Seating 5
Anti-Theft Device . . . . None
Parking Index Rating . . . . Very Easy
Where Made . . . . Hwasung, South Korea
Fuel Factor
 MPG Rating (city/hwy) Good-26/36
 Driving Range (mi.) Average-407.1
 Fuel Type . . . . Regular
 Annual Fuel Cost . . . . Very Low-$1631
 Gas Guzzler Tax . . . . No
 Greenhouse Gas Emissions (tons/yr.) Low-6.5
 Barrels of Oil Used per year Average-11.8

How the Competition Rates

Competitors	Rating	Pg.
Chevrolet Cruze	9	111
Honda Civic	–	146
Subaru Impreza	–	238

Price Range	Retail	Markup
LX Manual	$15,200	2%
LX Automatic	$16,200	2%
EX Automatic	$17,600	5%
SX Automatic	$19,100	5%

Safety Checklist

Crash Tests:
 Frontal . . . . Poor
 Side . . . . Poor**
Airbags:
 Head . . . . Fr. & Rr. Roof Curtain
 Torso . . . . Front Pelvis/Torso from Seat
 Pelvis . . . . Front Pelvis/Torso from Seat
 Roll Sensing . . . . No
 Knee Bolster . . . . None
Crash Avoidance:
 Frontal Collision Warning . . . . None
 Blind Spot Detection . . . . None
 Crash Imminent Braking . . . . None
 Lane Departure Warning . . . . None
General:
 Auto. Crash Notification . . . . None
 Day Running Lamps . . . . None
Safety Belt/Restraint:
 Dynamic Head Restraints . . . . . . Standard Front
 Adjustable Belt . . . . Standard Front
 Pretensioners . . . . Standard Front

Kia Forte

Specifications

Drive . . . . FWD
Engine 2.0-liter I4
Transmission . . . . 6-sp. Auto. w/ Overdrive
Tow Rating (lbs.) . . . . –
Head/Leg Room (in.) . . . . . Very Roomy-40/43.3
Interior Space (cu. ft.) Cramped-96.8
Cargo Space (cu. ft.) Cramped-14.7
Wheelbase/Length (in.) 104.3/178.3

**Additional injury potential in side test. See asterisked footnote (**) on page 20.

Kia Optima

Ratings—10 Best, 1 Worst	
Combo Crash Tests	9
Safety Features	4
Rollover	9
Preventative Maintenance	7
Repair Costs	9
Warranty	8
Fuel Economy	7
Complaints	2
Insurance Costs	1
OVERALL RATING	8

Kia Optima

At-a-Glance

Status/Year Series Started Unchanged/2011
Twins . . . . –
Body Styles . . . . Sedan
Seating 5
Anti-Theft Device . Opt. Pass. Immobil. & Active Alarm
Parking Index Rating . . . . Easy
Where Made . . . . West Point, GA
Fuel Factor
MPG Rating (city/hwy) Good-24/34
Driving Range (mi.) . . . . Very Long-511.7
Fuel Type . . . . Regular
Annual Fuel Cost . . . . Low-$1752
Gas Guzzler Tax . . . . No
Greenhouse Gas Emissions (tons/yr.) . . Average-6.7
Barrels of Oil Used per year Average-12.2

How the Competition Rates

Competitors	Rating	Pg.
Honda Accord	8	144
Mitsubishi Galant	–	211
Toyota Camry	10	246

Price Range	Retail	Markup
LX Manual	$19,500	2%
EX	$23,200	7%
EX Turbo	$25,100	7%
SX	$26,500	7%

Safety Checklist

Crash Tests:
Frontal . . . . Very Good
Side . . . . Average
Airbags:
Head . . . . Fr. & Rr. Roof Curtain
Torso . . . . Front Pelvis/Torso from Seat
Pelvis . . . . Front Pelvis/Torso from Seat
Roll Sensing . . . . No
Knee Bolster . . . . None
Crash Avoidance:
Frontal Collision Warning . . . . None
Blind Spot Detection . . . . None
Crash Imminent Braking . . . . None
Lane Departure Warning . . . . None
General:
Auto. Crash Notification . . . . None
Day Running Lamps . . . . None
Safety Belt/Restraint:
Dynamic Head Restraints . . . . . . Standard Front
Adjustable Belt . . . . Standard Front
Pretensioners . . . . Standard Front

Kia Optima

Specifications

Drive . . . . FWD
Engine 2.4-liter I4
Transmission . . . . 6-sp. Auto. w/ Overdrive
Tow Rating (lbs.) . . . . –
Head/Leg Room (in.) . . . . Very Roomy-40/45.5
Interior Space (cu. ft.) Average-102.2
Cargo Space (cu. ft.) Cramped-15.4
Wheelbase/Length (in.) 110/190.7

Ratings—10 Best, 1 Worst	
Combo Crash Tests	–
Safety Features	2
Rollover	7
Preventative Maintenance	6
Repair Costs	9
Warranty	8
Fuel Economy	10
Complaints	–
Insurance Costs	1
OVERALL RATING	–

Kia Rio

Kia Rio

At-a-Glance	
Status/Year Series Started	All New/2012
Twins	Hyundai Accent
Body Styles	Sedan, Hatchback
Seating	5
Anti-Theft Device	None
Parking Index Rating	Very Easy
Where Made	St. Petersburg, Russia
Fuel Factor	
MPG Rating (city/hwy)	Very Good-30/40
Driving Range (mi.)	Short-385.4
Fuel Type	Regular
Annual Fuel Cost	Very Low-$1433
Gas Guzzler Tax	No
Greenhouse Gas Emissions (tons/yr.)	Low-5.7
Barrels of Oil Used per year	Low-10.4

How the Competition Rates

Competitors	Rating	Pg.
Chevrolet Sonic	9	116
Hyundai Accent	9	155
Suzuki SX4	–	243

Price Range	Retail	Markup
LX Manual	$13,300	2%
LX Automatic	$14,400	3%
EX	$16,200	5%
SX	$17,400	5%

Safety Checklist

Crash Tests:
Frontal ... –
Side ... –

Airbags:
Head ... Fr. & Rr. Roof Curtain
Torso ... Front Pelvis/Torso from Seat
Pelvis ... Front Pelvis/Torso from Seat
Roll Sensing ... No
Knee Bolster ... None

Crash Avoidance:
Frontal Collision Warning ... None
Blind Spot Detection ... None
Crash Imminent Braking ... None
Lane Departure Warning ... None

General:
Auto. Crash Notification ... None
Day Running Lamps ... None

Safety Belt/Restraint:
Dynamic Head Restraints ... None
Adjustable Belt ... Standard Front
Pretensioners ... Standard Front

Kia Rio

Specifications

Drive	FWD
Engine	1.6-liter I4
Transmission	6-sp. Automatic
Tow Rating (lbs.)	–
Head/Leg Room (in.)	Very Roomy-40/43.8
Interior Space (cu. ft.)	Very Cramped-88.6
Cargo Space (cu. ft.)	Cramped-13.7
Wheelbase/Length (in.)	101.2/171.9

Ratings—10 Best, 1 Worst

Combo Crash Tests	–
Safety Features	4
Rollover	4
Preventative Maintenance	4
Repair Costs	5
Warranty	8
Fuel Economy	3
Complaints	4
Insurance Costs	8
OVERALL RATING	–

Kia Sedona

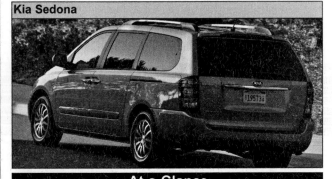

Kia Sedona

At-a-Glance

Status/Year Series Started Unchanged/2006
Twins . . . . –
Body Styles . . . . Minivan
Seating. 7
Anti-Theft Device . Opt. Pass. Immobil. & Active Alarm
Parking Index Rating . . . . Very Hard
Where Made . . . . Sohari, South Korea

Fuel Factor
MPG Rating (city/hwy) Poor-18/25
Driving Range (mi.) Long-434.6
Fuel Type. . . . . Regular
Annual Fuel Cost. . . . . High-$2353
Gas Guzzler Tax . . . . No
Greenhouse Gas Emissions (tons/yr.) High-8.9
Barrels of Oil Used per year. High-16.3

How the Competition Rates

Competitors	Rating	Pg.
Honda Odyssey	7	152
Toyota Sienna	1	254
Volkswagen Routan	–	264

Price Range	Retail	Markup
LX	$24,900	3%
EX	$29,190	7%

Safety Checklist

Crash Tests:
Frontal . . . . –
Side . . . . –
Airbags:
Head. . . . . Fr. & Rr. Roof Curtain
Torso. . . . . Front Pelvis/Torso from Seat
Pelvis . . . . Front Pelvis/Torso from Seat
Roll Sensing. . . . . No
Knee Bolster . . . . None
Crash Avoidance:
Frontal Collision Warning. . . . . None
Blind Spot Detection . . . . None
Crash Imminent Braking . . . . None
Lane Departure Warning . . . . None
General:
Auto. Crash Notification. . . . . None
Day Running Lamps . . . . None
Safety Belt/Restraint:
Dynamic Head Restraints. . . . . . Standard Front
Adjustable Belt . . . . . . Standard Front and Rear
Pretensioners . . . . Standard Front

Kia Sedona

Specifications

Drive . . . . FWD
Engine 3.5-liter V6
Transmission . . . . 5-sp. Auto. w/Overdrive
Tow Rating (lbs.) Low-3500
Head/Leg Room (in.) Roomy-40.9/41.7
Interior Space (cu. ft.) . . . . Very Roomy-172.3
Cargo Space (cu. ft.). . . . . Very Roomy-32.2
Wheelbase/Length (in.). 118.9/202

Kia Sorento | Mid-Size SUV

Kia Sorento

Ratings—10 Best, 1 Worst

Combo Crash Tests	5
Safety Features	7
Rollover	4
Preventative Maintenance	–
Repair Costs	7
Warranty	8
Fuel Economy	4
Complaints	1
Insurance Costs	8
OVERALL RATING	**5**

Kia Sorento

At-a-Glance

Status/Year Series Started Unchanged/2011
Twins . . . . Hyundai Santa Fe
Body Styles . . . . SUV
Seating 5/7
Anti-Theft Device . Opt. Pass. Immobil. & Active Alarm
Parking Index Rating . . . . Easy
Where Made . . . . West Point, GA
Fuel Factor
MPG Rating (city/hwy) Poor-20/26
Driving Range (mi.) Average-401.7
Fuel Type . . . . Regular
Annual Fuel Cost . . . . Average-$2171
Gas Guzzler Tax . . . . No
Greenhouse Gas Emissions (tons/yr.) High-8.5
Barrels of Oil Used per year High-15.6

How the Competition Rates

Competitors	Rating	Pg.
Ford Edge	5	132
Nissan Rogue	5	225
Toyota Venza	1	257

Price Range	Retail	Markup
Base	$21,250	4%
LX	$25,350	3%
EX	$27,950	6%
SX	$34,850	7%

Safety Checklist

Crash Tests:
Frontal . . . . Average
Side . . . . Poor
Airbags:
Head . . . . Fr. & Rr. Roof Curtain
Torso . . . . Front Pelvis/Torso from Seat
Pelvis . . . . Front Pelvis/Torso from Seat
Roll Sensing . . . . Yes
Knee Bolster . . . . None
Crash Avoidance:
Frontal Collision Warning . . . . None
Blind Spot Detection . . . . Optional
Crash Imminent Braking . . . . None
Lane Departure Warning . . . . None
General:
Auto. Crash Notification . . . . None
Day Running Lamps . . . . None
Safety Belt/Restraint:
Dynamic Head Restraints . . . . . . Standard Front
Adjustable Belt . . . . Standard Front
Pretensioners . . . . Standard Front

Kia Sorento

Specifications

Drive . . . . FWD
Engine 3.5-liter V6
Transmission . . . . 6-sp. Automatic
Tow Rating (lbs.) Low-3500
Head/Leg Room (in.) Cramped-39.2/41.3
Interior Space (cu. ft.) . . . . . . Very Roomy-149.4
Cargo Space (cu. ft.) . . . . Very Cramped-9.1
Wheelbase/Length (in.) 106.3/183.9

181

Ratings—10 Best, 1 Worst	
Combo Crash Tests	4
Safety Features	4
Rollover	6
Preventative Maintenance	5
Repair Costs	9
Warranty	8
Fuel Economy	9
Complaints	6
Insurance Costs	3
OVERALL RATING	7

Kia Soul

Kia Soul

At-a-Glance

Status/Year Series Started . Appearance Change/2010
Twins . . . . –
Body Styles . . . . Wagon
Seating 5
Anti-Theft Device . . . . None
Parking Index Rating . . . . Very Easy
Where Made . . . . Hwasung, South Korea

Fuel Factor
MPG Rating (city/hwy) . . . . Very Good-27/35
Driving Range (mi.) Short-382.2
Fuel Type . . . . Regular
Annual Fuel Cost . . . . Very Low-$1610
Gas Guzzler Tax . . . . No
Greenhouse Gas Emissions (tons/yr.) Low-6.2
Barrels of Oil Used per year Low-11.4

How the Competition Rates

Competitors	Rating	Pg.
Honda Fit	–	150
Nissan Cube	–	218
Scion xB	–	234

Price Range	Retail	Markup
Base	$13,900	2%
+ MT	$16,300	4%
+ AT	$17,300	4%
!	$19,600	5%

Safety Checklist

Crash Tests:
Frontal . . . . Poor
Side . . . . Average
Airbags:
Head . . . . Fr. & Rr. Roof Curtain
Torso . . . . Front Pelvis/Torso from Seat
Pelvis . . . . Front Pelvis/Torso from Seat
Roll Sensing . . . . No
Knee Bolster . . . . None
Crash Avoidance:
Frontal Collision Warning . . . . None
Blind Spot Detection . . . . None
Crash Imminent Braking . . . . None
Lane Departure Warning . . . . None
General:
Auto. Crash Notification . . . . None
Day Running Lamps . . . . None
Safety Belt/Restraint:
Dynamic Head Restraints . . . . . . Standard Front
Adjustable Belt . . . . Standard Front
Pretensioners . . . . Standard Front

Kia Soul

Specifications

Drive . . . . FWD
Engine 1.6-liter I4
Transmission . . . . 6-sp. Auto. w/ Overdrive
Tow Rating (lbs.) . . . . –
Head/Leg Room (in.) Roomy-40.2/42.1
Interior Space (cu. ft.) Average-102.3
Cargo Space (cu. ft.) Average-19.3
Wheelbase/Length (in.) 100.4/162.2

Kia Sportage

Ratings—10 Best, 1 Worst

Combo Crash Tests	–
Safety Features	6
Rollover	5
Preventative Maintenance	5
Repair Costs	10
Warranty	8
Fuel Economy	6
Complaints	5
Insurance Costs	5
OVERALL RATING	–

Kia Sportage

Kia Sportage

Safety Checklist

Crash Tests:
Frontal . . . . –
Side . . . . –
Airbags:
Head . . . . Fr. & Rr. Roof Curtain
Torso . . . . Front Pelvis/Torso from Seat
Pelvis . . . . Front Pelvis/Torso from Seat
Roll Sensing . . . . Yes
Knee Bolster . . . . None
Crash Avoidance:
Frontal Collision Warning . . . . None
Blind Spot Detection . . . . None
Crash Imminent Braking . . . . None
Lane Departure Warning . . . . None
General:
Auto. Crash Notification . . . . None
Day Running Lamps . . . . Optional
Safety Belt/Restraint:
Dynamic Head Restraints . . . . . . Standard Front
Adjustable Belt . . . . Standard Front
Pretensioners . . . . Standard Front

At-a-Glance

Status/Year Series Started Unchanged/2011
Twins . . . . –
Body Styles . . . . SUV
Seating 5
Anti-Theft Device . Opt. Pass. Immobil. & Active Alarm
Parking Index Rating . . . . Very Easy
Where Made . . . . Gwangju, South Korea
Fuel Factor
MPG Rating (city/hwy) Average-22/32
Driving Range (mi.) Average-391.7
Fuel Type . . . . Regular
Annual Fuel Cost . . . . Low-$1893
Gas Guzzler Tax . . . . No
Greenhouse Gas Emissions (tons/yr.) . . Average-7.5
Barrels of Oil Used per year Average-13.7

How the Competition Rates

Competitors	Rating	Pg.
Ford Escape	2	133
Jeep Liberty	–	174
Toyota RAV4	1	252

Price Range

Price Range	Retail	Markup
Base	$18,500	2%
LX	$20,800	4%
EX	$23,900	7%
SX	$26,900	7%

Specifications

Drive . . . . FWD
Engine 2.4-liter I4
Transmission . . . . 6-sp. Automatic
Tow Rating (lbs.) . . . . Very Low-2000
Head/Leg Room (in.) Cramped-39.1/41.4
Interior Space (cu. ft.) Average-100
Cargo Space (cu. ft.) Roomy-26.1
Wheelbase/Length (in.) 103.9/174.8

Ratings—10 Best, 1 Worst	
Combo Crash Tests	–
Safety Features	5
Rollover	2
Preventative Maintenance	4
Repair Costs	1
Warranty	4
Fuel Economy	1
Complaints	10
Insurance Costs	10
OVERALL RATING	**–**

Land Rover LR4

Land Rover LR4

Land Rover LR4

At-a-Glance

Status/Year Series Started Unchanged/2005	
Twins . . . . –	
Body Styles. . . . . SUV	
Seating 5/7	
Anti-Theft Device . Std. Pass. Immobil. & Active Alarm	
Parking Index Rating . . . . Average	
Where Made . . . . Solihull, England	

Fuel Factor

MPG Rating (city/hwy). . . . . Very Poor-12/17	
Driving Range (mi.). . . . . Very Short-315.3	
Fuel Type. . . . . Premium	
Annual Fuel Cost. . . . . Very High-$3796	
Gas Guzzler Tax . . . . No	
Greenhouse Gas Emissions (tons/yr.) Very High-13.3	
Barrels of Oil Used per year . . . . Very High-24.5	

How the Competition Rates

Competitors	Rating	Pg.
Chevrolet Tahoe	6	118
Ford Expedition	–	134
Infiniti QX56	–	169

Price Range	Retail	Markup
Base	$49,750	10%
HSE	$53,975	10%
HSE LUX	$58,995	10%

Safety Checklist

Crash Tests:
Frontal . . . . –
Side . . . . –
Airbags:
Head. . . . . Fr. & Rr. Roof Curtain
Torso. . . . . Front Pelvis/Torso from Seat
Pelvis . . . . Front Pelvis/Torso from Seat
Roll Sensing . . . . Yes
Knee Bolster . . . . None
Crash Avoidance:
Frontal Collision Warning. . . . . None
Blind Spot Detection . . . . None
Crash Imminent Braking . . . . None
Lane Departure Warning . . . . None
General:
Auto. Crash Notification. . . . . None
Day Running Lamps . . . . Optional
Safety Belt/Restraint:
Dynamic Head Restraints . . . . None
Adjustable Belt . . . . Standard Front
Pretensioners . . . . Standard Front

Land Rover LR4

Specifications

Drive 4WD	
Engine 5.0-liter V8	
Transmission. . . . . 6-sp Automatic	
Tow Rating (lbs.) High-7716	
Head/Leg Room (in.) Roomy-40.4/42.4	
Interior Space (cu. ft.) . . . . –	
Cargo Space (cu. ft.) . . . . Very Cramped-9.9	
Wheelbase/Length (in.) 113.6/190.1	

Land Rover Range Rover

Large SUV

Ratings—10 Best, 1 Worst

Combo Crash Tests	–
Safety Features	8
Rollover	2
Preventative Maintenance	5
Repair Costs	1
Warranty	4
Fuel Economy	1
Complaints	9
Insurance Costs	–
OVERALL RATING	**–**

Land Rover Range Rover

Land Rover Range Rover

At-a-Glance

Status/Year Series Started Unchanged/2006
Twins . . . . –
Body Styles . . . . SUV
Seating 5
Anti-Theft Device . Std. Pass. Immobil. & Active Alarm
Parking Index Rating . . . . Hard
Where Made . . . . Solihull, England
Fuel Factor
MPG Rating (city/hwy) . . . . Very Poor-12/18
Driving Range (mi.) Average-389.6
Fuel Type . . . . Premium
Annual Fuel Cost . . . . Very High-$3719
Gas Guzzler Tax . . . . No
Greenhouse Gas Emissions (tons/yr.) Very High-13.3
Barrels of Oil Used per year . . . . Very High-24.5

How the Competition Rates

Competitors	Rating	Pg.
Audi Q7	–	93
Cadillac Escalade	6	118
Mercedes-Benz GL-Class	–	205

Price Range	Retail	Markup
HSE	$79,425	10%
Supercharged	$94,820	10%

Safety Checklist

Crash Tests:
Frontal . . . . –
Side . . . . –
Airbags:
Head . . . . Fr. & Rr. Roof Curtain
Torso . . . . Front Pelvis/Torso from Seat
Pelvis . . . . Front Pelvis/Torso from Seat
Roll Sensing . . . . Yes
Knee Bolster . . . . Standard Driver
Crash Avoidance:
Frontal Collision Warning . . . . None
Blind Spot Detection . . . . Optional
Crash Imminent Braking . . . . None
Lane Departure Warning . . . . None
General:
Auto. Crash Notification . . . . None
Day Running Lamps . . . . Optional
Safety Belt/Restraint:
Dynamic Head Restraints . . . . . Standard Front
Adjustable Belt . . . . . . Standard Front and Rear
Pretensioners . . . . Standard Front

Land Rover Range Rover

Specifications

Drive 4WD
Engine 5.0-liter V8
Transmission . . . . 6-sp. Automatic
Tow Rating (lbs.) Low-3500
Head/Leg Room (in.) . . . . . Very Cramped-39.3/38.9
Interior Space (cu. ft.) . . . . –
Cargo Space (cu. ft.) . . . . Very Roomy-35.1
Wheelbase/Length (in.) 113.4/195.7

Ratings—10 Best, 1 Worst

Combo Crash Tests	–
Safety Features	6
Rollover	7
Preventative Maintenance	–
Repair Costs	–
Warranty	6
Fuel Economy	10
Complaints	–
Insurance Costs	5
OVERALL RATING	**–**

Lexus CT

Lexus CT

At-a-Glance

Status/Year Series Started Unchanged/2011
Twins . . . . –
Body Styles . . . . Hybrid Hatchback
Seating. 5
Anti-Theft Device. . . . . . . Std. Pass. Immobil. & Alarm
Parking Index Rating . . . . Easy
Where Made. Kyushu, Japan
Fuel Factor
 MPG Rating (city/hwy) . . . . Very Good-43/40
 Driving Range (mi.) . . . . Very Long-495.0
 Fuel Type. . . . . Regular
 Annual Fuel Cost . . . . Very Low-$1165
 Gas Guzzler Tax . . . . No
 Greenhouse Gas Emissions (tons/yr.) . Very Low-4.5
 Barrels of Oil Used per year . . . . Very Low-8.2

How the Competition Rates

Competitors	Rating	Pg.
Audi A3	–	86
BMW 1 Series	–	94
Volkswagen Golf	–	261

Price Range	Retail	Markup
Base	$29,120	
Premium	$31,750	

Safety Checklist

Crash Tests:
 Frontal . . . . –
 Side . . . . –
Airbags:
 Head. . . . . Fr. & Rr. Roof Curtain
 Torso. . . . . Front Pelvis/Torso from Seat
 Pelvis . . . . Front Pelvis/Torso from Seat
 Roll Sensing. . . . . No
 Knee Bolster. . . . . Standard Front
Crash Avoidance:
 Frontal Collision Warning. . . . . None
 Blind Spot Detection . . . . None
 Crash Imminent Braking . . . . Optional
 Lane Departure Warning . . . . None
General:
 Auto. Crash Notification . . . . Optional
 Day Running Lamps . . . . Standard
Safety Belt/Restraint:
 Dynamic Head Restraints . . . . None
 Adjustable Belt . . . . Standard Front
 Pretensioners . . . . Standard Front

Lexus CT

Specifications

Drive . . . . FWD
Engine. 1.8-liter I4
Transmission . . . . ECVT
Tow Rating (lbs.) . . . . –
Head/Leg Room (in.) Cramped-38.3/42.1
Interior Space (cu. ft.) . . . . Very Cramped-86.1
Cargo Space (cu. ft.) Cramped-14.3
Wheelbase/Length (in.) 102.4/170.1

Ratings—10 Best, 1 Worst

Combo Crash Tests	–
Safety Features	7
Rollover	8
Preventative Maintenance	3
Repair Costs	1
Warranty	6
Fuel Economy	4
Complaints	6
Insurance Costs	5
OVERALL RATING	–

Lexus ES

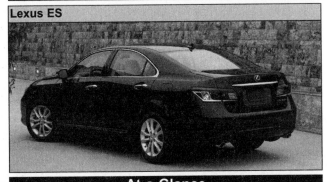
Lexus ES

At-a-Glance

Status/Year Series Started Unchanged/2007
Twins . . . . Toyota Camry
Body Styles . . . . Sedan
Seating 5
Anti-Theft Device . . . . Std. Pass. Immobil. & Alarm
Parking Index Rating . . . . Average
Where Made . . . . Kyushu, Japan
Fuel Factor
  MPG Rating (city/hwy) Poor-19/27
  Driving Range (mi.) Average-405.6
  Fuel Type . . . . Regular
  Annual Fuel Cost . . . . Average-$2210
  Gas Guzzler Tax . . . . No
  Greenhouse Gas Emissions (tons/yr.) High-8.5
  Barrels of Oil Used per year High-15.6

How the Competition Rates

Competitors	Rating	Pg.
Acura TL	–	83
Hyundai Sonata	10	161
Infiniti EX	–	165

Price Range	Retail	Markup
350	$36,725	10%

Safety Checklist

Crash Tests:
  Frontal . . . . –
  Side . . . . –
Airbags:
  Head . . . . Fr. & Rr. Roof Curtain
  Torso . . . . Fr. & Rr. Torso from Seat
  Pelvis . . . . None
  Roll Sensing . . . . No
  Knee Bolster . . . . Standard Front
Crash Avoidance:
  Frontal Collision Warning . . . . None
  Blind Spot Detection . . . . None
  Crash Imminent Braking . . . . None
  Lane Departure Warning . . . . None
General:
  Auto. Crash Notification . . . . Optional
  Day Running Lamps . . . . Standard
Safety Belt/Restraint:
  Dynamic Head Restraints . . . . None
  Adjustable Belt . . . . Standard Front
  Pretensioners . . . . Standard Front & Rear

Lexus ES

Specifications

Drive . . . . FWD
Engine 3.5-liter V6
Transmission . . . . 6-sp. Automatic
Tow Rating (lbs.) . . . . –
Head/Leg Room (in.) . . . . . Very Cramped-37.4/42.2
Interior Space (cu. ft.) Cramped-95.4
Cargo Space (cu. ft.) Cramped-14.8
Wheelbase/Length (in.) 109.3/191.7

Ratings—10 Best, 1 Worst

Combo Crash Tests	–
Safety Features	–
Rollover	8
Preventative Maintenance	6
Repair Costs	1
Warranty	6
Fuel Economy	4
Complaints	–
Insurance Costs	5
OVERALL RATING	**–**

Lexus GS

Lexus GS

Safety Checklist

Crash Tests:
Frontal . . . . –
Side . . . . –

Airbags:
Head. . . . . –
Torso. . . . . –
Pelvis . . . . –
Roll Sensing . . . . –
Knee Bolster. . . . . –

Crash Avoidance:
Frontal Collision Warning . . . . –
Blind Spot Detection. . . . . –
Crash Imminent Braking. . . . . –
Lane Departure Warning . . . . –

General:
Auto. Crash Notification . . . . –
Day Running Lamps. . . . . –

Safety Belt/Restraint:
Dynamic Head Restraints . . . . –
Adjustable Belt . . . . –
Pretensioners . . . . –

At-a-Glance

Status/Year Series Started . . . . All New/2012
Twins . . . . –
Body Styles . . . . Sedan
Seating 5
Anti-Theft Device . . . . –
Parking Index Rating . . . . Very Easy
Where Made . . . . Tahara, Japan
Fuel Factor
MPG Rating (city/hwy) Poor-19/28
Driving Range (mi.) Short-386.5
Fuel Type. . . . . Premium
Annual Fuel Cost. . . . . High-$2363
Gas Guzzler Tax . . . . No
Greenhouse Gas Emissions (tons/yr.). . . . . –
Barrels of Oil Used per year . . . . –

Lexus GS

How the Competition Rates

Competitors	Rating	Pg.
BMW 5 Series	9	96
Hyundai Genesis	–	159
Mercedes-Benz E-Class	–	204

Price Range

	Retail	Markup

Specifications

Drive. . . . . RWD
Engine 3.5-liter V6
Transmission . . . . 6-sp. Automatic
Tow Rating (lbs.). . . . . –
Head/Leg Room (in.) Cramped-38/42.3
Interior Space (cu. ft.) Roomy-109.1
Cargo Space (cu. ft.) Cramped-14.3
Wheelbase/Length (in.) 112.2/190.7

Ratings—10 Best, 1 Worst

Combo Crash Tests	–
Safety Features	9
Rollover	1
Preventative Maintenance	6
Repair Costs	2
Warranty	6
Fuel Economy	1
Complaints	7
Insurance Costs	8
OVERALL RATING	**–**

Lexus GX

At-a-Glance

Status/Year Series Started Unchanged/2003
Twins. . . . . Toyota 4Runner
Body Styles. . . . . SUV
Seating. 7
Anti-Theft Device. . . . . . . Std. Pass. Immobil. & Alarm
Parking Index Rating . . . . Average
Where Made . . . . Tahara, Japan
Fuel Factor
MPG Rating (city/hwy). . . . . Very Poor-15/20
Driving Range (mi.) Average-388.7
Fuel Type. . . . . Premium
Annual Fuel Cost. . . . . Very High-$3106
Gas Guzzler Tax . . . . No
Greenhouse Gas Emissions (tons/yr.) Very High-11.0
Barrels of Oil Used per year . . . . Very High-20.1

How the Competition Rates

Competitors	Rating	Pg.
Audi Q5	–	92
BMW X5	–	99
Volvo XC90	–	270

Price Range	Retail	Markup
Base	$53,245	12%
Premium	$58,040	12%

Lexus GX

Safety Checklist

Crash Tests:
Frontal . . . . –
Side . . . . –
Airbags:
Head. . . . . Fr. & Rr. Roof Curtain
Torso . . . . Rear Torso from Seat
Pelvis . . . . Front Pelvis/Torso from Seat
Roll Sensing . . . . Yes
Knee Bolster. . . . . Standard Front
Crash Avoidance:
Frontal Collision Warning. . . . . None
Blind Spot Detection . . . . None
Crash Imminent Braking . . . . Optional
Lane Departure Warning . . . . None
General:
Auto. Crash Notification . . . . Optional
Day Running Lamps . . . . Standard
Safety Belt/Restraint:
Dynamic Head Restraints. . . . . . Standard Front
Adjustable Belt . . . . . . Standard Front and Rear
Pretensioners. . . . . Standard Front & Rear

Lexus GX

Specifications

Drive 4WD
Engine 4.6-liter V8
Transmission . . . . 6-sp. Automatic
Tow Rating (lbs.) High-6500
Head/Leg Room (in.) Cramped-38/41.7
Interior Space (cu. ft.) . . . . Very Roomy-129.7
Cargo Space (cu. ft.) . . . . Very Cramped-11.6
Wheelbase/Length (in.) 109.8/189.2

Ratings—10 Best, 1 Worst

Combo Crash Tests	–
Safety Features	9
Rollover	6
Preventative Maintenance	8
Repair Costs	–
Warranty	6
Fuel Economy	10
Complaints	1
Insurance Costs	5
OVERALL RATING	–

Lexus HS

Lexus HS

At-a-Glance

Status/Year Series Started Unchanged/2010
Twins . . . . –
Body Styles . . . . Sedan
Seating. 5
Anti-Theft Device . . . . Std. Pass. Immobil. & Alarm
Parking Index Rating . . . . Average
Where Made. . . . . Kyushu, Japan
Fuel Factor
  MPG Rating (city/hwy) . . . . Very Good-35/34
  Driving Range (mi.). . . . . Very Long-500.9
  Fuel Type. . . . . Regular
  Annual Fuel Cost . . . . Very Low-$1403
  Gas Guzzler Tax . . . . No
  Greenhouse Gas Emissions (tons/yr.) . Very Low-5.4
  Barrels of Oil Used per year Low-9.8

How the Competition Rates

Competitors	Rating	Pg.
Acura TSX	–	84
Chevrolet Malibu	4	114
Ford Fusion	5	140

Price Range

	Retail	Markup
Base	$36,330	10%
Premium	$39,100	10%

Safety Checklist

Crash Tests:
  Frontal . . . . –
  Side . . . . –
Airbags:
  Head. . . . . Fr. & Rr. Roof Curtain
  Torso . . . . Fr. & Rr. Torso from Seat
  Pelvis. . . . . None
  Roll Sensing. . . . . No
  Knee Bolster. . . . . Standard Front
Crash Avoidance:
  Frontal Collision Warning. . . . . None
  Blind Spot Detection . . . . None
  Crash Imminent Braking . . . . Optional
  Lane Departure Warning . . . . None
General:
  Auto. Crash Notification . . . . Optional
  Day Running Lamps . . . . Standard
Safety Belt/Restraint:
  Dynamic Head Restraints. . . . . . Standard Front
  Adjustable Belt . . . . Standard Front
  Pretensioners. . . . . Standard Front & Rear

Lexus HS

Specifications

Drive . . . . FWD
Engine. 2.4-liter I4
Transmission. . . . . ECVT
Tow Rating (lbs.). . . . . –
Head/Leg Room (in.) Cramped-38/42.6
Interior Space (cu. ft.) Cramped-90.2
Cargo Space (cu. ft.) . . . . Very Cramped-12.1
Wheelbase/Length (in.) 106.3/184.8

Lexus IS

Ratings—10 Best, 1 Worst

Combo Crash Tests	–
Safety Features	5
Rollover	8
Preventative Maintenance	7
Repair Costs	1
Warranty	6
Fuel Economy	5
Complaints	7
Insurance Costs	5
OVERALL RATING	**–**

Lexus IS

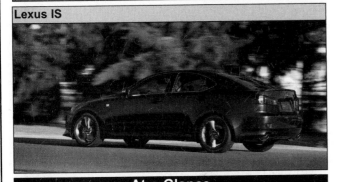

Lexus IS

At-a-Glance

Status/Year Series Started Unchanged/2006
Twins . . . . –
Body Styles . . . . Sedan, Convertible
Seating 5
Anti-Theft Device . . . . . . Std. Pass. Immobil. & Alarm
Parking Index Rating . . . . Very Easy
Where Made . . . . Kokura, Japan / Miyata, Japan

Fuel Factor
MPG Rating (city/hwy) Average-21/30
Driving Range (mi.) Long-415.1
Fuel Type . . . . Premium
Annual Fuel Cost . . . . Average-$2163
Gas Guzzler Tax . . . . No
Greenhouse Gas Emissions (tons/yr.) . . Average-7.5
Barrels of Oil Used per year Average-13.7

How the Competition Rates

Competitors	Rating	Pg.
Acura TSX	–	84
BMW 3 Series	–	95
Infiniti G	–	167

Price Range	Retail	Markup
Sport Manual	$33,595	11%
Base RWD	$40,020	11%
Base AWD	$42,480	11%
Convertible Automatic	$46,640	11%

Safety Checklist

Crash Tests:
Frontal . . . . –
Side . . . . –
Airbags:
Head . . . . Fr. & Rr. Roof Curtain
Torso . . . . Front Pelvis/Torso from Seat
Pelvis . . . . Front Pelvis/Torso from Seat
Roll Sensing . . . . No
Knee Bolster . . . . Standard Front
Crash Avoidance:
Frontal Collision Warning . . . . None
Blind Spot Detection . . . . None
Crash Imminent Braking . . . . None
Lane Departure Warning . . . . None
General:
Auto. Crash Notification . . . . Optional
Day Running Lamps . . . . Standard
Safety Belt/Restraint:
Dynamic Head Restraints . . . . None
Adjustable Belt . . . . Standard Front
Pretensioners . . . . Standard Front & Rear

Lexus IS

Specifications

Drive . . . . RWD
Engine 2.5-liter V6
Transmission . . . . 6-sp. Automatic
Tow Rating (lbs.) . . . . –
Head/Leg Room (in.) Average-37.2/43.9
Interior Space (cu. ft.) . . . . Very Cramped-85.7
Cargo Space (cu. ft.) Cramped-13
Wheelbase/Length (in.) 107.5/180.3

Ratings—10 Best, 1 Worst

Combo Crash Tests	–
Safety Features	7
Rollover	8
Preventative Maintenance	4
Repair Costs	1
Warranty	6
Fuel Economy	2
Complaints	9
Insurance Costs	5
OVERALL RATING	–

Lexus LS

Lexus LS

At-a-Glance

Status/Year Series Started Unchanged/2007
Twins . . . . –
Body Styles . . . . Sedan
Seating. 5
Anti-Theft Device. . . . . . . Std. Pass. Immobil. & Alarm
Parking Index Rating . . . . Average
Where Made . . . . Tahara, Japan
Fuel Factor
MPG Rating (city/hwy). . . . . Very Poor-16/24
Driving Range (mi.) Long-417.9
Fuel Type. . . . . Premium
Annual Fuel Cost. . . . . Very High-$2789
Gas Guzzler Tax . . . . No
Greenhouse Gas Emissions (tons/yr.) High-9.8
Barrels of Oil Used per year. High-18.0

How the Competition Rates

Competitors	Rating	Pg.
BMW 7 Series	–	97
Jaguar XF	–	170
Mercedes-Benz S-Class	–	208

Price Range

Price Range	Retail	Markup
460	$67,130	10%
460 AWD	$69,435	10%
460L AWD	$74,980	10%
600h L	$112,250	10%

Safety Checklist

Crash Tests:
Frontal . . . . –
Side . . . . –
Airbags:
Head. . . . . Fr. & Rr. Roof Curtain
Torso . . . . Rear Torso from Seat
Pelvis . . . . Front Pelvis/Torso from Seat
Roll Sensing. . . . . No
Knee Bolster. . . . . Standard Front
Crash Avoidance:
Frontal Collision Warning. . . . . None
Blind Spot Detection . . . . None
Crash Imminent Braking . . . . Optional
Lane Departure Warning . . . . None
General:
Auto. Crash Notification . . . . Optional
Day Running Lamps . . . . Standard
Safety Belt/Restraint:
Dynamic Head Restraints. . . . . . Standard Front
Adjustable Belt . . . . Standard Front
Pretensioners. . . . . Standard Front & Rear

Lexus LS

Specifications

Drive. . . . . RWD
Engine 4.6-liter V8
Transmission . . . . 8-sp. Automatic
Tow Rating (lbs.). . . . . –
Head/Leg Room (in.) Average-38/43.7
Interior Space (cu. ft.). Average-103
Cargo Space (cu. ft.) Average-18
Wheelbase/Length (in.) 116.9/199.2

Ratings—10 Best, 1 Worst

Combo Crash Tests	5
Safety Features	8
Rollover	3
Preventative Maintenance	7
Repair Costs	1
Warranty	6
Fuel Economy	3
Complaints	6
Insurance Costs	8
OVERALL RATING	**5**

Lexus RX

Lexus RX

At-a-Glance

Status/Year Series Started	Unchanged/2010
Twins	–
Body Styles	SUV
Seating	5
Anti-Theft Device	Std. Pass. Immobil. & Alarm
Parking Index Rating	Hard
Where Made	Kokura, Japan / Cambridge, Ontario

Fuel Factor

MPG Rating (city/hwy)	Poor-18/24
Driving Range (mi.)	Average-389.4
Fuel Type	Regular
Annual Fuel Cost	High-$2389
Gas Guzzler Tax	No
Greenhouse Gas Emissions (tons/yr.)	High-9.3
Barrels of Oil Used per year	High-17.1

How the Competition Rates

Competitors	Rating	Pg.
Acura ZDX	8	85
Audi Q5	–	92
Mercedes-Benz GLK-Class	–	206

Price Range

Price Range	Retail	Markup
350 FWD	$39,075	10%
350 AWD	$40,475	10%
450h FWD	$45,235	10%
450h AWD	$46,825	10%

Safety Checklist

Crash Tests:

Frontal	Average
Side	Poor

Airbags:

Head	Fr. & Rr. Roof Curtain
Torso	Rear Torso from Seat
Pelvis	Front Pelvis/Torso from Seat
Roll Sensing	Yes
Knee Bolster	Standard Front

Crash Avoidance:

Frontal Collision Warning	None
Blind Spot Detection	None
Crash Imminent Braking	None
Lane Departure Warning	None

General:

Auto. Crash Notification	Optional
Day Running Lamps	Standard

Safety Belt/Restraint:

Dynamic Head Restraints	Standard Front
Adjustable Belt	Standard Front
Pretensioners	Standard Front & Rear

Lexus RX

Specifications

Drive	AWD
Engine	3.5-liter V6
Transmission	6-sp. Automatic
Tow Rating (lbs.)	Low-3500
Head/Leg Room (in.)	Roomy-39.1/43.1
Interior Space (cu. ft.)	Very Roomy-139.7
Cargo Space (cu. ft.)	Very Roomy-40
Wheelbase/Length (in.)	107.9/187.8

Ratings—10 Best, 1 Worst

Combo Crash Tests	–
Safety Features	6
Rollover	7
Preventative Maintenance	6
Repair Costs	2
Warranty	6
Fuel Economy	3
Complaints	4
Insurance Costs	3
OVERALL RATING	**–**

Lincoln MKS

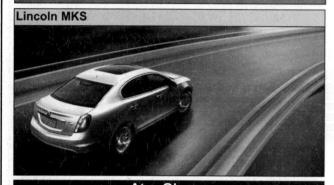

At-a-Glance

Status/Year Series Started Unchanged/2009
Twins . . . . –
Body Styles . . . . Sedan
Seating 5
Anti-Theft Device . . . . Std. Pass. Immobil. & Alarm
Parking Index Rating . . . . Very Hard
Where Made . . . . Chicago, IL
Fuel Factor
MPG Rating (city/hwy) Poor-17/25
Driving Range (mi.) Short-377.3
Fuel Type . . . . Regular
Annual Fuel Cost . . . . High-$2440
Gas Guzzler Tax . . . . No
Greenhouse Gas Emissions (tons/yr.) High-9.3
Barrels of Oil Used per year High-17.1

How the Competition Rates

Competitors	Rating	Pg.
Chrysler 300	–	122
Infiniti G	–	167
Lexus ES	–	187

Price Range	Retail	Markup
FWD	$41,500	6%
AWD	$43,390	6%
EcoBoost AWD	$48,390	6%

Lincoln MKS

Safety Checklist

Crash Tests:
Frontal . . . . –
Side . . . . –
Airbags:
Head . . . . Fr. & Rr. Roof Curtain
Torso . . . . Front Torso from Seat
Pelvis . . . . None
Roll Sensing . . . . Yes
Knee Bolster . . . . None
Crash Avoidance:
Frontal Collision Warning . . . . None
Blind Spot Detection . . . . Optional
Crash Imminent Braking . . . . None
Lane Departure Warning . . . . None
General:
Auto. Crash Notification . . . . Standard
Day Running Lamps . . . . None
Safety Belt/Restraint:
Dynamic Head Restraints . . . . None
Adjustable Belt . . . . Standard Front
Pretensioners . . . . Standard Front

Lincoln MKS

Specifications

Drive . . . . FWD
Engine 3.7-liter V6
Transmission . . . . 6-sp. Automatic
Tow Rating (lbs.) . . . . Very Low-1000
Head/Leg Room (in.) Average-39.7/41.9
Interior Space (cu. ft.) Roomy-105.8
Cargo Space (cu. ft.) Average-18.7
Wheelbase/Length (in.) 112.9/204.1

Ratings—10 Best, 1 Worst

Combo Crash Tests	–
Safety Features	6
Rollover	4
Preventative Maintenance	5
Repair Costs	1
Warranty	6
Fuel Economy	3
Complaints	2
Insurance Costs	8

OVERALL RATING — –

Lincoln MKT

Lincoln MKT

At-a-Glance

Status/Year Series Started Unchanged/2010
Twins . . . . –
Body Styles. . . . . SUV
Seating 6/7
Anti-Theft Device. . . . . . . Std. Pass. Immobil. & Alarm
Parking Index Rating . . . . Very Hard
Where Made . . . . Oakville, Ontario
Fuel Factor
MPG Rating (city/hwy) Poor-17/24
Driving Range (mi.). Short-364.0
Fuel Type. . . . . Regular
Annual Fuel Cost. . . . . High-$2476
Gas Guzzler Tax . . . . No
Greenhouse Gas Emissions (tons/yr.) High-9.3
Barrels of Oil Used per year. High-17.1

How the Competition Rates

Competitors	Rating	Pg.
Audi Q7	–	93
Cadillac Escalade	6	118
Nissan Armada	–	217

Price Range

Price Range	Retail	Markup
Base FWD	$44,300	6%
Base AWD	$46,295	6%

Safety Checklist

Crash Tests:
Frontal . . . . –
Side . . . . –
Airbags:
Head. . . . . Fr. & Rr. Roof Curtain
Torso . . . . Front Torso from Seat
Pelvis. . . . . None
Roll Sensing . . . . Yes
Knee Bolster . . . . None
Crash Avoidance:
Frontal Collision Warning. . . . . None
Blind Spot Detection . . . . Optional
Crash Imminent Braking . . . . None
Lane Departure Warning . . . . None
General:
Auto. Crash Notification . . . . Optional
Day Running Lamps . . . . None
Safety Belt/Restraint:
Dynamic Head Restraints . . . . None
Adjustable Belt . . . . Standard Front
Pretensioners . . . . Standard Front

Lincoln MKT

Specifications

Drive. . . . . FWD
Engine 3.7-liter V6
Transmission . . . . 6-sp. Automatic
Tow Rating (lbs.). Low-4500
Head/Leg Room (in.). Average-40.1/41.3
Interior Space (cu. ft.) . . . . Very Roomy-142.3
Cargo Space (cu. ft.) Average-17.9
Wheelbase/Length (in.) 117.9/207.6

Ratings—10 Best, 1 Worst

Combo Crash Tests	–
Safety Features	2
Rollover	6
Preventative Maintenance	–
Repair Costs	–
Warranty	2
Fuel Economy	9
Complaints	10
Insurance Costs	3
OVERALL RATING	**–**

Mazda 2

Mazda 2

At-a-Glance

Status/Year Series Started Unchanged/2011
Twins . . . . –
Body Styles . . . . Hatchback
Seating 5
Anti-Theft Device . . . . Std. Pass. Immobil.
Parking Index Rating . . . . Very Easy
Where Made . . . . Nui Thanh, Vietnam
Fuel Factor
  MPG Rating (city/hwy) . . . . Very Good-28/34
  Driving Range (mi.) . . . . Very Short-343.7
  Fuel Type . . . . Regular
  Annual Fuel Cost . . . . Very Low-$1593
  Gas Guzzler Tax . . . . No
  Greenhouse Gas Emissions (tons/yr.) Low-6.2
  Barrels of Oil Used per year Low-11.4

How the Competition Rates

Competitors	Rating	Pg.
Honda Fit	–	150
Nissan Versa	1	228
Toyota Yaris	–	258

Price Range	Retail	Markup
Sport MT	$14,370	1%
Sport AT	$15,210	1%
Touring MT	$15,855	1%
Touring AT	$16,695	1%

Safety Checklist

Crash Tests:
  Frontal . . . . –
  Side . . . . –
Airbags:
  Head . . . . Fr. & Rr. Roof Curtain
  Torso . . . . Front Torso from Seat
  Pelvis . . . . None
  Roll Sensing . . . . No
  Knee Bolster . . . . None
Crash Avoidance:
  Frontal Collision Warning . . . . None
  Blind Spot Detection . . . . None
  Crash Imminent Braking . . . . None
  Lane Departure Warning . . . . None
General:
  Auto. Crash Notification . . . . None
  Day Running Lamps . . . . None
Safety Belt/Restraint:
  Dynamic Head Restraints . . . . None
  Adjustable Belt . . . . Standard Front
  Pretensioners . . . . Standard Front

Mazda 2

Specifications

Drive . . . . FWD
Engine 1.5-liter I4
Transmission . . . . 4-sp. Automatic
Tow Rating (lbs.) . . . . –
Head/Leg Room (in.) Average-39.1/42.6
Interior Space (cu. ft.) . . . . Very Cramped-87.1
Cargo Space (cu. ft.) Cramped-13.3
Wheelbase/Length (in.) 98/155.5

Ratings—10 Best, 1 Worst

Combo Crash Tests	7
Safety Features	4
Rollover	7
Preventative Maintenance	6
Repair Costs	9
Warranty	2
Fuel Economy	7
Complaints	7
Insurance Costs	1
OVERALL RATING	**6**

Mazda 3

Mazda 3

At-a-Glance

Status/Year Series Started	Unchanged/2004
Twins	–
Body Styles	Sedan, Hatchback
Seating	5
Anti-Theft Device	Std. Pass. Immobil. & Alarm
Parking Index Rating	Easy
Where Made	Chongqing, China

Fuel Factor

MPG Rating (city/hwy)	Good-24/33
Driving Range (mi.)	Average-396.7
Fuel Type	Regular
Annual Fuel Cost	Low-$1771
Gas Guzzler Tax	No
Greenhouse Gas Emissions (tons/yr.)	Average-6.9
Barrels of Oil Used per year	Average-12.7

How the Competition Rates

Competitors	Rating	Pg.
Mitsubishi Lancer	–	212
Scion tC	7	233
Subaru Impreza	–	238

Price Range

	Retail	Markup
i	$15,800	7%
s Touring	$20,700	7%
s Grand Touring	$22,770	7%
Mazdaspeed3	$23,700	7%

Safety Checklist

Crash Tests:
Frontal	Very Good
Side	Very Poor

Airbags:
Head	Fr. & Rr. Roof Curtain
Torso	Front Pelvis/Torso from Seat
Pelvis	Front Pelvis/Torso from Seat
Roll Sensing	No
Knee Bolster	None

Crash Avoidance:
Frontal Collision Warning	None
Blind Spot Detection	None
Crash Imminent Braking	None
Lane Departure Warning	None

General:
Auto. Crash Notification	None
Day Running Lamps	None

Safety Belt/Restraint:
Dynamic Head Restraints	Standard Front
Adjustable Belt	Standard Front
Pretensioners	Standard Front

Mazda 3

Specifications

Drive	FWD
Engine	2.0-liter I4
Transmission	5-sp. Automatic
Tow Rating (lbs.)	–
Head/Leg Room (in.)	Average-38.9/42
Interior Space (cu. ft.)	Cramped-94.1
Cargo Space (cu. ft.)	Very Cramped-11.8
Wheelbase/Length (in.)	103.9/180.9

Ratings—10 Best, 1 Worst

Combo Crash Tests	–
Safety Features	2
Rollover	4
Preventative Maintenance	6
Repair Costs	7
Warranty	2
Fuel Economy	5
Complaints	2
Insurance Costs	1
OVERALL RATING	**–**

Mazda 5

Mazda 5

At-a-Glance

Status/Year Series Started . . . . All New/2012
Twins . . . . –
Body Styles . . . . Minivan
Seating 7
Anti-Theft Device . . . . Std. Pass. Immobil. & Alarm
Parking Index Rating . . . . Easy
Where Made . . . . Hiroshima, Japan
Fuel Factor
MPG Rating (city/hwy) Average-21/28
Driving Range (mi.) Short-376.2
Fuel Type . . . . Regular
Annual Fuel Cost . . . . Average-$2048
Gas Guzzler Tax . . . . No
Greenhouse Gas Emissions (tons/yr.) . . Average-7.8
Barrels of Oil Used per year High-14.3

How the Competition Rates

Competitors	Rating	Pg.
Mitsubishi Outlander	–	213
Nissan Rogue	5	225
Subaru Forester	5	237

Price Range

	Retail	Markup
Sport Manual	$19,345	7%
Sport Automatic	$20,345	7%
Touring	$21,345	7%
Grand Touring	$24,025	7%

Safety Checklist

Crash Tests:
Frontal . . . . –
Side . . . . –
Airbags:
Head . . . . Fr. & Rr. Roof Curtain
Torso . . . . Front Pelvis/Torso from Seat
Pelvis . . . . Front Pelvis/Torso from Seat
Roll Sensing . . . . No
Knee Bolster . . . . None
Crash Avoidance:
Frontal Collision Warning . . . . None
Blind Spot Detection . . . . None
Crash Imminent Braking . . . . None
Lane Departure Warning . . . . None
General:
Auto. Crash Notification . . . . None
Day Running Lamps . . . . None
Safety Belt/Restraint:
Dynamic Head Restraints . . . . None
Adjustable Belt . . . . Standard Front
Pretensioners . . . . Standard Front

Mazda 5

Specifications

Drive . . . . FWD
Engine 2.5-liter I4
Transmission . . . . 5-sp. Auto. w/Overdrive
Tow Rating (lbs.) . . . . –
Head/Leg Room (in.) Average-40.7/40.7
Interior Space (cu. ft.) Cramped-97.7
Cargo Space (cu. ft.) Roomy-27.5
Wheelbase/Length (in.) 108.3/180.5

Ratings—10 Best, 1 Worst

Combo Crash Tests	6
Safety Features	2
Rollover	8
Preventative Maintenance	6
Repair Costs	8
Warranty	2
Fuel Economy	6
Complaints	9
Insurance Costs	5
OVERALL RATING	**7**

Mazda 6

Mazda 6

At-a-Glance

Status/Year Series Started Unchanged/2009
Twins . . . . –
Body Styles . . . . Sedan
Seating 5
Anti-Theft Device . . . . Std. Pass. Immobil. & Alarm
Parking Index Rating . . . . Easy
Where Made . . . . Flat Rock, MI
Fuel Factor
  MPG Rating (city/hwy) Average-22/31
  Driving Range (mi.) . . . . Very Long-468.2
  Fuel Type. . . . . Regular
  Annual Fuel Cost . . . . Low-$1915
  Gas Guzzler Tax . . . . No
  Greenhouse Gas Emissions (tons/yr.) . . Average-7.5
  Barrels of Oil Used per year Average-13.7

How the Competition Rates

Competitors	Rating	Pg.
Mitsubishi Galant	–	211
Nissan Altima	6	215
Toyota Camry	10	246

Price Range	Retail	Markup
i Sport	$20,240	8%
i Touring Plus	$24,490	8%
i Grand Touring	$27,070	8%
s Grand Touring	$29,570	8%

Safety Checklist

Crash Tests:
  Frontal. . . . . Poor
  Side . . . . Very Good
Airbags:
  Head . . . . Fr. & Rr. Roof Curtain
  Torso . . . . Front Pelvis/Torso from Seat
  Pelvis . . . . Front Pelvis/Torso from Seat
  Roll Sensing. . . . . No
  Knee Bolster . . . . None
Crash Avoidance:
  Frontal Collision Warning. . . . . None
  Blind Spot Detection . . . . Optional
  Crash Imminent Braking . . . . None
  Lane Departure Warning . . . . None
General:
  Auto. Crash Notification . . . . None
  Day Running Lamps . . . . None
Safety Belt/Restraint:
  Dynamic Head Restraints . . . . None
  Adjustable Belt . . . . Standard Front
  Pretensioners . . . . Standard Front

Mazda 6

Specifications

Drive . . . . FWD
Engine. 2.5-liter I4
Transmission . . . . 5-sp. Automatic
Tow Rating (lbs.) . . . . –
Head/Leg Room (in.). Average-39.4/42.5
Interior Space (cu. ft.) Average-101.9
Cargo Space (cu. ft.) Average-16.6
Wheelbase/Length (in.) 109.8/193.7

Ratings—10 Best, 1 Worst

Combo Crash Tests	–
Safety Features	5
Rollover	5
Preventative Maintenance	6
Repair Costs	6
Warranty	2
Fuel Economy	4
Complaints	3
Insurance Costs	5
OVERALL RATING	–

Mazda CX-7

Mazda CX-7

At-a-Glance

Status/Year Series Started Unchanged/2007
Twins . . . . –
Body Styles. . . . . SUV
Seating. 5
Anti-Theft Device. . . . . . . Std. Pass. Immobil. & Alarm
Parking Index Rating . . . . Average
Where Made. . . . . Hiroshima, Japan
Fuel Factor
MPG Rating (city/hwy) Poor-20/28
Driving Range (mi.). Short-376.4
Fuel Type. . . . . Regular
Annual Fuel Cost . . . . Average-$2111
Gas Guzzler Tax . . . . No
Greenhouse Gas Emissions (tons/yr.) . . Average-8.1
Barrels of Oil Used per year. High-14.9

How the Competition Rates

Competitors	Rating	Pg.
Honda Pilot	4	153
Nissan Murano	3	223
Toyota Highlander	4	249

Price Range

	Retail	Markup

Safety Checklist

Crash Tests:
Frontal . . . . –
Side . . . . –
Airbags:
Head. . . . . Fr. & Rr. Roof Curtain
Torso . . . . Front Torso from Seat
Pelvis. . . . . None
Roll Sensing . . . . Yes
Knee Bolster . . . . None
Crash Avoidance:
Frontal Collision Warning. . . . . None
Blind Spot Detection . . . . Optional
Crash Imminent Braking . . . . None
Lane Departure Warning . . . . None
General:
Auto. Crash Notification . . . . None
Day Running Lamps . . . . None
Safety Belt/Restraint:
Dynamic Head Restraints . . . . None
Adjustable Belt . . . . Standard Front
Pretensioners . . . . Standard Front

Mazda CX-7

Specifications

Drive . . . . FWD
Engine. 2.5-liter I4
Transmission . . . . 5-sp. Automatic
Tow Rating (lbs.). . . . . Very Low-1500
Head/Leg Room (in.). Average-39.7/41.7
Interior Space (cu. ft.) Average-101.7
Cargo Space (cu. ft.) Roomy-29.9
Wheelbase/Length (in.) 108.3/184.3

Mazda CX-9

Mid-Size SUV

Ratings—10 Best, 1 Worst	
Combo Crash Tests	–
Safety Features	7
Rollover	4
Preventative Maintenance	6
Repair Costs	5
Warranty	2
Fuel Economy	3
Complaints	10
Insurance Costs	8
OVERALL RATING	**–**

Mazda CX-9

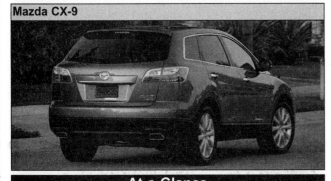
Mazda CX-9

At-a-Glance

Status/Year Series Started Unchanged/2007
Twins . . . . –
Body Styles. . . . . SUV
Seating. 7
Anti-Theft Device. . . . . . . Std. Pass. Immobil. & Alarm
Parking Index Rating . . . . Very Easy
Where Made. . . . . Hiroshima, Japan

Fuel Factor
MPG Rating (city/hwy). Poor-17/24
Driving Range (mi.) Average-393.3
Fuel Type. . . . . Regular
Annual Fuel Cost. . . . . High-$2476
Gas Guzzler Tax . . . . No
Greenhouse Gas Emissions (tons/yr.) High-9.8
Barrels of Oil Used per year. High-18.0

How the Competition Rates

Competitors	Rating	Pg.
Acura MDX	9	81
Chevrolet Equinox	3	112
Nissan Murano	3	223

Price Range	Retail	Markup
Sport FWD	$29,385	8%
Sport AWD	$30,775	8%
Touring FWD	$31,305	8%
Grand Touring	$34,785	8%

Safety Checklist

Crash Tests:
Frontal . . . . –
Side . . . . –
Airbags:
Head. . . . . Fr. & Rr. Roof Curtain
Torso . . . . Front Torso from Seat
Pelvis. . . . . None
Roll Sensing . . . . Yes
Knee Bolster . . . . None
Crash Avoidance:
Frontal Collision Warning. . . . . None
Blind Spot Detection . . . . Optional
Crash Imminent Braking . . . . None
Lane Departure Warning . . . . None
General:
Auto. Crash Notification. . . . . None
Day Running Lamps . . . . None
Safety Belt/Restraint:
Dynamic Head Restraints. . . . . . Standard Front
Adjustable Belt . . . . Standard Front
Pretensioners . . . . Standard Front

Mazda CX-9

Specifications

Drive . . . . FWD
Engine 3.7-liter V6
Transmission . . . . 6-sp. Automatic
Tow Rating (lbs.). . . . . Very Low-2000
Head/Leg Room (in.) Cramped-39.6/40.9
Interior Space (cu. ft.) . . . . Very Roomy-139.4
Cargo Space (cu. ft.) Average-17.2
Wheelbase/Length (in.) 113.2/200.2

Day Running

Ratings—10 Best, 1 Worst	
Combo Crash Tests	–
Safety Features	1
Rollover	10
Preventative Maintenance	6
Repair Costs	8
Warranty	2
Fuel Economy	5
Complaints	10
Insurance Costs	8
OVERALL RATING	–

Mazda MX-5 Miata

Safety Checklist

Crash Tests:
Frontal . . . . –
Side . . . . –
Airbags:
Head . . . . Front Head from Seat
Torso . . . . Front Head/Torso from Seat
Pelvis . . . . None
Roll Sensing. . . . . No
Knee Bolster . . . . None
Crash Avoidance:
Frontal Collision Warning. . . . . None
Blind Spot Detection . . . . None
Crash Imminent Braking . . . . None
Lane Departure Warning . . . . None
General:
Auto. Crash Notification. . . . . None
Day Running Lamps . . . . None
Safety Belt/Restraint:
Dynamic Head Restraints . . . . None
Adjustable Belt. None
Pretensioners . . . . Standard Front

Mazda MX-5 Miata

At-a-Glance

Status/Year Series Started Unchanged/2006
Twins . . . . –
Body Styles. . . . . Two Seater Convertible
Seating. 2
Anti-Theft Device . . . . Std. Pass. Immobil. & Alarm
Parking Index Rating . . . . Very Easy
Where Made. . . . . Hiroshima, Japan
Fuel Factor
MPG Rating (city/hwy) Average-21/28
Driving Range (mi.). . . . . Very Short-300.5
Fuel Type. . . . . Premium
Annual Fuel Cost . . . . Average-$2219
Gas Guzzler Tax . . . . No
Greenhouse Gas Emissions (tons/yr.) . . Average-8.1
Barrels of Oil Used per year. High-14.9

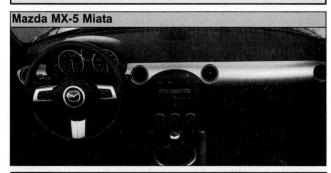

Mazda MX-5 Miata

How the Competition Rates

Competitors	Rating	Pg.
Ford Mustang	2	141
Hyundai Genesis	–	159
Nissan 370Z	–	214

Price Range	Retail	Markup
Sport	$24,350	14%
Touring Convertible	$26,650	8%
Touring Hardtop	$27,250	8%
Grand Touring	$29,760	8%

Specifications

Drive. . . . . RWD
Engine. 2.0-liter I4
Transmission . . . . 6-sp. Automatic
Tow Rating (lbs.). . . . . –
Head/Leg Room (in.) Cramped-37.4/43.1
Interior Space (cu. ft.) . . . . –
Cargo Space (cu. ft.) . . . . Very Cramped-5.3
Wheelbase/Length (in.) 91.7/157.3

Ratings—10 Best, 1 Worst

Combo Crash Tests	3
Safety Features	8
Rollover	8
Preventative Maintenance	4
Repair Costs	3
Warranty	3
Fuel Economy	3
Complaints	10
Insurance Costs	3
OVERALL RATING	**3**

Mercedes-Benz C-Class

At-a-Glance

Status/Year Series Started . Appearance Change/2008
Twins . . . . –
Body Styles . . . . Sedan
Seating 5
Anti-Theft Device . Std. Active Immobil. & Pass. Alarm
Parking Index Rating . . . . Easy
Where Made . . . . Bremen, Germany
Fuel Factor
MPG Rating (city/hwy) Poor-18/25
Driving Range (mi.) . . . . Very Short-358.4
Fuel Type . . . . Premium
Annual Fuel Cost . . . . High-$2549
Gas Guzzler Tax . . . . No
Greenhouse Gas Emissions (tons/yr.) High-9.3
Barrels of Oil Used per year High-17.1

How the Competition Rates

Competitors	Rating	Pg.
Audi A4	5	87
BMW 3 Series	–	95
Lexus IS	–	191

Price Range

	Retail	Markup
C250 Sport	$34,800	8%
C300 Sport	$38,020	8%
C300 Luxury	$38,430	8%
C350 Coupe	$42,370	8%

Mercedes-Benz C-Class

Safety Checklist

Crash Tests:
Frontal . . . . Very Poor
Side . . . . Average
Airbags:
Head . . . . Fr. & Rr. Roof Curtain
Torso . . . . Front Torso from Seat
Pelvis . . . . Front Pelvis from Seat
Roll Sensing . . . . No
Knee Bolster . . . . Standard Driver
Crash Avoidance:
Frontal Collision Warning . . . . None
Blind Spot Detection . . . . Optional
Crash Imminent Braking . . . . None
Lane Departure Warning . . . . Optional
General:
Auto. Crash Notification . . . . Optional
Day Running Lamps . . . . Standard
Safety Belt/Restraint:
Dynamic Head Restraints . . . . . Standard Front
Adjustable Belt . . . . Standard Front
Pretensioners . . . . Standard Front & Rear

Mercedes-Benz C-Class

Specifications

Drive . . . . RWD
Engine 3.0-liter V6
Transmission . . . . 7-sp. Automatic
Tow Rating (lbs.) . . . . –
Head/Leg Room (in.) . . . . . Very Cramped-37.1/41.7
Interior Space (cu. ft.) . . . . Very Cramped-88.2
Cargo Space (cu. ft.) Cramped-12.4
Wheelbase/Length (in.) 108.7/180.75

Mercedes-Benz E-Class

Ratings—10 Best, 1 Worst

Combo Crash Tests	–
Safety Features	10
Rollover	8
Preventative Maintenance	3
Repair Costs	1
Warranty	3
Fuel Economy	4
Complaints	9
Insurance Costs	5
OVERALL RATING	–

Mercedes-Benz E-Class

Mercedes-Benz E-Class

At-a-Glance

Status/Year Series Started Unchanged/2010
Twins . . . . –
Body Styles . . . . Sedan, Coupe, Wagon
Seating 5
Anti-Theft Device . Std. Active Immobil. & Pass. Alarm
Parking Index Rating . . . . Average
Where Made . . . . Germany

Fuel Factor
MPG Rating (city/hwy) Poor-19/28
Driving Range (mi.) . . . . Very Long-468.7
Fuel Type . . . . Premium
Annual Fuel Cost . . . . High-$2363
Gas Guzzler Tax . . . . No
Greenhouse Gas Emissions (tons/yr.) High-8.5
Barrels of Oil Used per year High-15.6

How the Competition Rates

Competitors	Rating	Pg.
BMW 5 Series	9	96
Infiniti G	–	167
Lexus GS	–	188

Price Range

	Retail	Markup
350 Coupe	$50,675	8%
350 4MATIC Luxury Sedan	$53,865	8%
550 Cabriolet	$65,675	8%
63 AMG Wagon	$92,375	8%

Safety Checklist

Crash Tests:
 Frontal . . . . –
 Side . . . . –
Airbags:
 Head . . . . Fr. & Rr. Roof Curtain
 Torso . . . . Fr. & Opt. Rr. Torso from Seat
 Pelvis . . . . Front Pelvis from Seat
 Roll Sensing . . . . Yes
 Knee Bolster . . . . Standard Driver
Crash Avoidance:
 Frontal Collision Warning . . . . Optional
 Blind Spot Detection . . . . Optional
 Crash Imminent Braking . . . . Optional
 Lane Departure Warning . . . . Optional
General:
 Auto. Crash Notification . . . . Optional
 Day Running Lamps . . . . Standard
Safety Belt/Restraint:
 Dynamic Head Restraints . . . . . . Standard Front
 Adjustable Belt . . . . . . Standard Front and Rear
 Pretensioners . . . . Standard Front & Rear

Mercedes-Benz E-Class

Specifications

Drive . . . . RWD
Engine 3.5-liter V6
Transmission . . . . 7-sp. Automatic
Tow Rating (lbs.) . . . . Very Low-1655
Head/Leg Room (in.) . . . . . Very Cramped-37.9/41.3
Interior Space (cu. ft.) . . . . Very Cramped-81
Cargo Space (cu. ft.) Average-15.9
Wheelbase/Length (in.) 113.2/191.7

Mercedes-Benz GL-Class | Large SUV

Ratings—10 Best, 1 Worst

Combo Crash Tests	–
Safety Features	10
Rollover	2
Preventative Maintenance	1
Repair Costs	1
Warranty	3
Fuel Economy	1
Complaints	7
Insurance Costs	5
OVERALL RATING	**–**

Mercedes-Benz GL-Class

Mercedes-Benz GL-Class

At-a-Glance

Status/Year Series Started Unchanged/2007
Twins . . . . –
Body Styles. . . . . SUV
Seating. 7
Anti-Theft Device . Std. Active Immobil. & Pass. Alarm
Parking Index Rating . . . . Very Hard
Where Made . . . . Vance, AL

Fuel Factor
MPG Rating (city/hwy). . . . . Very Poor-13/18
Driving Range (mi.) Average-392.2
Fuel Type. . . . . Premium
Annual Fuel Cost. . . . . Very High-$3534
Gas Guzzler Tax . . . . No
Greenhouse Gas Emissions (tons/yr.) Very High-12.4
Barrels of Oil Used per year . . . . Very High-22.8

How the Competition Rates

Competitors	Rating	Pg.
Audi Q7	–	93
Ford Expedition	–	134
Toyota Sequoia	–	253

Price Range	Retail	Markup
GL350 BlueTEC	$61,570	8%
GL450	$62,570	8%
GL550	$85,300	8%

Safety Checklist

Crash Tests:
Frontal . . . . –
Side . . . . –
Airbags:
Head. . . . . Fr. & Rr. Roof Curtain
Torso . . . . Fr. & Rr. Torso from Seat
Pelvis . . . . None
Roll Sensing . . . . Yes
Knee Bolster . . . . Standard Driver
Crash Avoidance:
Frontal Collision Warning. . . . . None
Blind Spot Detection . . . . Optional
Crash Imminent Braking . . . . None
Lane Departure Warning . . . . None
General:
Auto. Crash Notification . . . . Optional
Day Running Lamps. . . . . Optional
Safety Belt/Restraint:
Dynamic Head Restraints. . . . . Standard Front
Adjustable Belt . . . . Standard Front
Pretensioners. . . . . Standard Front & Rear

Mercedes-Benz GL-Class

Specifications

Drive 4WD
Engine 4.5-liter V8
Transmission . . . . 7-sp. Automatic
Tow Rating (lbs.) High-7500
Head/Leg Room (in.) Cramped-40.1/40.3
Interior Space (cu. ft.) . . . . Very Roomy-143
Cargo Space (cu. ft.) Cramped-14.3
Wheelbase/Length (in.) 121.1/200.6

Ratings—10 Best, 1 Worst

Combo Crash Tests	–
Safety Features	9
Rollover	3
Preventative Maintenance	1
Repair Costs	2
Warranty	3
Fuel Economy	2
Complaints	2
Insurance Costs	8
OVERALL RATING	–

Mercedes-Benz GLK-Class

Mercedes-Benz GLK-Class

At-a-Glance

Status/Year Series Started Unchanged/2010
Twins . . . . –
Body Styles. . . . . SUV
Seating. 5
Anti-Theft Device . Std. Active Immobil. & Pass. Alarm
Parking Index Rating . . . . Average
Where Made. . . . . Bremen, Germany
Fuel Factor
  MPG Rating (city/hwy). . . . . Very Poor-16/21
  Driving Range (mi.). . . . . Very Short-311.8
  Fuel Type. . . . . Premium
  Annual Fuel Cost. . . . . Very High-$2930
  Gas Guzzler Tax . . . . No
  Greenhouse Gas Emissions (tons/yr.). . . . High-10.4
  Barrels of Oil Used per year . . . . Very High-19.0

How the Competition Rates

Competitors	Rating	Pg.
Acura ZDX	8	85
Audi Q5	–	92
Lexus RX	4	193

Price Range	Retail	Markup
GLK350	$35,500	8%
GLK350 4MATIC	$37,500	8%

Safety Checklist

Crash Tests:
  Frontal . . . . –
  Side . . . . –
Airbags:
  Head. . . . . Fr. & Rr. Roof Curtain
  Torso . . . . Front Torso from Seat
  Pelvis . . . . Front Pelvis from Seat
  Roll Sensing . . . . Yes
  Knee Bolster . . . . Standard Driver
Crash Avoidance:
  Frontal Collision Warning. . . . . None
  Blind Spot Detection . . . . None
  Crash Imminent Braking . . . . None
  Lane Departure Warning . . . . None
General:
  Auto. Crash Notification . . . . Optional
  Day Running Lamps . . . . None
Safety Belt/Restraint:
  Dynamic Head Restraints. . . . . . Standard Front
  Adjustable Belt . . . . Standard Front
  Pretensioners. . . . . Standard Front & Rear

Mercedes-Benz GLK-Class

Specifications

Drive. . . . . RWD
Engine. 3.5-liter V6
Transmission . . . . 7-sp. Automatic
Tow Rating (lbs.). Low-3500
Head/Leg Room (in.) Cramped-39.02/41.4
Interior Space (cu. ft.) Average-102.9
Cargo Space (cu. ft.) Roomy-23.3
Wheelbase/Length (in.) 108.5/178.3

Ratings—10 Best, 1 Worst

Combo Crash Tests	–
Safety Features	10
Rollover	3
Preventative Maintenance	2
Repair Costs	2
Warranty	3
Fuel Economy	2
Complaints	6
Insurance Costs	8
OVERALL RATING	**–**

Mercedes-Benz M-Class

Mercedes-Benz M-Class

At-a-Glance

Status/Year Series Started . . . . All New/2012
Twins . . . . –
Body Styles. . . . . .SUV
Seating 5
Anti-Theft Device . Std. Active Immobil. & Pass. Alarm
Parking Index Rating . . . . Hard
Where Made . . . . Vance, AL

Fuel Factor
MPG Rating (city/hwy). . . . . Very Poor-17/22
Driving Range (mi.) . . . . Very Long-465.8
Fuel Type. . . . . Premium
Annual Fuel Cost. . . . . Very High-$2772
Gas Guzzler Tax . . . . No
Greenhouse Gas Emissions (tons/yr.) High-9.8
Barrels of Oil Used per year. High-18.0

How the Competition Rates

Competitors	Rating	Pg.
BMW X5	–	99
Infiniti FX	–	166
Volvo XC90	–	270

Price Range	Retail	Markup
350 4MATIC	$49,865	8%
350 BlueTEC 4MATIC	$51,365	8%
550 4MATIC	$57,865	8%

Safety Checklist

Crash Tests:
Frontal . . . . –
Side . . . . –
Airbags:
Head. . . . . Fr. & Rr. Roof Curtain
Torso . . . . Front Torso from Seat
Pelvis . . . . None
Roll Sensing . . . . Yes
Knee Bolster . . . . Standard Driver
Crash Avoidance:
Frontal Collision Warning . . . . Optional
Blind Spot Detection . . . . Optional
Crash Imminent Braking . . . . Optional
Lane Departure Warning. . . . . Optional
General:
Auto. Crash Notification . . . . Optional
Day Running Lamps . . . . Standard
Safety Belt/Restraint:
Dynamic Head Restraints. . . . . . Standard Front
Adjustable Belt . . . . Standard Front
Pretensioners . . . . Standard Front & Rear

Mercedes-Benz M-Class

Specifications

Drive . . . . AWD
Engine 3.5-liter V6
Transmission . . . . 7-sp. Automatic
Tow Rating (lbs.) High-7200
Head/Leg Room (in.). . . . . . Very Cramped-38.9/40.3
Interior Space (cu. ft.) . . . . Very Roomy-162
Cargo Space (cu. ft.). . . . . Very Roomy-36.2
Wheelbase/Length (in.) 114.8/189.1

Ratings—10 Best, 1 Worst

Combo Crash Tests	–
Safety Features	10
Rollover	8
Preventative Maintenance	1
Repair Costs	1
Warranty	3
Fuel Economy	2
Complaints	9
Insurance Costs	5
OVERALL RATING	**–**

Mercedes-Benz S-Class

Mercedes-Benz S-Class

At-a-Glance

Status/Year Series Started Unchanged/2007
Twins . . . . –
Body Styles . . . . Sedan
Seating 5
Anti-Theft Device . Std. Active Immobil. & Pass. Alarm
Parking Index Rating . . . . Very Hard
Where Made . . . . Sindelfingen, Germany
Fuel Factor
  MPG Rating (city/hwy) . . . . Very Poor-15/25
  Driving Range (mi.) Long-435.4
  Fuel Type . . . . Premium
  Annual Fuel Cost . . . . Very High-$2870
  Gas Guzzler Tax . . . . No
  Greenhouse Gas Emissions (tons/yr.) High-9.8
  Barrels of Oil Used per year High-18.0

How the Competition Rates

Competitors	Rating	Pg.
BMW 7 Series	–	97
Jaguar XF	–	170
Lexus LS	–	192

Price Range	Retail	Markup
400 Hybrid	$92,725	8%
550 4MATIC	$98,375	8%
63 AMG	$140,175	8%
65 AMG	$211,775	8%

Safety Checklist

Crash Tests:
  Frontal . . . . –
  Side . . . . –
Airbags:
  Head . . . . Fr. & Rr. Roof Curtain
  Torso . . . . Fr. & Rr. Torso from Seat
  Pelvis . . . . None
  Roll Sensing . . . . Yes
  Knee Bolster . . . . None
Crash Avoidance:
  Frontal Collision Warning . . . . Optional
  Blind Spot Detection . . . . Optional
  Crash Imminent Braking . . . . Optional
  Lane Departure Warning . . . . Optional
General:
  Auto. Crash Notification . . . . Optional
  Day Running Lamps . . . . Standard
Safety Belt/Restraint:
  Dynamic Head Restraints . . . . . . Standard Front
  Adjustable Belt . . . . Standard Front
  Pretensioners . . . . Standard Front & Rear

Mercedes-Benz S-Class

Specifications

Drive . . . . RWD
Engine 4.7-liter V8
Transmission . . . . 7-sp. Automatic
Tow Rating (lbs.) . . . . –
Head/Leg Room (in.) Cramped-37.8/41.9
Interior Space (cu. ft.) Roomy-125
Cargo Space (cu. ft.) Average-16.4
Wheelbase/Length (in.) 124.6/206.5

Ratings—10 Best, 1 Worst

Combo Crash Tests	–
Safety Features	2
Rollover	7
Preventative Maintenance	1
Repair Costs	6
Warranty	9
Fuel Economy	9
Complaints	1
Insurance Costs	3
OVERALL RATING	**–**

Mini Cooper

Mini Cooper

At-a-Glance

Status/Year Series Started Unchanged/2002
Twins . . . . –
Body Styles. . . . . Hatchback, Convertible
Seating. 4
Anti-Theft Device . . . . Std. Pass. Immobil.
Parking Index Rating. . . . . Very Easy
Where Made . . . . Oxford, England
Fuel Factor
MPG Rating (city/hwy) . . . . Very Good-28/36
Driving Range (mi.) Average-410.7
Fuel Type . . . . Premium
Annual Fuel Cost. . . . . Very Low-$1688
Gas Guzzler Tax . . . . No
Greenhouse Gas Emissions (tons/yr.) . . . Low-6.0
Barrels of Oil Used per year Low-11.0

How the Competition Rates

Competitors	Rating	Pg.
Kia Soul	6	182
Nissan Cube	–	218
Scion xD	–	235

Price Range

Price Range	Retail	Markup
Base	$24,950	11%
S	$27,950	11%
John Cooper Works	$35,100	11%

Safety Checklist

Crash Tests:
Frontal . . . . –
Side . . . . –
Airbags:
Head. . . . . Fr. & Rr. Roof Curtain
Torso. . . . . Front Torso from Seat
Pelvis. . . . . None
Roll Sensing. . . . . No
Knee Bolster . . . . None
Crash Avoidance:
Frontal Collision Warning. . . . . None
Blind Spot Detection . . . . None
Crash Imminent Braking . . . . None
Lane Departure Warning . . . . None
General:
Auto. Crash Notification. . . . . None
Day Running Lamps . . . . Standard
Safety Belt/Restraint:
Dynamic Head Restraints . . . . None
Adjustable Belt. None
Pretensioners . . . . Standard Front

Mini Cooper

Specifications

Drive . . . . FWD
Engine. 1.6-liter I4
Transmission . . . . 6-sp. Automatic
Tow Rating (lbs.). . . . . –
Head/Leg Room (in.) Cramped-38.8/41.4
Interior Space (cu. ft.) . . . . Very Cramped-76
Cargo Space (cu. ft.) . . . . Very Cramped-5.7
Wheelbase/Length (in.) 97.1/145.2

Ratings—10 Best, 1 Worst

Combo Crash Tests	–
Safety Features	3
Rollover	6
Preventative Maintenance	–
Repair Costs	–
Warranty	9
Fuel Economy	7
Complaints	–
Insurance Costs	3
OVERALL RATING	–

Mini Countryman

Mini Countryman

At-a-Glance

Status/Year Series Started Unchanged/2009
Twins . . . . –
Body Styles . . . . Hatchback
Seating 5
Anti-Theft Device . . . . Std. Pass. Immobil.
Parking Index Rating . . . . Very Easy
Where Made . . . . Oxford, England

Fuel Factor
  MPG Rating (city/hwy) Good-25/30
  Driving Range (mi.) . . . . Very Short-335.1
  Fuel Type . . . . Premium
  Annual Fuel Cost . . . . Low-$1943
  Gas Guzzler Tax . . . . No
  Greenhouse Gas Emissions (tons/yr.) Average-6.9
  Barrels of Oil Used per year Average-12.7

How the Competition Rates

Competitors	Rating	Pg.
Nissan Rogue	5	225
Subaru Forester	5	237
Toyota RAV4	1	252

Price Range	Retail	Markup

Safety Checklist

Crash Tests:
  Frontal . . . . –
  Side . . . . –
Airbags:
  Head . . . . Fr. & Rr. Roof Curtain
  Torso . . . . Front Torso from Seat
  Pelvis . . . . None
  Roll Sensing . . . . No
  Knee Bolster . . . . Standard Passenger
Crash Avoidance:
  Frontal Collision Warning . . . . None
  Blind Spot Detection . . . . None
  Crash Imminent Braking . . . . None
  Lane Departure Warning . . . . None
General:
  Auto. Crash Notification . . . . None
  Day Running Lamps . . . . Standard
Safety Belt/Restraint:
  Dynamic Head Restraints . . . . None
  Adjustable Belt . . . . None
  Pretensioners . . . . Standard Front

Mini Countryman

Specifications

Drive . . . . AWD
Engine 1.6-liter I4
Transmission . . . . 6-sp. Automatic
Tow Rating (lbs.) . . . . –
Head/Leg Room (in.) Cramped-39.9/40.4
Interior Space (cu. ft.) . . . . Very Cramped-87
Cargo Space (cu. ft.) . . . . Very Cramped-12.2
Wheelbase/Length (in.) 102.2/161.8

Ratings—10 Best, 1 Worst

Combo Crash Tests	–
Safety Features	2
Rollover	8
Preventative Maintenance	8
Repair Costs	10
Warranty	9
Fuel Economy	5
Complaints	10
Insurance Costs	3
OVERALL RATING	**–**

Mitsubishi Galant

Safety Checklist

Crash Tests:
Frontal . . . . –
Side . . . . –

Airbags:
Head . . . . Fr. & Rr. Roof Curtain
Torso . . . . Front Torso from Seat
Pelvis . . . . None
Roll Sensing . . . . No
Knee Bolster . . . . None

Crash Avoidance:
Frontal Collision Warning . . . . None
Blind Spot Detection . . . . None
Crash Imminent Braking . . . . None
Lane Departure Warning . . . . None

General:
Auto. Crash Notification . . . . None
Day Running Lamps . . . . None

Safety Belt/Restraint:
Dynamic Head Restraints . . . . None
Adjustable Belt . . . . Standard Front
Pretensioners . . . . Standard Front

Mitsubishi Galant

At-a-Glance

Status/Year Series Started Unchanged/2004
Twins . . . . –
Body Styles . . . . Sedan
Seating 5
Anti-Theft Device Std. Pass. Immobil. & Alarm or Active Alarm
Parking Index Rating . . . . Hard
Where Made . . . . Normal, IL

Fuel Factor
MPG Rating (city/hwy) Average-21/30
Driving Range (mi.) Long-429.7
Fuel Type . . . . Regular
Annual Fuel Cost . . . . Average-$1996
Gas Guzzler Tax . . . . No
Greenhouse Gas Emissions (tons/yr.) Average-7.8
Barrels of Oil Used per year High-14.3

How the Competition Rates

Competitors	Rating	Pg.
Ford Fusion	5	140
Mazda 6	7	199
Nissan Maxima	4	222

Price Range	Retail	Markup
ES	$21,899	4%
SE	$24,299	4%

Mitsubishi Galant

Specifications

Drive . . . . FWD
Engine 2.4-liter I4
Transmission . . . . 4-sp. Automatic
Tow Rating (lbs.) . . . . –
Head/Leg Room (in.) Roomy-39.6/42.6
Interior Space (cu. ft.) Average-101
Cargo Space (cu. ft.) Cramped-13.3
Wheelbase/Length (in.) 108.3/191.1

Ratings—10 Best, 1 Worst

Combo Crash Tests	–
Safety Features	4
Rollover	7
Preventative Maintenance	8
Repair Costs	7
Warranty	9
Fuel Economy	8
Complaints	5
Insurance Costs	1
OVERALL RATING	**–**

Mitsubishi Lancer

Mitsubishi Lancer

At-a-Glance

Status/Year Series Started Unchanged/2008
Twins . . . . –
Body Styles . . . . Sedan
Seating. 5
Anti-Theft Device Std. Pass. Immobil. & Alarm or Active Alarm
Parking Index Rating . . . . Very Easy
Where Made. Mizushima, Japan / Okayama, Japan
Fuel Factor
  MPG Rating (city/hwy) Good-25/33
  Driving Range (mi.) Long-434.9
  Fuel Type . . . . Regular
  Annual Fuel Cost . . . . Low-$1727
  Gas Guzzler Tax . . . . No
  Greenhouse Gas Emissions (tons/yr.) Average-6.7
  Barrels of Oil Used per year Average-12.2

How the Competition Rates

Competitors	Rating	Pg.
Honda Civic	–	146
Mazda 3	6	197
Subaru Impreza	–	238

Price Range	Retail	Markup
DE	$15,695	5%
ES	$17,895	5%
GT	$20,845	5%
Ralliart	$27,995	5%

Safety Checklist

Crash Tests:
  Frontal . . . . –
  Side . . . . –
Airbags:
  Head. . . . . Fr. & Rr. Roof Curtain
  Torso. . . . . Front Pelvis/Torso from Seat
  Pelvis . . . . Front Pelvis/Torso from Seat
  Roll Sensing. . . . . No
  Knee Bolster . . . . Standard Driver
Crash Avoidance:
  Frontal Collision Warning. . . . . None
  Blind Spot Detection . . . . None
  Crash Imminent Braking . . . . None
  Lane Departure Warning . . . . None
General:
  Auto. Crash Notification. . . . . None
  Day Running Lamps . . . . Standard
Safety Belt/Restraint:
  Dynamic Head Restraints . . . . None
  Adjustable Belt . . . . Standard Front
  Pretensioners . . . . Standard Front

Mitsubishi Lancer

Specifications

Drive . . . . FWD
Engine. 2.0-liter I4
Transmission . . . . CVT
Tow Rating (lbs.). . . . . –
Head/Leg Room (in.) Average-39.6/42.3
Interior Space (cu. ft.) Cramped-93.5
Cargo Space (cu. ft.) Cramped-12.3
Wheelbase/Length (in.). 103.7/180

Ratings—10 Best, 1 Worst

Combo Crash Tests	–
Safety Features	5
Rollover	3
Preventative Maintenance	4
Repair Costs	6
Warranty	9
Fuel Economy	6
Complaints	7
Insurance Costs	3
OVERALL RATING	**–**

Mitsubishi Outlander

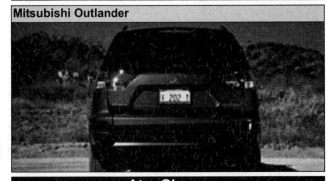
Mitsubishi Outlander

At-a-Glance

Status/Year Series Started Unchanged/2007
Twins . . . . –
Body Styles. . . . . SUV
Seating. 7
Anti-Theft Device . Std. Pass. Immobil. & Alarm or Active Alarm
Parking Index Rating . . . . Easy
Where Made . . . . Mizushima, Japan

Fuel Factor
MPG Rating (city/hwy) Average-23/28
Driving Range (mi.) Long-415.2
Fuel Type . . . . Regular
Annual Fuel Cost . . . . Low-$1937
Gas Guzzler Tax . . . . No
Greenhouse Gas Emissions (tons/yr.) Average-7.5
Barrels of Oil Used per year Average-13.7

How the Competition Rates

Competitors	Rating	Pg.
Honda CR-V	3	148
Hyundai Tucson	8	162
Toyota RAV4	1	252

Price Range	Retail	Markup
ES	$22,345	6%
SE AWC	$24,845	6%
GT 2WD	$25,895	6%
GT AWC	$27,895	6%

Safety Checklist

Crash Tests:
Frontal . . . . –
Side . . . . –
Airbags:
Head. . . . . Fr. & Rr. Roof Curtain
Torso. . . . . Front Pelvis/Torso from Seat
Pelvis . . . . Front Pelvis/Torso from Seat
Roll Sensing . . . . Yes
Knee Bolster . . . . None
Crash Avoidance:
Frontal Collision Warning. . . . . None
Blind Spot Detection . . . . None
Crash Imminent Braking . . . . None
Lane Departure Warning . . . . None
General:
Auto. Crash Notification. . . . . None
Day Running Lamps . . . . Standard
Safety Belt/Restraint:
Dynamic Head Restraints . . . . None
Adjustable Belt . . . . Standard Front
Pretensioners . . . . Standard Front

Mitsubishi Outlander

Specifications

Drive . . . . FWD
Engine. 2.4-liter I4
Transmission . . . . CVT
Tow Rating (lbs.). . . . . Very Low-1500
Head/Leg Room (in.). Average-40.3/41.6
Interior Space (cu. ft.) Average-100.4
Cargo Space (cu. ft.) Cramped-14.9
Wheelbase/Length (in.) 105.1/183.7

Ratings—10 Best, 1 Worst

Combo Crash Tests	–
Safety Features	2
Rollover	10
Preventative Maintenance	8
Repair Costs	2
Warranty	2
Fuel Economy	4
Complaints	–
Insurance Costs	1
OVERALL RATING	**–**

Nissan 370Z

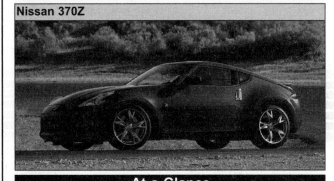

At-a-Glance

Status/Year Series Started Unchanged/2010
Twins . . . . –
Body Styles. . . . . Hatchback, Convertible
Seating. 2
Anti-Theft Device . . . . Std. Pass. Immobil. & Alarm
Parking Index Rating . . . . Very Easy
Where Made . . . . Tochigi, Japan
Fuel Factor
  MPG Rating (city/hwy) Poor-19/26
  Driving Range (mi.) Average-410.8
  Fuel Type . . . . Premium
  Annual Fuel Cost. . . . . High-$2428
  Gas Guzzler Tax . . . . No
  Greenhouse Gas Emissions (tons/yr.). . . High-8.5
  Barrels of Oil Used per year High-15.6

How the Competition Rates

Competitors	Rating	Pg.
Chevrolet Camaro	5	108
Ford Mustang	2	141
Mazda MX-5 Miata	–	202

Price Range	Retail	Markup
Base	$31,450	8%
Touring Manual	$36,150	8%
Touring Automatic	$37,450	8%
NISMO	$40,830	8%

Nissan 370Z

Safety Checklist

Crash Tests:
  Frontal . . . . –
  Side . . . . –
Airbags:
  Head . . . . Front Roof Curtain
  Torso . . . . Front Pelvis/Torso from Seat
  Pelvis . . . . Front Pelvis/Torso from Seat
  Roll Sensing . . . . No
  Knee Bolster . . . . None
Crash Avoidance:
  Frontal Collision Warning. . . . . None
  Blind Spot Detection . . . . None
  Crash Imminent Braking . . . . None
  Lane Departure Warning . . . . None
General:
  Auto. Crash Notification . . . . None
  Day Running Lamps . . . . None
Safety Belt/Restraint:
  Dynamic Head Restraints. . . . . . Standard Front
  Adjustable Belt. . . . . None
  Pretensioners . . . . Standard Front

Nissan 370Z

Specifications

Drive . . . . RWD
Engine 3.7-liter V6
Transmission . . . . 7-sp. Automatic
Tow Rating (lbs.) . . . . –
Head/Leg Room (in.). Average-38.2/42.9
Interior Space (cu. ft.) . . . . Very Cramped-51.6
Cargo Space (cu. ft.) . . . . Very Cramped-6.9
Wheelbase/Length (in.) 100.4/167.2

Ratings—10 Best, 1 Worst

Combo Crash Tests	5
Safety Features	4
Rollover	8
Preventative Maintenance	8
Repair Costs	7
Warranty	2
Fuel Economy	7
Complaints	9
Insurance Costs	1
OVERALL RATING	**6**

Nissan Altima

Nissan Altima

At-a-Glance

Status/Year Series Started Unchanged/2007
Twins . . . . –
Body Styles . . . . Sedan
Seating. 5
Anti-Theft Device . . . . Std. Pass. Immobil. & Alarm
Parking Index Rating . . . . Easy
Where Made. . . . . Canton, MS / Smyrna, TN
Fuel Factor
  MPG Rating (city/hwy) Good-23/32
  Driving Range (mi.). . . . . Very Long-526.7
  Fuel Type . . . . Regular
  Annual Fuel Cost . . . . Low-$1840
  Gas Guzzler Tax . . . . No
  Greenhouse Gas Emissions (tons/yr.) Average-6.9
  Barrels of Oil Used per year Average-12.7

How the Competition Rates

Competitors	Rating	Pg.
Honda Accord	8	144
Kia Optima	9	178
Toyota Camry	10	246

Price Range	Retail	Markup
2.5	$20,410	4%
2.5 S	$22,570	7%
3.5 SR	$25,430	8%

Safety Checklist

Crash Tests:
  Frontal . . . . Average
  Side . . . . Average
Airbags:
  Head . . . . Fr. & Rr. Roof Curtain
  Torso . . . . Front Torso from Seat
  Pelvis . . . . Front Pelvis/Torso from Seat
  Roll Sensing. . . . . No
  Knee Bolster . . . . None
Crash Avoidance:
  Frontal Collision Warning. . . . . None
  Blind Spot Detection . . . . None
  Crash Imminent Braking . . . . None
  Lane Departure Warning . . . . None
General:
  Auto. Crash Notification . . . . None
  Day Running Lamps . . . . None
Safety Belt/Restraint:
  Dynamic Head Restraints. . . . . . Standard Front
  Adjustable Belt . . . . Standard Front
  Pretensioners . . . . Standard Front

Nissan Altima

Specifications

Drive . . . . FWD
Engine. 2.5-liter I4
Transmission . . . . CVT
Tow Rating (lbs.). . . . . Very Low-1000
Head/Leg Room (in.) . . . . . . Very Roomy-40.6/44.1
Interior Space (cu. ft.) Average-100.7
Cargo Space (cu. ft.) Cramped-15.3
Wheelbase/Length (in.) 109.3/190.7

Ratings—10 Best, 1 Worst	
Combo Crash Tests	–
Safety Features	3
Rollover	8
Preventative Maintenance	8
Repair Costs	9
Warranty	2
Fuel Economy	7
Complaints	10
Insurance Costs	1
OVERALL RATING	**–**

Nissan Altima Coupe

Nissan Altima Coupe

At-a-Glance

Status/Year Series Started Unchanged/2008
Twins . . . . –
Body Styles . . . . Coupe
Seating. 5
Anti-Theft Device . . . . Std. Pass. Immobil. & Alarm
Parking Index Rating . . . . Easy
Where Made. . . . . Canton, MS / Smyrna, TN
Fuel Factor
  MPG Rating (city/hwy) Good-23/32
  Driving Range (mi.). . . . . Very Long-526.7
  Fuel Type . . . . Regular
  Annual Fuel Cost . . . . Low-$1840
  Gas Guzzler Tax . . . . No
  Greenhouse Gas Emissions (tons/yr.)Average-7.2
  Barrels of Oil Used per year Average-13.2

How the Competition Rates

Competitors	Rating	Pg.
Mitsubishi Lancer	–	212
Scion tC	7	233
Subaru Impreza	–	238

Price Range

Price Range	Retail	Markup
2.5 S Manual	$23,600	7%
2.5 S Automatic	$24,100	7%
3.5 SR Automatic	$28,430	8%
3.5 SR Manual	$30,760	8%

Safety Checklist

Crash Tests:
  Frontal . . . . –
  Side . . . . –
Airbags:
  Head. . . . . Fr. & Rr. Roof Curtain
  Torso . . . . Front Torso from Seat
  Pelvis . . . . Front Pelvis/Torso from Seat
  Roll Sensing. . . . . No
  Knee Bolster . . . . None
Crash Avoidance:
  Frontal Collision Warning. . . . . None
  Blind Spot Detection . . . . None
  Crash Imminent Braking . . . . None
  Lane Departure Warning . . . . None
General:
  Auto. Crash Notification. . . . . None
  Day Running Lamps . . . . None
Safety Belt/Restraint:
  Dynamic Head Restraints. . . . . . Standard Front
  Adjustable Belt. . . . . None
  Pretensioners . . . . Standard Front

Nissan Altima Coupe

Specifications

Drive . . . . FWD
Engine. 2.5-liter I4
Transmission . . . . CVT
Tow Rating (lbs.). . . . . Very Low-1000
Head/Leg Room (in.). Roomy-39.7/42.5
Interior Space (cu. ft.) . . . . . . Very Cramped-89.3
Cargo Space (cu. ft.) . . . . Very Cramped-8.2
Wheelbase/Length (in.) 105.3/180.9

Ratings—10 Best, 1 Worst

Combo Crash Tests	–
Safety Features	7
Rollover	2
Preventative Maintenance	3
Repair Costs	5
Warranty	2
Fuel Economy	1
Complaints	3
Insurance Costs	10
OVERALL RATING	**–**

Nissan Armada

Nissan Armada

At-a-Glance

Status/Year Series Started Unchanged/2004
Twins . . . . –
Body Styles. . . . . SUV
Seating 7/8
Anti-Theft Device . . . . Std. Pass. Immobil. & Alarm
Parking Index Rating . . . . Very Hard
Where Made. Canton, MS

Fuel Factor
MPG Rating (city/hwy). . . . . Very Poor-13/19
Driving Range (mi.) Long-424.3
Fuel Type . . . . Regular
Annual Fuel Cost . . . . Very High-$3197
Gas Guzzler Tax . . . . No
Greenhouse Gas Emissions (tons/yr.) Vry High-12.4
Barrels of Oil Used per year . . . . . Very High-22.8

How the Competition Rates

Competitors	Rating	Pg.
Chevrolet Tahoe	6	118
Ford Expedition	–	134
Toyota Sequoia	–	253

Price Range	Retail	Markup
4x2 SV	$38,790	10%
4x2 SL	$44,240	10%
4x4 SL	$47,140	10%
4x4 Platinum	$54,250	10%

Safety Checklist

Crash Tests:
Frontal . . . . –
Side . . . . –

Airbags:
Head. . . . . Fr. & Rr. Roof Curtain
Torso . . . . Front Torso from Seat
Pelvis . . . . None
Roll Sensing . . . . Yes
Knee Bolster . . . . None

Crash Avoidance:
Frontal Collision Warning. . . . . None
Blind Spot Detection . . . . None
Crash Imminent Braking . . . . None
Lane Departure Warning . . . . None

General:
Auto. Crash Notification . . . . None
Day Running Lamps . . . . None

Safety Belt/Restraint:
Dynamic Head Restraints. . . . . . Standard Front
Adjustable Belt . . . . . . Standard Front and Rear
Pretensioners . . . . Standard Front

Nissan Armada

Specifications

Drive . . . . RWD
Engine 5.6-liter V8
Transmission . . . . 5-sp. Auto. w/Overdrive
Tow Rating (lbs.) . . . . Very High-8200
Head/Leg Room (in.) Roomy-41/41.8
Interior Space (cu. ft.) Roomy-127.3
Cargo Space (cu. ft.) Average-20
Wheelbase/Length (in.) 123.2/207.7

Ratings—10 Best, 1 Worst

Combo Crash Tests	–
Safety Features	4
Rollover	3
Preventative Maintenance	8
Repair Costs	–
Warranty	2
Fuel Economy	8
Complaints	10
Insurance Costs	3
OVERALL RATING	**–**

Nissan Cube

Nissan Cube

At-a-Glance

Status/Year Series Started Unchanged/2009
Twins . . . . –
Body Styles 4-Door
Seating 5
Anti-Theft Device . . . . Std. Pass. Immobil. & Alarm
Parking Index Rating . . . . Very Easy
Where Made . . . . Oppama, Japan
Fuel Factor
  MPG Rating (city/hwy) Good-27/31
  Driving Range (mi.) Short-378.4
  Fuel Type . . . . Regular
  Annual Fuel Cost . . . . Low-$1690
  Gas Guzzler Tax . . . . No
  Greenhouse Gas Emissions (tons/yr.) Average-6.7
  Barrels of Oil Used per year Average-12.2

How the Competition Rates

Competitors	Rating	Pg.
Kia Soul	6	182
Mini Countryman	–	210
Scion xD	–	235

Price Range	Retail	Markup

Safety Checklist

Crash Tests:
  Frontal . . . . –
  Side . . . . –
Airbags:
  Head . . . . Fr. & Rr. Roof Curtain
  Torso . . . . Front Pelvis/Torso from Seat
  Pelvis . . . . Front Pelvis/Torso from Seat
  Roll Sensing . . . . No
  Knee Bolster . . . . None
Crash Avoidance:
  Frontal Collision Warning . . . . None
  Blind Spot Detection . . . . None
  Crash Imminent Braking . . . . None
  Lane Departure Warning . . . . None
General:
  Auto. Crash Notification . . . . None
  Day Running Lamps . . . . None
Safety Belt/Restraint:
  Dynamic Head Restraints . . . . . . Standard Front
  Adjustable Belt . . . . Standard Front
  Pretensioners . . . . Standard Front

Nissan Cube

Specifications

Drive . . . . FWD
Engine 1.8-liter I4
Transmission . . . . CVT
Tow Rating (lbs.) . . . . –
Head/Leg Room (in.) . . . . . . Very Roomy-42.6/42.4
Interior Space (cu. ft.) Cramped-97.7
Cargo Space (cu. ft.) . . . . Very Cramped-11.4
Wheelbase/Length (in.) 99.6/156.7

Nissan Frontier

Ratings—10 Best, 1 Worst

Combo Crash Tests	–
Safety Features	6
Rollover	2
Preventative Maintenance	3
Repair Costs	8
Warranty	2
Fuel Economy	1
Complaints	6
Insurance Costs	5
OVERALL RATING	**–**

Nissan Frontier

Nissan Frontier

At-a-Glance

```
Status/Year Series Started ...... Unchanged/2005
Twins . . . . . . . . . . . . . . . . . . . . . . . . . . . . . . . –
Body Styles. . . . . . . . . . . . . . . . . . Crew, King Cab
Seating. . . . . . . . . . . . . . . . . . . . . . . . . . . . . . . 5
Anti-Theft Device . . . . . . . . . . . Opt. Pass. Immobil.
Parking Index Rating. . . . . . . . . . . . . . . Very Hard
Where Made. . . . . . . . . . . . . . . . . . . . Smyrna, TN
```

Fuel Factor
```
MPG Rating (city/hwy). . . . . . . . Very Poor-14/19
Driving Range (mi.) . . . . . . . . . Very Short-335.1
Fuel Type . . . . . . . . . . . . . . . . . . . . . . . . Regular
Annual Fuel Cost . . . . . . . . . . . Very High-$3051
Gas Guzzler Tax. . . . . . . . . . . . . . . . . . . . . . . No
Greenhouse Gas Emissions (tons/yr.)Vry High-11.6
Barrels of Oil Used per year . . . . . Very High-21.4
```

How the Competition Rates

Competitors	Rating	Pg.
Chevrolet Colorado	–	109
Honda Ridgeline	–	154
Toyota Tacoma	1	255

Price Range	Retail	Markup
S CC 4x2	$22,510	6%
SL CC 4x2	$29,680	6%
Pro-4X CC 4x4	$30,360	8%
SL CC 4x4	$32,380	8%

Safety Checklist

Crash Tests:
```
Frontal . . . . . . . . . . . . . . . . . . . . . . . . . . . . . –
Side . . . . . . . . . . . . . . . . . . . . . . . . . . . . . . . –
```
Airbags:
```
Head. . . . . . . . . . . . . . . Fr. & Rr. Roof Curtain
Torso . . . . . . . Opt. Front Pelvis/Torso from Seat
Pelvis . . . . . . . . . Front Pelvis/Torso from Seat
Roll Sensing . . . . . . . . . . . . . . . . . . . . . . . . Yes
Knee Bolster . . . . . . . . . . . . . . . . . . . . . . None
```
Crash Avoidance:
```
Frontal Collision Warning. . . . . . . . . . . . . None
Blind Spot Detection . . . . . . . . . . . . . . . None
Crash Imminent Braking . . . . . . . . . . . . . None
Lane Departure Warning . . . . . . . . . . . . . None
```
General:
```
Auto. Crash Notification . . . . . . . . . . . . . None
Day Running Lamps . . . . . . . . . . . . . . . None
```
Safety Belt/Restraint:
```
Dynamic Head Restraints. . . . . . Standard Front
Adjustable Belt . . . . . . . . . . . . . Standard Front
Pretensioners . . . . . . . . . . . . . . Standard Front
```

Specifications

```
Drive . . . . . . . . . . . . . . . . . . . . . . . . . . . . . . 4WD
Engine. . . . . . . . . . . . . . . . . . . . . . . . 4.0-liter V6
Transmission . . . . . . . . . . . . . . . 5-sp. Automatic
Tow Rating (lbs.) . . . . . . . . . . . . . . Average-6100
Head/Leg Room (in.) . . . . . . . . Roomy-40/42.4
Interior Space (cu. ft.) . . . . . . . . . . Average-101.1
Cargo Space (cu. ft.) . . . . . . . . . . Roomy-27.1
Wheelbase/Length (in.) . . . . . . 125.9/205.5
```

Ratings—10 Best, 1 Worst

Combo Crash Tests	–
Safety Features	4
Rollover	5
Preventative Maintenance	–
Repair Costs	–
Warranty	2
Fuel Economy	8
Complaints	9
Insurance Costs	5
OVERALL RATING	–

Nissan Juke

Nissan Juke

At-a-Glance

Status/Year Series Started Unchanged/2011
Twins . . . . –
Body Styles . . . . Hatchback
Seating 5
Anti-Theft Device . . . . Std. Pass. Immobil. & Alarm
Parking Index Rating . . . . Easy
Where Made . . . . Oppama, Japan
Fuel Factor
MPG Rating (city/hwy) Good-27/32
Driving Range (mi.) Short-383.4
Fuel Type . . . . Premium
Annual Fuel Cost . . . . Low-$1808
Gas Guzzler Tax . . . . No
Greenhouse Gas Emissions (tons/yr.) . . . Low-6.5
Barrels of Oil Used per year Average-11.8

How the Competition Rates

Competitors	Rating	Pg.
Kia Soul	6	182
Nissan Versa	1	228
Scion xB	–	234

Price Range	Retail	Markup
S FWD	$19,770	5%
SV FWD	$21,580	5%
SV AWD	$23,230	6%
SL AWD	$25,550	6%

Safety Checklist

Crash Tests:
Frontal . . . . –
Side . . . . –
Airbags:
Head . . . . Fr. & Rr. Roof Curtain
Torso . . . . Front Pelvis/Torso from Seat
Pelvis . . . . Front Pelvis/Torso from Seat
Roll Sensing . . . . No
Knee Bolster . . . . None
Crash Avoidance:
Frontal Collision Warning . . . . None
Blind Spot Detection . . . . None
Crash Imminent Braking . . . . None
Lane Departure Warning . . . . None
General:
Auto. Crash Notification . . . . None
Day Running Lamps . . . . None
Safety Belt/Restraint:
Dynamic Head Restraints . . . . . . Standard Front
Adjustable Belt . . . . Standard Front
Pretensioners . . . . Standard Front

Nissan Juke

Specifications

Drive . . . . FWD
Engine 1.6-liter I4
Transmission . . . . CVT
Tow Rating (lbs.) . . . . –
Head/Leg Room (in.) Average-39.6/42.1
Interior Space (cu. ft.) . . . . . Very Cramped-86.7
Cargo Space (cu. ft.) . . . . . . Very Cramped-10.5
Wheelbase/Length (in.) 99.6/162.4

Ratings—10 Best, 1 Worst

Combo Crash Tests	8
Safety Features	4
Rollover	6
Preventative Maintenance	–
Repair Costs	–
Warranty	2
Fuel Economy	10
Complaints	1
Insurance Costs	5
OVERALL RATING	**6**

Nissan Leaf

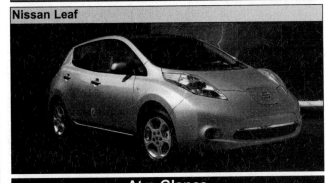

At-a-Glance

Status/Year Series Started Unchanged/2011
Twins . . . . –
Body Styles . . . . Hatchback
Seating 5
Anti-Theft Device . . . . Std. Pass. Immobil. & Alarm
Parking Index Rating . . . . Very Easy
Where Made . . . . Oppama, Japan
Fuel Factor
  MPG Rating (city/hwy) . . . . Very Good-106/92
  Driving Range (mi.) . . . . 73-100 miles/charge
  Fuel Type . . . . Electricity
  Annual Fuel Cost . . . . Very Low-$431
  Gas Guzzler Tax . . . . No
  Greenhouse Gas Emissions (tons/yr.) Very Low-0.0
  Barrels of Oil Used per year . . . . . . Very Low-0.4

How the Competition Rates

Competitors	Rating	Pg.
Chevrolet Volt	9	120
Honda Insight	–	151
Toyota Prius	7	251

Price Range	Retail	Markup
SV	$35,200	4.4%
SL	$37,250	4.4%

Nissan Leaf

Safety Checklist

Crash Tests:
  Frontal . . . . Good
  Side . . . . Very Good
Airbags:
  Head . . . . Fr. & Rr. Roof Curtain
  Torso . . . . Front Pelvis/Torso from Seat
  Pelvis . . . . Front Pelvis/Torso from Seat
  Roll Sensing . . . . No
  Knee Bolster . . . . None
Crash Avoidance:
  Frontal Collision Warning . . . . None
  Blind Spot Detection . . . . None
  Crash Imminent Braking . . . . None
  Lane Departure Warning . . . . None
General:
  Auto. Crash Notification . . . . None
  Day Running Lamps . . . . None
Safety Belt/Restraint:
  Dynamic Head Restraints . . . . . . Standard Front
  Adjustable Belt . . . . Standard Front
  Pretensioners . . . . Standard Front

Nissan Leaf

Specifications

Drive . . . . FWD
Engine . . . . 80-liter Electric
Transmission . . . . Single Speed Reducer
Tow Rating (lbs.) . . . . –
Head/Leg Room (in.) . . . . . . Very Roomy-41.2/42.1
Interior Space (cu. ft.) . . . . Very Cramped-90
Cargo Space (cu. ft.) Cramped-14.5
Wheelbase/Length (in.) 106.3/175

Ratings—10 Best, 1 Worst

Combo Crash Tests	3
Safety Features	4
Rollover	8
Preventative Maintenance	6
Repair Costs	7
Warranty	2
Fuel Economy	4
Complaints	8
Insurance Costs	5
OVERALL RATING	**4**

Nissan Maxima

Nissan Maxima

At-a-Glance

Status/Year Series Started Unchanged/2009
Twins . . . . –
Body Styles . . . . Sedan
Seating. 5
Anti-Theft Device . . . . Std. Pass. Immobil. & Alarm
Parking Index Rating . . . . Average
Where Made. Smyrna, TN

Fuel Factor
MPG Rating (city/hwy). Poor-19/26
Driving Range (mi.) Long-432.4
Fuel Type . . . . Premium
Annual Fuel Cost. . . . . High-$2428
Gas Guzzler Tax . . . . No
Greenhouse Gas Emissions (tons/yr.). . . High-8.5
Barrels of Oil Used per year High-15.6

Safety Checklist

Crash Tests:
Frontal . . . . Very Poor
Side. . . . . Average
Airbags:
Head. . . . . Fr. & Rr. Roof Curtain
Torso . . . . Front Torso from Seat
Pelvis . . . . Front Pelvis/Torso from Seat
Roll Sensing. . . . . No
Knee Bolster . . . . None
Crash Avoidance:
Frontal Collision Warning. . . . . None
Blind Spot Detection . . . . None
Crash Imminent Braking . . . . None
Lane Departure Warning . . . . None
General:
Auto. Crash Notification. . . . . None
Day Running Lamps . . . . None
Safety Belt/Restraint:
Dynamic Head Restraints. . . . . . Standard Front
Adjustable Belt . . . . Standard Front
Pretensioners . . . . Standard Front

Nissan Maxima

How the Competition Rates

Competitors	Rating	Pg.
Chevrolet Impala	4	113
Honda Accord	8	144
Toyota Camry	10	246

Price Range

	Retail	Markup
S	$31,750	9%
SV	$34,450	9%

Specifications

Drive . . . . FWD
Engine 3.5-liter V6
Transmission . . . . CVT
Tow Rating (lbs.). . . . . Very Low-1000
Head/Leg Room (in.). Roomy-38.5/43.8
Interior Space (cu. ft.) Cramped-95.8
Cargo Space (cu. ft.). Cramped-14
Wheelbase/Length (in.) 109.3/190.6

Ratings—10 Best, 1 Worst

Combo Crash Tests	2
Safety Features	7
Rollover	3
Preventative Maintenance	7
Repair Costs	5
Warranty	2
Fuel Economy	3
Complaints	7
Insurance Costs	10
OVERALL RATING	**3**

Nissan Murano

At-a-Glance

Status/Year Series Started Unchanged/2009
Twins . . . . –
Body Styles. . . . . SUV
Seating. 5
Anti-Theft Device . . . . Std. Pass. Immobil. & Alarm
Parking Index Rating . . . . Hard
Where Made . . . . Kyushu, Japan
Fuel Factor
MPG Rating (city/hwy). Poor-18/23
Driving Range (mi.) Long-433.0
Fuel Type . . . . Regular
Annual Fuel Cost. . . . . High-$2428
Gas Guzzler Tax . . . . No
Greenhouse Gas Emissions (tons/yr.) . . . High-9.3
Barrels of Oil Used per year High-17.1

How the Competition Rates

Competitors	Rating	Pg.
Acura MDX	9	81
Honda Pilot	4	153
Toyota Highlander	4	249

Price Range

Price Range	Retail	Markup
S FWD	$29,290	9%
SV AWD	$34,460	9%
SL FWD	$36,400	9%
LE AWD	$39,900	9%

Nissan Murano

Safety Checklist

Crash Tests:
Frontal. . . . . Poor
Side. . . . . Poor
Airbags:
Head. . . . . Fr. & Rr. Roof Curtain
Torso. . . . . Front Pelvis/Torso from Seat
Pelvis . . . . Front Pelvis/Torso from Seat
Roll Sensing . . . . Yes
Knee Bolster . . . . None
Crash Avoidance:
Frontal Collision Warning. . . . . None
Blind Spot Detection . . . . None
Crash Imminent Braking . . . . None
Lane Departure Warning . . . . None
General:
Auto. Crash Notification. . . . . None
Day Running Lamps . . . . None
Safety Belt/Restraint:
Dynamic Head Restraints. . . . . . Standard Front
Adjustable Belt . . . . . . Standard Front and Rear
Pretensioners . . . . Standard Front

Nissan Murano

Specifications

Drive . . . . AWD
Engine 3.5-liter V6
Transmission . . . . CVT
Tow Rating (lbs.) Low-3500
Head/Leg Room (in.) . . . . . . Very Roomy-40.1/43.6
Interior Space (cu. ft.) . . . . Very Roomy-140.4
Cargo Space (cu. ft.) . . . . Very Roomy-31.8
Wheelbase/Length (in.) 111.2/189.9

Ratings—10 Best, 1 Worst

Combo Crash Tests	–
Safety Features	7
Rollover	1
Preventative Maintenance	3
Repair Costs	7
Warranty	2
Fuel Economy	1
Complaints	4
Insurance Costs	10
OVERALL RATING	–

Nissan Pathfinder

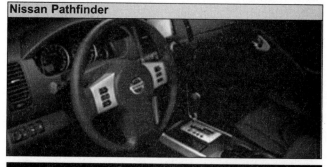

Nissan Pathfinder

At-a-Glance

Status/Year Series Started Unchanged/2005
Twins . . . . –
Body Styles. . . . . SUV
Seating. 7
Anti-Theft Device . . . . Std. Pass. Immobil. & Alarm
Parking Index Rating . . . . Hard
Where Made. . . . . Smyrna, TN

Fuel Factor
MPG Rating (city/hwy). . . . . Very Poor-14/20
Driving Range (mi.) . . . . Very Short-341.5
Fuel Type . . . . Premium
Annual Fuel Cost . . . . Very High-$3244
Gas Guzzler Tax . . . . No
Greenhouse Gas Emissions (tons/yr.)Vry High-11.6
Barrels of Oil Used per year . . . . . Very High-21.4

How the Competition Rates

Competitors	Rating	Pg.
Chevrolet Equinox	3	112
Toyota Highlander	4	249
Volvo XC90	–	270

Price Range	Retail	Markup
S 4x2	$28,570	7%
SV 4x4	$33,920	8%
Silver Edition 4x2	$35,910	8%
LE 4x4	$43,250	8%

Safety Checklist

Crash Tests:
Frontal . . . . –
Side . . . . –
Airbags:
Head. . . . . Fr. & Rr. Roof Curtain
Torso. . . . . Front Pelvis/Torso from Seat
Pelvis . . . . Front Pelvis/Torso from Seat
Roll Sensing . . . . Yes
Knee Bolster . . . . None
Crash Avoidance:
Frontal Collision Warning. . . . . None
Blind Spot Detection . . . . None
Crash Imminent Braking . . . . None
Lane Departure Warning . . . . None
General:
Auto. Crash Notification. . . . . None
Day Running Lamps . . . . None
Safety Belt/Restraint:
Dynamic Head Restraints. . . . . . Standard Front
Adjustable Belt . . . . . . Standard Front and Rear
Pretensioners . . . . Standard Front

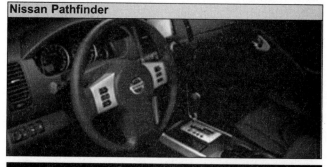

Nissan Pathfinder

Specifications

Drive 4WD
Engine. 4.0-liter V6
Transmission . . . . 5-sp. Automatic
Tow Rating (lbs.) Average-6000
Head/Leg Room (in.) Roomy-40/42.4
Interior Space (cu. ft.) Average-100.6
Cargo Space (cu. ft.). . . . . Very Roomy-48.9
Wheelbase/Length (in.) 112.2/192.3

Ratings—10 Best, 1 Worst

Combo Crash Tests	5
Safety Features	7
Rollover	3
Preventative Maintenance	7
Repair Costs	6
Warranty	2
Fuel Economy	5
Complaints	9
Insurance Costs	5
OVERALL RATING	**5**

Nissan Rogue

Nissan Rogue

At-a-Glance

Status/Year Series Started	Unchanged/2008
Twins	–
Body Styles	SUV
Seating	5
Anti-Theft Device	Std. Pass. Immobil. & Alarm
Parking Index Rating	Average
Where Made	Kyushu, Japan

Fuel Factor

MPG Rating (city/hwy)	Average-22/26
Driving Range (mi.)	Short-375.8
Fuel Type	Regular
Annual Fuel Cost	Average-$2050
Gas Guzzler Tax	No
Greenhouse Gas Emissions (tons/yr.)	Average-7.8
Barrels of Oil Used per year	High-14.3

How the Competition Rates

Competitors	Rating	Pg.
Kia Sorento	5	181
Toyota Venza	1	257
Volvo XC60	10	269

Price Range	Retail	Markup
S FWD	$21,580	5%
SV FWD	$24,020	5%
SV AWD	$25,270	5%
SV w/ SL Package	$29,170	5%

Safety Checklist

Crash Tests:

Frontal	Poor
Side	Good

Airbags:

Head	Fr. & Rr. Roof Curtain
Torso	Front Pelvis/Torso from Seat
Pelvis	Front Pelvis/Torso from Seat
Roll Sensing	Yes
Knee Bolster	None

Crash Avoidance:

Frontal Collision Warning	None
Blind Spot Detection	None
Crash Imminent Braking	None
Lane Departure Warning	None

General:

Auto. Crash Notification	None
Day Running Lamps	None

Safety Belt/Restraint:

Dynamic Head Restraints	Standard Front
Adjustable Belt	Standard Front and Rear
Pretensioners	Standard Front

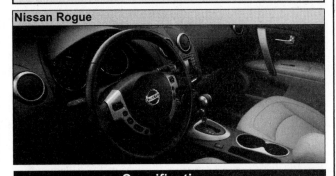

Nissan Rogue

Specifications

Drive	AWD
Engine	2.5-liter I4
Transmission	CVT
Tow Rating (lbs.)	Very Low-1500
Head/Leg Room (in.)	Roomy-40.4/42.5
Interior Space (cu. ft.)	Cramped-97.5
Cargo Space (cu. ft.)	Roomy-28.9
Wheelbase/Length (in.)	105.9/183.3

Ratings—10 Best, 1 Worst

Combo Crash Tests	2
Safety Features	4
Rollover	7
Preventative Maintenance	7
Repair Costs	9
Warranty	2
Fuel Economy	8
Complaints	9
Insurance Costs	1
OVERALL RATING	**4**

Nissan Sentra

Nissan Sentra

At-a-Glance

Status/Year Series Started Unchanged/2007
Twins . . . . –
Body Styles . . . . Sedan
Seating. 5
Anti-Theft Device . . . . Std. Pass. Immobil.
Parking Index Rating . . . . Easy
Where Made . . . . Aguascalientes, Mexico
Fuel Factor
  MPG Rating (city/hwy) Good-27/34
  Driving Range (mi.) Long-431.5
  Fuel Type . . . . Regular
  Annual Fuel Cost. . . . . Very Low-$1628
  Gas Guzzler Tax . . . . No
  Greenhouse Gas Emissions (tons/yr.) . . . Low-6.2
  Barrels of Oil Used per year Low-11.4

How the Competition Rates

Competitors	Rating	Pg.
Chevrolet Cruze	9	111
Honda Civic	–	146
Toyota Corolla	4	247

Price Range	Retail	Markup
Base Manual	$16,060	4%
S	$17,990	7%
SL	$19,390	7%
SE-R Spec V Manual Trans.	$20,620	7%

Safety Checklist

Crash Tests:
  Frontal. . . . . Poor
  Side . . . . Very Poor
Airbags:
  Head. . . . . Fr. & Rr. Roof Curtain
  Torso . . . . Front Torso from Seat
  Pelvis . . . . Front Pelvis/Torso from Seat
  Roll Sensing. . . . . No
  Knee Bolster . . . . None
Crash Avoidance:
  Frontal Collision Warning. . . . . None
  Blind Spot Detection . . . . None
  Crash Imminent Braking . . . . None
  Lane Departure Warning . . . . None
General:
  Auto. Crash Notification. . . . . None
  Day Running Lamps . . . . None
Safety Belt/Restraint:
  Dynamic Head Restraints. . . . . . . Standard Front
  Adjustable Belt . . . . Standard Front
  Pretensioners . . . . Standard Front

Nissan Sentra

Specifications

Drive . . . . FWD
Engine. 2.0-liter I4
Transmission . . . . CVT
Tow Rating (lbs.) . . . . Very Low-1000
Head/Leg Room (in.) Roomy-40.6/42.4
Interior Space (cu. ft.) Cramped-97.4
Cargo Space (cu. ft.) Cramped-13.1
Wheelbase/Length (in.) 105.7/179.8

Ratings—10 Best, 1 Worst

Combo Crash Tests	–
Safety Features	6
Rollover	3
Preventative Maintenance	3
Repair Costs	5
Warranty	2
Fuel Economy	1
Complaints	2
Insurance Costs	8
OVERALL RATING	**–**

Nissan Titan

Nissan Titan

At-a-Glance

Status/Year Series Started	Unchanged/2004
Twins	–
Body Styles	Crew, King Cab
Seating	5
Anti-Theft Device	Std. Pass. Immobil. & Alarm
Parking Index Rating	Very Hard
Where Made	Canton, MS

Fuel Factor

MPG Rating (city/hwy)	Very Poor-13/18
Driving Range (mi.)	Long-416.0
Fuel Type	Regular
Annual Fuel Cost	Very High-$3261
Gas Guzzler Tax	No
Greenhouse Gas Emissions (tons/yr.)	Vry High-12.4
Barrels of Oil Used per year	Very High-22.8

How the Competition Rates

Competitors	Rating	Pg.
Chevrolet Silverado Ext.	5	115
Ford F-150 Super Cab	4	136
Honda Ridgeline	–	154

Price Range	Retail	Markup
S King 2WD	$27,710	10%
SV King 4WD	$29,710	10%
SL Crew 2WD	$37,810	10%
SL Crew 4WD	$40,510	10%

Safety Checklist

Crash Tests:
Frontal . . . . –
Side . . . . –

Airbags:
Head . . . . Fr. & Rr. Roof Curtain
Torso . . . . Front Pelvis/Torso from Seat
Pelvis . . . . Front Pelvis/Torso from Seat
Roll Sensing . . . . Yes
Knee Bolster . . . . None

Crash Avoidance:
Frontal Collision Warning . . . . None
Blind Spot Detection . . . . None
Crash Imminent Braking . . . . None
Lane Departure Warning . . . . None

General:
Auto. Crash Notification . . . . None
Day Running Lamps . . . . None

Safety Belt/Restraint:
Dynamic Head Restraints . . . . . . Standard Front
Adjustable Belt . . . . Standard Front
Pretensioners . . . . Standard Front

Nissan Titan

Specifications

Drive	RWD
Engine	5.6-liter V8
Transmission	5-sp. Automatic
Tow Rating (lbs.)	High-7400
Head/Leg Room (in.)	Roomy-41/41.8
Interior Space (cu. ft.)	Roomy-112.8
Cargo Space (cu. ft.)	–
Wheelbase/Length (in.)	139.8/224.6

227

Ratings—10 Best, 1 Worst

Combo Crash Tests	1
Safety Features	4
Rollover	5
Preventative Maintenance	2
Repair Costs	9
Warranty	2
Fuel Economy	9
Complaints	8
Insurance Costs	1
OVERALL RATING	**1**

Nissan Versa

At-a-Glance

Status/Year Series Started Appearance Change/2006
Twins . . . . –
Body Styles . . . . Sedan, Hatchback
Seating. 5
Anti-Theft Device. None
Parking Index Rating. . . . . Very Easy
Where Made . . . . Aguascalientes, Mexico
Fuel Factor
  MPG Rating (city/hwy) . . . . Very Good-28/34
  Driving Range (mi.) Average-401.5
  Fuel Type . . . . Regular
  Annual Fuel Cost. . . . . Very Low-$1593
  Gas Guzzler Tax . . . . No
  Greenhouse Gas Emissions (tons/yr.) . . . Low-6.2
  Barrels of Oil Used per year Low-11.4

How the Competition Rates

Competitors	Rating	Pg.
Honda Fit	–	150
Hyundai Accent	9	155
Toyota Yaris	–	258

Price Range	Retail	Markup
Base Manual	$10,990	4%
SV Automatic	$14,560	4%
S Hatchback Automatic	$15,380	4%
SL	$15,560	4%

Nissan Versa

Safety Checklist

Crash Tests:
  Frontal . . . . Very Poor
  Side . . . . Very Poor
Airbags:
  Head. . . . . Fr. & Rr. Roof Curtain
  Torso . . . . Front Torso from Seat
  Pelvis. . . . . None
  Roll Sensing. . . . . No
  Knee Bolster . . . . None
Crash Avoidance:
  Frontal Collision Warning. . . . . None
  Blind Spot Detection . . . . None
  Crash Imminent Braking . . . . None
  Lane Departure Warning . . . . None
General:
  Auto. Crash Notification. . . . . None
  Day Running Lamps . . . . None
Safety Belt/Restraint:
  Dynamic Head Restraints. . . . . . Standard Front
  Adjustable Belt . . . . Standard Front
  Pretensioners . . . . Standard Front

Nissan Versa

Specifications

Drive. . . . . FWD
Engine. 1.8-liter I4
Transmission . . . . 4-sp. Automatic
Tow Rating (lbs.). . . . . –
Head/Leg Room (in.). Average-39.8/41.8
Interior Space (cu. ft.). . . . . Very Cramped-90
Cargo Space (cu. ft.) Cramped-14.8
Wheelbase/Length (in.) 102.4/175.4

Ratings—10 Best, 1 Worst

Combo Crash Tests	–
Safety Features	7
Rollover	1
Preventative Maintenance	3
Repair Costs	7
Warranty	2
Fuel Economy	1
Complaints	3
Insurance Costs	10
OVERALL RATING	–

Nissan Xterra

Nissan Xterra

At-a-Glance

Status/Year Series Started Unchanged/2005
Twins . . . . –
Body Styles. . . . . SUV
Seating. 5
Anti-Theft Device . . . . Std. Pass. Immobil. & Alarm
Parking Index Rating . . . . Easy
Where Made. . . . . Smyrna, TN

Fuel Factor
MPG Rating (city/hwy). . . . . Very Poor-15/20
Driving Range (mi.) . . . . Very Short-356.6
Fuel Type . . . . Regular
Annual Fuel Cost . . . . Very High-$2867
Gas Guzzler Tax. . . . . No
Greenhouse Gas Emissions (tons/yr.)Vry High-11.0
Barrels of Oil Used per year . . . . . Very High-20.1

How the Competition Rates

Competitors	Rating	Pg.
Hyundai Santa Fe	–	160
Mazda CX-7	–	200
Volvo XC90	–	270

Price Range	Retail	Markup
4x2 X	$24,560	6%
4x4 X	$26,610	6%
4x4 S	$28,600	6%
4x4 PRO-4X	$31,020	7%

Safety Checklist

Crash Tests:
  Frontal . . . . –
  Side . . . . –
Airbags:
  Head. . . . . Fr. & Rr. Roof Curtain
  Torso. . . . . Front Pelvis/Torso from Seat
  Pelvis . Fr. Seat Pelvis/Torso & Opt. Rr. Door Pelvis/Torso
  Roll Sensing . . . . Yes
  Knee Bolster . . . . None
Crash Avoidance:
  Frontal Collision Warning. . . . . None
  Blind Spot Detection . . . . None
  Crash Imminent Braking . . . . None
  Lane Departure Warning . . . . None
General:
  Auto. Crash Notification . . . . None
  Day Running Lamps . . . . None
Safety Belt/Restraint:
  Dynamic Head Restraints. . . . . Standard Front
  Adjustable Belt . . . . . . Standard Front and Rear
  Pretensioners . . . . Standard Front

Nissan Xterra

Specifications

Drive 4WD
Engine 4.0-liter V6
Transmission . . . . 5-sp. Automatic
Tow Rating (lbs.) Average-5000
Head/Leg Room (in.) Roomy-39.9/42.4
Interior Space (cu. ft.) Average-99.8
Cargo Space (cu. ft.). . . . . Very Roomy-36.3
Wheelbase/Length (in.) 106.3/178.7

#Additional injury potential in side test see footnote (2) on page 19.

Ratings—10 Best, 1 Worst

Combo Crash Tests	–
Safety Features	9
Rollover	4
Preventative Maintenance	8
Repair Costs	9
Warranty	7
Fuel Economy	2
Complaints	1
Insurance Costs	8
OVERALL RATING	–

Porsche Cayenne

Porsche Cayenne

At-a-Glance

Status/Year Series Started Unchanged/2011
Twins . . . . Volkswagen Touareg
Body Styles. . . . . SUV
Seating. 5
Anti-Theft DeviceStd. Pass. Immobil. & Active Alarm
Parking Index Rating . . . . Hard
Where Made . . . . Leipzig, Germany
Fuel Factor
  MPG Rating (city/hwy). . . . . Very Poor-16/23
  Driving Range (mi.). . . . . Very Long-489.4
  Fuel Type . . . . Premium
  Annual Fuel Cost . . . . Very High-$2832
  Gas Guzzler Tax . . . . No
  Greenhouse Gas Emissions (tons/yr.). . . High-9.8
  Barrels of Oil Used per year High-18.0

How the Competition Rates

Competitors	Rating	Pg.
Audi Q7	–	93
Infiniti FX	–	166
Land Rover Range Rover	–	185

Price Range	Retail	Markup
Base	$48,200	
S	$65,000	
S Hybrid	$69,000	
Turbo	$107,100	

Safety Checklist

Crash Tests:
  Frontal . . . . –
  Side . . . . –
Airbags:
  Head. . . . . Fr. & Rr. Roof Curtain
  Torso . . . . Fr. & Rr. Torso from Seat
  Pelvis. . . . . None
  Roll Sensing . . . . Yes
  Knee Bolster . . . . Standard Driver
Crash Avoidance:
  Frontal Collision Warning. . . . . None
  Blind Spot Detection . . . . Optional
  Crash Imminent Braking . . . . None
  Lane Departure Warning . . . . None
General:
  Auto. Crash Notification. . . . . None
  Day Running Lamps . . . . Standard
Safety Belt/Restraint:
  Dynamic Head Restraints . . . . None
  Adjustable Belt . . . . . . Standard Front and Rear
  Pretensioners. . . . . Standard Front & Rear

Porsche Cayenne

Specifications

Drive . . . . AWD
Engine 3.6-liter V6
Transmission . . . . 8-sp. Automatic
Tow Rating (lbs.) High-7700
Head/Leg Room (in.) . . . . –
Interior Space (cu. ft.) . . . . –
Cargo Space (cu. ft.) Roomy-23.7
Wheelbase/Length (in.). 114/190.8

Ratings—10 Best, 1 Worst	Crew	Reg.	Quad
Combo Crash Tests	1	5	4
Safety Features	1	1	1
Rollover	3	3	3
Preventative Maintenance	1	1	1
Repair Costs	10	10	10
Warranty	4	4	4
Fuel Economy	1	1	1
Complaints	9	9	9
Insurance Costs	8	8	8
OVERALL RATING	**1**	**2**	**3**

Ram 1500

Ram 1500

At-a-Glance

Status/Year Series Started Unchanged/2009
Twins . . . . –
Body Styles . . . . Quad, Regular, Crew Cabs
Seating 5/6
Anti-Theft Device . . . . Std. Pass. Immobil. & Alarm
Parking Index Rating . . . . Very Hard
Where Made . . . . Warren, MI
Fuel Factor
  MPG Rating (city/hwy) . . . . Very Poor-14/19
  Driving Range (mi.) Long-412.9
  Fuel Type Regular/E85
  Annual Fuel Cost . . . . Very High-$3051
  Gas Guzzler Tax . . . . No
  Greenhouse Gas Emissions (tons/yr.)Vry High-11.6
  Barrels of Oil Used per year . . . . . Very High-21.4

How the Competition Rates

Competitors	Rating	Pg.
Chevrolet Silverado Ext.	5	115
Ford F-150 Super Cab	4	136
Toyota Tundra	3	256

Price Range	Retail	Markup
ST Reg Cab SWB 2WD	$21,475	7%
SLT Reg Cab SWB 4WD	$29,225	8%
Sport Quad Cab SWB 2WD	$34,035	8%
Laramie Longhorn Crew Cab 4WD	$46,270	9%

Safety Checklist

Crash Tests:
  Frontal . . . . Very Poor
  Side . . . . Very Poor***
Airbags:
  Head . . . . Front Roof Curtain
  Torso . . . . None
  Pelvis . . . . None
  Roll Sensing . . . . No
  Knee Bolster . . . . None
Crash Avoidance:
  Frontal Collision Warning . . . . None
  Blind Spot Detection . . . . None
  Crash Imminent Braking . . . . None
  Lane Departure Warning . . . . None
General:
  Auto. Crash Notification . . . . None
  Day Running Lamps . . . . None
Safety Belt/Restraint:
  Dynamic Head Restraints . . . . None
  Adjustable Belt . . . . Standard Front
  Pretensioners . . . . Standard Front

Ram 1500

Specifications

Drive 4WD
Engine 5.7-liter V8
Transmission . . . . 5-sp. Automatic
Tow Rating (lbs.) . . . . Very High-14000
Head/Leg Room (in.) Average-41/41
Interior Space (cu. ft.) Roomy-106.6
Cargo Space (cu. ft.) . . . . Very Roomy-57.5
Wheelbase/Length (in.) 140.5/229

*Additional injury potential in side test. See asterisked footnote (***) on page 27.

Ratings—10 Best, 1 Worst	
Combo Crash Tests	–
Safety Features	3
Rollover	5
Preventative Maintenance	–
Repair Costs	–
Warranty	2
Fuel Economy	10
Complaints	–
Insurance Costs	–
OVERALL RATING	–

Scion iQ

Scion iQ

Scion iQ

At-a-Glance

Status/Year Series Started	Unchanged/2011
Twins	–
Body Styles	Hatchback
Seating	4
Anti-Theft Device	None
Parking Index Rating	Very Easy
Where Made	Takaoka City, Japan

Fuel Factor

MPG Rating (city/hwy)	Very Good-36/37
Driving Range (mi.)	Very Short-309.8
Fuel Type	Regular
Annual Fuel Cost	Very Low-$1329
Gas Guzzler Tax	No
Greenhouse Gas Emissions (tons/yr.)	Very Low-5.1
Barrels of Oil Used per year	Very Low-9.3

How the Competition Rates

Competitors	Rating	Pg.
Mazda 2	–	196
Smart ForTwo	–	236
Volkswagen Beetle	–	259

Price Range	Retail	Markup
Base	$15,265	5%

Safety Checklist

Crash Tests:

Frontal	–
Side	–

Airbags:

Head	Fr. & Rr. Roof Curtain
Torso	Front Pelvis/Torso from Seat
Pelvis	Front Pelvis/Torso from Seat
Roll Sensing	No
Knee Bolster	Standard Front

Crash Avoidance:

Frontal Collision Warning	None
Blind Spot Detection	None
Crash Imminent Braking	None
Lane Departure Warning	None

General:

Auto. Crash Notification	None
Day Running Lamps	None

Safety Belt/Restraint:

Dynamic Head Restraints	None
Adjustable Belt	None
Pretensioners	Standard Front

Scion iQ

Specifications

Drive	FWD
Engine	1.3-liter I4
Transmission	CVT
Tow Rating (lbs.)	–
Head/Leg Room (in.)	Very Cramped-37.7/40.9
Interior Space (cu. ft.)	Very Cramped-73.8
Cargo Space (cu. ft.)	Very Cramped-3.5
Wheelbase/Length (in.)	78.7/120.1

Scion tC

Ratings—10 Best, 1 Worst

Combo Crash Tests	9
Safety Features	5
Rollover	7
Preventative Maintenance	9
Repair Costs	–
Warranty	2
Fuel Economy	6
Complaints	6
Insurance Costs	1
OVERALL RATING	**7**

Scion tC

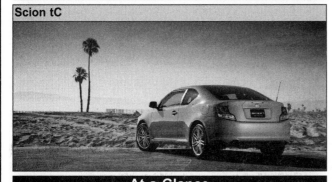
Scion tC

At-a-Glance

Status/Year Series Started Unchanged/2011
Twins . . . . –
Body Styles. . . . . Sedan, Coupe
Seating. 5
Anti-Theft Device . . . . Std. Pass. Immobil.
Parking Index Rating . . . . Easy
Where Made . . . . Tsutsumi, Japan
Fuel Factor
  MPG Rating (city/hwy) Average-23/31
  Driving Range (mi.) Short-377.3
  Fuel Type . . . . Regular
  Annual Fuel Cost . . . . Low-$1862
  Gas Guzzler Tax . . . . No
  Greenhouse Gas Emissions (tons/yr.) Average-7.2
  Barrels of Oil Used per year Average-13.2

How the Competition Rates

Competitors	Rating	Pg.
Mazda 3	6	197
Mitsubishi Lancer	–	212
Subaru Impreza	–	238

Price Range

	Retail	Markup
MT	$18,575	5%
AT	$19,575	5%

Safety Checklist

Crash Tests:
  Frontal . . . . Good
  Side . . . . Very Good
Airbags:
  Head . . . . Fr. & Rr. Roof Curtain
  Torso . . . . Front Pelvis/Torso from Seat
  Pelvis . . . . Front Pelvis/Torso from Seat
  Roll Sensing. . . . . No
  Knee Bolster . . . . Standard Front
Crash Avoidance:
  Frontal Collision Warning. . . . . None
  Blind Spot Detection . . . . None
  Crash Imminent Braking . . . . None
  Lane Departure Warning . . . . None
General:
  Auto. Crash Notification . . . . None
  Day Running Lamps . . . . None
Safety Belt/Restraint:
  Dynamic Head Restraints. . . . . . Standard Front
  Adjustable Belt. . . . . None
  Pretensioners . . . . Standard Front

Scion tC

Specifications

Drive . . . . FWD
Engine. 2.5-liter I4
Transmission . . . . 6-sp. Automatic
Tow Rating (lbs.) . . . . –
Head/Leg Room (in.) . . . . . Very Cramped-37.7/41.8
Interior Space (cu. ft.) . . . . Very Cramped-88.4
Cargo Space (cu. ft.) . . . . Very Roomy-34.5
Wheelbase/Length (in.) 106.3/174

Ratings—10 Best, 1 Worst

Combo Crash Tests	–
Safety Features	2
Rollover	4
Preventative Maintenance	7
Repair Costs	8
Warranty	2
Fuel Economy	5
Complaints	4
Insurance Costs	1
OVERALL RATING	**–**

Scion xB

Scion xB

Safety Checklist

Crash Tests:
Frontal . . . . –
Side . . . . –
Airbags:
Head . . . . Fr. & Rr. Roof Curtain
Torso . . . . Front Pelvis/Torso from Seat
Pelvis . . . . Front Pelvis/Torso from Seat
Roll Sensing . . . . No
Knee Bolster . . . . None
Crash Avoidance:
Frontal Collision Warning . . . . None
Blind Spot Detection . . . . None
Crash Imminent Braking . . . . None
Lane Departure Warning . . . . None
General:
Auto. Crash Notification . . . . None
Day Running Lamps . . . . None
Safety Belt/Restraint:
Dynamic Head Restraints . . . . None
Adjustable Belt . . . . Standard Front
Pretensioners . . . . Standard Front

At-a-Glance

Status/Year Series Started Unchanged/2008
Twins . . . . –
Body Styles . . . . Hatchback
Seating 5
Anti-Theft Device . . . . None
Parking Index Rating . . . . Very Easy
Where Made . . . . Iwata, Japan
Fuel Factor
MPG Rating (city/hwy) Average-22/28
Driving Range (mi.) . . . . Very Short-340.9
Fuel Type . . . . Regular
Annual Fuel Cost . . . . Average-$1990
Gas Guzzler Tax . . . . No
Greenhouse Gas Emissions (tons/yr.) Average-7.8
Barrels of Oil Used per year High-14.3

How the Competition Rates

Competitors	Rating	Pg.
Kia Soul	6	182
Nissan Cube	–	218
Toyota Yaris	–	258

Price Range

Price Range	Retail	Markup
MT	$16,300	5%
AT	$17,250	5%

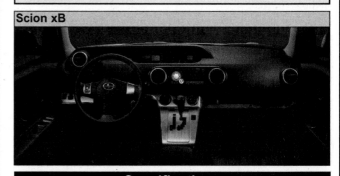

Scion xB

Specifications

Drive . . . . FWD
Engine 2.4-liter I4
Transmission . . . . 4-sp. Automatic
Tow Rating (lbs.) . . . . –
Head/Leg Room (in.) Cramped-40/40.7
Interior Space (cu. ft.) Average-100.8
Cargo Space (cu. ft.) Average-21.7
Wheelbase/Length (in.) 102.4/167.3

Ratings—10 Best, 1 Worst

Combo Crash Tests	–
Safety Features	4
Rollover	5
Preventative Maintenance	10
Repair Costs	6
Warranty	2
Fuel Economy	8
Complaints	9
Insurance Costs	1
OVERALL RATING	**–**

Scion xD

Scion xD

At-a-Glance

Status/Year Series Started Unchanged/2008
Twins . . . . –
Body Styles . . . . Hatchback
Seating 5
Anti-Theft Device . . . . None
Parking Index Rating . . . . Very Easy
Where Made . . . . Takaoka City, Japan
Fuel Factor
MPG Rating (city/hwy) Good-27/33
Driving Range (mi.) . . . . Very Short-326.4
Fuel Type . . . . Regular
Annual Fuel Cost . . . . Very Low-$1648
Gas Guzzler Tax . . . . No
Greenhouse Gas Emissions (tons/yr.) . . . Low-6.5
Barrels of Oil Used per year Average-11.8

How the Competition Rates

Competitors	Rating	Pg.
Hyundai Accent	9	155
Kia Rio	–	179
Suzuki SX4	–	243

Price Range	Retail	Markup
MT	$15,345	5%
AT	$16,145	5%

Safety Checklist

Crash Tests:
Frontal . . . . –
Side . . . . –
Airbags:
Head . . . . Fr. & Rr. Roof Curtain
Torso . . . . Front Torso from Seat
Pelvis . . . . None
Roll Sensing . . . . No
Knee Bolster . . . . None
Crash Avoidance:
Frontal Collision Warning . . . . None
Blind Spot Detection . . . . None
Crash Imminent Braking . . . . None
Lane Departure Warning . . . . None
General:
Auto. Crash Notification . . . . None
Day Running Lamps . . . . None
Safety Belt/Restraint:
Dynamic Head Restraints . . . . . . Standard Front
Adjustable Belt . . . . Standard Front
Pretensioners . . . . Standard Front

Scion xD

Specifications

Drive . . . . FWD
Engine 1.8-liter I4
Transmission . . . . 4-sp. Automatic
Tow Rating (lbs.) . . . . –
Head/Leg Room (in.) . . . . . Very Cramped-38.9/40.3
Interior Space (cu. ft.) . . . . Very Cramped-84.5
Cargo Space (cu. ft.) . . . . Very Cramped-10.5
Wheelbase/Length (in.) 96.9/154.7

Ratings—10 Best, 1 Worst	
Combo Crash Tests	–
Safety Features	2
Rollover	2
Preventative Maintenance	–
Repair Costs	–
Warranty	1
Fuel Economy	10
Complaints	6
Insurance Costs	3
OVERALL RATING	–

Smart ForTwo

Smart ForTwo

At-a-Glance

Status/Year Series Started Unchanged/2008
Twins . . . . –
Body Styles . . . . . . Two Seater Coupe, Convertible
Seating. 2
Anti-Theft DeviceStd. Pass. Immobil. & Active Alarm
Parking Index Rating. . . . . Very Easy
Where Made . . . . Hambach, France
Fuel Factor
  MPG Rating (city/hwy) . . . . Very Good-33/41
  Driving Range (mi.) . . . . Very Short-314.7
  Fuel Type . . . . Premium
  Annual Fuel Cost. . . . . Very Low-$1451
  Gas Guzzler Tax . . . . No
  Greenhouse Gas Emissions (tons/yr.)Very Low-5.2
  Barrels of Oil Used per year Low-9.5

How the Competition Rates

Competitors	Rating	Pg.
Fiat 500	2	131
Ford Fiesta	5	137
Scion iQ	–	232

Price Range	Retail	Markup
pure coupe	$12,490	8%
passion coupe	$14,690	8%
passion cabriolet	$17,690	8%

Safety Checklist

Crash Tests:
  Frontal . . . . –
  Side . . . . –
Airbags:
  Head. . . . . Front Roof Curtain
  Torso . . . . Front Torso from Seat
  Pelvis. . . . . None
  Roll Sensing. . . . . No
  Knee Bolster. . . . . Standard Front
Crash Avoidance:
  Frontal Collision Warning. . . . . None
  Blind Spot Detection . . . . None
  Crash Imminent Braking . . . . None
  Lane Departure Warning . . . . None
General:
  Auto. Crash Notification . . . . Optional
  Day Running Lamps . . . . Optional
Safety Belt/Restraint:
  Dynamic Head Restraints . . . . None
  Adjustable Belt. None
  Pretensioners . . . . Standard Front

Smart ForTwo

Specifications

Drive . . . . FWD
Engine. 1.0-liter I3
Transmission . . . . 5-sp. Manual
Tow Rating (lbs.). . . . . –
Head/Leg Room (in.) Average-39.7/41.2
Interior Space (cu. ft.) . . . . Very Cramped-45.4
Cargo Space (cu. ft.) . . . . Very Cramped-7.8
Wheelbase/Length (in.) 73.5/106.1

Ratings—10 Best, 1 Worst	
Combo Crash Tests	5
Safety Features	7
Rollover	3
Preventative Maintenance	4
Repair Costs	8
Warranty	3
Fuel Economy	5
Complaints	8
Insurance Costs	5
OVERALL RATING	**5**

Subaru Forester

At-a-Glance

Status/Year Series Started Unchanged/2009
Twins . . . . –
Body Styles. . . . . Wagon
Seating. 5
Anti-Theft DeviceStd. Pass. Immobil. & Active Alarm
Parking Index Rating. . . . . Very Easy
Where Made. . . . . Gunma, Japan
Fuel Factor
  MPG Rating (city/hwy) Average-21/27
  Driving Range (mi.) Average-394.3
  Fuel Type . . . . Regular
  Annual Fuel Cost. . . . . Average-$2076
  Gas Guzzler Tax . . . . No
  Greenhouse Gas Emissions (tons/yr.) Average-8.1
  Barrels of Oil Used per year High-14.9

How the Competition Rates

Competitors	Rating	Pg.
Hyundai Tucson	8	162
Mini Countryman	–	210
Toyota RAV4	1	252

Price Range	Retail	Markup
2.5X	$20,595	6%
2.5X Limited	$26,595	6%
2.5X Touring	$27,895	6%
2.5XT Touring	$29,895	6%

Subaru Forester

Safety Checklist

Crash Tests:
  Frontal . . . . Good
  Side . . . . Very Poor
Airbags:
  Head. . . . . Fr. & Rr. Roof Curtain
  Torso. . . . . Front Pelvis/Torso from Seat
  Pelvis . . . . Front Pelvis/Torso from Seat
  Roll Sensing . . . . Yes
  Knee Bolster . . . . None
Crash Avoidance:
  Frontal Collision Warning. . . . . None
  Blind Spot Detection . . . . None
  Crash Imminent Braking . . . . None
  Lane Departure Warning . . . . None
General:
  Auto. Crash Notification . . . . None
  Day Running Lamps . . . . Standard
Safety Belt/Restraint:
  Dynamic Head Restraints. . . . . . Standard Front
  Adjustable Belt . . . . Standard Front
  Pretensioners . . . . Standard Front

Subaru Forester

Specifications

Drive . . . . AWD
Engine. 2.5-liter I4
Transmission . . . . 4-sp. Automatic
Tow Rating (lbs.). . . . . Very Low-2400
Head/Leg Room (in.) . . . . . . Very Roomy-41.6/43.1
Interior Space (cu. ft.) Roomy-107.6
Cargo Space (cu. ft.). . . . . Very Roomy-33.5
Wheelbase/Length (in.). 103/179.5

Subaru Impreza

Ratings—10 Best, 1 Worst	
Combo Crash Tests	–
Safety Features	4
Rollover	7
Preventative Maintenance	4
Repair Costs	9
Warranty	3
Fuel Economy	9
Complaints	–
Insurance Costs	1
OVERALL RATING	–

Subaru Impreza

At-a-Glance

Status/Year Series Started . . . . All New/2012
Twins . . . . –
Body Styles . . . . Sedan, Wagon
Seating. 5
Anti-Theft DeviceStd. Pass. Immobil. & Active Alarm
Parking Index Rating . . . . Easy
Where Made. . . . . Gunma, Japan
Fuel Factor
  MPG Rating (city/hwy) . . . . Very Good-27/36
  Driving Range (mi.). . . . . Very Long-514.1
  Fuel Type . . . . Regular
  Annual Fuel Cost. . . . . Very Low-$1593
  Gas Guzzler Tax . . . . No
  Greenhouse Gas Emissions (tons/yr.) . . . Low-6.2
  Barrels of Oil Used per year Low-11.4

How the Competition Rates

Competitors	Rating	Pg.
Honda Civic	–	146
Mazda 3	6	197
Mitsubishi Lancer	–	212

Price Range	Retail	Markup
Base	$17,495	5%
Premium	$19,795	5%
Limited	$21,595	5%
Sport Limited	$22,595	5%

Safety Checklist

Crash Tests:
  Frontal . . . . –
  Side . . . . –
Airbags:
  Head. . . . . Fr. & Rr. Roof Curtain
  Torso. . . . . Front Pelvis/Torso from Seat
  Pelvis . . . . Front Pelvis/Torso from Seat
  Roll Sensing. . . . . No
  Knee Bolster . . . . Standard Driver
Crash Avoidance:
  Frontal Collision Warning. . . . . None
  Blind Spot Detection . . . . None
  Crash Imminent Braking . . . . None
  Lane Departure Warning . . . . None
General:
  Auto. Crash Notification . . . . None
  Day Running Lamps . . . . Standard
Safety Belt/Restraint:
  Dynamic Head Restraints . . . . None
  Adjustable Belt . . . . Standard Front
  Pretensioners . . . . Standard Front

Subaru Impreza

Specifications

Drive . . . . AWD
Engine. 2.0-liter I4
Transmission . . . . CVT
Tow Rating (lbs.). . . . . –
Head/Leg Room (in.) Roomy-39.7/43.5
Interior Space (cu. ft.) Cramped-96.4
Cargo Space (cu. ft.) . . . . Very Cramped-12
Wheelbase/Length (in.) 104.1/180.3

Ratings—10 Best, 1 Worst

Combo Crash Tests	5
Safety Features	2
Rollover	7
Preventative Maintenance	2
Repair Costs	8
Warranty	3
Fuel Economy	6
Complaints	2
Insurance Costs	3
OVERALL RATING	**2**

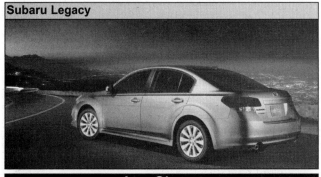
Subaru Legacy

At-a-Glance

Status/Year Series Started Unchanged/2010
Twins . . . . –
Body Styles . . . . Sedan
Seating. 5
Anti-Theft DeviceStd. Pass. Immobil. & Active Alarm
Parking Index Rating . . . . Easy
Where Made . . . . Lafayette, IN
Fuel Factor
 MPG Rating (city/hwy) Average-23/31
 Driving Range (mi.). . . . . Very Long-481.4
 Fuel Type . . . . Regular
 Annual Fuel Cost . . . . Low-$1862
 Gas Guzzler Tax . . . . No
 Greenhouse Gas Emissions (tons/yr.) Average-7.2
 Barrels of Oil Used per year Average-13.2

How the Competition Rates

Competitors	Rating	Pg.
Ford Fusion	5	140
Mazda 6	7	199
Mitsubishi Galant	–	211

Price Range

Price Range	Retail	Markup
2.5i	$19,995	5.5%
2.5i Limited	$25,595	6.5%
3.6R Premium	$26,298	6.5%
2.5GT	$31,595	7%

Subaru Legacy

Safety Checklist

Crash Tests:
 Frontal . . . . Average
 Side. . . . . Poor
Airbags:
 Head . . . . Fr. & Rr. Roof Curtain
 Torso . . . . Front Pelvis/Torso from Seat
 Pelvis . . . . Front Pelvis/Torso from Seat
 Roll Sensing. . . . . No
 Knee Bolster . . . . None
Crash Avoidance:
 Frontal Collision Warning. . . . . None
 Blind Spot Detection . . . . None
 Crash Imminent Braking . . . . None
 Lane Departure Warning . . . . None
General:
 Auto. Crash Notification . . . . None
 Day Running Lamps . . . . Standard
Safety Belt/Restraint:
 Dynamic Head Restraints . . . . None
 Adjustable Belt . . . . Standard Front
 Pretensioners . . . . Standard Front

Subaru Legacy

Specifications

Drive . . . . AWD
Engine. 2.5-liter I4
Transmission . . . . CVT
Tow Rating (lbs.) . . . . –
Head/Leg Room (in.) . . . . Very Roomy-40.3/43
Interior Space (cu. ft.) Average-103
Cargo Space (cu. ft.) Cramped-14.7
Wheelbase/Length (in.) 108.3/186.4

Ratings—10 Best, 1 Worst

Combo Crash Tests	–
Safety Features	5
Rollover	5
Preventative Maintenance	2
Repair Costs	9
Warranty	3
Fuel Economy	6
Complaints	2
Insurance Costs	8
OVERALL RATING	**–**

Subaru Outback

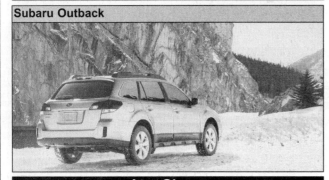

Subaru Outback

At-a-Glance

Status/Year Series Started Unchanged/2010
Twins . . . . –
Body Styles. . . . . Wagon
Seating. 5
Anti-Theft DeviceStd. Pass. Immobil. & Active Alarm
Parking Index Rating . . . . Average
Where Made . . . . Lafayette, IN

Fuel Factor
MPG Rating (city/hwy) Average-22/29
Driving Range (mi.). . . . . Very Long-456.6
Fuel Type . . . . Regular
Annual Fuel Cost . . . . Low-$1963
Gas Guzzler Tax . . . . No
Greenhouse Gas Emissions (tons/yr.) Average-7.8
Barrels of Oil Used per year High-14.3

How the Competition Rates

Competitors	Rating	Pg.
Honda Accord	8	144
Kia Optima	9	178
Volkswagen Passat	10	263

Price Range	Retail	Markup
Base	$23,295	6%
Premium	$25,795	6%
3.6R	$28,295	7%
3.6R Limited	$31,695	7%

Safety Checklist

Crash Tests:
Frontal. . . . . Average
Side. . . . . Poor
Airbags:
Head. . . . . Fr. & Rr. Roof Curtain
Torso. . . . . Front Pelvis/Torso from Seat
Pelvis . . . . Front Pelvis/Torso from Seat
Roll Sensing . . . . Yes
Knee Bolster . . . . None
Crash Avoidance:
Frontal Collision Warning. . . . . None
Blind Spot Detection . . . . None
Crash Imminent Braking . . . . None
Lane Departure Warning . . . . None
General:
Auto. Crash Notification. . . . . None
Day Running Lamps . . . . Standard
Safety Belt/Restraint:
Dynamic Head Restraints . . . . None
Adjustable Belt . . . . Standard Front
Pretensioners . . . . Standard Front

Subaru Outback

Specifications

Drive . . . . AWD
Engine. 2.5-liter I4
Transmission . . . . CVT
Tow Rating (lbs.) Low-3000
Head/Leg Room (in.) . . . . . . Very Roomy-40.8/43
Interior Space (cu. ft.) Roomy-105.4
Cargo Space (cu. ft.). . . . . Very Roomy-34.3
Wheelbase/Length (in.) 107.9/188.2

Ratings—10 Best, 1 Worst

Combo Crash Tests	–
Safety Features	5
Rollover	3
Preventative Maintenance	1
Repair Costs	3
Warranty	4
Fuel Economy	3
Complaints	4
Insurance Costs	3
OVERALL RATING	**–**

Suzuki Grand Vitara

Suzuki Grand Vitara

At-a-Glance

Status/Year Series Started Unchanged/2006
Twins . . . . –
Body Styles. . . . . SUV
Seating. 5
Anti-Theft Device. . . . . None
Parking Index Rating . . . . Easy
Where Made . . . . Iwata, Japan

Fuel Factor
MPG Rating (city/hwy). Poor-19/25
Driving Range (mi.). Short-370.6
Fuel Type . . . . Regular
Annual Fuel Cost. . . . . High-$2275
Gas Guzzler Tax . . . . No
Greenhouse Gas Emissions (tons/yr.) . . . High-8.9
Barrels of Oil Used per year High-16.3

How the Competition Rates

Competitors	Rating	Pg.
Jeep Patriot	–	175
Kia Sportage	–	183
Toyota RAV4	1	252

Price Range	Retail	Markup

Safety Checklist

Crash Tests:
  Frontal . . . . –
  Side . . . . –
Airbags:
  Head. . . . . Fr. & Rr. Roof Curtain
  Torso . . . . Front Torso from Seat
  Pelvis . . . . None
  Roll Sensing . . . . Yes
  Knee Bolster . . . . None
Crash Avoidance:
  Frontal Collision Warning. . . . . None
  Blind Spot Detection . . . . None
  Crash Imminent Braking . . . . None
  Lane Departure Warning . . . . None
General:
  Auto. Crash Notification. . . . . None
  Day Running Lamps . . . . Standard
Safety Belt/Restraint:
  Dynamic Head Restraints . . . . None
  Adjustable Belt . . . . Standard Front
  Pretensioners . . . . Standard Front

Suzuki Grand Vitara

Specifications

Drive. . . . . RWD
Engine. 2.4-liter I4
Transmission . . . . 4-sp. Automatic
Tow Rating (lbs.). Low-3000
Head/Leg Room (in.) Average-40/41.3
Interior Space (cu. ft.) Roomy-111.1
Cargo Space (cu. ft.) Cramped-12.5
Wheelbase/Length (in.) 103.9/175.8

Ratings—10 Best, 1 Worst

Combo Crash Tests	–
Safety Features	6
Rollover	7
Preventative Maintenance	5
Repair Costs	3
Warranty	4
Fuel Economy	6
Complaints	–
Insurance Costs	3
OVERALL RATING	–

Suzuki Kizashi

Suzuki Kizashi

At-a-Glance

Status/Year Series Started Unchanged/2010
Twins . . . . –
Body Styles . . . . Sedan
Seating. 5
Anti-Theft Device . . . . Std. Pass. Immobil. & Alarm
Parking Index Rating. . . . . Very Easy
Where Made. . . . . Sagara, Japan
Fuel Factor
 MPG Rating (city/hwy). Average-23/30
 Driving Range (mi.). Long-426.6
 Fuel Type . . . . Regular
 Annual Fuel Cost . . . . Low-$1885
 Gas Guzzler Tax . . . . No
 Greenhouse Gas Emissions (tons/yr.) Average-7.2
 Barrels of Oil Used per year Average-13.2

How the Competition Rates

Competitors	Rating	Pg.
Mazda 3	6	197
Mitsubishi Lancer	–	212
Subaru Impreza	–	238

Price Range	Retail	Markup

Safety Checklist

Crash Tests:
 Frontal . . . . –
 Side . . . . –
Airbags:
 Head. . . . . Fr. & Rr. Roof Curtain
 Torso. . . . . Fr. & Rr. Pelvis/Torso from Seat
 Pelvis . . . . Front Pelvis/Torso from Seat
 Roll Sensing. . . . . No
 Knee Bolster . . . . None
Crash Avoidance:
 Frontal Collision Warning. . . . . None
 Blind Spot Detection . . . . Optional
 Crash Imminent Braking . . . . None
 Lane Departure Warning . . . . None
General:
 Auto. Crash Notification. . . . . None
 Day Running Lamps . . . . Standard
Safety Belt/Restraint:
 Dynamic Head Restraints . . . . None
 Adjustable Belt . . . . Standard Front
 Pretensioners . . . . Standard Front

Suzuki Kizashi

Specifications

Drive . . . . FWD
Engine. 2.4-liter I4
Transmission . . . . CVT
Tow Rating (lbs.). . . . . –
Head/Leg Room (in.) Average-39.3/41.7
Interior Space (cu. ft.) Cramped-92.1
Cargo Space (cu. ft.) Cramped-13.3
Wheelbase/Length (in.) 106.3/183.1

Ratings—10 Best, 1 Worst

Combo Crash Tests	–
Safety Features	4
Rollover	5
Preventative Maintenance	1
Repair Costs	4
Warranty	4
Fuel Economy	6
Complaints	4
Insurance Costs	1
OVERALL RATING	**–**

Suzuki SX4

At-a-Glance

Status/Year Series Started Unchanged/2007
Twins . . . . –
Body Styles . . . . Sedan, Hatchback
Seating. 5
Anti-Theft Device. . . . . None
Parking Index Rating . . . . Very Easy
Where Made . . . . Esztergom, Hungary
Fuel Factor
MPG Rating (city/hwy) Average-23/30
Driving Range (mi.) . . . . Very Short-339.2
Fuel Type . . . . Regular
Annual Fuel Cost . . . . Low-$1885
Gas Guzzler Tax . . . . No
Greenhouse Gas Emissions (tons/yr.) Average-7.2
Barrels of Oil Used per year Average-13.2

How the Competition Rates

Competitors	Rating	Pg.
Honda Fit	–	150
Hyundai Accent	9	155
Kia Rio	–	179

Price Range

Price Range	Retail	Markup

Suzuki SX4

Safety Checklist

Crash Tests:
Frontal . . . . –
Side . . . . –
Airbags:
Head. . . . . Fr. & Rr. Roof Curtain
Torso . . . . Fr. & Rr. Torso from Seat
Pelvis . . . . None
Roll Sensing. . . . . No
Knee Bolster . . . . None
Crash Avoidance:
Frontal Collision Warning. . . . . None
Blind Spot Detection . . . . None
Crash Imminent Braking . . . . None
Lane Departure Warning . . . . None
General:
Auto. Crash Notification. . . . . None
Day Running Lamps . . . . Standard
Safety Belt/Restraint:
Dynamic Head Restraints . . . . None
Adjustable Belt . . . . Standard Front
Pretensioners . . . . Standard Front

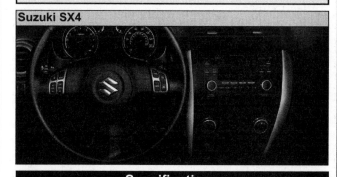

Suzuki SX4

Specifications

Drive . . . . FWD
Engine. 2.0-liter I4
Transmission . . . . CVT
Tow Rating (lbs.). . . . . Very Low-1000
Head/Leg Room (in.). Average-39.6/41.4
Interior Space (cu. ft.). . . . . Very Cramped-88
Cargo Space (cu. ft.) Cramped-15.5
Wheelbase/Length (in.) 98.4/177.6

Ratings—10 Best, 1 Worst

Combo Crash Tests	–
Safety Features	9
Rollover	2
Preventative Maintenance	9
Repair Costs	4
Warranty	2
Fuel Economy	3
Complaints	8
Insurance Costs	10
OVERALL RATING	**–**

Toyota 4Runner

At-a-Glance

Status/Year Series Started Unchanged/2006
Twins . . . . Lexus GX
Body Styles. . . . . SUV
Seating 5/7
Anti-Theft Device Std. Pass. Immobil. & Opt. Pass. Alarm
Parking Index Rating . . . . Average
Where Made . . . . Tahara, Japan
Fuel Factor
  MPG Rating (city/hwy). Poor-17/23
  Driving Range (mi.). . . . . Very Long-443.0
  Fuel Type . . . . Regular
  Annual Fuel Cost. . . . . High-$2515
  Gas Guzzler Tax . . . . No
  Greenhouse Gas Emissions (tons/yr.). . . High-9.8
  Barrels of Oil Used per year High-18.0

How the Competition Rates

Competitors	Rating	Pg.
Ford Explorer	6	135
Honda Pilot	4	153
Nissan Pathfinder	–	224

Price Range	Retail	Markup
2WD SR5	$31,090	9%
4WD SR5	$32,830	9%
4WD Trail	$36,755	9%
4WD Limited	$40,630	9%

Toyota 4Runner

Safety Checklist

Crash Tests:
  Frontal . . . . –
  Side . . . . –
Airbags:
  Head. . . . . Fr. & Rr. Roof Curtain
  Torso. . . . . Front Pelvis/Torso from Seat
  Pelvis . . . . Front Pelvis/Torso from Seat
  Roll Sensing . . . . Yes
  Knee Bolster. . . . . Standard Front
Crash Avoidance:
  Frontal Collision Warning. . . . . None
  Blind Spot Detection . . . . None
  Crash Imminent Braking . . . . None
  Lane Departure Warning . . . . None
General:
  Auto. Crash Notification . . . . Optional
  Day Running Lamps . . . . Standard
Safety Belt/Restraint:
  Dynamic Head Restraints. . . . . . Standard Front
  Adjustable Belt . . . . Standard Front
  Pretensioners . . . . Standard Front

Toyota 4Runner

Specifications

Drive. . . . . RWD
Engine 4.0-liter V6
Transmission . . . . 5-sp. Automatic
Tow Rating (lbs.) Average-5000
Head/Leg Room (in.). Average-39.3/41.7
Interior Space (cu. ft.). Roomy-128
Cargo Space (cu. ft.) . . . . Very Cramped-9
Wheelbase/Length (in.) 109.8/189.9

Ratings—10 Best, 1 Worst

Combo Crash Tests	–
Safety Features	8
Rollover	7
Preventative Maintenance	10
Repair Costs	4
Warranty	2
Fuel Economy	5
Complaints	2
Insurance Costs	8
OVERALL RATING	**–**

Toyota Avalon

Toyota Avalon

Safety Checklist

Crash Tests:
Frontal . . . . –
Side . . . . –
Airbags:
Head. . . . . Fr. & Rr. Roof Curtain
Torso. . . . . Fr. & Rr. Pelvis/Torso from Seat
Pelvis . . . . Fr. & Rr. Pelvis/Torso from Seat
Roll Sensing. . . . . No
Knee Bolster . . . . Standard Driver
Crash Avoidance:
Frontal Collision Warning. . . . . None
Blind Spot Detection . . . . None
Crash Imminent Braking . . . . None
Lane Departure Warning . . . . None
General:
Auto. Crash Notification . . . . Optional
Day Running Lamps . . . . Standard
Safety Belt/Restraint:
Dynamic Head Restraints. . . . . . Standard Front
Adjustable Belt . . . . Standard Front
Pretensioners . . . . Standard Front

At-a-Glance

Status/Year Series Started Unchanged/2006
Twins . . . . –
Body Styles . . . . Sedan
Seating. 5
Anti-Theft Device . . . . Std. Pass. Immobil. & Alarm
Parking Index Rating . . . . Average
Where Made . . . . Georgetown, KY
Fuel Factor
MPG Rating (city/hwy). Average-20/29
Driving Range (mi.) Long-430.1
Fuel Type . . . . Regular
Annual Fuel Cost. . . . . Average-$2084
Gas Guzzler Tax . . . . No
Greenhouse Gas Emissions (tons/yr.) Average-8.1
Barrels of Oil Used per year High-14.9

Toyota Avalon

How the Competition Rates

Competitors	Rating	Pg.
Chevrolet Impala	4	113
Ford Fusion	5	140
Nissan Altima	6	215

Price Range

	Retail	Markup
Base	$33,195	12%
Limited	$36,435	12%

Specifications

Drive . . . . FWD
Engine 3.5-liter V6
Transmission . . . . 6-sp. Automatic
Tow Rating (lbs.). . . . . Very Low-1000
Head/Leg Room (in.) Cramped-38.9/41.3
Interior Space (cu. ft.) Roomy-106.9
Cargo Space (cu. ft.) Cramped-14.4
Wheelbase/Length (in.) 111/197.6

Toyota Camry | Intermediate

Ratings—10 Best, 1 Worst

Ratings—10 Best, 1 Worst	
Combo Crash Tests	8
Safety Features	8
Rollover	8
Preventative Maintenance	10
Repair Costs	6
Warranty	2
Fuel Economy	8
Complaints	–
Insurance Costs	8
OVERALL RATING	**10**

Toyota Camry

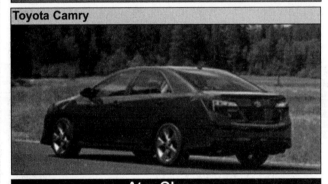
Toyota Camry

At-a-Glance

Status/Year Series Started . . . . All New/2012
Twins . . . . Lexus ES
Body Styles . . . . Sedan
Seating. 5
Anti-Theft Device . . . . Std. Pass. Immobil. & Alarm
Parking Index Rating . . . . Average
Where Made . . . . Georgetown, KY
Fuel Factor
  MPG Rating (city/hwy) Good-25/35
  Driving Range (mi.). . . . . Very Long-487.7
  Fuel Type . . . . Regular
  Annual Fuel Cost . . . . Low-$1689
  Gas Guzzler Tax . . . . No
  Greenhouse Gas Emissions (tons/yr.) Average-6.7
  Barrels of Oil Used per year Average-12.2

How the Competition Rates

Competitors	Rating	Pg.
Chevrolet Malibu	4	114
Ford Fusion	5	140
Scion tC	7	233

Price Range

Price Range	Retail	Markup
Base	$21,955	9%
SE	$23,000	10%
XLE	$24,725	10%
Hybrid XLE	$27,400	9%

Safety Checklist

Crash Tests:
  Frontal . . . . Good
  Side . . . . Good
Airbags:
  Head. . . . . Fr. & Rr. Roof Curtain
  Torso. . . . . Fr. & Rr. Pelvis/Torso from Seat
  Pelvis . . . . Fr. & Rr. Pelvis/Torso from Seat
  Roll Sensing. . . . . No
  Knee Bolster. . . . . Standard Front
Crash Avoidance:
  Frontal Collision Warning. . . . . None
  Blind Spot Detection . . . . Optional
  Crash Imminent Braking . . . . None
  Lane Departure Warning . . . . None
General:
  Auto. Crash Notification . . . . Optional
  Day Running Lamps . . . . Standard
Safety Belt/Restraint:
  Dynamic Head Restraints . . . . None
  Adjustable Belt . . . . Standard Front
  Pretensioners . . . . Standard Front

Toyota Camry

Specifications

Drive . . . . FWD
Engine. 2.5-liter I4
Transmission . . . . 6-sp. Automatic
Tow Rating (lbs.). . . . . Very Low-1000
Head/Leg Room (in.) Cramped-38.8/41.6
Interior Space (cu. ft.) Average-102.7
Cargo Space (cu. ft.) Cramped-15.4
Wheelbase/Length (in.) 109.3/189.2

Ratings—10 Best, 1 Worst

Combo Crash Tests	5
Safety Features	4
Rollover	6
Preventative Maintenance	9
Repair Costs	9
Warranty	2
Fuel Economy	8
Complaints	3
Insurance Costs	1
OVERALL RATING	**5**

Toyota Corolla

Toyota Corolla

At-a-Glance

Status/Year Series Started	Unchanged/2003
Twins	–
Body Styles	Sedan
Seating	5
Anti-Theft Device	Std. Pass. Immobil.
Parking Index Rating	Easy
Where Made	Ontario, Canada

Fuel Factor

MPG Rating (city/hwy)	Good-26/34
Driving Range (mi.)	Short-383.8
Fuel Type	Regular
Annual Fuel Cost	Very Low-$1666
Gas Guzzler Tax	No
Greenhouse Gas Emissions (tons/yr.)	Low-6.5
Barrels of Oil Used per year	Average-11.8

How the Competition Rates

Competitors	Rating	Pg.
Honda Civic	–	146
Mazda 3	6	197
Volkswagen Jetta	5	262

Price Range	Retail	Markup
L	$16,130	6%
LE	$17,910	9%
S	$18,820	9%

Safety Checklist

Crash Tests:

Frontal	Good
Side	Very Poor

Airbags:

Head	Fr. & Rr. Roof Curtain
Torso	Front Torso from Seat
Pelvis	None
Roll Sensing	No
Knee Bolster	None

Crash Avoidance:

Frontal Collision Warning	None
Blind Spot Detection	None
Crash Imminent Braking	None
Lane Departure Warning	None

General:

Auto. Crash Notification	None
Day Running Lamps	Standard

Safety Belt/Restraint:

Dynamic Head Restraints	Standard Front
Adjustable Belt	Standard Front
Pretensioners	Standard Front

Toyota Corolla

Specifications

Drive	FWD
Engine	1.8-liter I4
Transmission	4-sp. Automatic
Tow Rating (lbs.)	Very Low-1500
Head/Leg Room (in.)	Cramped-38.8/41.7
Interior Space (cu. ft.)	Cramped-92.1
Cargo Space (cu. ft.)	Cramped-12.3
Wheelbase/Length (in.)	102.4/180

#Additional injury potential in side test see footnote (7) on page 21.

Ratings—10 Best, 1 Worst

Combo Crash Tests	–
Safety Features	6
Rollover	2
Preventative Maintenance	9
Repair Costs	4
Warranty	2
Fuel Economy	2
Complaints	2
Insurance Costs	5
OVERALL RATING	**–**

Toyota FJ Cruiser

Toyota FJ Cruiser

Safety Checklist

Crash Tests:
Frontal . . . . –
Side . . . . –
Airbags:
Head . . . . Fr. & Rr. Roof Curtain
Torso . . . . Front Torso from Seat
Pelvis . . . . None
Roll Sensing . . . . Yes
Knee Bolster . . . . None
Crash Avoidance:
Frontal Collision Warning. . . . . None
Blind Spot Detection . . . . None
Crash Imminent Braking . . . . None
Lane Departure Warning . . . . None
General:
Auto. Crash Notification . . . . None
Day Running Lamps . . . . Optional
Safety Belt/Restraint:
Dynamic Head Restraints . . . . . . Standard Front
Adjustable Belt . . . . Standard Front
Pretensioners . . . . Standard Front

At-a-Glance

Status/Year Series Started Unchanged/2007
Twins . . . . –
Body Styles. . . . . SUV
Seating. 5
Anti-Theft Device . . . . Std. Pass. Immobil.
Parking Index Rating . . . . Hard
Where Made . . . . Hamura, Japan
Fuel Factor
MPG Rating (city/hwy). . . . . Very Poor-17/20
Driving Range (mi.) . . . . Very Short-346.4
Fuel Type . . . . Regular
Annual Fuel Cost . . . . Very High-$2658
Gas Guzzler Tax . . . . No
Greenhouse Gas Emissions (tons/yr.) . . High-10.4
Barrels of Oil Used per year . . . . . Very High-19.0

Toyota FJ Cruiser

How the Competition Rates

Competitors	Rating	Pg.
Chevrolet Tahoe	6	118
GMC Acadia	6	143
Jeep Grand Cherokee	6	173

Price Range	Retail	Markup
2WD AT	$25,990	8%
4WD MT	$27,170	8%
4WD AT	$27,580	8%

Specifications

Drive 4WD
Engine 4.0-liter V6
Transmission . . . . 5-sp. Automatic
Tow Rating (lbs.) Average-5000
Head/Leg Room (in.) Roomy-41.3/41.9
Interior Space (cu. ft.) . . . . –
Cargo Space (cu. ft.) Roomy-27.9
Wheelbase/Length (in.) 105.9/183.9

Toyota Highlander

Ratings—10 Best, 1 Worst

Combo Crash Tests	5
Safety Features	8
Rollover	4
Preventative Maintenance	7
Repair Costs	2
Warranty	2
Fuel Economy	2
Complaints	5
Insurance Costs	10
OVERALL RATING	**4**

Toyota Highlander

Toyota Highlander

At-a-Glance

Status/Year Series Started Unchanged/2008
Twins . . . . –
Body Styles. . . . . SUV
Seating. 7
Anti-Theft Device . . Opt. Pass. Immobil. &/or Alarm
Parking Index Rating . . . . Hard
Where Made . . . . Princeton, IN
Fuel Factor
  MPG Rating (city/hwy). . . . . Very Poor-17/22
  Driving Range (mi.). Short-363.6
  Fuel Type . . . . Regular
  Annual Fuel Cost. . . . . High-$2559
  Gas Guzzler Tax . . . . No
  Greenhouse Gas Emissions (tons/yr.) . . . High-9.8
  Barrels of Oil Used per year High-18.0

How the Competition Rates

Competitors	Rating	Pg.
Audi Q5	–	92
Honda Pilot	4	153
Nissan Murano	3	223

Price Range	Retail	Markup
Limited Hybrid	$	
Base	$28,090	10%
SE	$35,300	10%
Limited	$35,595	10%

Safety Checklist

Crash Tests:
  Frontal. . . . . Poor
  Side . . . . Good
Airbags:
  Head. . . . . Fr. & Rr. Roof Curtain
  Torso. . . . . Front Pelvis/Torso from Seat
  Pelvis . . . . Front Pelvis/Torso from Seat
  Roll Sensing . . . . Yes
  Knee Bolster . . . . Standard Driver
Crash Avoidance:
  Frontal Collision Warning. . . . . None
  Blind Spot Detection . . . . None
  Crash Imminent Braking . . . . None
  Lane Departure Warning . . . . None
General:
  Auto. Crash Notification. . . . . None
  Day Running Lamps . . . . Optional
Safety Belt/Restraint:
  Dynamic Head Restraints. . . . . . Standard Front
  Adjustable Belt . . . . Standard Front
  Pretensioners . . . . Standard Front

Toyota Highlander

Specifications

Drive 4WD
Engine 3.5-liter V6
Transmission . . . . 5-sp. Automatic
Tow Rating (lbs.). . . . . Very Low-2000
Head/Leg Room (in.) . . . . . . Very Roomy-40.6/43.2
Interior Space (cu. ft.) . . . . Very Roomy-145.7
Cargo Space (cu. ft.) . . . . Very Cramped-10.3
Wheelbase/Length (in.) 109.8/188.4

Toyota Matrix — Compact

Ratings—10 Best, 1 Worst

Combo Crash Tests	–
Safety Features	4
Rollover	6
Preventative Maintenance	9
Repair Costs	8
Warranty	2
Fuel Economy	7
Complaints	5
Insurance Costs	3
OVERALL RATING	**–**

Toyota Matrix

Toyota Matrix

At-a-Glance

Status/Year Series Started Unchanged/2003
Twins . . . . –
Body Styles. . . . . Hatchback
Seating. 5
Anti-Theft Device . . . . Std. Pass. Immobil.
Parking Index Rating . . . . Easy
Where Made . . . . Ontario, Canada

Fuel Factor
MPG Rating (city/hwy) Good-25/32
Driving Range (mi.). Short-366.0
Fuel Type . . . . Regular
Annual Fuel Cost . . . . Low-$1747
Gas Guzzler Tax . . . . No
Greenhouse Gas Emissions (tons/yr.) Average-6.7
Barrels of Oil Used per year. . . . . . . Very Low-1.2

How the Competition Rates

Competitors	Rating	Pg.
Dodge Caliber	2	125
Mazda 3	6	197
Volkswagen Golf	–	261

Price Range	Retail	Markup
L	$18,845	7%
S	$20,755	9%
S AWD	$21,715	9%

Safety Checklist

Crash Tests:
Frontal . . . . –
Side . . . . –
Airbags:
Head. . . . . Fr. & Rr. Roof Curtain
Torso . . . . Front Torso from Seat
Pelvis . . . . None
Roll Sensing. . . . . No
Knee Bolster . . . . None
Crash Avoidance:
Frontal Collision Warning. . . . . None
Blind Spot Detection . . . . None
Crash Imminent Braking . . . . None
Lane Departure Warning . . . . None
General:
Auto. Crash Notification . . . . None
Day Running Lamps . . . . Standard
Safety Belt/Restraint:
Dynamic Head Restraints. . . . . . Standard Front
Adjustable Belt . . . . Standard Front
Pretensioners . . . . Standard Front

Toyota Matrix

Specifications

Drive . . . . FWD
Engine. 1.8-liter I4
Transmission . . . . 4-sp. Automatic
Tow Rating (lbs.). . . . . Very Low-1500
Head/Leg Room (in.). Roomy-40.5/41.6
Interior Space (cu. ft.) Cramped-94.2
Cargo Space (cu. ft.) Average-19.8
Wheelbase/Length (in.) 102.4/171.9

Ratings—10 Best, 1 Worst

Combo Crash Tests	9
Safety Features	7
Rollover	6
Preventative Maintenance	9
Repair Costs	–
Warranty	2
Fuel Economy	10
Complaints	1
Insurance Costs	3
OVERALL RATING	**7**

Toyota Prius

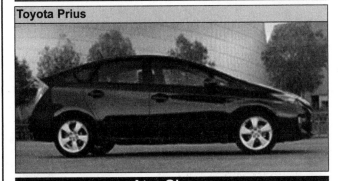

At-a-Glance

Status/Year Series Started Unchanged/2010
Twins . . . . –
Body Styles . . . . Hatchback
Seating 5
Anti-Theft Device . . . . Std. Pass. Immobil.
Parking Index Rating . . . . Very Easy
Where Made . . . . Tsutsumi, Japan
Fuel Factor
MPG Rating (city/hwy) . . . . Very Good-51/48
Driving Range (mi.) . . . . Very Long-590.3
Fuel Type . . . . Regular
Annual Fuel Cost . . . . Very Low-$977
Gas Guzzler Tax . . . . No
Greenhouse Gas Emissions (tons/yr.) Very Low-3.8
Barrels of Oil Used per year . . . . . . Very Low-6.9

How the Competition Rates

Competitors	Rating	Pg.
Scion xD	–	235
Toyota Matrix	–	250
Volkswagen Golf	–	261

Price Range	Retail	Markup

Toyota Prius

Safety Checklist

Crash Tests:
  Frontal . . . . Very Good
  Side . . . . Good
Airbags:
  Head . . . . Fr. & Rr. Roof Curtain
  Torso . . . . Front Torso from Seat
  Pelvis . . . . None
  Roll Sensing . . . . No
  Knee Bolster . . . . Standard Driver
Crash Avoidance:
  Frontal Collision Warning . . . . None
  Blind Spot Detection . . . . None
  Crash Imminent Braking . . . . Optional
  Lane Departure Warning . . . . None
General:
  Auto. Crash Notification . . . . Optional
  Day Running Lamps . . . . Standard
Safety Belt/Restraint:
  Dynamic Head Restraints . . . . . . Standard Front
  Adjustable Belt . . . . Standard Front
  Pretensioners . . . . Standard Front

Toyota Prius

Specifications

Drive . . . . FWD
Engine 1.8-liter I4
Transmission . . . . ECVT
Tow Rating (lbs.) . . . . –
Head/Leg Room (in.) Average-38.6/42.5
Interior Space (cu. ft.) Cramped-93.7
Cargo Space (cu. ft.) Average-21.6
Wheelbase/Length (in.) 106.3/176.4

Ratings—10 Best, 1 Worst

Combo Crash Tests	1
Safety Features	6
Rollover	3
Preventative Maintenance	10
Repair Costs	4
Warranty	2
Fuel Economy	5
Complaints	5
Insurance Costs	5
OVERALL RATING	**1**

Toyota RAV4

Toyota RAV4

At-a-Glance

Status/Year Series Started	Unchanged/2006
Twins	–
Body Styles	SUV
Seating	5/7
Anti-Theft Device	Std. Pass. Immobil.
Parking Index Rating	Easy
Where Made	Tahara, Japan
Fuel Factor	
MPG Rating (city/hwy)	Average-21/27
Driving Range (mi.)	Short-371.0
Fuel Type	Regular
Annual Fuel Cost	Average-$2076
Gas Guzzler Tax	No
Greenhouse Gas Emissions (tons/yr.)	Average-7.8
Barrels of Oil Used per year	High-14.3

How the Competition Rates

Competitors	Rating	Pg.
Ford Escape	2	133
Honda CR-V	3	148
Hyundai Tucson	8	162

Price Range	Retail	Markup

Safety Checklist

Crash Tests:
Frontal	Very Poor
Side	Very Poor

Airbags:
Head	Fr. & Rr. Roof Curtain
Torso	Front Torso from Seat
Pelvis	None
Roll Sensing	Yes
Knee Bolster	None

Crash Avoidance:
Frontal Collision Warning	None
Blind Spot Detection	None
Crash Imminent Braking	None
Lane Departure Warning	None

General:
Auto. Crash Notification	None
Day Running Lamps	Optional

Safety Belt/Restraint:
Dynamic Head Restraints	Standard Front
Adjustable Belt	Standard Front
Pretensioners	Standard Front

Toyota RAV4

Specifications

Drive	4WD
Engine	2.5-liter I4
Transmission	4-sp. Automatic
Tow Rating (lbs.)	Very Low-1500
Head/Leg Room (in.)	Roomy-40.8/41.8
Interior Space (cu. ft.)	Very Roomy-144.5
Cargo Space (cu. ft.)	Cramped-12.3
Wheelbase/Length (in.)	104.7/181.9

Ratings—10 Best, 1 Worst

Combo Crash Tests	–
Safety Features	8
Rollover	3
Preventative Maintenance	9
Repair Costs	3
Warranty	2
Fuel Economy	1
Complaints	5
Insurance Costs	10
OVERALL RATING	**–**

Toyota Sequoia

Toyota Sequoia

At-a-Glance

Status/Year Series Started Unchanged/2008
Twins . . . . –
Body Styles. . . . . SUV
Seating. 8
Anti-Theft Device . . . . Std. Pass. Immobil. & Alarm
Parking Index Rating . . . . Very Hard
Where Made . . . . Princeton, IN
Fuel Factor
  MPG Rating (city/hwy). . . . . Very Poor-13/17
  Driving Range (mi.). Short-383.8
  Fuel Type . . . . Regular
  Annual Fuel Cost . . . . Very High-$3332
  Gas Guzzler Tax . . . . No
  Greenhouse Gas Emissions (tons/yr.)Vry High-13.3
  Barrels of Oil Used per year . . . . . Very High-24.5

How the Competition Rates

Competitors	Rating	Pg.
Chevrolet Tahoe	6	118
Nissan Armada	–	217
Cadillac Escalade	6	118

Price Range

Price Range	Retail	Markup
SR5 2WD 4.6L	$40,930	11%
SR5 4WD 5.7L FFV	$44,780	11%
Limited 4WD	$54,265	11%
Platinum 4WD FFV	$61,805	11%

Safety Checklist

Crash Tests:
  Frontal . . . . –
  Side . . . . –
Airbags:
  Head. . . . . Fr. & Rr. Roof Curtain
  Torso . . . . Front Torso from Seat
  Pelvis . . . . None
  Roll Sensing . . . . Yes
  Knee Bolster. . . . . Standard Front
Crash Avoidance:
  Frontal Collision Warning. . . . . None
  Blind Spot Detection . . . . Optional
  Crash Imminent Braking . . . . None
  Lane Departure Warning . . . . None
General:
  Auto. Crash Notification . . . . None
  Day Running Lamps . . . . Optional
Safety Belt/Restraint:
  Dynamic Head Restraints . . . . None
  Adjustable Belt . . . . . . Standard Front and Rear
  Pretensioners . . . . Standard Front

Toyota Sequoia

Specifications

Drive 4WD
Engine 5.7-liter V8
Transmission . . . . 6-sp. Automatic
Tow Rating (lbs.) High-7100
Head/Leg Room (in.) Roomy-39.7/42.5
Interior Space (cu. ft.) . . . . –
Cargo Space (cu. ft.) Average-18.9
Wheelbase/Length (in.). 122/205.1

Ratings—10 Best, 1 Worst

Combo Crash Tests	2
Safety Features	6
Rollover	5
Preventative Maintenance	6
Repair Costs	5
Warranty	2
Fuel Economy	3
Complaints	2
Insurance Costs	8
OVERALL RATING	**1**

Toyota Sienna

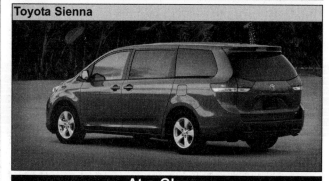
Toyota Sienna

At-a-Glance

Status/Year Series Started Unchanged/2004
Twins . . . . –
Body Styles . . . . Minivan
Seating 7/8
Anti-Theft Device . . . Std. Pass. Immobil. & Opt. Pass. Alarm
Parking Index Rating . . . . Hard
Where Made . . . . Princeton, IN

Fuel Factor
  MPG Rating (city/hwy) Poor-19/24
  Driving Range (mi.) Long-419.3
  Fuel Type . . . . Regular
  Annual Fuel Cost . . . . High-$2311
  Gas Guzzler Tax . . . . No
  Greenhouse Gas Emissions (tons/yr.) . . . High-8.9
  Barrels of Oil Used per year High-16.3

How the Competition Rates

Competitors	Rating	Pg.
Dodge Grand Caravan	5	129
Honda Odyssey	7	152
Kia Sedona	–	180

Price Range	Retail	Markup
Base 7-Pass. FWD 4cyl.	$25,060	7%
LE 8-Pass. FWD	$29,700	8%
XLE 7-Pass. AWD	$35,545	9%
Limited 7-Pass. AWD	$40,570	9%

Safety Checklist

Crash Tests:
  Frontal . . . . Very Poor
  Side . . . . Average
Airbags:
  Head . . . . Fr. & Rr. Roof Curtain
  Torso . . . . Front Torso from Seat
  Pelvis . . . . None
  Roll Sensing . . . . No
  Knee Bolster . . . . Standard Driver
Crash Avoidance:
  Frontal Collision Warning . . . . None
  Blind Spot Detection . . . . None
  Crash Imminent Braking . . . . Optional
  Lane Departure Warning . . . . None
General:
  Auto. Crash Notification . . . . Optional
  Day Running Lamps . . . . Standard
Safety Belt/Restraint:
  Dynamic Head Restraints . . . . . . Standard Front
  Adjustable Belt . . . . Standard Front & Rear
  Pretensioners . . . . Standard Front

Toyota Sienna

Specifications

Drive . . . . FWD
Engine 2.7-liter I4
Transmission . . . . 6-sp. Automatic
Tow Rating (lbs.) Low-3500
Head/Leg Room (in.) Average-41/40.5
Interior Space (cu. ft.) . . . . Very Roomy-164.4
Cargo Space (cu. ft.) . . . . Very Roomy-39.1
Wheelbase/Length (in.) 119.3/200.2

Ratings—10 Best, 1 Worst

Combo Crash Tests	3
Safety Features	5
Rollover	5
Preventative Maintenance	10
Repair Costs	4
Warranty	2
Fuel Economy	2
Complaints	5
Insurance Costs	3
OVERALL RATING	**1**

Toyota Tacoma

Toyota Tacoma

At-a-Glance

Status/Year Series Started	Unchanged/2009
Twins	–
Body Styles	Access, Regular, Double Cabs
Seating	4
Anti-Theft Device	None
Parking Index Rating	Very Hard
Where Made	San Antonio, TX

Fuel Factor

MPG Rating (city/hwy)	Very Poor-16/21
Driving Range (mi.)	Short-378.1
Fuel Type	Regular
Annual Fuel Cost	Very High-$2704
Gas Guzzler Tax	No
Greenhouse Gas Emissions (tons/yr.)	High-9.8
Barrels of Oil Used per year	High-18.0

How the Competition Rates

Competitors	Rating	Pg.
Chevrolet Colorado	–	109
Honda Ridgeline	–	154
Nissan Frontier	–	219

Price Range

Price Range	Retail	Markup
Base Reg. Cab 2WD Manual	$16,875	8%
Prerunner Dbl. Cab 2WD V6 Automatic	$24,260	8%
Base Access Cab 4WD V6 Automatic	$25,935	8%
Base LB 4WD V6 Automatic	$27,835	8%

Toyota Tacoma

Safety Checklist

Crash Tests:

Frontal	Poor
Side	Poor

Airbags:

Head	Front Roof Curtain
Torso	Front Torso from Seat
Pelvis	None
Roll Sensing	Yes
Knee Bolster	None

Crash Avoidance:

Frontal Collision Warning	None
Blind Spot Detection	None
Crash Imminent Braking	None
Lane Departure Warning	None

General:

Auto. Crash Notification	None
Day Running Lamps	Optional

Safety Belt/Restraint:

Dynamic Head Restraints	Standard Front
Adjustable Belt	Standard Front
Pretensioners	Standard Front

Toyota Tacoma

Specifications

Drive	4WD
Engine	4.0-liter V6
Transmission	5-sp. Automatic
Tow Rating (lbs.)	Low-3500
Head/Leg Room (in.)	Average-40/41.7
Interior Space (cu. ft.)	Very Cramped-88.7
Cargo Space (cu. ft.)	Very Roomy-38
Wheelbase/Length (in.)	127.4/208.1

Ratings—10 Best, 1 Worst

Combo Crash Tests	6
Safety Features	4
Rollover	3
Preventative Maintenance	9
Repair Costs	5
Warranty	2
Fuel Economy	1
Complaints	7
Insurance Costs	5
OVERALL RATING	**3**

Toyota Tundra

Toyota Tundra

At-a-Glance

Status/Year Series Started Unchanged/2007
Twins . . . . –
Body Styles . . . Crew, Double, Regular Cab Pickup
Seating 5/6
Anti-Theft Device . . . Opt. Pass. Alarm &/or only Immobil.
Parking Index Rating . . . . Very Hard
Where Made . . . . San Antonio, TX
Fuel Factor
MPG Rating (city/hwy) . . . . Very Poor-15/20
Driving Range (mi.) . . . . Very Long-446.2
Fuel Type . . . . Regular
Annual Fuel Cost . . . . Very High-$2867
Gas Guzzler Tax . . . . No
Greenhouse Gas Emissions (tons/yr.)Vry High-11.0
Barrels of Oil Used per year . . . . . Very High-20.1

How the Competition Rates

Competitors	Rating	Pg.
Chevrolet Colorado	–	109
Ram 1500 Quad Cab	2	231
Ford F-150 Super Cab	4	136

Price Range

Price Range	Retail	Markup
Reg. Cab 2WD V6	$25,155	9%
Double 4WD 5.7L V6	$27,365	9%
CrewMax 4WD 4.6L V8	$30,335	9%
CrewMax 4WD 5.7L V8 FFV	$43,345	9%

Safety Checklist

Crash Tests:
Frontal . . . . Poor
Side . . . . Very Good
Airbags:
Head . . . . Front Roof Curtain
Torso . . . . Front Torso from Seat
Pelvis . . . . None
Roll Sensing . . . . Yes
Knee Bolster . . . . Standard Front
Crash Avoidance:
Frontal Collision Warning . . . . None
Blind Spot Detection . . . . None
Crash Imminent Braking . . . . None
Lane Departure Warning . . . . None
General:
Auto. Crash Notification . . . . None
Day Running Lamps . . . . Standard
Safety Belt/Restraint:
Dynamic Head Restraints . . . . None
Adjustable Belt . . . . None
Pretensioners . . . . Standard Front

Toyota Tundra

Specifications

Drive . . . . RWD
Engine 4.6-liter V8
Transmission . . . . 6-sp. Auto. w/ Overdrive
Tow Rating (lbs.) . . . . Very High-9900
Head/Leg Room (in.) Roomy-40.2/42.5
Interior Space (cu. ft.) . . . . Very Roomy-131
Cargo Space (cu. ft.) . . . . Very Roomy-42
Wheelbase/Length (in.) 145.7/228.7

Ratings—10 Best, 1 Worst

Combo Crash Tests	3
Safety Features	6
Rollover	5
Preventative Maintenance	3
Repair Costs	3
Warranty	2
Fuel Economy	3
Complaints	5
Insurance Costs	8
OVERALL RATING	**1**

Toyota Venza

Toyota Venza

At-a-Glance

Status/Year Series Started Unchanged/2009
Twins . . . . –
Body Styles . . . . Crossover
Seating. 5
Anti-Theft Device . Std. Pass. Immobil. & Opt. Pass. Alarm
Parking Index Rating . . . . Very Hard
Where Made . . . . Georgetown, KY
Fuel Factor
MPG Rating (city/hwy). Poor-18/25
Driving Range (mi.). Short-364.5
Fuel Type . . . . Regular
Annual Fuel Cost. . . . . High-$2353
Gas Guzzler Tax . . . . No
Greenhouse Gas Emissions (tons/yr.) . . . High-8.9
Barrels of Oil Used per year High-16.3

How the Competition Rates

Competitors	Rating	Pg.
Honda Pilot	4	153
Mazda CX-7	–	200
Nissan Murano	3	223

Price Range

Price Range	Retail	Markup
LE L4 FWD	$27,425	11%
LE V6 AWD	$30,700	11%
XLE V6 AWD	$33,050	11%
Limited V6 AWD	$37,915	11%

Safety Checklist

Crash Tests:
Frontal . . . . Very Poor
Side. . . . . Average
Airbags:
Head. . . . . Fr. & Rr. Roof Curtain
Torso . . . . Front Torso from Seat
Pelvis . . . . None
Roll Sensing. . . . . No
Knee Bolster . . . . Standard Driver
Crash Avoidance:
Frontal Collision Warning. . . . . None
Blind Spot Detection . . . . None
Crash Imminent Braking . . . . None
Lane Departure Warning . . . . None
General:
Auto. Crash Notification . . . . None
Day Running Lamps . . . . Standard
Safety Belt/Restraint:
Dynamic Head Restraints. . . . . . Standard Front
Adjustable Belt . . . . Standard Front
Pretensioners . . . . Standard Front

Toyota Venza

Specifications

Drive. . . . . AWD
Engine 3.5-liter V6
Transmission . . . . 6-sp. Automatic
Tow Rating (lbs.) Low-3500
Head/Leg Room (in.) Cramped-39.6/40.3
Interior Space (cu. ft.). Roomy-108
Cargo Space (cu. ft.). Roomy-30.7
Wheelbase/Length (in.). 109.3/189

Ratings—10 Best, 1 Worst

Combo Crash Tests	–
Safety Features	2
Rollover	6
Preventative Maintenance	10
Repair Costs	10
Warranty	2
Fuel Economy	9
Complaints	–
Insurance Costs	1
OVERALL RATING	**–**

Toyota Yaris

Toyota Yaris

At-a-Glance

Status/Year Series Started . Appearance Change/2012
Twins . . . . –
Body Styles . . . . Sedan, Coupe, Hatchback
Seating. 5
Anti-Theft Device . . . . Std. Pass. Immobil.
Parking Index Rating. . . . . Very Easy
Where Made . . . . Miyagi, Japan
Fuel Factor
 MPG Rating (city/hwy) . . . . Very Good-30/35
 Driving Range (mi.) . . . . Very Short-355.9
 Fuel Type . . . . Regular
 Annual Fuel Cost . . . . Very Low-$1511
 Gas Guzzler Tax . . . . No
 Greenhouse Gas Emissions (tons/yr.) . . . Low-5.8
 Barrels of Oil Used per year. Low-10.7

How the Competition Rates

Competitors	Rating	Pg.
Honda Fit	–	150
Kia Rio	–	179
Nissan Versa	1	228

Price Range	Retail	Markup
L 2D	$14,115	4%
L 4D	$15,140	4%
LE	$16,100	4%
SE	$17,200	4%

Safety Checklist

Crash Tests:
 Frontal . . . . –
 Side . . . . –
Airbags:
 Head. . . . . Fr. & Rr. Roof Curtain
 Torso. . . . . Front Pelvis/Torso from Seat
 Pelvis . . . . Front Pelvis/Torso from Seat
 Roll Sensing. . . . . No
 Knee Bolster . . . . None
Crash Avoidance:
 Frontal Collision Warning. . . . . None
 Blind Spot Detection . . . . None
 Crash Imminent Braking . . . . None
 Lane Departure Warning . . . . None
General:
 Auto. Crash Notification. . . . . None
 Day Running Lamps . . . . None
Safety Belt/Restraint:
 Dynamic Head Restraints . . . . None
 Adjustable Belt. None
 Pretensioners . . . . Standard Front

Toyota Yaris

Specifications

Drive . . . . FWD
Engine. 1.5-liter I4
Transmission . . . . 4-sp. Automatic
Tow Rating (lbs.). . . . . –
Head/Leg Room (in.) Cramped-39.3/40.6
Interior Space (cu. ft.) . . . . Very Cramped-85.1
Cargo Space (cu. ft.) Cramped-15.6
Wheelbase/Length (in.) 98.8/153.5

Ratings—10 Best, 1 Worst

Combo Crash Tests	–
Safety Features	1
Rollover	7
Preventative Maintenance	–
Repair Costs	7
Warranty	8
Fuel Economy	6
Complaints	–
Insurance Costs	3
OVERALL RATING	–

Volkswagen Beetle

At-a-Glance

Status/Year Series Started	All New/2012
Twins	–
Body Styles	Coupe, Convertible
Seating	4
Anti-Theft Device	Std. Pass. Immobil. & Alarm
Parking Index Rating	Very Easy
Where Made	Puebla, Mexico

Fuel Factor

MPG Rating (city/hwy)	Average-22/29
Driving Range (mi.)	Very Short-357.9
Fuel Type	Regular
Annual Fuel Cost	Low-$1963
Gas Guzzler Tax	No
Greenhouse Gas Emissions (tons/yr.)	Average-7.5
Barrels of Oil Used per year	Average-13.7

How the Competition Rates

Competitors	Rating	Pg.
Scion iQ	–	232
Smart ForTwo	–	236
Suzuki SX4	–	243

Price Range	Retail	Markup
Base	$18,995	4%
2.5L PZEV	$20,895	4%
Black Turbo Launch	$24,950	4%
DSG 2.0T Turbo w/Sun/Snd/Nav	$29,095	4%

Volkswagen Beetle

Safety Checklist

Crash Tests:

Frontal	–
Side	–

Airbags:

Head	Front Head from Seat
Torso	Front Head/Torso from Seat
Pelvis	Front Pelvis/Torso from Seat
Roll Sensing	–
Knee Bolster	None

Crash Avoidance:

Frontal Collision Warning	None
Blind Spot Detection	None
Crash Imminent Braking	None
Lane Departure Warning	None

General:

Auto. Crash Notification	None
Day Running Lamps	Standard

Safety Belt/Restraint:

Dynamic Head Restraints	–
Adjustable Belt	None
Pretensioners	Standard Front

Volkswagen Beetle

Specifications

Drive	FWD
Engine	2.5-liter I5
Transmission	Automatic
Tow Rating (lbs.)	–
Head/Leg Room (in.)	Cramped-39.4/41.3
Interior Space (cu. ft.)	Very Cramped-85.1
Cargo Space (cu. ft.)	Cramped-15.4
Wheelbase/Length (in.)	99.9/168.4

Ratings—10 Best, 1 Worst

Combo Crash Tests	–
Safety Features	3
Rollover	8
Preventative Maintenance	7
Repair Costs	5
Warranty	8
Fuel Economy	6
Complaints	7
Insurance Costs	5
OVERALL RATING	**–**

Volkswagen CC

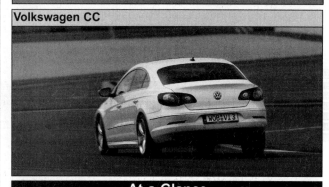

Volkswagen CC

At-a-Glance

Status/Year Series Started Unchanged/2009
Twins . . . . –
Body Styles . . . . Sedan
Seating 4
Anti-Theft Device . . . . Std. Pass. Immobil. & Alarm
Parking Index Rating . . . . Average
Where Made . . . . Emden, Germany
Fuel Factor
  MPG Rating (city/hwy) Average-22/31
  Driving Range (mi.) . . . . Very Long-468.2
  Fuel Type . . . . Premium
  Annual Fuel Cost . . . . Average-$2075
  Gas Guzzler Tax . . . . No
  Greenhouse Gas Emissions (tons/yr.) Average-7.5
  Barrels of Oil Used per year Average-13.7

How the Competition Rates

Competitors	Rating	Pg.
Acura TSX	–	84
Subaru Legacy	2	239
Toyota Camry	10	246

Price Range	Retail	Markup
Sport	$28,515	4%
Luxury	$31,420	4%
Luxury Plus	$33,865	4%
VR6 4Motion	$40,390	4%

Safety Checklist

Crash Tests:
  Frontal . . . . –
  Side . . . . –
Airbags:
  Head . . . . Fr. & Rr. Roof Curtain
  Torso . . . . Front Pelvis/Torso from Seat
  Pelvis . . . . Front Pelvis/Torso from Seat
  Roll Sensing . . . . No
  Knee Bolster . . . . None
Crash Avoidance:
  Frontal Collision Warning . . . . None
  Blind Spot Detection . . . . None
  Crash Imminent Braking . . . . None
  Lane Departure Warning . . . . None
General:
  Auto. Crash Notification . . . . None
  Day Running Lamps . . . . Standard
Safety Belt/Restraint:
  Dynamic Head Restraints . . . . –
  Adjustable Belt . . . . Standard Front
  Pretensioners . . . . Standard Front & Rear

Volkswagen CC

Specifications

Drive . . . . FWD
Engine 2.0-liter I4
Transmission . . . . 6-sp. Automatic
Tow Rating (lbs.) . . . . –
Head/Leg Room (in.) . . . . . Very Cramped-37.4/41.6
Interior Space (cu. ft.) Cramped-96.3
Cargo Space (cu. ft.) Cramped-13.2
Wheelbase/Length (in.) 106.7/188.9

Ratings—10 Best, 1 Worst

Combo Crash Tests	–
Safety Features	4
Rollover	7
Preventative Maintenance	7
Repair Costs	6
Warranty	8
Fuel Economy	7
Complaints	1
Insurance Costs	1
OVERALL RATING	–

Volkswagen Golf

Volkswagen Golf

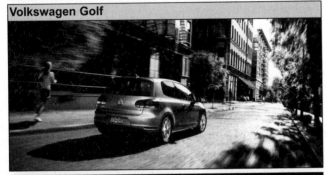
Volkswagen Golf

At-a-Glance

Status/Year Series Started Unchanged/2010
Twins . . . . –
Body Styles. . . . . Hatchback
Seating. 5
Anti-Theft Device . . . . Std. Pass. Immobil. & Alarm
Parking Index Rating. . . . . Very Easy
Where Made . . . . Wolfsburg, Germany
Fuel Factor
  MPG Rating (city/hwy) Good-24/31
  Driving Range (mi.). Short-387.4
  Fuel Type . . . . Regular
  Annual Fuel Cost . . . . Low-$1814
  Gas Guzzler Tax . . . . No
  Greenhouse Gas Emissions (tons/yr.) Average-7.2
  Barrels of Oil Used per year Average-13.2

How the Competition Rates

Competitors	Rating	Pg.
Mazda 3	6	197
Subaru Impreza	–	238
Toyota Matrix	–	250

Price Range

Price Range	Retail	Markup
Base 2D Manual Trans.	$17,995	4%
2D TDI Manual Trans.	$23,995	4%
4D TDI Auto. Trans.	$25,795	4%
4D TDI w/Tech Pkg Auto. Trans.	$29,165	4%

Safety Checklist

Crash Tests:
  Frontal . . . . –
  Side . . . . –
Airbags:
  Head. . . . . Fr. & Rr. Roof Curtain
  Torso . . . . Fr. & Opt. Rr. Pelvis/Torso from Seat
  Pelvis . . . Fr. & Opt. Rr. Pelvis/Torso from Seat
  Roll Sensing. . . . . No
  Knee Bolster . . . . None
Crash Avoidance:
  Frontal Collision Warning. . . . . None
  Blind Spot Detection . . . . None
  Crash Imminent Braking . . . . None
  Lane Departure Warning . . . . None
General:
  Auto. Crash Notification. . . . . None
  Day Running Lamps . . . . Standard
Safety Belt/Restraint:
  Dynamic Head Restraints . . . . –
  Adjustable Belt . . . . Standard Front
  Pretensioners . . . . Std. Front & Opt. Rear

Volkswagen Golf

Specifications

Drive . . . . FWD
Engine. 2.5-liter I5
Transmission . . . . 6-sp. Automatic
Tow Rating (lbs.). . . . . –
Head/Leg Room (in.) Cramped-39.3/41.2
Interior Space (cu. ft.) Cramped-93
Cargo Space (cu. ft.) Cramped-15.2
Wheelbase/Length (in.) 101.5/165.4

Ratings—10 Best, 1 Worst

Combo Crash Tests	7
Safety Features	2
Rollover	7
Preventative Maintenance	8
Repair Costs	7
Warranty	8
Fuel Economy	7
Complaints	1
Insurance Costs	1
OVERALL RATING	**6**

Volkswagen Jetta

Volkswagen Jetta

At-a-Glance

Status/Year Series Started Unchanged/2011
Twins . . . . –
Body Styles . . . . Sedan, Wagon
Seating. 5
Anti-Theft Device . . . . Std. Pass. Immobil. & Alarm
Parking Index Rating . . . . Easy
Where Made . . . . Puebla, Mexico
Fuel Factor
MPG Rating (city/hwy) Good-24/32
Driving Range (mi.) Average-392.1
Fuel Type . . . . Premium
Annual Fuel Cost . . . . Low-$1941
Gas Guzzler Tax . . . . No
Greenhouse Gas Emissions (tons/yr.) Average-6.9
Barrels of Oil Used per year Average-12.7

How the Competition Rates

Competitors	Rating	Pg.
Ford Focus	6	139
Honda Civic	–	146
Toyota Corolla	4	247

Price Range

Price Range	Retail	Markup
S Manual	$16,495	4%
SE Manual	$18,495	4%
DSG TDI	$23,625	4%
DSG TDI w/Premium & Nav	$26,195	4%

Safety Checklist

Crash Tests:
Frontal . . . . Good
Side. . . . . Average
Airbags:
Head. . . . . Fr. & Rr. Roof Curtain
Torso. . . . . Front Pelvis/Torso from Seat
Pelvis . . . . Front Pelvis/Torso from Seat
Roll Sensing. . . . . No
Knee Bolster . . . . None
Crash Avoidance:
Frontal Collision Warning. . . . . None
Blind Spot Detection . . . . None
Crash Imminent Braking . . . . None
Lane Departure Warning . . . . None
General:
Auto. Crash Notification. . . . . None
Day Running Lamps . . . . Standard
Safety Belt/Restraint:
Dynamic Head Restraints . . . . –
Adjustable Belt . . . . Standard Front
Pretensioners . . . . Standard Front

Volkswagen Jetta

Specifications

Drive . . . . FWD
Engine. 2.0-liter I4
Transmission . . . . 6-sp. Automatic
Tow Rating (lbs.). . . . . –
Head/Leg Room (in.) . . . . . Very Cramped-38.2/41.2
Interior Space (cu. ft.) Cramped-94.1
Cargo Space (cu. ft.) Cramped-15.5
Wheelbase/Length (in.) 104.4/182.2

Ratings—10 Best, 1 Worst

Combo Crash Tests	10
Safety Features	3
Rollover	7
Preventative Maintenance	8
Repair Costs	7
Warranty	8
Fuel Economy	6
Complaints	–
Insurance Costs	5
OVERALL RATING	**9**

Volkswagen Passat

Volkswagen Passat

At-a-Glance

Status/Year Series Started . . . . All New/2012
Twins . . . . –
Body Styles . . . . Sedan
Seating. 5
Anti-Theft Device . . . . Std. Pass. Immobil. & Alarm
Parking Index Rating . . . . Average
Where Made. . . . . Chattanooga, TN
Fuel Factor
  MPG Rating (city/hwy) Average-22/31
  Driving Range (mi.) . . . . Very Long-468.2
  Fuel Type . . . . Regular
  Annual Fuel Cost . . . . Low-$1915
  Gas Guzzler Tax . . . . No
  Greenhouse Gas Emissions (tons/yr.) Average-7.5
  Barrels of Oil Used per year Average-13.7

How the Competition Rates

Competitors	Rating	Pg.
Honda Accord	8	144
Hyundai Sonata	10	161
Nissan Altima	6	215

Price Range	Retail	Markup
S	$19,995	4%
SE 2.0 TDI	$25,995	4%
SEL	$28,395	4%
SEL 3.6L	$32,950	4%

Safety Checklist

Crash Tests:
  Frontal . . . . Very Good
  Side . . . . Good
Airbags:
  Head . . . . Fr. & Rr. Roof Curtain
  Torso . . . . Front Pelvis/Torso from Seat
  Pelvis . . . . Front Pelvis/Torso from Seat
  Roll Sensing. . . . . No
  Knee Bolster . . . . None
Crash Avoidance:
  Frontal Collision Warning. . . . . None
  Blind Spot Detection . . . . None
  Crash Imminent Braking . . . . None
  Lane Departure Warning . . . . None
General:
  Auto. Crash Notification . . . . None
  Day Running Lamps . . . . Standard
Safety Belt/Restraint:
  Dynamic Head Restraints . . . . –
  Adjustable Belt . . . . Standard Front
  Pretensioners . . . . Standard Front & Rear

Volkswagen Passat

Specifications

Drive . . . . FWD
Engine. 2.5-liter I5
Transmission . . . . 6 sp. Automatic
Tow Rating (lbs.) . . . . –
Head/Leg Room (in.) Cramped-38.3/42.4
Interior Space (cu. ft.) Average-102
Cargo Space (cu. ft.) Average-15.9
Wheelbase/Length (in.) 110.4/191.6

Ratings—10 Best, 1 Worst	
Combo Crash Tests	−
Safety Features	8
Rollover	4
Preventative Maintenance	8
Repair Costs	8
Warranty	8
Fuel Economy	3
Complaints	1
Insurance Costs	10
OVERALL RATING	−

Volkswagen Routan

Volkswagen Routan

At-a-Glance

Status/Year Series Started Unchanged/2009
Twins . . . . −
Body Styles . . . . Minivan
Seating. 7
Anti-Theft Device . . . . Std. Pass. Immobil. & Alarm
Parking Index Rating . . . . Hard
Where Made . . . . Windsor, Ontario

Fuel Factor
MPG Rating (city/hwy). Poor-17/25
Driving Range (mi.) Average-397.2
Fuel Type . . . . Regular
Annual Fuel Cost. . . . . High-$2440
Gas Guzzler Tax . . . . No
Greenhouse Gas Emissions (tons/yr.) . . . High-9.3
Barrels of Oil Used per year High-17.1

How the Competition Rates

Competitors	Rating	Pg.
Dodge Grand Caravan	5	129
Mazda 5	−	198
Toyota Sienna	1	254

Price Range	Retail	Markup
S	$27,020	4%
SE w/RSE	$33,490	4%
SEL w/ Nav	$37,890	4%
SEL Premium	$44,280	4%

Safety Checklist

Crash Tests:
　Frontal . . . . −
　Side . . . . −
Airbags:
　Head. . . . . Fr. & Rr. Roof Curtain
　Torso. . . . . Front Pelvis/Torso from Seat
　Pelvis . . . . Front Pelvis/Torso from Seat
　Roll Sensing . . . . .Yes
　Knee Bolster . . . . Standard Driver
Crash Avoidance:
　Frontal Collision Warning. . . . . None
　Blind Spot Detection . . . . Optional
　Crash Imminent Braking . . . . None
　Lane Departure Warning . . . . None
General:
　Auto. Crash Notification. . . . . None
　Day Running Lamps . . . . Optional
Safety Belt/Restraint:
　Dynamic Head Restraints. . . . . . Standard Front
　Adjustable Belt . . . . . . Standard Front and Rear
　Pretensioners . . . . Standard Front

Volkswagen Routan

Specifications

Drive . . . . FWD
Engine 3.6-liter V6
Transmission . . . . 6-sp. Automatic
Tow Rating (lbs.). . . . . Very Low-2000
Head/Leg Room (in.). . . . . Very Cramped-37.2/40.6
Interior Space (cu. ft.) . . . . Very Roomy-163.5
Cargo Space (cu. ft.). −
Wheelbase/Length (in.) 121.4/202.5

Ratings—10 Best, 1 Worst

Combo Crash Tests	–
Safety Features	5
Rollover	4
Preventative Maintenance	7
Repair Costs	6
Warranty	8
Fuel Economy	5
Complaints	5
Insurance Costs	8
OVERALL RATING	**–**

Volkswagen Tiguan

Volkswagen Tiguan

At-a-Glance

Status/Year Series Started Unchanged/2009
Twins . . . . –
Body Styles. . . . . SUV
Seating. 5
Anti-Theft Device . . . . Std. Pass. Immobil. & Alarm
Parking Index Rating . . . . Average
Where Made Wolfsburg, Germany / Kaluga, Russia

Fuel Factor
  MPG Rating (city/hwy) Average-22/27
  Driving Range (mi.) Average-403.2
  Fuel Type . . . . Premium
  Annual Fuel Cost. . . . . Average-$2188
  Gas Guzzler Tax . . . . No
  Greenhouse Gas Emissions (tons/yr.) Average-7.8
  Barrels of Oil Used per year High-14.3

How the Competition Rates

Competitors	Rating	Pg.
Hyundai Tucson	8	162
Subaru Forester	5	237
Toyota RAV4	1	252

Price Range	Retail	Markup
S	$22,840	4%
SE	$28,635	4%
SEL	$33,975	4%
SEL w/Prem. Nav. & Dyn.	$37,780	4%

Safety Checklist

Crash Tests:
  Frontal . . . . –
  Side . . . . –
Airbags:
  Head . . . . Fr. & Rr. Roof Curtain
  Torso. . . . . Front Pelvis/Torso from Seat
  Pelvis . . . . Front Pelvis/Torso from Seat
  Roll Sensing . . . . Yes
  Knee Bolster . . . . None
Crash Avoidance:
  Frontal Collision Warning. . . . . None
  Blind Spot Detection . . . . None
  Crash Imminent Braking . . . . None
  Lane Departure Warning . . . . None
General:
  Auto. Crash Notification . . . . None
  Day Running Lamps . . . . Standard
Safety Belt/Restraint:
  Dynamic Head Restraints . . . . –
  Adjustable Belt . . . . Standard Front
  Pretensioners . . . . Standard Front

Volkswagen Tiguan

Specifications

Drive . . . . FWD
Engine. 2.0-liter I4
Transmission . . . . 6-sp. Automatic
Tow Rating (lbs.). . . . . Very Low-2200
Head/Leg Room (in.) . . . . . Very Cramped-39.1/40.1
Interior Space (cu. ft.) Cramped-95.4
Cargo Space (cu. ft.) Roomy-23.8
Wheelbase/Length (in.) 102.5/174.3

Ratings—10 Best, 1 Worst

Combo Crash Tests	–
Safety Features	3
Rollover	9
Preventative Maintenance	10
Repair Costs	6
Warranty	10
Fuel Economy	4
Complaints	10
Insurance Costs	8
OVERALL RATING	**–**

Volvo C70

Volvo C70

At-a-Glance

Status/Year Series Started Unchanged/2006
Twins . . . . –
Body Styles . . . . Coupe, Convertible
Seating 4
Anti-Theft DeviceStd. Pass. Immobil. & Active Alarm
Parking Index Rating . . . . Average
Where Made . . . . Udevalla, Sweden
Fuel Factor
  MPG Rating (city/hwy) Poor-18/28
  Driving Range (mi.) . . . . Very Short-341.0
  Fuel Type . . . . Regular
  Annual Fuel Cost . . . . High-$2259
  Gas Guzzler Tax . . . . No
  Greenhouse Gas Emissions (tons/yr.) . . . High-8.9
  Barrels of Oil Used per year High-16.3

How the Competition Rates

Competitors	Rating	Pg.
Audi A5	–	88
BMW 1 Series	–	94
Mitsubishi Lancer	–	212

Price Range	Retail	Markup
T5	$39,950	6%
T5 Premier Plus	$40,950	6%
T5 Platinum	$43,550	6%

Safety Checklist

Crash Tests:
  Frontal . . . . –
  Side . . . . –
Airbags:
  Head . . . . Front Curtain from Door
  Torso . . . . Front Torso from Seat
  Pelvis . . . . None
  Roll Sensing . . . . Yes
  Knee Bolster . . . . None
Crash Avoidance:
  Frontal Collision Warning . . . . None
  Blind Spot Detection . . . . Optional
  Crash Imminent Braking . . . . None
  Lane Departure Warning . . . . None
General:
  Auto. Crash Notification . . . . None
  Day Running Lamps . . . . Standard
Safety Belt/Restraint:
  Dynamic Head Restraints . . . . None
  Adjustable Belt . . . . None
  Pretensioners . . . . Standard Front & Rear

Volvo C70

Specifications

Drive . . . . FWD
Engine 2.5-liter I5
Transmission . . . . 5-sp. Automatic
Tow Rating (lbs.) . . . . Very Low-2000
Head/Leg Room (in.) Cramped-38.2/42.3
Interior Space (cu. ft.) . . . . Very Cramped-84
Cargo Space (cu. ft.) Cramped-12.8
Wheelbase/Length (in.) 103.9/181.7

Volvo S60

Ratings—10 Best, 1 Worst

Combo Crash Tests	–
Safety Features	8
Rollover	8
Preventative Maintenance	10
Repair Costs	7
Warranty	10
Fuel Economy	3
Complaints	10
Insurance Costs	5
OVERALL RATING	**–**

Volvo S60

Safety Checklist

Crash Tests:
Frontal . . . . –
Side . . . . –
Airbags:
Head . . . . Fr. & Rr. Roof Curtain
Torso . . . . Front Pelvis/Torso from Seat
Pelvis . . . . Front Pelvis/Torso from Seat
Roll Sensing . . . . Yes
Knee Bolster . . . . None
Crash Avoidance:
Frontal Collision Warning . . . . Optional
Blind Spot Detection . . . . Optional
Crash Imminent Braking . . . . Optional
Lane Departure Warning . . . . Optional
General:
Auto. Crash Notification . . . . None
Day Running Lamps . . . . Standard
Safety Belt/Restraint:
Dynamic Head Restraints . . . . None
Adjustable Belt . . . . Standard
Pretensioners . . . . Standard Front & Rear

At-a-Glance

Status/Year Series Started Unchanged/2011
Twins . . . . –
Body Styles . . . . Sedan
Seating 5
Anti-Theft Device Std. Pass. Immobil. & Active Alarm
Parking Index Rating . . . . Hard
Where Made . . . . Ghent, Belgium
Fuel Factor
MPG Rating (city/hwy) Poor-18/26
Driving Range (mi.) Short-371.9
Fuel Type . . . . Regular
Annual Fuel Cost . . . . High-$2319
Gas Guzzler Tax . . . . No
Greenhouse Gas Emissions (tons/yr.) . . . High-8.9
Barrels of Oil Used per year High-16.3

How the Competition Rates

Competitors	Rating	Pg.
Acura TL	–	83
Hyundai Sonata	10	161
Infiniti EX	–	165

Price Range	Retail	Markup
T5	$30,975	6%
T6	$37,700	6%
T6 R	$42,275	6%

Volvo S60

Specifications

Drive . . . . AWD
Engine 3.0-liter I6
Transmission . . . . 6-sp. Automatic
Tow Rating (lbs.) Low-3300
Head/Leg Room (in.) Cramped-38.3/41.9
Interior Space (cu. ft.) Cramped-92
Cargo Space (cu. ft.) . . . . Very Cramped-12
Wheelbase/Length (in.) 109.3/182.2

Ratings—10 Best, 1 Worst

Combo Crash Tests	–
Safety Features	6
Rollover	7
Preventative Maintenance	10
Repair Costs	5
Warranty	10
Fuel Economy	5
Complaints	6
Insurance Costs	5
OVERALL RATING	**–**

Volvo S80

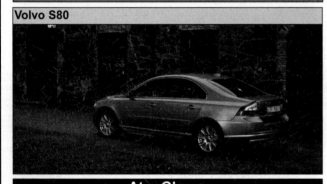

At-a-Glance

Status/Year Series Started Unchanged/2008
Twins . . . . –
Body Styles . . . . Sedan
Seating. 5
Anti-Theft DeviceStd. Pass. Immobil. & Active Alarm
Parking Index Rating . . . . Average
Where Made . . . . Gothenburg, Sweden
Fuel Factor
 MPG Rating (city/hwy) Average-20/29
 Driving Range (mi.) Long-430.1
 Fuel Type . . . . Regular
 Annual Fuel Cost. . . . . Average-$2084
 Gas Guzzler Tax . . . . No
 Greenhouse Gas Emissions (tons/yr.) Average-8.1
 Barrels of Oil Used per year High-14.9

How the Competition Rates

Competitors	Rating	Pg.
BMW 7 Series	–	97
Infiniti M	6	168
Lexus LS	–	192

Price Range	Retail	Markup
Base	$37,550	6%
Premier Plus	$38,550	6%
Platinum	$41,250	6%
Platinum Turbo	$45,000	6%

Volvo S80

Safety Checklist

Crash Tests:
 Frontal . . . . –
 Side . . . . –
Airbags:
 Head. . . . . Fr. & Rr. Roof Curtain
 Torso. . . . . Front Pelvis/Torso from Seat
 Pelvis . . . . Front Pelvis/Torso from Seat
 Roll Sensing. . . . . No
 Knee Bolster . . . . None
Crash Avoidance:
 Frontal Collision Warning . . . . Optional
 Blind Spot Detection . . . . Optional
 Crash Imminent Braking . . . . Optional
 Lane Departure Warning. . . . . Optional
General:
 Auto. Crash Notification. . . . . None
 Day Running Lamps . . . . Standard
Safety Belt/Restraint:
 Dynamic Head Restraints . . . . None
 Adjustable Belt. . . . . Standard
 Pretensioners. . . . . Standard Front & Rear

Volvo S80

Specifications

Drive . . . . FWD
Engine. 3.2-liter I6
Transmission . . . . 6-sp. Automatic
Tow Rating (lbs.) Low-3300
Head/Leg Room (in.) Cramped-37.8/41.9
Interior Space (cu. ft.). Average-98
Cargo Space (cu. ft.) Cramped-14.9
Wheelbase/Length (in.). 111.6/191

Ratings—10 Best, 1 Worst

Combo Crash Tests	10
Safety Features	8
Rollover	4
Preventative Maintenance	10
Repair Costs	5
Warranty	10
Fuel Economy	3
Complaints	4
Insurance Costs	10
OVERALL RATING	**10**

Volvo XC60

Volvo XC60

At-a-Glance

Status/Year Series Started Unchanged/2009
Twins . . . . –
Body Styles. . . . . SUV
Seating. 5
Anti-Theft DeviceStd. Pass. Immobil. & Active Alarm
Parking Index Rating . . . . Average
Where Made . . . . Ghent, Belgium

Fuel Factor
MPG Rating (city/hwy). Poor-17/23
Driving Range (mi.) . . . . Very Short-356.3
Fuel Type . . . . Regular
Annual Fuel Cost. . . . . High-$2515
Gas Guzzler Tax . . . . No
Greenhouse Gas Emissions (tons/yr.). . . High-9.3
Barrels of Oil Used per year High-17.1

How the Competition Rates

Competitors	Rating	Pg.
Acura MDX	9	81
Honda Pilot	4	153
Toyota 4Runner	–	244

Price Range	Retail	Markup
Base 3.2L	$32,900	6%
Premier Plus 3.2L	$37,150	6%
R-Design 3.0L	$43,150	6%
R-Design Platinum 3.0L	$47,600	6%

Safety Checklist

Crash Tests:
Frontal . . . . Very Good
Side . . . . Good
Airbags:
Head. . . . . Fr. & Rr. Roof Curtain
Torso. . . . . Front Pelvis/Torso from Seat
Pelvis . . . . Front Pelvis/Torso from Seat
Roll Sensing . . . . Yes
Knee Bolster . . . . None
Crash Avoidance:
Frontal Collision Warning . . . . Optional
Blind Spot Detection . . . . Optional
Crash Imminent Braking . . . . Optional
Lane Departure Warning. . . . . Optional
General:
Auto. Crash Notification. . . . . None
Day Running Lamps . . . . Standard
Safety Belt/Restraint:
Dynamic Head Restraints . . . . None
Adjustable Belt. . . . . Standard
Pretensioners. . . . . Standard Front & Rear

Volvo XC60

Specifications

Drive . . . . AWD
Engine. 3.0-liter I6
Transmission . . . . 6-sp. Automatic
Tow Rating (lbs.). Low-3300
Head/Leg Room (in.) . . . . . . Very Cramped-38/41.2
Interior Space (cu. ft.). Average-99
Cargo Space (cu. ft.). Roomy-30.8
Wheelbase/Length (in.) 109.2/182.2

Ratings—10 Best, 1 Worst

Combo Crash Tests	–
Safety Features	6
Rollover	3
Preventative Maintenance	10
Repair Costs	5
Warranty ·	10
Fuel Economy	2
Complaints	3
Insurance Costs	10

OVERALL RATING — —

Volvo XC90

Volvo XC90

At-a-Glance

Status/Year Series Started Unchanged/2003
Twins . . . . –
Body Styles. . . . . SUV
Seating. 7
Anti-Theft DeviceStd. Pass. Immobil. & Active Alarm
Parking Index Rating . . . . Hard
Where Made . . . . Gothenburg, Sweden

Fuel Factor
MPG Rating (city/hwy). . . . . Very Poor-16/22
Driving Range (mi.). Short-384.8
Fuel Type . . . . Regular
Annual Fuel Cost . . . . Very High-$2656
Gas Guzzler Tax . . . . No
Greenhouse Gas Emissions (tons/yr.). . High-10.4
Barrels of Oil Used per year. . . . . . . Very Low-0.0

How the Competition Rates

Competitors	Rating	Pg.
BMW X5	–	99
Infiniti FX	–	166
Mercedes-Benz M-Class	–	207

Price Range	Retail	Markup
Base ·	$38,400	6%
Premier Plus	$39,600	6%
R-Design Premier Plus	$41,600	6%
R-Design Platinum	$44,300	6%

Safety Checklist

Crash Tests:
Frontal . . . . –
Side . . . . –
Airbags:
Head. . . . . Fr. & Rr. Roof Curtain
Torso . . . . Front Torso from Seat
Pelvis . . . . None
Roll Sensing . . . . Yes
Knee Bolster . . . . None
Crash Avoidance:
Frontal Collision Warning. . . . . None
Blind Spot Detection . . . . Optional
Crash Imminent Braking . . . . None
Lane Departure Warning . . . . None
General:
Auto. Crash Notification . . . . None
Day Running Lamps . . . . Standard
Safety Belt/Restraint:
Dynamic Head Restraints . . . . None
Adjustable Belt . . . . Standard
Pretensioners . . . . Standard Front & Rear

Volvo XC90

Specifications

Drive . . . . FWD
Engine. 3.2-liter I6
Transmission . . . . 6-sp. Automatic
Tow Rating (lbs.) Low-3970
Head/Leg Room (in.) Cramped-39.7/41
Interior Space (cu. ft.) Average-100.9
Cargo Space (cu. ft.) . . . . Very Cramped-8.8
Wheelbase/Length (in.) 112.6/189.3

Use this page to keep some notes on the choices you are considering. Include any comments your friends make, statements made by the dealer that may be important later, and your own personal reactions to the car and the test drive. After you've looked at 4 or 5 cars, it's easy to mix up the details.

MAKE/MODEL:_____ **PRICE RANGE:**_____ **PAGE:** _____

PROS:

CONS:

NOTES:

MAKE/MODEL:_____ **PRICE RANGE:**_____ **PAGE:** _____

PROS:

CONS:

NOTES:

MAKE/MODEL:_____ **PRICE RANGE:**_____ **PAGE:** _____

PROS:

CONS:

NOTES:

Airbags; *see Safety,* 78
Anti-Lock Brakes, 79
Auto Brokers, 68
Auto Manufacturers, 58
Auto Safety Hotline, 54
Bumpers; *see Insurance,* 52
Child Safety Seats; *see Safety,* 29
  Recalls, 29
Complaints
  Best and Worst, 55
  resolving, 53
  under warranty, 67; *see also*
    Warranty, 54
Consumer Groups, 57
  Advocates for Highway & Auto
    Safety, 57
  Center for Auto Safety, 4, 38,
    54, *56-57,* 73
  Consumer Action, 57
  Center for the Study of Services,
    66-68, 73
  CarBargains, 68
  Consumers for Auto Reliability
    and Safety, 57
  Kids And Cars, 57
Corporate Twins, 75
Crash Test; *see Safety,* 18-28, 76
  crash protection, 28
  telematics, 28
Depreciation, 74
Financing, 69
Fuel Economy, 33
  factors affecting, 33
  fuel saving tips, 34
  misers and guzzlers, 35
  octane rating, 33
  website, 34
Government Agencies
  Department of Justice, 57
  Department of Transportation
    (DOT), 30, 57
  Environmental Protection
    Agency (EPA), 57, 73
  Federal Trade Commission
    (FTC), 57
  Highway Loss Data Institute
    (HLDI), 51
  National Highway Traffic
    Safety Administration
    (NHTSA), 29, 55, 57, 73
Insurance, 49
  auto theft, 51
  bumpers, 52

Insurance Institute for
    Highway Safety (IIHS), 50, 52
  reducing costs, 50-51
  speeding, 50
  types of coverage, 49
Internet, 73
  using, 70
  web information, 70
Leasing
  capitalized cost, 71
  Leasewise, 71
  questions to ask, 71-72
  residual value, 72
  versus buying, 71-72
Legal Action
  arbitration; *see Complaints,* 53
  lemon laws, 59-63
    avoiding lemons, 67
  Lemon Book, 54
Maintenance, 39
  costs, 40-43
  dealing with a mechanic, 45
  preventative, 39
  repair protection, 45
  service contract, 44
National Institute for Automotive
  Service Excellence, 45
Operating costs; *see Maintenance,*
  40, 43
  typical, 70
Policy Adjustments; *see Warranty,*
  secret, 38, 56
Price
  auto brokers, 68
  avoiding lemons, 67
  dealer markup, 78
  depreciation, 74
  negotiating, 64-67
  price shopping service, 68
  tires, 46
Ratings
  car ratings, 81-270
  explanation, 76-80
Recall Information, 54
  child seat, 29
Repair
  complaints; *see Complaints,* 54
  costs, 39, 40-43
  dealing with a mechanic, 45
  payment by credit card, 45
Resale Value; *see Depreciation,* 74
Rollover, 30
  Roof Crush, 31

Static Stability Factor, 32
Safety, 18
  airbag types, 78
  automatic crash protection, 28
  children & airbags, 29
  children & seatbelts, 29
  child safety seats
    recalls, 29
    tips on use, 29
  crash test
    explanation, 18
    ratings, 19-28
    rollover, 30-32
    roll sensing SAB 30, 79
    roof crush, 31
  equipment, 78-79
  young drivers, 51
Service Bulletins, 38
Service Contracts, 44
Thefts, 51
Tires
  care, 46
  heat resistance, 55
  how to read, 47
  NHTSA hotline, 57
  pricing, 46
  ratings program, 48
  traction, 46
  treadwear, 46
Warranty, 36
  best and worst, 37
  comparing, 37
  corrosion, 36
  emission system, 36
  legal rights, 38
  Magnuson-Moss Warranty Act,
    54
  power train, 36
  roadside assistance, 36
  secret, 38